The Failure
of
U.S. Tax Policy

The Failure
of
U.S. Tax Policy

Revenue and Politics

Sheldon D. Pollack

The Pennsylvania State University Press
University Park, Pennsylvania

Library of Congress Cataloging-in-Publication Data

Pollack, Sheldon David.
   The failure of U.S. tax policy: revenue and politics / Sheldon D. Pollack.
      p.   cm.
   Includes bibliographical references and index.
   ISBN 0-271-01582-9 (alk. paper)
   ISBN 0-271-01583-7 (pbk. : alk. paper)
   1. Taxation–United States–History.   2. Revenue–United States
   –History.   I. Title.
   HJ2362.P65   1996
   336.2′00973–dc20   95-26110
                                                                       CIP

Copyright ©1996 The Pennsylvania State University
All rights reserved
Printed in the United States of America
Published by The Pennsylvania State University Press,
University Park, PA 16802-1003

It is the policy of The Pennsylvania State University Press to use acid-free
paper for the first printing of all clothbound books. Publications on uncoated
stock satisfy the minimum requirements of American National Standard for
Information Sciences–Permanence of Paper for Printed Library Materials,
ANSI Z39.48-1992.

For
Alyssa and Seth

Contents

Preface

As a practicing tax lawyer in the 1980s, I was forced on a daily basis to confront the consequences of a tax policy out of control. The income tax regime as it had evolved over the previous half century was radically and unexpectedly restructured under the Tax Reform Act of 1986 – much to the dismay of seasoned tax lawyers who had practiced for decades under the old regime but now were forced to relearn the income tax laws. Of course, this is precisely what made the 1980s an exciting time to practice tax law. Unfortunately, private legal practice does not allow for many moments of quiet reflection and contemplation on the merits and theories behind such major tax legislation as was enacted during the decade. For this reason, I personally found the practice of law to be suffocating, stultifying, and painful. Later, I decided to return to the academy to commence this study of tax policymaking.

The starting point of my analysis was the question why tax policy had floundered in the 1980s. The success of the tax reform movement in 1986 turned out to be an isolated event, and tax policy seemed to revert to prior patterns by the end of the decade. But by the early 1990s, tax policy was again moving in new directions. The only thing certain was that the income tax laws had become even more complicated as a consequence of the decade-long deluge of tax legislation. Although this study goes beyond this initial concern with tax policy in the 1980s, it always returns to the underlying question why tax policy is so erratic, complicated, unstable, and unprincipled. As such, I have attempted to identify those features of contemporary American politics that account for the serious deficiencies in U.S. tax policy. The result is a rather broad study of how the income tax, which raises much of the revenue of the federal government, impinges upon the national economy and is used by policymakers to implement public policies.

My belief is that this widespread nonpartisan infatuation of policymakers with the tax code has undesirable consequences for the

American polity—not the least of which is that the federal government intrudes into nearly every sphere of political, social, and economic activity through the tax laws. But that is a subject for another day. The concern here is with uncovering the origins of the quagmire that tax policy has become.

My intellectual debts are many. I learned much of what I know about American politics and public policy from Theodore J. Lowi of Cornell University. I am also grateful to Ted for standing behind me during my long sabbatical from academia—the dreary decade when I practiced law. It is no coincidence that Ted has legions of loyal colleagues and former students who owe him an incomparable debt for his friendship and support. Special thanks also go to Youssef Cohen of New York University, who read portions of this book in manuscript and made his usual insightful comments. He also provided fifteen years of sustained and interesting conversation—if only one could get a word in edgewise. Paul J. Quirk of the University of Illinois expressed an irrational faith in my ability to complete this project. He read portions of an early draft and contributed valuable suggestions for its improvement. Robert E. McQuiston, Chairman of the Tax Department at the law firm of Ballard Sphar Andrews & Ingersoll, provided much support and friendship over the years. Andrew Dubroff, former tax legislative counsel in the Treasury Department and now with the accounting firm of Ernst & Young, has generously shared with me his expertise in tax law. Sandy Thatcher, Director of Penn State Press, stood behind this project from the beginning and helped bring it to fruition. Portions of this book previously appeared in the *New Republic, American Journal of Tax Policy, Tax Notes, George Mason Independent Law Review*, and the *Tax Law Review*. The editors of those journals contributed much to improving this work, as did Keith Monley, my copyeditor from Penn State Press, and Eileen Pollack of the University of Michigan.

I greatly benefited from the comments of the many scholars who read portions of this book in manuscript. These include Jerrold Schneider of the University of Delaware, John Kingdon of the University of Michigan, and William Gale of the Brookings Institution. John Witte of the University of Wisconsin, who knows as much about the politics of the federal income tax as anyone, took an early interest in this work and throughout the course of its development provided many valuable recommendations toward improvement of the analysis. James Curtis of Pennsylvania State University and Euell Elliot of the University of Texas at Dallas both read the book in manuscript and offered many helpful suggestions.

Kent St. Pierre, Chairman of the Accounting Department, and Kenneth Biederman, Dean of the College of Business and Economics at the University of Delaware, encouraged, supported, and helped finance this project. My research assistant at the University of Delaware, Joshua Chapman, provided invaluable research assistance. The librarians of the Brookings Institution and of the Hugh M. Morris Library of the University of Delaware were of great assistance in tracking down hard-to-find materials. The Gowen Fellowship of the University of Pennsylvania Law School, the General University Research Fund of the University of Delaware, and the College of Business and Economics at the University of Delaware afforded me generous financial support during the course of this project.

Thomas E. Mann, Director of the Governmental Studies Program at the Brookings Institution, provided me the opportunity to spend some time in Washington during the summer of 1995 observing tax policymaking firsthand as well as making use of the invaluable resources of the Brookings Institution itself—the most important being the many talented scholars who reside there. While at the Brookings Institution, I particularly enjoyed and benefited from my conversations with Bill Frenzel, former congressman from Minnesota and now a senior fellow at Brookings, who was particularly generous in sharing his time and thoughts with me. During that summer, several members of the staffs of the Senate Finance and House Ways and Means Committees who wish to remain anonymous provided me their insights into the federal tax-policymaking process as well as the labyrinths of Washington politics.

My parents, Abraham and Wilma Pollack, supported and helped finance my many academic adventures over the course of the past four decades. That is but one of many indulgences for which I must thank them. Lastly, I thank my wife, Patti Werther, and my children, Seth and Alyssa, for their great patience and understanding during the long hours spent away from them in isolation (in my basement office as well as in Washington) writing this book. Only their love allowed me to complete this project. Alas, its many shortcomings are attributable to the limits of human reasoning—most specifically, my own. For these, I must regrettably take full responsibility.

Introduction

[M]odern taxation or tax making in its most characteristic aspect is a group contest in which powerful interests vigorously endeavor to rid themselves of present or proposed tax burdens. It is, first of all, a hard game in which he who trusts wholly to economics, reason, and justice, will in the end retire beaten and disillusioned. Class politics is the essence of taxation.

−T. S. Adams (1927)

[T]he tax system is more than a revenue-raising device, it is an instrument of national policy.

−Walter Heller (1961)

During the 1980s, the income tax laws of the United States were revised, reformed, and rewritten to a greater extent than during any other period in the history of the tax. The federal courts, the IRS, taxpayers, and the private tax bar all struggled just to keep up with the deluge of increasingly complex tax statutes and regulations. The Tax Reform Act of 1986 (TRA) was the most important bill ever enacted in the history of the federal income tax, and it completely changed the landscape of tax practice. Contrary to all expectations, "tax reform" became the centerpiece of domestic policy during the Reagan administration, and TRA was a massive tax-reform bill. Other significant tax legislation was also enacted during the 1980s−much of which contradicted the underlying philosophy and policies behind TRA. By the end of the decade, tax policy was adrift. That changed with the triumph of the Republican Party in the 1994 mid-term elections; tax policy very much found a direction. Nevertheless, it remains to be seen whether any long-term stability and coherence will return to federal tax policy as a result of Republican domination of Congress, or whether the next few years will witness the same pattern of erratic policymaking that characterized the 1980s.

The goal of this study is to explain the many diverse and often conflicting demands made upon the federal income tax by policymakers, who at once use the tax to raise revenue, manage the national economy, further partisan politics, and implement a wide assortment of public policies. American policymakers themselves are subjected to diverse and conflicting demands with respect to satisfying the revenue needs of the American state. In addition, policymakers have individual interests and goals, as well as partisan affiliations, which are expressed and satisfied through the tax bills they write. Our constantly changing and extraordinarily complex tax laws reflect the fact that so much is attempted through the Internal Revenue Code.

First and foremost, a "revenue imperative" motivates federal tax policymaking. For two centuries, political elites have struggled to satisfy the revenue demands of the American state. Officials of any state must "negotiate" for revenue with the major social and economic interests of civil society. However, the American state was expressly designed through its original constitutional structure to deny the federal government easy access to revenue. Furthermore, the prevailing liberal political culture has limited the capacity of state officials to "extract" revenue from civil society. Taxation, after all, is both one of the most important and coercive activities of the state and one of the dominant themes of American political liberalism has been the restriction of such coercive state powers.

Despite the limitations on the fiscal powers of state officials, the "traditional" sources of federal revenue (customs duties, excise taxes, the sale of public land, and the tariff) were generally adequate in financing the limited activities of the nineteenth-century American state. Nevertheless, the deficiencies in the fiscal organization of the central state became apparent during crucial periods of American history, particularly during military crises, beginning with the Revolutionary War, the War of 1812, and the Civil War, and then again during the two world wars of the twentieth century. It is during military conflicts that the revenue imperative is felt most keenly by state officials, who are forced to accommodate a dramatic increase in the revenue needs of the state.[1] During

---

1. The connection between the great cost of military warfare and the development of the modern state has been well noted. See, e.g., Joseph A. Schumpeter, "The Crisis of the Tax State" (1918), reprinted in *International Economic Papers, No. 4* (New York: Macmillan, 1954), 13: "The most important cause of the financial difficulties [of fourteenth- and fifteenth-century European monarchs] consisted in the growing expenses of warfare." An interesting version of this theme is found in Charles Tilly, "War Making and

such periods of crisis, policymakers must search out and cultivate new sources of revenue and experiment with new and often radical policies. The U.S. income tax was such a wartime innovation – one that raised unprecedented revenue and at the same time radically altered the development of the American state. To a large extent, the great revenue brought in by the income tax made possible the expansion of the American state in the twentieth century, the establishment of a social welfare state beginning in the 1930s, and the creation of a dominant American military organization.

But just as the revenue imperative has played a primary role in shaping American tax policy, so, periodically, have various ideological imperatives. For instance, populism and radical egalitarianism inspired the politics behind the adoption of the federal income taxes of 1894 and 1913. Surprisingly, once the income tax was adopted and became institutionalized, these ideological movements tended to play a more minor role in the development of income tax policy, which fell under the sway of mainstream politicians who recognized that the great potential of the income tax was in the revenue that it would bring in for the American state, and not in its capacity to redistribute wealth among social classes. Nevertheless, questions of "equity" and redistribution have pervaded the debate over income tax policy, often under the cover of partisan politics. In a speech on the floor of the Senate during debate over the 1913 income tax, Henry Cabot Lodge of Massachusetts demonstrated how income taxation, even when justified in terms of the revenue it raises, continues to invoke deep-rooted "class" issues: "It will be an evil day for us when we enter on confiscation of property under the guise of taxation. What we want to do is raise money for the support of the Government. . . . But to have the Government undertake, for vindictive reasons, to punish a man simply because he has succeeded and has accumulated property by thrift and intelligence and character, or has inherited it honestly under the law, is entering upon a dangerous path. It would convert this tax from the imposition of a tax to a pillage of a class."[2] Over the next eight decades, tax policy never actually manifested the kind of overt class warfare that Senator Lodge so intensely

---

State Making as Organized Crime," in *Bringing the State Back In,* ed. Theda Skocpol, Peter Evans, and Dietrich Rueschemeyer (New York: Cambridge University Press, 1985); see also Bruce D. Porter, *War and the Rise of the State: The Military Foundations of Modern Politics* (New York: Free Press, 1994).

2. *Congressional Record,* 63d Cong., 1st sess. (August 28, 1913), 50, pt. 4, 3840.

feared. But tax policy has expressed a level of partisanship certainly no less intense than that which otherwise prevails in American politics.

Since the adoption of the modern twentieth-century income tax in 1913, both of the major national political parties have had their own unique visions of how the burden of income taxation should be imposed upon and shared among the citizenry. As distinct from economics and public finance, which are generally concerned with the aggregate level of tax revenue extracted from the private sector to support the public sphere, partisan tax policy is often little more than a veiled attempt to shift the incidence of taxation from one particular social or economic class to another. This is evidenced by the often-heard demand that the income tax (as well as other taxes, such as estate and inheritance taxes) be used to effect a redistribution of wealth among social classes. Similarly, the attempt to shift the burden of taxation onto the "wealthy" would seem to be the primary political impetus behind the corporate-level income tax, as well as that behind increasing the rates at which the corporate income tax is imposed. There is great uncertainty regarding who actually bears the economic burden of corporate taxes. But ideological impulses, rather than sound economic theory, have more often informed policy with respect to the taxation of the business corporation in the United States. The claims made to defend or castigate such policies reflect and express partisan political rhetoric as applied to the federal income tax. Sadly, this constitutes a good deal of what passes for "tax policy" in the United States.

Tax policy has also accommodated a "functional" nonpartisan use of the income tax by elected representatives intent upon currying favor with constituents as well as implementing social and economic policies through the tax laws. As the role of the congressmen changed during the twentieth century, so too did their use of the federal income tax. The congressman as "ombudsman" introduces amendments to the income tax that are intended to protect and enhance the economic well-being of local interests and constituents. As such, the income tax code becomes an effective vehicle for politicians, Democrats and Republicans alike, looking to curry favor with the home district. At times, this amounts to little more than political grandstanding; at other times, it produces "special-interest" provisions buried within the arcane language of the income tax code. The latter explains why the tax committees are such attractive assignments for congressmen and why the leading members of the tax committees have such full coffers at election time.

In the decades following World War II, American tax policy has also been shaped by a very distinct and particular vision—one traditionally enunciated by tax academics and professionals. Tax experts share a faith that the ideal income tax can be achieved through "tax reform." Their understanding of what is demanded by tax reform constitutes a distinct worldview—one that is dominant among the executive and congressional staffs charged with formulating policy initiatives and drafting tax legislation. In this way, the principles of tax reform have influenced the kind of tax proposals that are advanced and the kind of choices offered to policymakers by their own professional tax advisers. This often puts the congressman's professional advisers in conflict with his own basic motives and interests as a politician. Most of the time, the political impulses of congressional policymakers prevail, but occasionally the interests of these politicians and the worldview of the tax experts converge. This was most apparent in 1986, when congressional policymakers realized that tax reform could constitute a viable and convenient political issue. As a result of the momentary convergence of the interests of tax professionals and policymakers, the tax code was restructured under the Tax Reform Act of 1986 according to the general dictates of the movement for tax reform.

These many disparate uses and ideological imperatives that drive the politics of the income tax have resulted in an unstable and internally inconsistent tax policy. The incoherence and complexity of the tax code can be attributed to much the same source—a "pluralist" tax-policymaking process that accommodates nearly every organized economic interest at once, almost always preserving prior tax policies while constantly grafting new and often contradictory policies onto the same tax code through "incremental" development. The instability of federal tax policy is attributable to the American political system itself—a system of divided and shared powers, institutional fragmentation, and structural incoherence. And while instability has marked tax policy for decades as contemporary political coalitions (and their attendant tax policies) have come and gone, it was particularly intense during the 1980s, when federal tax policy dramatically shifted direction several times—first following the broad dictates of supply-side economics in 1981 then tax reform in 1986, and, by the end of the decade, no clear direction at all.

The major tax bill enacted in 1993, during the first year of the Clinton administration, seemed to signal a return to pre-1986 patterns of tax policy. But any such movement came to a screeching halt in 1994 with the electoral triumph of the Republican Party in Congress. The new Republican tax policy codified during the first one hundred days of the 104th Congress evidenced the high degree of partisanship underlying contemporary tax policy, as well as the continued volatility and lack of principle behind the enterprise as a whole.

This study begins with a survey of the historical origins of the federal income tax, focusing in particular on income tax legislation enacted during the postwar period. Special attention is paid to developments during the 1980s (in particular, the enactment of the historic Tax Reform Act of 1986) and the 1990s (especially the "new" Republican tax policy that dominated the policy agenda following the November 1994 elections). The pessimistic conclusion here is that the deficiencies and shortcomings of contemporary federal tax policy can be traced to the "constitution" of the American regime and the political system as a whole. As such, the shortcomings of the tax-policymaking process are likely to endure as an endemic problem.

Chapter 1 presents the overall theme of the book—that contemporary American tax policy has been generally unstable, unpredictable, highly partisan, and excessively complex because federal policymakers use the federal income tax for disparate and often contradictory purposes. Such use of tax law, generally to the detriment of income tax policy, is a consequence of the rules of the "tax game" established by the overall structure of American politics and institutions (i.e., the "constitution" of the regime). The "normal" rules of the tax game are defined by the pluralist structure of political power that prevails in American politics and usually results in a process of incremental development for the income tax. Within the confines of this constitutional structure, congressional policymakers use the tax code as a *political instrument* in pursuit of what are in essence political aims—constituency service, reelection, and partisanship. While not inherently undesirable, this political use does place great strains on the income tax as a source of revenue and impinges upon the underlying coherence of tax policy.

Chapter 2 presents a brief historical account of the fiscal organization of the early American state, the adoption during the Civil War of the first federal income tax, the subsequent reenactment of an income tax in 1913, the dramatic expansion of the income tax during World War I, and the transformation of the income tax into a broad-based "mass" tax during World War II. I argue herein that the fiscal crises provoked by these military conflicts led to the most dramatic and important structural developments in the federal income tax. Unlike most domestic programs and policies, the income tax expands, rather than contracts, during periods of military crisis as policymakers scramble for new revenues.

Federal income tax policy in the decades following World War II is examined in Chapter 3. During this sustained period of politics-as-usual, Congress learned and perfected the art of policymaking through manipulating the income tax code. The first expression of many of the problems that haunt contemporary American tax policy—excessive complexity, incoherence, and instability—can be traced to the major legislative efforts of the 1960s and 1970s. The extraordinarily high marginal tax rates that survived World War II provided the foundation for the instrumental tax policymaking wherein congressmen introduce special-interest provisions as relief for constituents. At the same time, postwar tax policy has always reflected the underlying partisan divisions that emerged in the wake of the New Deal "critical realignment."

In Chapters 4 and 5, the focus is on tax policy in the 1980s and 1990s. During these decades, tax policy clearly evidenced an inherent conflict between an unrestrained political use of the income tax by the tax policymaker qua politician and the revenue imperative that drives so much of our fiscal policy. The resulting tax policy was particularly unstable and erratic, even by contemporary American standards. Political pressure for tax cuts eventually undermined the great capacity of even the federal income tax to raise revenue. This has resulted in unprecedented peacetime budget deficits, which in turn have limited the options available to policymakers. In Chapter 6, I consider the special factors that characterized and contributed to the peculiar pattern of tax policymaking that emerged during the 1980s.

The overuse of the tax code to achieve disparate goals and objectives has also resulted in excessive complexity in the tax laws. Tax professionals have made their own special contribution to the quagmire that tax policy has become by inflicting untold complexity on the income tax through Treasury regulations, thereby exacerbating the problem of overlegislating by Congress and the executive. The origins of the excessive complexity of the income tax and the problems associated with it are considered in Chapter 7.

The movement for tax reform was a significant political force behind the most important legislation in the history of the federal income tax—the Tax Reform Act of 1986. Tax experts in the bureaucracy shared a professional commitment to the principles advanced by the tax-reform movement. This had an important impact upon the choice of a bill to serve as the Reagan administration's first initiative for tax reform in 1985 (i.e., the so-called Treasury I tax-reform bill), an effort that culminated in TRA. The intellectual origins and ideological premises of the movement for tax reform and the manner of that movement's institutionalization within the tax bureaucracy and, hence, the tax-policymaking process are the subjects of Chapter 8.

The dominant theoretical models advanced to describe and explain the development and politics of the federal income tax are considered in Chapter 9. Pluralism has been the most comprehensive descriptive model of the structure of power in American politics. Incrementalism is a descriptive model of tax policymaking within the confines of the pluralist structure of politics; it is also a normative strategy for a particular mode of "rational" policymaking. Incrementalism and pluralism are often combined into a single unified model of "normal" congressional tax policymaking, which is said to advance through incremental or gradual departures from existing law. The incrementalist/pluralist model is highly descriptive of the normal policymaking for the income tax during most of the postwar period and generally expresses the rules of the tax game that prevail during such periods of politics-as-usual. Notwithstanding the considerable power of the incrementalist/pluralist model, it fails to explain the almost schizophrenic pattern of tax policy witnessed in the 1980s, as well as the highly partisan tax policy that has characterized the 1990s to date. Likewise, the model is not very helpful in describing tax policymaking during the periods of wartime crisis, when the most important and radical innovations in the income tax have appeared. In Chapter 9, I present the outline for an alternative typology to explain the long-term development of the federal income tax–a typology that takes into account those periods of systemic crisis during which the most radical and significant changes to the income tax laws are made.

The intention here is to present a broad picture of the tax-policymaking process, rather than to focus upon any one narrow aspect of the federal income tax, as is typical in the vast literature on taxation. Tax policy embraces questions of economics, law, public finance, and public policy. However, in the end the federal income tax is a *political instrument*, and tax policy is made by partisan politicians acting within the context and confines of the American political system. This is to say that tax policy is a political story–one that ultimately must be told in political terms.

1

Revenue, Politics, and the Income Tax

[P]oliticians want to be reelected, bureaucrats want to manage a stable and efficient tax policy, and interest groups want to promote the well-being of their constituents. But how these general desires get translated into specific policy preferences and specific political strategies depends upon the rules of the game; and the rules of the game are written by the institutions through which the game is played.

— Sven Steimo, *Taxation and Democracy* (1993)

The overall theme of this book is that federal policymakers use the income tax for a wide variety of political purposes, resulting in a tax policy that is generally unstable, unpredictable, highly partisan, and excessively complex. In so using the tax laws for such disparate and often contradictory purposes, congressional policymakers are simply following the rules of the "tax game" established by the overall structure of American politics and institutions. Within this "constitutional" structure, the tax code is transformed into a political instrument. This use of the federal income tax compromises its capacity to raise revenue and undermines the coherence of tax policy.

Revenue and the Income Tax

For decades the U.S. income tax has been the single most important source of revenue for the federal government, providing an extraordinarily fertile and stable means of financing the activities of the American state. Revenue derived from the federal income tax (corporate and individual combined) has increased from $28 million in 1913 (the first half year of the tax) to $29 billion in 1945, during the height of World War II, to $587 billion in 1990, to a projected $781 billion for fiscal 1996. In 1914, the federal income tax provided 9.7 percent of total receipts of the federal government; by 1985, the figure was 55 percent. In 1950, revenue from the federal income tax constituted 45 percent of federal receipts from all taxes; by 1985, the figure had risen to nearly 73 percent.[1]

Income taxation would be of paramount importance to the American state if only on account of this immense revenue that it raises. A modern income tax makes possible a state's institutional development because it provides a viable means to tap the great wealth produced by modern, advanced market economies. Income taxation is both an exercise of and prerequisite to a modern state. A successful income tax is conceivable only within the context of an advanced market society such as that which had emerged in the United States and Great Britain by the turn of the century; at the same time, only a well-developed state is capable of administering and enforcing the kind of income tax that will generate such massive revenue. The significance of the state's capacity to "extract" revenue from civil society to sustain its own institutional development has been described as follows: " 'Extraction' is an ugly but necessary term that neatly summarizes the complex strategies governments adopt to assure themselves adequate flows of revenue. . . . [R]ulers cannot develop a central state apparatus without some degree of capacity to extract revenues from the subject population of a nation."[2] It was the federal income tax that provided the twentieth-century American state with the capacity to extract revenue from the private economy to finance two worldwide military campaigns and (along with the Social Security wage tax) the modern social welfare

---

1. Federal receipts from all forms of taxation (income, excise, estate, etc.) reached $1 trillion for the first time in 1990. The individual income tax alone raised $476.5 billion in 1992. As a percentage of gross domestic product (GDP), receipts from the individual income tax increased dramatically during World War II, declined after the war, and remained relatively constant (in the range from 8 to 9 percent of GDP) thereafter. Revenue from the corporate income tax has declined steadily from 30 percent of federal revenue in the early 1950s to a fairly constant 20 to 25 percent in the 1960s to the current figure, which hovers at or below 10 percent. This is partly on account of the increase in other taxes, such as Social Security. See House Committee on Ways and Means, *Overview of the Federal Tax System*, 103d Cong., 1st sess. (Washington, D.C.: Government Printing Office, 1993); *Statistical Abstract of the United States* (Washington, D.C.: Government Printing Office, 1985), table 488, p. 307.

2. Dall W. Forsythe, *Taxation and Political Change in the Young Nation, 1781–1833* (New York: Columbia University Press, 1977), 1.

state. If, as Edmund Burke once declared, the "revenue of the state is the state," then surely the U.S. income tax has been at the heart of the twentieth-century American state.

A federal income tax was first contemplated by national policymakers during the revenue crisis caused by the War of 1812. However, the war ended before any final political action was taken. That was not the case during the 1860s, when the Civil War forced policymakers reluctantly to adopt the first U.S. income tax in 1861 in the face of a deepening fiscal crisis attributable to the military conflict. The regional, economic, and partisan resistance to income taxation, suppressed during the crisis of the Civil War, was reasserted once the conflict ended. Facing intense opposition from Northern industrial interests aggregated within the Republican Party, the tax was allowed to expire in 1872. However, ideological backing for income taxation gained support again in the closing decades of the nineteenth century, especially among the more radical agrarian political parties of the South and Midwest. Sentiment in favor of an income tax remained strong, notwithstanding the opposition of the U.S. Supreme Court, and a new income tax was enacted in 1913 soon after the ratification of the Sixteenth Amendment. This new income tax was significantly expanded during the revenue crisis of World War I and again during World War II. During these military crises of the twentieth century, the income tax emerged as the primary source of revenue for the American state. However, the relationship between income taxation and the American state goes far beyond revenue.

The Income Tax as a Political Instrument

An examination of the vast body of the Internal Revenue Code from a broad historical perspective reveals that the drive for revenue has been the single most important force behind the adoption and subsequent expansion of the income tax. However, similar examination of the congressional politics-as-usual through which the federal tax laws are made indicates that a significant portion of income tax policy is dedicated *not* to raising revenue, but rather to implementing public policies that effectively reduce federal revenue. During periods of peace and domestic tranquillity, revenue is but one among many concerns pursued by federal policymakers—and not always the dominant or overriding one at that.

For instance, the income tax is used by American policymakers as an easy, albeit crude, means for manipulating private economic and social behavior. Through taxation, a state is able to alter the allocation of goods and services that otherwise results from the unrestrained expression of human wants and desires. In this way, the income tax establishes a broad system of economic incentives and disincentives through which the state can direct, and thereby subtly control, a wide sphere of private economic and social activity. Liberal capitalist states that otherwise maintain relatively free markets and adhere to general principles favoring a minimum of governmental intrusion into private economic matters routinely use income taxation to direct the private economic sphere, although few so extensively as the United States. Since the American state is particularly lacking in the institutions and powers of centralized planning and economic management found elsewhere among the Western industrial democracies and Japan, political elites here have found taxation to be one of the best means at their disposal for implementing macroeconomic policy. For this reason, taxation has become an important, if not the primary, fiscal tool of the American state.

In the years following World War II, political elites, labor, and capitalists all came to regard the income tax as a means for stimulating long-term investment and the accumulation of capital. "Beginning with the Employment Act of 1946, the federal government undertook to oversee the economy and maintain a stable business climate through macroeconomic stabilization policies that involved the income tax structure among other tools."[3] This consensus was informed by a "neo-Keynesian" faith in the central government's capacity to manage the national economy for purposes of long-term growth, job creation, and prosperity for capital and labor alike. As Ronald King puts it: "Public finance increasingly became an arena devoted to government efforts at non-zero-sum macroeconomic regulation, and taxation was thus transformed into an instrument promising class coordination, not polariza-

---

3. Cathie J. Martin, *Shifting the Burden: The Struggle over Growth and Corporate Taxation* (Chicago: University of Chicago Press, 1991), 18. Martin's interesting study focuses upon the ways in which the corporate income tax was turned into a system of deductions and credits "to create incentives to stimulate savings and investment." She also focuses upon the politics behind the decline of the corporate income tax as a source of federal revenue from the 1950s to the 1980s (i.e., "shifting the burden" away from corporate taxpayers). However, Martin cannot really prove that this trend amounted to shifting the burden (or incidence) of taxation from the wealthy to the middle class, since it remains uncertain who bears the economic cost, or incidence, of the corporate income tax.

tion."[4] Federal tax policy has reflected this undoubtedly overly optimistic belief that the federal government can manage the national economy through the tax laws. Walter Heller, economist and member of John F. Kennedy's Council of Economic Advisers, observed this "important truth" in declaring that "the tax system is more than a revenue-raising device, it is an instrument of national policy."[5]

So for decades now the federal income tax has been used (for better or worse) as an "instrument" for managing the national economy. Federal policymakers in Congress and the White House routinely use the income tax to implement a wide array of public policies. Some of these are broad national public policies. Others are narrow provisions inserted into the tax laws strictly for the benefit of "special interests"–many of which, not surprisingly, are located in the home district of some member of Congress with a strategic seat on one of the tax committees. Nevertheless, though special interests often prevail in influencing tax policy decisions, this is only one side of the story, one greatly exaggerated in journalistic accounts of tax politics, as well as in the general public's perception of how Congress works. But whether used to implement broad national economic policy or

4. Ronald F. King, *Money, Time, and Politics: Investment Tax Subsidies and American Democracy* (New Haven: Yale University Press, 1993), 121. This is the central theme of King's important interpretation of the development of postwar income tax policy. See also Barry P. Bosworth, *Tax Incentives and Economic Growth* (Washington, D.C.: Brookings Institution, 1984), 5: "The neo-Keynsian or neoclassical synthesis–bringing together long-held views of the determinants of supply and Keynsian views on the need to manage aggregate demand–has provided the framework for the discussion and conduct of economic policy for the last several decades. . . . On the demand side, fiscal and monetary policies were aimed at moving actual output closer to potential and avoiding the fluctuations that had been so costly in the past. On the supply side, new tax incentives and an accommodative monetary policy were major elements of an effort to encourage new investment."

5. Quoted in King, *Money, Time, and Politics*, 268. Three decades later, this observation seems trite; textbooks take it as a given fact of tax policy. See, e.g., Joseph A. Pechman, *Federal Tax Policy*, 5th ed. (Washington, D.C.: Brookings Institution, 1987), 5: "Taxation is a major instrument of social and economic policy. It has three goals: to transfer resources from the private to the public sector; to distribute the cost of government fairly . . . and to promote economic growth, stability and efficiency." See also John K. McNulty, *Federal Income Taxation of Individuals*, 4th ed. (St. Paul, Minn.: West Publishing Co., 1988), 1–2: "The income tax serves several functions in addition to financing federal government expenditures. It also allocates resources, encourages or discourages certain kinds of economic and social behavior, redistributes wealth, stimulates or stabilizes economic growth, helps maintain our federalism, and helps solve some specific social problems such as pollution and urban decay."

to benefit narrow special interests, the income tax is an important tool of federal policymakers in making public policy.

The many provisions in the tax code *not* dedicated to raising revenue enact a curious assortment of social and economic policies, often in a rather haphazard fashion. This is the source of much of the incoherence found in the tax code. Old policies are seldom repealed by the "incremental" policymaking that prevails in the tax arena; new policies (very often at cross-purposes to the old) are simply grafted onto the tax code. This instrumental use of the federal income tax is a relatively recent phenomenon of the postwar period. While the great revenue-raising potential of the modern income tax was almost immediately recognized by political elites during the wartime fiscal crisis of World War I, it took several decades more for congressional policymakers to comprehend the great possibilities of the income tax as a nonpartisan tool for serving constituents. But since World War II, Congress has perfected the art of policymaking through the income tax laws.

At the same time, a distinctly partisan use of the federal income tax reflects the fact that early in the history of the nation the major political parties cultivated their own very distinct fiscal and tax policies. During the first decades of the nineteenth century, this was evidenced by the split between Federalists and Jeffersonian Republicans, a split in substantial part occasioned by deep-rooted ideological differences over tariff policy. Later in the nineteenth century, the parties were divided over the fundamental question of an income tax. Ever since, Democrats and Republicans have disagreed on the substantive issues of income tax policy and on the overall structure of the tax system, with Republicans generally favoring lower and flatter tax rates since the 1860s. In the 1920s, Warren Harding's treasury secretary, Andrew W. Mellon, was instrumental in cultivating the Republican Party's first income tax policy and rhetoric, both of which were resurrected intact during the 1994 congressional elections. None of this should come as much of a surprise, since partisan affiliation was, and remains, the single most significant division within Congress.[6] Differences over tax policy simply reflect the dominant partisan cleavage of the day.

While there are fundamental differences in the visions of tax policy that prevail among Republicans and Democrats, congressional policymakers share a nonpartisan inclination to implement their respective policies through the income tax. Democrats have traditionally favored

6. See, e.g., Jerrold E. Schneider, *Ideological Coalitions in Congress* (Westport, Conn.: Greenwood Press, 1979).

such policies as offering tax credits for low-income earners and for housing for the poor, encouraging employee stock ownership plans (ESOPs) and retirement plans through tax preferences, limiting executive compensation, and providing preferential tax treatment for employer-provided health insurance and pension plans. Republicans pursue a similarly wide range of social and economic policies through the tax code: income tax cuts, preferential tax treatment for capital gains, tax-favored economic "enterprise zones" as a cure for urban blight, and various tax credits and expenditures aimed at encouraging savings, investment, and the accumulation of capital. The list goes on and on. The very first week that he was elected Speaker of the House of Representatives, Republican Newt Gingrich proposed (apparently in all seriousness, but what later was described by Gingrich himself as a "dumb idea") a tax credit for the "poor" to enable them to purchase laptop computers.[7] More absurd proposals have found their way into the tax code.

Conservatives who otherwise extol the virtues of "voluntary" private action, fiscal responsibility, and governmental noninterference in the private social and economic spheres showed great eagerness in the 1980s to use the tax laws to implement their favored social and economic policies. Condemning the institutional approaches of New Deal liberalism, conservatives find the tax code a convenient alternative vehicle for public policymaking—assuming that governmental controls imposed through tax credits and tax preferences are somehow less coercive than programs relying upon direct budgetary outlays and enforcement through administrative agencies other than the Internal Revenue Service. In many respects, the most significant difference between the tax policies of congressional Democrats and Republicans lies in the particular policies that they choose to write into the tax laws. Both sides of the political spectrum appear equally enamored of the electoral benefits derived from using the tax code to provide nonpartisan constituency service to the home district. The resulting tax policy has left the tax code riddled through and through by a dizzying array of tax credits, preferences, and deductions.

A number of factors contributed to the general increase in this use of the federal income tax to make public policy. First, the development of an American social welfare state during the 1930s greatly increased the overall magnitude of all public policies pursued by the federal

7. Testimony of Speaker of the House Newt Gingrich before a joint meeting of the House Ways and Means and Senate Finance Committees, January 5, 1995, as reported in "104th Congress: The First 100 Days," *N.Y. Times*, January 6, 1995, A20, col. 1.

government. Perhaps it was inevitable that some of these new policies would find their way into the federal tax code; more than a few did. Second, the tax legislative arena, as compared to that of budgeting and appropriations, proved to be generally more accessible and hospitable to the personal interests, ambitions, and goals of individual congressmen. It simply proved politically easier to provide constituents with benefits through the tax code than through direct budgetary expenditures.[8] On top of this, the overall rise of interest-group politics and the related decline in political parties following World War II left individual congressmen relatively free to pursue special-interest tax provisions on behalf of their constituents. The post-Watergate "reforms" of the congressional-committee hierarchy (discussed further in Chapters 3 and 6) only contributed to this trend, since they radically altered the political arena within which tax policy is made—in particular, weakening the control over the tax legislative process formerly exerted by the chairman of the House Ways and Means Committee. As a result, congressional policymakers were increasingly able to use the tax code as a vehicle for satisfying their own individual political goals and aspirations. Few in the legislative branch had much interest in protecting the integrity of the tax code or the interest of the Treasury in revenue.

The most common means of enacting public policy through the tax code is through tax preferences of one sort or another. Such tax preferences are now often referred to as "tax expenditures" to emphasize the extent to which they are functionally equivalent (at least in respect to the net effect upon the Treasury) to direct expenditures or outlays. The concept of tax expenditures was first formally introduced to budget analysis by the Treasury Department in 1968. Subsequently recognized by statute, tax expenditures are defined as "those revenue losses attributable to provisions of the Federal tax laws which allow a special exclusion, exemption, or deduction from gross income or which provide a special credit, a preferential rate of tax, or a deferral of tax liability."[9]

8. One main difference between the tax arena and that of appropriations is that an appropriations bill must first clear a subcommittee with pertinent technical expertise and jurisdiction over the bill before it reaches the appropriations committee, whereas a comparable tax expenditure proceeds directly out of the tax committee. For a summary of other relevant differences between the tax and appropriating processes, see Thomas J. Reese, *The Politics of Taxation* (Westport, Conn.: Quorum Books, 1980), 198–201.

9. Congressional Budget and Impoundment Act, Pub. L. No. 93-344, sec. 3(a)(3), 88 Stat. 298, 299 (1974). For a comprehensive discussion of the political process of legislating tax expenditures, see Stanley S. Surrey, *Pathways to Tax Reform: The Concept of Tax Expenditures* (Cambridge: Harvard University Press, 1973); see also Stanley S. Surrey and

Tax expenditures grant relief from taxation on specific terms, with the express intention of altering the behavior of those who wish to claim the benefit of such exemption, deferral, or tax credit. Thus, rather than "loopholes"—a term that suggests a glitch or tax benefit unintentionally conferred by Congress upon taxpayers (or at least those astute enough to recognize them)—tax expenditures are preferences intentionally adopted precisely to allow taxpayers to escape some measure of taxation by complying with the dictates of the particular favored policy. Of course, there also are genuine loopholes in the tax code—unintended tax benefits derived from the intersection of different provisions of the tax code that, when combined by tax attorneys, produce significant tax advantages. Some of the more clever (and perfectly legal) tax shelters devised during the 1970s and early 1980s would fall into this category.[10]

Notwithstanding the relatively recent awareness of the importance of tax expenditures in the budgetary process, the use of sanctioned tax preferences in the political process was already understood by the 1950s and common by the 1960s. Congressional policymakers, as well as those in the White House, routinely offered tax incentives to specific groups, interests, or classes of individuals, with the goal of promoting social and economic policies favored by such policymakers, as well as satisfying constituents. When tax preferences are used by members of Congress for purposes of constituency service, the class of taxpayers who benefit may be so narrow as to consist of a single individual—as is the class of taxpayers affected by the "transition rules" for new tax legislation.[11]

Because policymaking through tax expenditures is relatively easy and generally conducive to the political and electoral needs of representatives in Congress, it has become a common mode of congressional policymaking. As a result, the revenue-raising capacity of the tax code has been undermined by special tax preferences generated by the political process, and no end to the practice is in sight. Stanley Surrey and Paul McDaniel calculated that the volume of government "spending"

Paul McDaniel, *Tax Expenditures* (Cambridge: Harvard University Press, 1985), and Pechman, *Federal Tax Policy*, 355–63.

10. It is not as easy as many would think to define a "tax shelter." See, e.g., Calvin H. Johnson, "What's a Tax Shelter?" 68 *Tax Notes* 879 (August 14, 1995).

11. For a discussion of such narrow tax preferences granted to individuals in the transition rules to the Tax Reform Act of 1986, see Donald L. Barlett and James B. Steele, "The Great Tax Giveaway," *Phila. Inquirer*, April 10, 1988; see also Lawrence Zelenak, "Are Rifle Shot Transition Rules and Other Ad Hoc Tax Legislation Constitutional?" 44 *Tax L. Rev.* 563 (1989).

through tax expenditures increased by 179 percent from fiscal year 1974 to fiscal year 1981.[12] The tax expenditure spending spree continued even after 1981, notwithstanding the success of tax-reform efforts in 1986. A recent study by the General Accounting Office estimated that tax expenditures totaled almost $402 billion in 1993 and will continue to increase annually by 4 percent.[13]

Every tax expenditure represents a discrete departure from a pure revenue-driven tax policy. As tax reformers like to remind us, the cumulative affect of all the many tax expenditures, credits, exemptions, deferrals, and other tax preferences has been to "erode" the revenue-raising capabilities of the federal income tax. According to the president's budget for fiscal year 1997, the revenue loss attributable to federal income tax expenditures will be $544 billion – a 4.1 percent increase over 1996.[14] To the extent that the income tax succeeds in redirecting social and economic behavior toward preferred activities enshrined in the tax code, it becomes less capable of raising revenue. In turn, the revenue loss attributable to the increase in tax expenditures increases pressure for higher overall tax rates. For this reason, the distinctive characteristic of the postwar federal income tax has been high marginal tax rates with an abundance of tax preferences provided by congressional policymakers eager to alleviate the burden of such rates as they apply to favored constituents. This proliferation of tax expenditures has even led some to question whether the federal income tax can continue as the primary source of federal revenue.[15]

During the 1950s, the revenue loss attributable to the use of the federal income tax for such instrumental political purposes was much less critical. Congressional policymakers enjoyed the luxury of unprecedented, sustained economic prosperity during the immediate postwar era. Buoyed by the effect of long-term inflationary trends and the strong economy, federal policymakers enjoyed a constantly increasing source of revenue attributable to so-called bracket creep. The relative stability of

---

12. Surrey and McDaniel, *Tax Expenditures*, 6.

13. General Accounting Office, "Tax Policy: Tax Expenditures Deserve More Scrutiny" (GAO/GGD-AIMD-94-122) (June 3, 1994).

14. Budget of the United States Government, Fiscal Year 1997 (submitted to Congress by President Clinton, March 19, 1996), "Analytical Perspectives," chap. 5 ("Tax Expenditures").

15. See, e.g., Michael J. Graetz, "Can the Income Tax Continue to Be the Major Revenue Source?" in *Options for Tax Reform*, ed. Joseph A. Pechman (Washington, D.C.: Brookings Institution, 1984).

institutional structures and partisan politics in Congress contributed to the persistence of this pattern of tax policymaking throughout the 1960s and into the 1970s. At that time, the postwar economic boom began to stall out, denying policymakers the luxury of the automatic tax increases to which they had become accustomed. Then, in 1981 the income tax brackets were indexed for inflation, and policymakers were forced to confront serious revenue constraints. As discussed further in Chapters 4 and 5, this fiscal restraint, along with the enormous budget deficits that followed in the wake of the 1981 tax act, had a profound impact upon tax policymaking in the 1980s and 1990s, when the rules of the "tax game" were radically altered. While it is unclear whether any substantive changes in tax policy are attributable to the ongoing budget shortfalls, the structures and processes of federal tax policymaking have changed dramatically in the face of a heightened revenue imperative.

Rules of the Tax Game

The fiscal policies of any state inevitably reflect a complicated calculus of decisionmaking. A comparative study of the revenue policies of even relatively similar states will reveal very different fiscal policies, which are informed by the unique political institutions, cultures, and histories of each state. To paraphrase one prominent theorist of political change, tax policy is ultimately "rooted in and mediated by preestablished institutional arrangements."[16] This is the underlying theme of the historical account of American fiscal and tax policy that follows in subsequent chapters. A recent comparative study of the tax policies of Sweden, England, and the United States illustrates how the "preestablished regime" can determine the development of tax policy. The study reveals very different patterns of policymaking attributable to the individual political histories and institutions of these states. "Fundamentally, the various actors in the tax policy process in these three countries want similar things: politicians want to be reelected, bureaucrats want to

16. Stephen Skowronek, *Building A New American State: The Expansion of National Administrative Capacities, 1877–1920* (New York: Cambridge University Press, 1982), ix. Skowronek's study focuses on the relationship between political (or state) change and "the structure of the preestablished regime, the struggle for political power and institutional position that it frames, and the disjunction in time between environmental changes and new governing arrangements."

manage a stable and efficient tax policy, and interest groups want to promote the well-being of their constituents. But how these general desires get translated into specific policy preferences and specific political strategies depends upon the rules of the game; and the rules of the game are written by the institutions through which the game is played."[17] Accordingly, to make any sense of American tax policy, it is necessary first to understand how the rules of the "tax game" are played out within the political processes and institutions of American government.

The institutions and procedures established under the U.S. Constitution are important, but do not alone define the rules of the American tax game. The extraconstitutional democratic electoral party system that evolved in the early nineteenth century defines much of significance in American politics and, hence, implicitly affects the way the tax game is played. Likewise, the American political culture is important in defining the rules and setting the boundaries for the tax game; the revenue demands of the state, and the behavior of political elites, are bound and restrained by the liberal political tradition. At the same time, the motives and interests of the individual policymakers are very much relevant in determining the course of tax policymaking.

For instance, an unrestrained political use of the federal income tax makes little sense from the perspective of the state's abstract interest in maximizing revenue.[18] However, it makes all the sense in the world from the perspective, interests, motives, and goals of individual policymakers—most particularly, members of Congress seeking reelection. The political interests of individual congressional policymakers, defined within the context of the given political system and the unique American political tradition, lie most immediately in using the income tax to cultivate support among constituents and to implement public policies. This dictates in favor of tax expenditures, rather than tax increases and unrestrained revenue extraction.

Elected representatives must eventually confront the political reality of an electorate with an apparently insatiable appetite for "public goods" that at the same time harbors a deep-rooted intolerance for the levels of taxation sufficient to support its own proclivities. This creates

17. Sven Steinmo, *Taxation and Democracy: Swedish, British, and American Approaches to Financing the Modern State* (New Haven: Yale University Press, 1993), 10.
18. That the rulers of a state have such an interest in maximizing revenue is the central theme of Margaret Levi, *Of Rule and Revenue* (Berkeley and Los Angeles: University of California Press, 1988), and idem, "A Theory of Predatory Rule," 10 *Pol. & Soc'y* 431 (1981).

a dilemma for elected officials subject to the mixed pressures of the democratic politics within which the tax regime is located. Popular resistance to tax increases is strong within the political culture, and these sentiments are translated into political commands by the electoral process that dominates the political system.[19] At the same time, the dynamics of American electoral politics creates strong incentives for congressional policymakers constantly to offer up greater quantities of public goods (as well as tax expenditures) for the benefit of constituents, thereby increasing overall pressure for higher taxes.[20] Over the long run, the "electoral connection" compels congressional policymakers to adopt ever more tax preferences and budget expenditures and concurrently avoid raising taxes to finance all the many policies that are now commonly referred to as "revenue losers." Indeed, there is enormous political pressure to *reduce* taxes even in the face of significant budget shortfalls—a lesson learned all too well by President Clinton. Clinton was forced to offer his own tax-cut proposals in an effort to quiet the thunder of Republicans in the wake of their significant electoral successes in the 1994 midterm elections, during which tax-reduction rhetoric ran rampant. Political incentives lead politicians to postpone paying the piper for as long as possible; budget deficits are the direct and inescapable consequence.

Accordingly, the overall operative tendency is for members of Congress (as well as the executive) to increase expenditures and thus aggravate the demand for revenue beyond what the federal income tax can readily accommodate within the limits imposed by the prevailing democratic/populist politics—at least, absent the extraordinary national unity occasioned by a military crisis. This has suggested to some an inherent structural defect in the democratic/liberal state, rendering it

19. For example, the grassroots, populist antitax movement that began in California with Proposition 13. For a discussion of antitax politics, see Susan B. Hansen, *The Politics of Taxation: Revenue Without Representation* (New York: Praeger, 1983), chap. 7, and David O. Sears and Jack Citrin, *Tax Revolt: Something for Nothing in California* (Cambridge: Harvard University Press, 1982). Much the same antitax sentiment was expressed in the 1977 Kemp-Roth proposal, as well as the politics leading up to the 1981 tax act. Antitax rhetoric heated up again during the fall of 1994, when conservative Republicans made tax cuts a central campaign theme.

20. James Buchanan describes this dynamics as follows: "[T]hose citizens and their legislative agents who enjoy the current benefits of spending without paying current taxes impose costs on all taxpayers who will be around in future periods." James M. Buchanan, "Clarifying Confusion About the Balanced Budget Amendment," 48 *Nat'l Tax J.* 347, 350 (1995).

incapable of adequately financing its own activities.[21] Whether this constitutes a "structural deficit" is a matter open to serious debate. Certainly the "Deficit" has become a constant presence looming over and influencing the course of contemporary American politics.[22] Even still, both the Republican and the Democratic Parties exert strong political pressure to reduce taxes, rather than raise them. The tension between the state's pressures for revenue and the citizenry's appetite for public goods imposes a peculiar (and perverse) dynamics on American tax policymaking.

In less open and democratic politics, political elites may escape this dynamics altogether, encountering fewer barriers and obstacles to the pure pursuit of revenue – perhaps even enjoying the outright unrestrained freedom to plunder their own societies. The sad history of the former Soviet Union suggests that political elites in control of an authoritarian state, unrestrained by popular controls, will extract the maximum wealth from civil society, even to the point where private economic activity is suppressed to the obvious detriment of the state itself. Pursuit of the state's wealth at the expense of civil society may be self-destructive in the long run, but the political elites who for decades dined on caviar and vodka in Moscow did not worry about the long run. They left behind an economy and society ravaged and decimated by the Soviet state itself. However, in the Western liberal democracies, political elites are continually subjected to popular controls exerted through electoral politics and the open expression of public opinion. Electoral competition and public opinion impose a significant degree of popular control over elected political elites and render them in some way accountable to the citizenry.[23] The need for American political elites to raise revenue for the

21. This is James O'Connor's premise, derived from his neo-Marxist perspective, that there is an inherent tendency of the liberal democratic state to spend beyond its fiscal capacities. James O'Connor, *The Fiscal Crisis of the State* (New York: St. Martin's Press, 1973).

22. Joseph White and Aaron Wildavsky described the looming presence of the budget deficit in American politics as follows: "Now we are living in the era of the budget .... Virtually all other issues are discussed and decided in terms of the impacts on the deficit." Aaron B. Wildavsky and Joseph White, *The Deficit and the Public Interest: The Search for Responsible Budgeting in the 1980s* (Berkeley and Los Angeles: University of California Press, 1989), xv–xvi. The politics of the budget deficit is the focus of a new study, John H. Makin and Norman J. Ornstein, *Debt and Taxes* (New York: Random House, 1994); see also James D. Savage, *Balanced Budgets and American Politics* (Ithaca, N.Y.: Cornell University Press, 1988).

23. The seminal statement of this view of electoral politics is found in Joseph A.

state is tempered by such electoral pressures and controls, exerted through the peculiar arrangement of American political institutions operating within the traditional liberal political culture.

One of the most significant achievements of American constitutionalism has been to devise and put in place structures and procedures that effectively restrain the federal government from imposing arbitrary, exploitative, and onerous controls over the private sphere. The prevailing democratic electoral politics has generally limited the capacity of the state to maximize its revenue at the expense of civil society. The power of the liberal state to tax, like all the other coercive powers of the state, has for the most part been contained within constitutionally prescribed boundaries. This has effectively prevented American political elites from behaving as bona fide "revenue predators."[24] However, the same institutional arrangements and democratic politics have also contributed to a fragmented and internally inconsistent tax policy. This is the real "structural" problem of contemporary American tax policy.

Political Structures and the Tax Game

As noted above, there are significant incentives for politicians to use the federal income tax for purely instrumental political purposes. This politically motivated use of the federal income tax is but one consequence of the lack of institutional resistance to interest-group pressures; an unstable and inconsistent tax policy is another. In addition, the simultaneous efforts to raise revenue, make public policy, serve special interests, and direct the national economy through the federal income tax all leave tax policy without any singular purpose or body of unified and coherent

---

Schumpeter, *Capitalism, Socialism, and Democracy* (New York: Harper & Row, 1950), chap. 22. Robert Dahl built upon Schumpeter's theme, arguing that elections ensure that "political leaders will be somewhat responsive to the preferences of some ordinary citizens." Robert A. Dahl, *A Preface to Democratic Theory* (Chicago: University of Chicago Press, 1956), 131.

24. Again, the reference is to Margaret Levi's "theory of predatory rule," which holds that "rulers are predatory in that they try to extract as much revenue as they can from the population." Levi, *Of Rule and Revenue*, 3. Notwithstanding the significant insights of Levi's theory, the conclusion here is that it is not particularly useful in describing or predicting the actions or motives of American policymakers with respect to the politics of the U.S. income tax.

organizational principles.[25] It has also made American tax law an incredibly complicated affair. Stanley Surrey once described contemporary tax legislation as "a catch-as-catch-can affair that produces complexities, unfairness, conflicting moves in all directions, almost mindless provisions."[26] Amazingly, Surrey wrote those words *before* the great deluge of tax legislation enacted during the 1980s, wherein the complexities, conflicting moves, and mindless provisions proliferated beyond anything previously experienced or imagined.

The instability, incoherence, and great complexity of contemporary tax policy can be traced to a number of factors. First, American political institutions designed to restrain the coercive powers of the federal government have simultaneously introduced conflict into the legislative process. As constitutional scholar Edwin Corwin once observed, the separation of powers built into the structure of national political institutions by the U.S. Constitution proved to be an invitation to two hundred years of conflict. This separation of the executive and legislative functions has similarly contributed to the instability and incoherence of contemporary American tax policy. Major tax policy initiatives tend to originate with the executive branch, but tax legislation is very much a product of a congressional policymaking process dominated by a relatively small number of key players on the House Ways and Means and Senate Finance Committees. The divergence of interests between the executive and legislative branches, even when these are controlled by the same national party, is evidenced in the final legislative product and is one notable source of the incoherence of contemporary tax policy.

Second, the pluralist structure of American political institutions affords private interests considerable access to public policymaking. It is generally recognized that on account of this pluralist structure, federal policymakers have been highly accessible (or, more pessimistically, susceptible) to the entreaties of private interests located outside the formal processes of government. The input of constituents, special interests, so-called public-interest groups, as well as the media, is felt most intensely in congressional committees. The pressures from these various interests play an important role in shaping tax policy outcomes, securing enactment of special provisions, or merely in vetoing some

25. That interest-group politics (or "interest-group liberalism") generally lacks coherence and principle is a major theme of Theodore J. Lowi, *The End of Liberalism* (New York: W. W. Norton, 1969).

26. Stanley S. Surrey, "Our Troubled Tax Policy," 12 *Tax Notes* 179 (February 2, 1981).

executive initiative adverse to their interests, thereby robbing tax policy initiatives of any overall perspective or ideological coherence. The tax code becomes a collection of disconnected and occasionally contradictory provisions as congressional policymaking degenerates into this peculiar brand of tax-"pork-barrel" politics.

There have been moments in political time when broad national partisan coalitions have emerged and overwhelmed this congressional "politics-as-usual"—such as during the first years of the New Deal, immediately following Lyndon Johnson's triumph in 1964, in the years following Ronald Reagan's overwhelming and decisive electoral victory in 1981, and during the opening days of the 104th Congress following the Republican victory in the 1994 midterm elections. During these rare moments of consensus, broad tax policy initiatives have prevailed. However, such moments of tax policy consensus have turned out to be temporary and invariably short-lived. Notwithstanding the apparent strength of commitment to a particular political alliance at some given moment, coalitions melt away quickly and the course of tax policy shifts once again. During the periods of stability between critical elections and realignments, American tax policy has floundered.

Thus, the fundamental problem of contemporary American tax policymaking is that it seldom has any overall direction and is simply too accessible to too many private interests at once. This is a direct consequence of the constitutional structure of American politics. John Witte has observed that the "inability of the [tax] system to resist change create[s] a policy morass that is perpetuated by its own structure."[27] The underlying problem of American tax policy then relates to the failings of American politics and cannot simply be blamed upon the failure of individual "politicians" or "special interests" that are said to control congressional policymaking—as reformers so often hold. The failure of American tax policy reflects the fragmented structure of the American political system out of which it originates. Ironically, efforts in the early 1970s to "reform" the hierarchical organization and legislative procedures of Congress only exacerbated the problems of tax policy by further weakening the institutions of decisionmaking. With the weakening of these institutions, tax policymaking became an even more unprincipled and unstable enterprise, even more susceptible to pressures and interests external to the congressional apparatus of decisionmaking.

27. John F. Witte, *The Politics and Development of the Federal Income Tax* (Madison: University of Wisconsin Press, 1985), 20.

A Pattern of Erratic Tax Policy

The many failings of contemporary American policymaking regarding the income tax seemed to come to a head in the 1980s, when a "pattern of erratic tax policy" prevailed.[28] The tax legislation of the 1980s reflected the inability of the political system to adopt a single coherent tax policy to the exclusion of all others. In the 1980s, policymakers seemed intent upon accommodating nearly every organized political and economic interest—if not in the same tax bill, then eventually over time through their constant tinkering with the tax code. During the decade, the tax-policymaking process was particularly open and accessible to pressures from outside the formal legislative process and generally was unrestrained by fiscal reality or the inherent limits of public policy. For example, tax legislation enacted in 1981 slashed taxes and revenues, both out of ideological conviction (i.e., supply-side economics) and to appease pro-business constituents within the Republican Party. In sharp contrast, the Tax Reform Act of 1986 represented the greatest success of tax professionals in their quest to achieve a more perfect tax code through "tax reform." In this respect, the spirit of the 1986 bill was very much at odds with that of the 1981 legislation. In a matter of only five years, federal tax policy entirely reversed course—and this under the tutelage of the very same president.[29]

Not only is contemporary American tax policy unstable, but the tax laws have also become incredibly complex on account of the overuse of the income tax laws for instrumental political purposes. American tax laws are by far the most complex of all the Western industrial nations. One of the purported goals of tax reformers in 1986 was to strip out the many tax preferences and expenditures that contribute so much to the excessive complexity of the enterprise. However, the already arcane tax laws actually grew more complex precisely because the 1986 act sought an aesthetically purer income tax regime; policymakers (first congressmen through their statutes, and then "tax experts" through their administrative regulations) drew increasingly subtle distinctions between

28. Charles A. McLure Jr., "The Budget Process and Tax Simplification/Complication," 45 *Tax L. Rev.* 25, 28 (1989).

29. Witte has pointed out the irony of President Reagan's political support for both the 1981 and 1986 tax acts: "Ronald Reagan thus has the unique historical position of supporting both the largest tax reform and the largest anti-tax reform legislation in the history of the United States." John F. Witte, "The Tax Reform Act of 1986: A New Era in Tax Politics?" 19 *Am. Pol. Q.* 438, 443 (1991).

what is allowed and what is disallowed under the tax laws. This constant overlegislating, so aptly described as "hyperlexis,"[30] threatens to swamp the tax code with the accumulated weight of such subtle distinctions.

While the reform of excessive complexity has emerged as a perennial issue on the tax policy agenda, the tax laws themselves have continued to grow ever more complex, becoming a serious consideration for taxpayers and practitioners who must cope with a system of rules and regulations spiraling out of control. However, for the politicians who are ultimately responsible for the excessive complexity, tax simplification provides an attractive political theme for currying favor with constituents. Indeed, it is unclear whether policymakers have any real interest in simplifying the tax laws. To paraphrase a theme familiar in the political science literature on Congress: the political interests of policymakers may very well be served best by acting in Congress to increase the complexity of the tax laws and, at the very same time, campaigning for reform and simplification before their constituents in the home district.[31]

The Study of the Federal Income Tax

Given the political uses of the federal income tax, as well as the obvious importance of the tax in financing the activities of the American state, one would expect political scientists to have paid considerably more attention to federal tax policy. Yet, the discipline as a whole has failed to appreciate the importance of income taxation. The complex way in which the state regulates and organizes private interests through income taxation has been left largely unexplored. Only in recent years

30. The term was coined to define "a pathological condition caused by an overactive law-making gland." Bayless Manning, "Hyperlexis: Our National Disease," 71 *Nw. U. L. Rev.* 767 (1977). Manning went on to describe and lament the consequences of hyperlexis: "Statutory codes, such as those in the fields of commercial law and taxation, are becoming ever more particularistic, longer, more complex, and less comprehensible. We are drowning in law."

31. The reference is to the proposition, set forth by political scientists Morris Fiorina and David Mayhew, that politicians will constantly rail against the "bureaucracy," though their political interest lies in creating the very same. See Morris P. Fiorina, *Congress: Keystone of the Washington Establishment* (New Haven: Yale University Press, 1977), and David R. Mayhew, *Congress: The Electoral Connection* (New Haven: Yale University Press, 1974).

have political scientists contributed much of substance to the vast literature on the federal income tax.[32] When they have concerned themselves with the income tax, political scientists have tended to focus upon the legislative process – the familiar story of Congress, committees, and the interest-group politics that is said to characterize tax policymaking. The classic account of this side of tax policymaking was first given almost forty years ago, and little new has been added since then.[33]

However, the political importance of the federal income tax goes beyond this interest-group politics exerted in Congress. The tax laws and political institutions constitute a unified "tax system," a steering mechanism for the liberal state through which political institutions exert control over civil society and the private economic sphere. If the income tax is used as a tool of the American state to regulate and control private interests, the relationship runs both ways, since private interests also use the open and porous tax-policymaking process to shape and define public policy to their own interest. For those who can read its arcane language, the tax code provides a virtual architectural blueprint of the American state.

Any study that treats the federal income tax as a self-contained body of law or economic principles will inevitably miss the important political and ideological dimensions of tax policy. For instance, economists have mostly concerned themselves with the fiscal and macroeconomic aspects of federal taxation. Applying formal theories at the systemic level, economists look to predict the impact of tax policy on mass economic behavior: "The principal question which economics raises is what effect will the tax policies have on economic growth, and on the efficient use of resources in the national economy."[34] Such an approach is important, but not very fruitful for explaining the politics or development of the income tax.

32. The following are some of the most recent and best contributions to the literature on the federal income tax from political scientists: John F. Witte, *The Politics and Development of the Federal Income Tax*; Timothy J. Conlan, Margaret T. Wrightson, and David R. Beam, *Taxing Choices: The Politics of Tax Reform* (Washington, D.C.: Congressional Quarterly Press, 1990); Cathie J. Martin, *Shifting the Burden: The Struggle over Growth and Corporate Taxation*; Ronald F. King, *Money, Time, and Politics: Investment Tax Subsidies and American Democracy*; Sven Steinmo, *Taxation and Democracy: Swedish, British, and American Approaches to Financing the Modern State*.

33. The seminal account is Stanley S. Surrey, "The Congress and the Tax Lobbyist – How Special Tax Provisions Get Enacted," 70 *Harv. L. Rev.* 1145 (1957).

34. B. Guy Peters, *The Politics of Taxation: A Comparative Perspective* (Cambridge: Blackwell, 1991), 1–2.

The goal here is to pursue a broader historical and theoretical perspective, viewing tax policy as the outcome of the dynamic interaction between the various political interests, ideologies, and, most significantly, the revenue imperative that drives American policymakers. The attempt is to delineate the sources of the conflicting demands made upon the federal income tax and to show how these account for the internal inconsistency, incoherence, instability, and excessive complexity that has plagued contemporary American tax policymaking. As such, this study raises issues central to contemporary American politics.

2

The Fiscal Organization of the American State

Taxes are the source of life for the bureaucracy, the army, the priests and the court, in short, for the whole apparatus of the executive power.
— Karl Marx, *The Eighteenth Brumaire of Louis Bonaparte* (1852)

The fiscal history of a people is above all an essential part of its general history.
— Joseph A. Schumpeter, "The Crisis of the Tax State" (1918)

The decisionmaking process in the American political system is defined to a large extent by the constitutional structure of the regime. Institutional arrangements adopted during the eighteenth century continue to influence contemporary policymaking. Likewise, contemporary policymaking reflects the accumulated weight of prior policy decisions. Policymakers seldom enjoy the luxury of writing on a clean slate, and the options at any given moment are defined by and, hence, limited by the choices made by prior generations. In this respect, policymaking is bound by political history. Accordingly, this study of contemporary American tax policy sets forth a brief account of the constitutional structure of the regime, as well as the historical origins of the federal income tax and its subsequent transformation into the U.S. government's most important source of revenue.

Revenue and the New American Regime

Even before the outbreak of the military hostilities that culminated in the American Revolution, indigenous political thought was already greatly hostile to centralized political power. A pervasive and deep-rooted strain of native antistatism has been traced to the radical antinomianism that pervaded colonial religious thought during the seventeenth and eighteenth centuries.[1] The antistatism of colonial political thought provided the theoretical underpinnings for the historical event of utmost significance, the severing of the constitutional tie with the English monarchy.[2] Following the Revolution, the fundamental concern of political theorists and statesmen alike was how to reconstitute the constitutional order destroyed by the Revolution.

The Articles of Confederation, while only formally ratified by the state governments in 1781, served as the constitution of the new American regime from 1777. The scant powers entrusted to the new central government by the state governments under the Articles reflected the prevailing consensus within the former colonies against creating a strong national entity. As the constitutional blueprint for the new unified regime, the Articles mandated a weak central state, establishing little more than the "firm league of friendship" it proclaimed to the world.[3] The decentralized federal structure established under the Articles stood in sharp contrast with the strong state development already evident in Europe by that time. American political institutions were borrowed from the English constitutional tradition, took root here in the eighteenth century, and "were given new life precisely at the time that they were being abandoned in the home country."[4] This was especially

---

1. The origins of colonial political thought are diverse. Among the best discussions of the interconnection between eighteenth-century American religious dogma and democratic political thought are Perry Miller, *Life in the Mind in America: From the Revolution to the Civil War* (New York: Harcourt, Brace & World, 1965); idem, *Errand into the Wilderness* (Cambridge: Harvard University Press, 1956); Alan Heimert, *Religion and the American Mind: From the Great Awakening to the Revolution* (Cambridge: Harvard University Press, 1966). Among the best accounts of political thought during the Revolutionary period are Bernard Bailyn, *Ideological Origins of the American Revolution* (Cambridge: Harvard University Press, 1967); Gordon S. Wood, *The Creation of the American Republic, 1776–1787* (New York: W. W. Norton, 1972); idem, *The Radicalism of the American Revolution* (New York: Knopf, 1992).

2. Not all were able to take the great intellectual leap to revolution. The reluctance was most clearly expressed in the political writings of John Adams. See, e.g., "A Dissertation on the Canon and Feudal Law," in *The Political Writings of John Adams* (Indianapolis: Bobbs-Merrill, 1954), 3–21; "Novanglus Papers," in *The Works of John Adams* (Boston: Little, Brown, 1856), 1:166, 2:405, 4:3, 9:354, 10:179.

3. Articles of Confederation, art. 3.

4. Samuel P. Huntington, *Political Order in Changing Societies* (New Haven: Yale University Press, 1968), 96.

the case with respect to the revenue powers granted to the national government. The fiscal organization of the new regime reflected the overall weakness of its central state vis-à-vis the constituent members of the confederation.

The separate constituent states already possessed their own independent sources of revenue. In some cases, state governments had been relatively autonomous political entities for over a century. Since the colonies were separated from the king's ministers by thousands of miles of ocean, officials of the local governments had long exercised a quasi-autonomous power of taxation.[5] None too surprisingly, the state governments retained for themselves this power as they struck the political bargain for the Articles; the central state was denied any comparable independent source of revenue. Under the Articles, the national government was strictly forced to rely upon the state governments to collect its revenue.[6] Such revenue assessments required a good deal of voluntary compliance by the state legislatures, something that was not always forthcoming. "Under the Articles of Confederation, extractive capacity was severely limited, and neither legal authority nor bureaucratic machinery existed to enforce the demands of the Continental Congress for revenues."[7] Rather than revenue predators, the officials of the national government under the Articles of Confederation more closely resembled revenue paupers or beggars.

This lack of an independent source of revenue for the central government severely inhibited the institutional development of the early American state. Compounding the problems attributable to the weak fiscal powers of the central state, the national military was also largely inadequate, composed of state militia with only officers in federal uniform. Thus, under the Articles of Confederation, the central state lacked both its own army and an independent source of revenue, the two most

5. A detailed discussion of colonial taxation is found in Edwin R. A. Seligman, *The Income Tax: A Study of the History, Theory, and Practice of Income Taxation at Home and Abroad* (New York: Macmillan, 1911), pt. 2, chap. 1, 367–87. The leading history of colonial taxation and the power of taxation under the Articles of Confederation is Robert A. Becker, *Revolution, Reform, and the Politics of American Taxation, 1763–1783* (Baton Rouge: Louisiana State University Press, 1980).

6. Articles of Confederation, art. 8. The most comprehensive discussion of the political regime established under the Articles of Confederation is Merrill Jensen, *The Articles of Confederation* (Madison: University of Wisconsin Press, 1940).

7. Dall W. Forsythe, *Taxation and Political Change in the Young Nation, 1781–1833* (New York: Columbia University Press, 1977), 14.

significant prerequisites to and indices of strong state development.[8] These deficiencies were the cause of the endemic institutional crisis that persisted throughout the 1780s. Revenue and currency problems were exacerbated by the $54 million debt that the Congress had amassed during the Revolutionary War. The central government was unable adequately to finance even the minimal activity granted it under the Articles, let alone retire the national debt previously incurred to finance the War.[9] The limited powers of the national government to raise revenue and its lack of an independent power to tax left the new regime forever teetering on the brink of fiscal collapse. At the same time, the constitutional structures created under the Articles prevented political elites from expanding national powers. The inherent institutional, fiscal, and military inadequacies of the new regime precipitated what an earlier generation of American historians referred to as the Critical Period.[10]

These weaknesses of the regime ultimately led the state legislators of Virginia to call for a convention in Annapolis in the fall of 1786 for the purpose of reforming the Articles of Confederation. The subsequent wholesale abandonment of the Articles and adoption of a new constitution at the Philadelphia Convention in 1787 represented the culmination of a decade of dissatisfaction with the Articles. The new Constitution of 1789 was supported by political elites with aspirations and visions of a strong national state, most notably, Alexander Hamilton and James Madison. These nationalists favored a radical restructuring of the regime to grant the central state enhanced military and fiscal powers. Local and state political elites were generally less favorably inclined toward such an expansion of the powers of the central state — a radical innovation that they understood was directly at their expense — although among local political elites in border states, support for a strong national military was a strong contributing factor behind the movement for an enhanced national entity.[11]

8. For a description of these indices of "strong" state development, see the well-known essay by J. P. Nettle, "The State as a Conceptual Variable," 20 *World Pol* 559 (1968).

9. An excellent recent account of the weaknesses of the fiscal organization of the central government during the period of the Articles of Confederation is found in James D. Savage, *Balanced Budgets and American Politics* (Ithaca, N.Y.: Cornell University Press, 1988), 54–84.

10. John Fiske, *The Critical Period of American History, 1783–1789* (Boston: Houghton, Mifflin & Co., 1888).

11. According to William Riker, border states were most exposed to attack by the British from Canada and by hostile Indian forces in Florida and the Southwest. Riker argues that this explains support among political elites in these regions for an enhanced

The local elites who opposed the expansion of national powers, pejoratively labeled Antifederalists by their political opponents, ultimately lost the political battle over ratification of the new Constitution to the nationalists.[12] The authors of *The Federalist Papers* were instrumental in securing the political coalition that abandoned the weak confederacy and greatly expanded national powers, especially those related to the central state's power to raise revenue independent of the state governments. In Alexander Hamilton's concise assessment, "A nation cannot long exist without revenue."[13] Later, Hamilton and Madison would personally exercise political powers within the new national government. However, though the Antifederalists lost the political battle over the Constitution to those with a vision of a more powerful national government, the reconstituted central state actually remained confined within such a narrow political space that the local state governments survived for the next two centuries as semi-autonomous political entities. The retention of an independent power of taxation for the local state governments under the Constitution of 1789 contributed much to preserving their autonomy.[14] Contrary to the notion that adoption of the new constitution solved the problem of the weakness at the center, the triumph was as much political rhetoric as reality.

What the Constitution of 1789 did successfully strengthen was the fiscal organization of the national government, which, most importantly, was no longer beholden to the constituent state governments for its revenue. However, even then the central state still only possessed what can at best be characterized as rather limited powers, especially with respect to stimulating and orchestrating the expansion of the nascent national economy. Furthermore, the national government's

---

military and more centralized confederation. William H. Riker, *Federalism: Origin, Operation, Significance* (Boston: Little, Brown, 1964), 12–25.

12. The classic study of the Antifederalists is Jackson Turner Main, *The Antifederalists: Critics of the Constitution, 1781–1788* (Chicago: Quadrangle Books, 1961); see also Herbert J. Storing, ed., *The Anti-Federalist* (Chicago: University of Chicago Press, 1985).

13. Alexander Hamilton, Paper No. 12, in *The Federalist Papers,* by James Madison, Alexander Hamilton, and John Jay (New York: New American Library, 1961); see also Hamilton in Paper No. 30 ("[T]here must be interwoven in the frame of the government a general power of taxation"), Paper No. 32, and Paper No. 34. Madison expressed similar sentiments in Paper No. 41.

14. For an account of nineteenth-century state taxation, see Seligman, *The Income Tax,* pt. 2, chap. 2, 388–429; see also Randolph E. Paul, *Taxation in the United States* (Boston: Little, Brown, 1954), 7.

limited financial resources remained inadequate to cope with the huge public debt amassed during the Revolutionary War. In 1789, tariff and various customs duties raised approximately $2 million annually, a significant amount, but dwarfed by the national debt, then in excess of $77 million. By the end of the decade, federal revenues had risen to approximately $8 million annually, producing surpluses over current expenditures in the range of $2 million, but still quite insufficient to retire the debt.

As the first secretary of the treasury, Hamilton argued that it was critical for the central state to consolidate and pay off the war debt. This led him to propose a broad program of institutional innovations for overcoming the revenue crisis. Hamilton's well-known proposals provided for the consolidation and repayment at face value of the war debt, the establishment of a strong national banking system and a program for public projects and internal development, and the use of protective tariffs for the benefit of emerging domestic industries.[15] Much of Hamilton's plan met with concerted opposition from significant sectors of civil society for which the competing national vision of Jeffersonian democracy still held much greater appeal. However, the bulk of Hamilton's program was eventually adopted in some form or another. Most important with respect to the fiscal organization of the new American state, a national bank was chartered, and the debt was consolidated and assumed by a federal government with expanded powers of taxation. Notwithstanding these Hamiltonian innovations in the organization of the American state, the national government still possessed only rather limited fiscal powers. Furthermore, the political battles over Hamilton's fiscal "reforms" (especially high protective tariffs) contributed to the split in Federalist ranks that led to the emergence of a new national party system and, later, Republican hegemony. The agrarian Jeffersonian republic, rather than the strong Hamiltonian fiscal state, emerged as the model for the American polity for the first half of the nineteenth century. The activities of this Jeffersonian state were financed through a piecemeal system of excise taxes, customs duties, the occasional sale of public lands, and, most significantly, the tariff.

---

15. Alexander Hamilton, "Report Relative to a Provision for the Support of Public Credit" (1790), "Second Report on the Further Provision Necessary for Establishing Public Credit" (1790), and "Report on Manufacturers" (1791), in *Reports of Alexander Hamilton* (New York: Harper & Row, 1964).

The tariff was at the heart of nineteenth-century public finance and, indeed, constituted the single most significant source of federal revenue up to World War I. The tariff was also used during the decades following the War of 1812 to implement a Hamiltonian policy of state protectionism that largely benefited Northern industrial interests and greatly offended Southern agriculture.[16] The irony is that the tariff was central to Hamilton's strong nationalist vision and anathema to Jeffersonian agrarian republicanism. The tariff provoked intense political conflict for over one hundred years as it pitted regional and economic interests against one another. Nevertheless, the nineteenth-century Jeffersonian state was entirely dependent upon the tariff for its finances. Later, in the face of a Hamiltonian expansion of state functions during the Civil War and again during the period of intense state-building orchestrated by Progressives during the first decades of the twentieth century, the tariff would prove inadequate for financing the development of a modern state. The tariff was a particularly inefficient means of raising federal revenue, since its yield fluctuated greatly in response to the success of business and the health of the economy, rather than in relation to the government's fiscal needs. This often resulted in surpluses one year and deficits the next.[17] The fiscal organization of the nineteenth-century American state would prove problematic because political elites were denied access by the Constitution to the revenue needed to support a modern, centralized administrative state.

Still, the fiscal powers of the early-nineteenth-century Jeffersonian state were adequate to finance its limited activities during periods of peace. Jefferson's secretary of treasury Albert Gallatin had considerable success in reducing the national debt and increasing Treasury reserves, even with the repeal of the "odious" Federalist internal taxes.[18] However, the fiscal stability of the Jeffersonian republic was greatly upset by the War of 1812. At first, Gallatin believed that borrowing and the tariff would be sufficient for financing the war with Britain; however, that

16. The best account of how the tariff was used to implement protectionist policies from 1816 through the Civil War is found in Forsythe, *Taxation and Political Change*, 62–106.

17. For a discussion of the inadequacies of the tariff as a source of federal revenue, see Roy G. Blakely and Gladys C. Blakely, *The Federal Income Tax* (New York: Longmans, Green & Co., 1940), 2.

18. The best account of Gallatin's fiscal policies is Alexander Balinky, *Albert Gallatin: Fiscal Theories and Policies* (New Brunswick, N.J.: Rutgers University Press, 1958).

proved not to be the case. Already by early 1813, the national government was having great difficulty in raising sufficient revenue to finance the war effort. The tariff was particularly sensitive to levels of international trade, and hence, the war itself caused a significant decline in federal revenue as foreign commerce declined. On account of the British naval blockade of the American coast, receipts from the tariff fell from $13 million in 1813 to only $6 million in 1814.[19] In response, a federal income tax was proposed by Treasury secretary Alexander J. Dallas in January 1815, but the war ended by December, before the tax was taken up by Congress.[20]

After the war, Federalists and Republicans joined to support a new system of internal protection under the Tariff Act of 1816. This system served the federal government well for the next forty-five years, since revenue usually exceeded governmental expenditures. When revenues came up short, the federal government simply borrowed to make up the difference, and usually repaid the loans within a matter of a few years. From 1817 to 1857, the Treasury Department issued notes or borrowed fourteen times, quickly paying off such debts out of subsequent budget surpluses. The revenue derived from the tariff was supplemented by revenue from the sale of public land. Such sales, though sporadic, produced significant revenue – amounting to $1 million in 1811, $5 million in 1834, $15 million in 1835, and $25 million in 1836.[21] Thus, even after the wartime excise and property taxes enacted during the War of 1812 were repealed, the federal government not only survived but prospered.

The Civil War: Regime Crisis and Income Taxation

Fiscal prosperity continued for four decades, at which time national institutions were pushed to the breaking point by the political crisis over states' rights and slavery. In 1860, the Jeffersonian institutions faced the most severe test in the history of the Republic. With the outbreak of overt military hostilities, the traditional nineteenth-century system of public finance was strained to the limit by the increased level of state activity

19. Sidney Ratner, *American Taxation: Its History as a Social Force in Democracy* (New York: W. W. Norton, 1942), 34.
20. Secretary of Treasury A. J. Dallas's proposal for a federal income tax is found in "Special Report on the State of the Finance, January 17, 1815," reprinted in *American State Papers* (Washington, D.C.: Gales and Seaton, 1832), 6:885–87.
21. Ratner, *American Taxation*, 35–39.

necessitated by the military crisis. As such, the Civil War was the great stimulus for institutional innovation as well as a watershed event in the history of the fiscal organization of the American state.

During the first year of the Civil War, Lincoln and his first secretary of treasury, Salmon Chase, believed that the necessary expansion of the military could be funded through increases in the tariff and excise taxes, expanded sales of public lands, and increased public borrowing effected through the sale of federal debt instruments. However, the federal government had already run three successive deficits following the Panic of 1857, mounting a deficit of $50 million by the end of fiscal year 1860. Thus, the financial resources of the Republic were already severely strained, and the traditional nineteenth-century means of raising federal revenue proved insufficient. Early in 1861, confronting a widening military conflict and deepening budget deficit, Republicans in the Senate ushered through Congress the Morrill Tariff Act, which broadly increased the tariff on most items. But by then, the federal government faced a $75 million deficit, and revenue continued to lag far behind the expenditures required to support the war effort. This trend would continue, and the federal deficit would eventually grow to $1 billion by 1865.[22]

By mid-1861, it became apparent that the traditional nineteenth-century sources of federal revenue were insufficient to finance the war. This was recognized by the editors of the *New York Times*, who lamented the passing of the Jeffersonian state: "[W]e must bid adieu to the golden era in our history in which we were scarcely conscious that we had a Government, so lightly did its burdens rest upon us, and enter upon that in which the almost sole problem of a statesman will be to make the credit balance the debt side of the national ledger."[23]

Lincoln, beleaguered Treasury officials, and the Republican leadership in Congress all recognized that they faced the most severe fiscal crisis that had ever confronted the young Republic. Finding new sources of revenue was imperative. In April 1861, Secretary Chase embarked upon an effort to raise some $15 million of new revenue by selling Treasury bonds and notes. When Congress reconvened on July 4, 1861, Secretary Chase issued a report calling for $20 million more to be raised by direct taxes, internal duties, and excise taxes. Later in July, Thaddeus Stevens of Pennsylvania, powerful Republican chairman of the

22. For a more detailed account of budget deficits and fiscal policy during the Civil War, see Savage, *Balanced Budgets and American Politics*, 123–31.

23. *N.Y. Times*, January 8, 1862, 4.

House Ways and Means Committee, proposed a direct land tax to be allocated to each state in proportion to its population. Stevens's proposal for a direct tax on land provoked intense opposition among representatives from the South and West, where agricultural interests were predominant.[24] Later in July, Justin Morrill, an abolitionist and one of the founders of the Republican Party in Vermont, as well as an influential member of the Ways and Means Committee, offered a compromise proposal that included a national income tax to supplement the revenue to be derived from a reduced land tax.

Like the tariff, income taxation was a highly controversial issue that provoked deep political divisions exacerbated by regional conflicts. Opposition to an income tax centered in the Northeast, while support was strongest in the South and Midwest.[25] Throughout the nineteenth century, political conflict over the income tax would follow much these same geographical lines, reflecting the underlying economic division between Southern agriculture and Northern manufacturing interests. Ironically, in July 1861 politicians believed that with the compromise of income taxation they would avoid provoking the more intense regional conflict that would inevitably be triggered by increases in the tariff and federal excise taxes. Since it proved impossible to fund the war effort solely through existing fiscal arrangements, Northern Republicans finally but still reluctantly acquiesced in the adoption of an income tax bill, which passed the House on July 29 by a 77 to 60 vote.[26]

Thereafter, it was the Senate's turn to choose between further increases in the tariff, the "direct" land tax, and the income tax (often

24. Relevant portions of the debate are found in the *Congressional Globe*, 37th Cong., 1st sess. (July 24, 1861), 246–55. House Ways and Means member Roscoe Conkling complained that the most "obnoxious" feature of the proposed tax was that it "creates an army of officers whose business it is to collect these taxes." Stevens defended the "disagreeable" aspects of his proposed real estate tax in terms of the need to "sustain the Government" against the attacks by the "rebels, who are now destroying or attempting to destroy this Government." Stevens acknowledged that the tax would have an impact on different states in different ways, but justified the revenue package as a whole as necessary in light of the Union's war effort. He declared that "the annihilation of the Government is the alternative."

25. The opposition to the income tax was led in the House by Representative Schuler Colfax, Republican of Indiana, later vice-president under Grant. The political cleavages that formed over the Civil War income tax are discussed in Paul, *Taxation in the United States*, 7–17; Blakely and Blakely, *The Federal Income Tax*, 1–8; Seligman, *The Income Tax*, pt. 2, chap. 3, 430–80.

26. *Congressional Globe*, 37th Cong., 1st sess. (July 24, 1861), 330–31.

referred to as an "income duty"). There was general agreement in the Senate that the government badly needed the revenue. However, the question remained, who would bear the economic burden of the war effort? Senator James F. Simmons of Rhode Island, chairman of the Finance Committee, defended an income tax with a high personal exemption based upon the relative "fairness" and equities of such a measure as compared with a land tax: "Let us tax property in the last resort, when we have to reach the poor as well as the rich, people of small means as well as those with large; but I do not believe this country has come to pass to be driven to a resource of such extreme measures."[27] Others agreed, declaring that the income tax would be "more equalized on all classes of the community, more especially on those who are able to bear them."[28] Based upon such sentiment, the bill passed the Senate and became law on August 5, 1861.[29] Public opinion was generally favorable to the new tax. The *New York Times* subsequently praised this new tax, "levied upon a person's purse," as "probably one of the most equitable and bearable taxes that can be imposed."[30]

This first federal income tax called for a relatively modest 3 percent tax on annual income above an $800 personal exemption. The income of U.S. citizens residing abroad was 5 percent, and the tax on interest income from securities was reduced to 1.5 percent. By virtue of the relatively high personal exemption, most of the population was effectively exempt from taxation. The new statute also evidenced Congress's general lack of experience with income taxation. For instance, the House and Senate bills left unclear whether the tax was imposed on gross or net income, and the statute made no express provision for the deduction of expenses attributable to the production of such income.[31]

The statute of 1861 was never actually put into effect and, thus, never raised a single dollar of revenue. Treasury secretary Chase objected to it on the grounds that the income to be derived from the tax was too uncertain, with most of the population exempt by virtue of the $800 personal exemption, and the cost of implementing the tax too

27. Ibid., 254.
28. Ibid., 255 (Senator William Pitt Fressenden, Republican of Maine).
29. Act of August 5, 1861, chap. 45, sec. 49, 12 Stat. 309.
30. *N.Y. Times*, January 8, 1862, 4.
31. The Conference Committee clarified that the tax was on net income, but the final bill left the details of computing such to the commissioner of Internal Revenue.

great.[32] Nevertheless, Morrill continued to defend the income tax as the "fairest" means for raising the revenue necessary to finance the war:

> The income duty is one, perhaps, of the least defensible that, on the whole, the Committee concluded to retain. . . . The income tax is an inquisitorial one at best; but upon looking into the considerable class of state officers, and the many thousands who are employed on a fixed salary, most of whom would not contribute a penny unless called upon through this tax, it has been thought best not to wholly abandon it. Ought not men, too, with large incomes, to pay more in proportion to what they have than those with limited means, who live by the work of their own hands, or that of their families?[33]

At Morrill's instigation, the Ways and Means Committee reported a bill for a new income tax statute in April 1862, and the Senate followed in May. The Senate bill introduced a graduated-rate structure to the bill, and this provision was accepted by the Conference Committee. The new income tax was signed into law by Lincoln on July 1, 1862, as part of a wide-ranging revenue act that imposed a federal inheritance tax and also taxed certain specific types of corporations (e.g., the gross receipts of railroads, banks, trust companies, and insurance companies).[34]

The income tax of 1862 provided for a 3 percent tax on the "annual gains, profits or incomes" above $600 of anyone residing in the United States, "whether derived from any kinds of property, rents, interest, dividends, salaries or from any profession, trade, employment or vocation carried on in the United States or elsewhere, or from any source whatever." The tax rate increased to 5 percent on income in excess of $10,000 and on all income earned by citizens residing abroad. The provision also provided for withholding on the salaries of government employees and expressly allowed limited business deductions. The conceptual distinction between ordinary income and gain from the sale of capital assets still baffled the drafters of the statute. Of course, that elusive distinction haunts economists, legislators, and the federal courts to this day.[35]

---

32. *Report of the Secretary of the Treasury for the Year 1861* (Washington, D.C., 1861), 15.

33. *Congressional Globe*, 37th Cong., 2d sess. (March 12, 1862), 1196.

34. Act of July 1, 1862, chap. 119, 12 Stat. 432, 469–71.

35. The Supreme Court and the Internal Revenue Service continue to grapple with the distinction. See, e.g., *Corn Prod. Ref. Co. v. Commissioner*, 350 U.S. 46 (1955); *Arkansas Best Corp. v. Commissioner*, 485 U.S. 212 (1988).

By 1862, the wartime debt had risen to $505 million and increased throughout 1863. A new and more comprehensive income tax statute was proposed in the spring of 1864. The Ways and Means Committee reported a bill that included a flat income tax of 5 percent. However, the House followed the recommendations of the commissioner of Internal Revenue in favor of a progressive rate structure.[36] This provoked intense objections on the grounds of the injustice the graduated tax would inflict upon the wealthy. Opposition to the progressive rate structure was led by Representatives Stevens and Morrill. Stevens objected to the tax as a "strange way to punish men because they are rich."[37] Morrill denounced the graduated tax as reflecting the "spirit of agrarianism" and as contrary to the "very theory of our institutions," wherein "we make no distinction between the rich man and the poor man." Morrill further declared that progressive tax rates "punish men because they are rich," and amount to nothing less than "seizing the property of men for the crime of having too much."[38]

The Senate bill followed that of the House with respect to progressive rates, imposing a maximum rate of 10 percent on annual income in excess of $25,000. In response to intense opposition, the Finance Committee reduced the top rate to 7.5 percent on annual income in excess of $10,000. However, a floor amendment again raised the top rate, and the Conference Committee finally agreed on a maximum rate of 10 percent on income in excess of $10,000. In the end, the new income tax of 1864 was imposed at 5 percent on income over $600, rose to 7.5 percent on income over $5,000, and reached 10 percent on income over $10,000.[39] Notwithstanding the emotional debate over the justice and equity of a graduated-rate structure, it was the state's need for additional revenue that was ultimately responsible for Congress's adoption of such a structure.[40] Continued pressure for revenue forced Northern Republicans to accept the graduated income tax rates along with an equally odious federal inheritance tax.

The income tax of 1864 was considerably more sophisticated than its predecessor statutes. Reflecting this, the number of preferences,

36. The first commissioner of Internal Revenue, George S. Boutwell of Massachusetts, had recommended that the tax rate rise to 5.5 percent on annual income in excess of $20,000. *Report of the Commissioner of Internal Revenue for the Year Ending June 30, 1863* (Washington, D.C., 1864), 183–84.

37. *Congressional Globe*, 38th Cong., 1st sess. (1864), 1876.

38. Ibid., 1940.

39. Act of June 30, 1864, chap. 173, sec. 116, 13 Stat. 223.

40. "The principle of progressivity was not adopted for its own sake but as a by-product of the increases in rates." Ratner, *American Taxation*, 72.

deductions, exclusions, and exemptions recognized by the government was greatly increased. Likewise, the income tax "base" was greatly expanded under the 1864 statute. Revenue from the income tax increased from $2.75 million in 1863 to $20 million in 1864, $61 million in 1865, and $73.5 million in 1866.[41] The revenue crisis of the Civil War had led national policymakers to experiment with income taxation, and as a result, the fiscal organization of the American state was expanded far beyond its Jeffersonian origins. Likewise, the Civil War had stimulated the creation of a vast military and administrative apparatus largely financed by the Civil War income tax. When the Civil War ended, the government was left with a $2.3 billion debt. However, the regional politics that had been suppressed during the national military crisis reemerged, and Northern business interests within the Republican Party pushed for rate reductions and the eventual repeal of the income tax. Revenue from the tax began to decline beginning in 1866, amounting to only $38 million by 1870. Under the act of July 14, 1870, rates were further reduced and the despised inheritance taxes were repealed altogether. The act also provided for a "sunset" expiration date in 1872 for the income tax. Over the next two years, considerable efforts were made by Senator John Sherman of Ohio, chairman of the Finance Committee, to make the income tax permanent; however, opposition from Northern Republicans blocked all such attempts. Budget surpluses were realized from 1870 to 1872, and these lent support to those who opposed extending the tax. Accordingly, the income tax was allowed to expire as scheduled in 1872. By that time, much of the enthusiasm for the tax, even among its original supporters, had waned considerably. For instance, notwithstanding their initial enthusiasm for the new income tax, the editors of the *New York Times* became increasingly hostile, finally declaring their support for outright repeal: "The most judicious management cannot divest [the income tax] of an inquisitorial character, or obviate inequalities and injustice from its practical operation. It has been tolerated, just as various other obnoxious taxes were tolerated—because it was one of the inevitable burdens entailed upon us by a great war.... Let Congress redeem the session from utter barrenness by averting the vexation and unpopularity which will inevitably arise from the continued infliction of the impost."[42]

Following the end of the war, the military/administrative state created by the Union government was slowly dismantled. The great

41. Figures cited in ibid., 141.
42. *N.Y. Times*, January 19, 1871, 4.

army of the North, the largest standing army in the world in 1865, stood down and was withdrawn from the South by the late 1870s, with many of the remaining units sent to the West to support an increasingly aggressive wave of territorial expansion. On the other hand, the activity of the federal government, as measured by federal expenditures, persisted at elevated levels even as the military state was dismantled. Before the Civil War, federal expenditures had never amounted to more than $65 million; after the war, they never again dropped below $240 million.[43] With the expiration of the income tax, policymakers returned to the traditional nineteenth-century sources of revenue – customs duties, excise taxes, the sale of public land, and the tariff. In fact, the tariff alone raised revenue in excess of federal expenditures, providing the federal government in the three decades following the Civil War with the luxury of significant budget surpluses, a large portion of which was used to increase pensions to Civil War veterans.[44]

In 1883, the eclectic economist Henry George pointedly observed that on account of the revenue brought into the federal Treasury by the tariff during this period, "the great question before Congress [was] what to do with the surplus."[45] This has suggested to one observer of fiscal policy that to "legitimize the need for high tariffs, Republicans dramatically increased public expenditures in the late nineteenth century."[46] In this respect, the revenue imperative continued to shape federal policymaking – only from the rare perspective of budget surpluses driving the increase in governmental spending.

Income Taxation, Ideology, and the Post–Civil War State

The last two decades of the nineteenth century was a period of "patchwork" state-building that resulted in a "reconstitution" of American

43. Figures cited in Savage, *Balanced Budgets*, 131.

44. See Robert Higgs, *Crisis and Leviathan: Critical Episodes in the Growth of American Government* (New York: Oxford University Press, 1987), 97: "In the absence of appreciable political leeway for tariff reduction the government's main response to the embarrassingly routine surpluses was to authorize greater and greater largess for the Civil War veterans and their (ever more distant) relatives . . . . Despite the prodigality of the pensions, the budgetary surpluses persisted, pouring into the Treasury in every fiscal year of the period 1866–1893."

45. Quoted in John H. Makin and Norman J. Ornstein, *Debt and Taxes* (New York: Random House, 1994), 75.

46. Savage, *Balanced Budgets*, 122.

national political institutions.[47] During this period, attempts were made to expand the fiscal and administrative powers of the American state beyond the traditional nineteenth-century constitution. The federal courts, with the Supreme Court leading the way, made a number of infamous, although largely unsuccessful, efforts to impose federal regulations on the nascent national economy during this period.[48] In the long run such attempts by the federal courts were doomed to failure because the federal judiciary–lacking administration, expertise, and enforcement capabilities–was, and remains, in so many respects the very antithesis of strong state power.

The American state continued to rely mostly upon the tariff to supply its revenue. However, use of the tariff to fund any further expansion of the American state reached its natural limits. At its historic high of 45 percent, the tariff was politically and economically intolerable to Southern and Midwestern agriculture interests. Likewise, wage laborers were severely harmed by such a duty, and grassroots opposition intensified as a consequence. Demands for a return to progressive income taxation became more and more common among the agrarian-based political parties, which increased in strength at the close of the nineteenth century. Populists, agrarian parties, and egalitarians embraced the income tax, following the more radical Communist Parties of Europe. (Marx had included a highly progressive income tax in the first-stage revolutionary program of the proletariat as set forth in the Communist Manifesto of 1848.) Calls for a graduated income tax first appeared in the 1877 and 1878 platforms of the Greenback Party, and then again in the 1880 platform of the National Greenback Party. The Greenback Labor and Anti-Monopoly Parties adopted similar proposals in 1884, and the Union Labor Party embraced the income tax in 1888. Grangers, Knights of Labor, and the Farmers Alliance all demanded restoration of the income tax, as did the Populist Party in each of its

47. For a provocative account of this expansion of the American state, see Stephen Skowronek, *Building a New American State: The Expansion of National Administrative Capacities, 1877–1920* (New York: Cambridge University Press, 1982), 39–162. The discussion in this chapter and throughout this study draws heavily upon Skowronek's narrative.

48. The most important cases were *Munn v. Illinois*, 94 U.S. 113 (1877); *Mugler v. Kansas*, 123 U.S. 623 (1887); *Allgeyer v. Louisiana*, 165 U.S. 578 (1897); *Lochner v. New York*, 198 U.S. 45 (1905). For a discussion of the principle of "substantive due process" expressed in these decisions, see Raoul Berger, *Government by Judiciary: The Transformation of the Fourteenth Amendment* (Cambridge: Harvard University Press, 1977), 193–220.

platforms. From 1874 to 1894, no less than sixty-eight bills were introduced to restore an income tax.

The federal income tax was finally resurrected in 1894, largely at the instigation of Populists, who by then exerted considerable influence within the Democratic Party, especially in the South and Midwest.[49] Like its Civil War predecessor, the new income tax was strongly opposed by commercial and manufacturing interests, including both Republicans and Democrats in the House from the eastern states wherein such interests dominated. On the other side, congressional support for the tax was orchestrated by Democrats William Jennings Bryan of Nebraska and Benton McMillin of Tennessee, chairman of the Ways and Means Subcommittee on Internal Revenue, who had been a strong supporter of a new income tax for over a decade. Support on Ways and Means for the income tax was strongest among Southern and Midwestern Democrats. The chairman of the House Ways and Means Committee, William L. Wilson of West Virginia, opposed the measure, preferring tariff reduction. Following strict partisan divisions, all six Republican members of Ways and Means opposed the income tax bill.

Debate over the bill persisted for months. The highlight was in January 1894, when Bryan successfully beat back Republican opposition to the tax, denouncing such opposition as "class" warfare. Responding to threats that the wealthy would simply depart from the United States if an income tax was adopted, Bryan responded with his famous quip: "Of all the mean men I have known, I have never known one so mean that I would be willing to say to him that his patriotism was less than 2 per cent deep. . . . If 'some of our best people' prefer to leave the country rather than pay a tax of 2 per cent, God pity the worst."[50] In the wake of Bryan's splendid oration, the income tax provision passed the House the following day by a 175-to-56 vote.

The political atmosphere in the Senate was quite different, although the regional/party splits were much the same. Because the income tax proposal was presented as an amendment to the tariff reform bill advanced by Representative Wilson, it was caught up in the intense partisan debate over protectionism that raged in the Senate throughout the summer of 1894. The Wilson tariff reform bill was initially supported by President Cleveland. But in the end, Cleveland refused to sign the

49. The best accounts of the enactment of the 1894 income tax are Seligman, *The Income Tax*, pt. 2, chap. 4, 493–530, and Ratner, *American Taxation*, 168–92.

50. *Congressional Record*, 53d Cong., 2d sess. (January 30, 1894), 26, pt. 2, app., 1658.

revenue measure (which passed both houses on August 28) after Senators from his own party emasculated the tariff reform provisions of the bill. The income tax provision (based entirely on the defunct Civil War statutes) imposed a 2 percent tax on the gains, profits, and income of individuals above the $4,000 exemption, and a 2 percent tax on the "net profits" or income of all corporations, companies, and associations doing business for profit in the United States.

The intense ideological conflict over the income tax was expressed by John Sherman, the prominent senator from Ohio, who denounced the new tax as "socialism, communism, [and] devilism."[51] Resistance to income taxation was soon rendered moot, however, when the U.S. Supreme Court in 1895 held the tax to be an unconstitutional "direct" tax in the case of *Pollock v. Farmer's Loan & Trust Co.*[52] The Constitution requires direct taxes to be apportioned among the states based upon population.[53] For over a century, the Court seemingly took the position that *only* poll and property taxes were "direct" taxes subject to this constitutional requirement.[54] The logic of the Supreme Court's decision in *Pollock*, as well as the Court's effort to draw a constitutional distinction between direct and indirect taxes, can be mystifying and largely unconvincing. Constitutional scholar Edwin Corwin once referred to the *Pollock* decision as "bad history and bad logic."[55] Whatever the merits of the Supreme Court's logic in the *Pollock* decision, for the moment it effectively checked the Populist zeal for the radical redistribution of wealth, a zeal that had surrounded the enactment of the tax in 1894.

51. Ibid. (June 22, 1894), 26, pt. 7, 6695 (Senator John Sherman of Ohio).

52. *Pollock v. Farmer's Loan & Trust Co.*, 157 U.S. 429c (1895); 158 U.S. 601 (1895) (rehearing). The U.S. Constitution seemingly disallowed such direct taxes, requiring the imposition of such taxes to be "uniform throughout the United States." U.S. Constitution, art. 1, sec. 8. For a discussion of the confusing debate over "direct" versus "indirect" taxes, see Boris I. Bittker and Lawrence Lokken, *Federal Taxation of Income, Estates and Gifts,* 2d. ed. (New York: Warren, Gorham & Lamont, 1989), ¶1.2.2.

53. U.S. Constitution, art. 1, sec. 2.

54. This was the position argued by the government's lawyers, led by Attorney General Olney. Indeed, when an income tax was considered during the War of 1812, the consensus was that it was *not* a direct tax. See Lawrence M. Friedman, *A History of American Law* (New York: Simon & Schuster, 1973), 496 n. 79; Paul, *Taxation in the United States,* 6. The Supreme Court had previously expressed this view in dictum in *Springer v. United States,* 102 U.S. 586 (1880). The debate over the constitutionality of direct taxation and of the income tax is discussed at length in Seligman, *The Income Tax,* pt. 2, chap. 5, 531–89.

55. Edwin S. Corwin, *Court Over Constitution* (New York: P. Smith, 1938), 188.

But the Supreme Court's restraint on the overzealous spirit of agrarian democracy turned out to be a short-lived defeat for Populist and radical Democrat interests. In 1909, Congress had the last word by adopting an "excise tax" on corporations pursuant to the Payne-Aldrich Tariff Act,[56] and then a new constitutional amendment sanctioning an income tax. Ironically, the income tax amendment was proposed by Nelson W. Aldrich, chairman of the Senate Finance Committee, and was supported by President Taft to deflect the rising campaign for a progressive income tax.[57] Democrats favoring the amendment were joined by Progressives within the Republican Party. Taft was particularly sympathetic to the Supreme Court's position, fearing any weakening of its legitimacy that would follow from the constitutional income tax controversy that was sure to arise again. Accordingly, he threw his support behind Aldrich's proposal for a constitutional amendment, hoping to settle the matter once and for all in favor of the federal power to impose an income tax:

> The decision of the Supreme Court in the income-tax cases deprived the National Government of a power which, by reason of previous decisions of the court, it was generally supposed that Government had. It is undoubtedly a power the National Government ought to have. It might be indispensable to the nation's life in great crises. Although I have not considered a constitutional amendment as necessary to the exercise of certain phases of this power, a mature consideration has convinced me that an amendment is the only proper course for its establishment to its full extent.[58]

Opposition to the constitutional amendment was strongest in the Northeast and mostly reflected economic interests. But some perceptively based their opposition on the grounds that a national income tax

56. Act of August 5, 1909, 36 Stat. 112. This corporate business privilege tax was imposed "with respect to the carrying on or doing business" of corporations. In *Flint v. Stone Tracy Co.*, 220 U.S. 107 (1911), the Supreme Court held the tax to be a business privilege tax, and not an income tax, which presumably would have been prohibited under Article 1, Section 9, of the U.S. Constitution as a "direct tax."

57. Jerold L. Waltman, *Political Origins of the U.S. Income Tax* (Jackson: University Press of Mississippi, 1985), 4–6.

58. President William Howard Taft to the Senate and House of Representatives, June 16, 1909, in *Messages and Papers of the Presidents* (Washington, D.C.: Bureau of National Literature, 1912), 7770.

would promote a significant shift in the delicate balance of power between the states and the federal government, as well as that between the state and citizenry in general. In 1910, Richard E. Byrd, Speaker of the Virginia Senate, proclaimed his opposition to the income tax amendment based upon his deep-rooted fear that it would lead to an intrusion by the federal government into local state government and the affairs of private citizens:

> A hand from Washington will be stretched out and placed upon every man's business; the eye of the Federal inspector will be in every man's counting house. . . . The law will of necessity have inquisitorial features, it will provide penalties, it will create complicated machinery. Under it men will be hailed into courts distant from their homes. Heavy fines imposed by distant and unfamiliar tribunals constantly will menace the tax payer. An army of Federal inspectors, spies and detectives will descend upon the state. . . . Who of us who have had knowledge of the doings of the Federal officials in the Internal Revenue service can be blind to what will follow?[59]

Notwithstanding Byrd's prophetic warning, the campaign for a constitutional amendment sanctioning an income tax gathered momentum following the stunning political victory of the Democrats in 1912, which gave the party control not only of the White House (for only the third time since the Civil War) but also of the House and Senate. Ratification by the necessary thirty-six states was achieved in February 1913, four years after the amendment had been proposed by Congress. The Sixteenth Amendment thus became part of the U.S. Constitution, marking *Pollock* as the only twentieth-century Supreme Court decision expressly overturned by constitutional amendment.

Immediately following his election in 1912, Woodrow Wilson pushed for a reduction in the tariff and adoption of a federal income tax statute under the authority of the new constitutional amendment. This was not exactly a radical position, since Taft and elements within the Republican Party had also supported both tariff reduction and an income tax during the 1908 presidential campaign. Soon after Wilson's inauguration, Democrats and Progressives in Congress joined forces behind a proposal for an income tax as part of the new tariff reduction bill. The

---

59. *Times-Dispatch* (Richmond), March 3, 1910, quoted in Blakely and Blakely, *The Federal Income Tax*, 70.

politics behind the 1913 income tax provision reflected and resulted from the defection of "insurgent" Republicans to the Progressive Party and the subsequent rise in power of congressional Democrats.[60] The income tax provision was buried in the massive tariff reduction bill and generated what now appears to have been remarkably little fanfare in the House. With the ratification of the Sixteenth Amendment, adoption of some form of income tax had become a foregone conclusion. Most of the discussion in Congress was over the rate structure and the magnitude of the personal exemption, much more controversial issues. A mildly progressive rate structure was added to the House bill by the Senate and was justified by Progressives (along with income taxation in general) as a "fairer" source of revenue than the tariff. All parties recognized that the very high personal exemption that both bills included would effectively exempt all but the wealthy from taxation. This too was defended on grounds of justice and equity. In the words of Democratic representative William H. Murray of Oklahoma: "The purpose of this tax is nothing more than to levy a tribute upon that surplus wealth which requires extra expense, and in doing so, it is nothing more than meting out even-handed justice."[61]

Others took a more practical position, recognizing the political liabilities that would follow from a lower personal exemption that subjected a greater portion of the population to the tax. Representative Richard Austin of Tennessee expressed the pragmatic view when, in response to a proposal by Frederick Gillett of Massachusetts to lower the personal exemption in the House bill, he declared, "Does the gentleman not think it would defeat every member who would vote for this amendment if the fact [lowering the personal exemption] were known at home?"[62] As one astute contemporary observer noted soon after the bill

60. The most comprehensive discussion of Progressive support for the income tax is John D. Buenker, *The Income Tax and the Progressive Era* (New York: Garland Publishing Co., 1985). For a general account of the politics behind the enactment of the 1913 income tax, see Ratner, *American Taxation*, chap. 5; Paul, *Taxation in the United States*, 90–104; Blakely and Blakely, *The Federal Income Tax*, 71–103. An excellent recent study of Progressive political thought is Eldon J. Eisenach, *The Lost Promise of Progressivism* (Lawrence: University Press of Kansas, 1994).

61. *Congressional Record*, 63d Cong., 1st sess. (May 6, 1913), 50, pt. 2, 1252. Murray went on to predict correctly that the income tax would supplant the tariff as the primary source of federal revenue: "I want to predict now that we are just entering upon a policy for the support of this Government which, in a few years, will be the only method of taxation for the support of the American Republic, and the days for protective-tariff favoritism will be over."

62. *Congressional Record*, 63d Cong., 1st sess. (May 6, 1913), 50, pt. 2, 1247.

was enacted, "[T]he controlling reasons for so high an exemption were primarily political."[63] In other words, although the chief motive for supporting the bill was revenue, tempered by progressive sentiments that only the rich should be subject to the tax, political constraints imposed limits upon the more radical elements (most particularly, Senator La Follette of Wisconsin) who preferred even more steeply graduated rates.

These political constraints were expressed by Democratic senator John Sharp Williams of Mississippi, who, in response to La Follette's proposal for a maximum individual income tax rate of 10 percent and an inheritance tax reaching a maximum rate of 75 percent, protested that "the object of taxation is not to leave men with equal incomes after you have taxed them."[64] Disavowing any radical pretensions behind the mildly progressive tax, Williams declared that "[n]o honest man can wage war upon great fortunes, *per se*. The Democratic party never has done it, and when the Democratic party begins to do it, it will cease to be the Democratic party and become the Socialistic party of the United States; or better expressed, the Communistic party, or Quasi-Communistic party of the United States."[65]

Thus, the capacity of income taxation to redistribute wealth was recognized and *repudiated* in Congress from the very beginning. Notwithstanding the protests of Senator Henry Cabot Lodge, who warned that the progressive income tax would result in the "pillage of a class,"[66] most members of Congress viewed the final proposal as relatively moderate in scope. The Conference Committee markup was approved by both houses on October 3, 1913, and the income tax became law pursuant to the Tariff Act of 1913.[67] The final version included a $3,000 personal exemption and a tax on personal income starting at 1 percent on income exceeding $3,000 and increasing to 6 percent on income over $500,000. The 1 percent surtax raised the maximum marginal tax rate to 7 percent on income over $500,000.

In 1916, the Supreme Court was again forced to address the question of the constitutionality of income taxation—specifically, with respect to the progressive rate structure of the income tax. In *Brushaber v. Union*

---

63. Seligman, *The Income Tax*, 687.
64. *Congressional Record*, 63d Cong., 1st sess. (August 27, 1913), 50, pt. 4, 3807.
65. Ibid., 3821.
66. Ibid., 3840.
67. Pub. L. No. 63-16, chap. 16, 38 Stat. 114, 166–81.

Pacific Railroad Co.,[68] the Supreme Court held that this aspect of the tax did not violate the "due process" clause of the Fifth Amendment to the Constitution and, notwithstanding claims that persist among fringe elements to this day, thereby settled once and for all issues pertaining to the constitutionality of the income tax.

The First World War and the Income Tax

As anticipated, the high personal exemption of $3,000 rendered only a relatively small and well-defined stratum of the citizenry subject to the federal income tax of 1913. For 1913, the first half year under the tax, only 0.8 percent of the population had sufficient income to subject them to taxation; only 358,000 individuals filed income tax returns reporting net taxable income.[69] This was significantly less than the 425,000 returns that the House Ways and Means Committee had predicted.[70] Furthermore, the tax due on the revenue reported made only a minor contribution to the federal Treasury. Revenue from the income tax for 1913 (which went into effect in March) amounted to $28 million–60 percent less than the $70 million the Ways and Means Committee had predicted.[71] Over the next few years revenue from the individual income tax increased slightly but was offset by a decrease in revenue from the corporate income tax. This all changed dramatically by the end of the decade.

The war that began in Europe in 1914 had a dramatic impact upon both the American economy generally and federal receipts in particular. The economic paralysis resulting from the European conflict led to a decline in federal receipts from $73.2 million in July 1914 to $44.5 million in October.[72] Congress responded by enacting the Emergency

---

68. *Brushaber v. Union Pac. R.R. Co.*, 240 U.S. 1 (1916).

69. Cited in Richard Goode, *The Individual Income Tax* (Washington, D.C.: Brookings Institution, 1976), 3–4.

70. House Committee on Ways and Means, 63d Cong., 1st sess. (April 21, 1913), H. Rept. 5, xxxix.

71. Ibid. The revenue collected under the first year of the income tax was reported in "Letter of the Secretary of the Treasury, William G. McAdoo," 63d Cong., 3d sess. (October 15, 1914), S. Doc. 623, 2.

72. Treasury Department, *Annual Report, 1915*, 228, cited in Charles Gilbert, *American Financing of World War I* (Westport, Conn.: Greenwood Publishing Co., 1970), 26.

Revenue Act of 1914,[73] a temporary measure that raised excise taxes while leaving the income tax untouched. The Emergency Revenue Act was projected to raise some $100 million in new revenue, but only produced $52 million. This pushed the Wilson administration (led by Treasury secretary McAdoo) to campaign for a new revenue bill. Wilson and McAdoo viewed the income tax as the major solution to the emerging fiscal crisis and proposed lowering exemptions and increasing the progressivity of the tax rates to raise additional revenue. In a speech to a joint session of Congress on December 7, 1915, Wilson spelled out this approach, condemning excessive borrowing to fund the increase in spending, while offering the income tax as the only viable alternative:

> I, for one, do not believe that the people of this country approve of postponing the payment of their bills. Borrowing money is short-sighted finance. . . . We should be following an almost universal example of modern governments if we were to draw the greater part or even the whole of the revenues we need from the income tax. By somewhat lowering the present limits of exemption and the figure at which the surtax shall begin to be imposed and by increasing, step by step throughout the graduation, the surtax itself, the income taxes as at present apportioned would yield sums sufficient to balance the books of the Treasury at the end of the fiscal year 1917 without making the burdens unreasonably or oppressively heavy.

Wilson further proposed increases in excise taxes on gasoline and the internal combustion engines used in automobiles, as well as on iron and steel production—this in order to be sure that "the industry of this generation should pay the bills of this generation."[74]

The Ways and Means Committee, chaired by Democrat Claude Kitchin of North Carolina, took up work on the measure in January 1916, with the House finally approving a complex omnibus revenue bill in July. Action proceeded slowly through the Senate, with final passage of the Revenue Act of 1916 coming in August.[75] The bill imposed a "normal" tax of 2 percent, with a surtax of 1 percent on income in excess of $20,000, rising to a rate of 13 percent on income in excess of $2 million.

---

73. Pub. L. No. 63-217, 38 Stat. 745.

74. *Messages and Papers of the Presidents* (New York: Bureau of National Literature, n.d.), 8113.

75. Pub. L. No. 64-271, 39 Stat. 756.

The 1916 measure proved inadequate, and a new revenue bill began to take shape early in 1917. The new bill, the Revenue Act of March 3, 1917,[76] raised estate taxes and imposed a new excess profits tax, but income tax rates remained at the same levels as under the 1916 act. With American entry into the war in April 1917, this all necessarily changed. McAdoo urged Congress to act quickly to close the anticipated increase in the already significant budget deficit, asking for $3.5 billion as an initial one-year appropriation. Since the economy had rebounded significantly in the years following the outbreak of the war in Europe, the income tax was viewed as the primary source of the desperately needed new revenue. As historian Jerold Waltman put it: "Congress and Treasury now faced the huge task of tapping the booming economy."[77] This task was accomplished pretty much through the modifications to the income tax that Wilson had suggested in his December 1915 speech. A revenue measure was passed early in October, after intense political maneuvering throughout the summer. The War Revenue Act of 1917 provided for a wartime surtax that reached 50 percent on individual income in excess of $1 million, and augmented the 1916 normal 2 percent tax with an additional 2 percent on income in excess of $3,000 for single persons and $4,000 for married persons.[78] In addition, personal exemptions were lowered to $1,000 for single taxpayers and $2,000 for married taxpayers (down from the $3,000 and $4,000 levels set by the 1916 act). The normal corporate rates were raised, and the excess profits tax rates were increased as well.

America's entry into World War I resulted in an increase in the federal government's demand for revenue that far exceeded all initial estimates. Revenue projections from Treasury were constantly revised upward as estimates by the military of the cost of war invariably proved to be understated. In fact, the cost of the first full year of American participation in the war was $26 billion—more than the total cost of the entire federal government from 1791 through 1917.[79] Such an

76. Pub. L. No. 64-377, 39 Stat. 1000.

77. Waltman, *Political Origins of the U.S. Income Tax*, 42. Waltman's study focuses upon the politics behind the revenue bills enacted immediately before, during, and following World War I.

78. Pub. L. No. 65-50, 40 Stat. 300. A concise account of the politics of the important Revenue Act of 1917 is found in Waltman, *Political Origins of the U.S. Income Tax*, 42–54.

79. Blakely and Blakely, *The Federal Income Tax*, 153. Charles Gilbert calculates that total war expenditures from 1917 to 1920 were approximately $38 billion. Gilbert, *American Financing of World War I*, 69.

explosion in federal expenditures could hardly have failed to occasion a fiscal revolution. As had been the case during the 1860s, the revenue crisis of war led to fundamental changes in the structure of the federal income tax.[80]

Congressional policymakers quickly learned an important lesson during the wartime fiscal crisis: great revenue could be raised relatively easily from the individual income tax through only minor tinkering and slight adjustments to tax rates and exemption levels. This allowed decisionmakers to produce quick changes in the overall revenue-raising capacity of the income tax. Now, as then, slight changes to only one or two provisions of the tax laws (those setting forth the tax rates or exemption levels) can produce significant increases in the level of revenue raised (e.g., billions of dollars can be raised merely by increasing a few numbers in a single provision of the tax code). In this way, decisionmakers are able to increase taxes quickly during a crisis of war, and then quickly reduce them to prewar levels once the crisis has passed. Indeed, the original proponents of the 1913 statute understood this crucial fact. The House Ways and Means Committee noted that revenues from income taxes "readily respond to changes of rates," and emphasized this as one of the most important aspects of the tax.[81] Senator John Sharp Williams had noted that given the "elasticity" of the income tax, the government would readily be able to "raise or lower revenue."[82]

During the first year of the war, policymakers turned to a more progressive rate structure in response to revenue demands of the war effort, as well as a desire to limit the anticipated wartime "excess profits" of business—but *not* to redistribute wealth. By the end of the war, the top tax rate reached 77 percent on income over $1 million, this from the

---

80. Government expenditures during the Civil War reached a peak of $1.298 billion in 1865, up 1,847 percent from prewar expenditures in 1861. During World War I, government expenditures increased from $742 million in 1916 to $18.952 billion in 1919—an increase of 2,454 percent. For a general discussion of the impact of the First World War on expenditures and revenues, see Gilbert, *American Financing of World War I*, 65–74.

81. House Committee on Ways and Means, 63d Cong., 1st sess. (April 21, 1913), H. Rept. 5, xxxvii.

82. *Congressional Record*, 63d Cong., 1st sess. (August 27, 1913), 50, pt. 4, 3806–7. Political scientist James Curtis argues that the "elasticity" of the income tax was the crucial feature that supported the development of a strong administrative state in the twentieth century. James L. Curtis, "Federal Deficits and the Boundaries of Democratic Politics" (paper delivered at the annual meeting of the American Political Science Association, New York, September 1994), 11.

initial 6 percent maximum rate adopted only six years earlier.[83] The "transformation" of the income tax during World War I has been described succinctly as follows: "The First World War had an important impact on the income tax, rapidly transforming it from a highly contested but insignificant source of revenue into a major tax. Rate and provision adjustments made over several years turned what was almost a proportional tax into one with a highly progressive nominal rate structure."[84] Most important, those changes in the rate structure of the income tax occasioned by the war shifted the burden of the tax from the very wealthy to middle- and low-income taxpayers. As a result, the steeply graduated income tax applied to a wide spectrum of the population and produced revenue beyond anything previously imagined by federal policymakers. This transformation of the income tax–and with it the radical restructuring of the fiscal organization of the American state–was made possible solely by the crisis of war, which suppressed political interests in the dominant Republican Party, whose hostility to income taxation would otherwise have been successful in blocking any such innovations.

Immediately before World War I, excise taxes and the tariff produced over 90 percent of the revenue of the federal government. In 1914, the federal income tax provided only 9.7 percent of total federal receipts; this figure rose to 16 percent by 1916. By 1918, revenue from the wartime income tax and excess profits tax supplied fully 63.1 percent of total federal receipts; for that year, revenue from the tariff and all other excise taxes declined to 28.7 percent of total federal receipts.[85] This is all the more remarkable given that even at the height of the war only a minority of the citizenry was subject to the tax; no more than 20 percent of the population was ever required to file tax returns. Even still, the income tax produced revenue that exceeded what anyone anticipated could ever be raised by the U.S. government; and accordingly, the income tax

---

83. Pub. L. No. 65-254, 40 Stat. 1057. The Revenue Act of 1918 (officially, Title 3 of the War Profits and Excess Profits Tax of 1918) provided for a surtax on the "normal" tax of 12 percent on income in excess of $4,000. The surtax started at 2 percent on income in excess of $6,000 and reached 65 percent on income in excess of $1 million. However, the combined tax reached 50 percent on income in excess of $78,000 and thus, was hardly a "millionaire's tax."

84. John F. Witte, *The Politics and Development of the Federal Income Tax* (Madison: University of Wisconsin Press, 1985), 110.

85. Figures cited in Ronald F. King, *Money, Time, and Politics: Investment Tax Subsidies and American Democracy* (New Haven: Yale University Press, 1993), 103.

emerged as the most important source of federal revenue, supplanting the tariff and excise taxes as the "cornerstone of the federal revenue system."[86] But to a large extent the dramatic impact of World War I on the structure of the federal income tax proved to be temporary. As the revenue requirements of the federal government declined after 1919, pressure increased within the Republican Party to reduce tax rates to prewar levels. On the other hand, following the armistice, there was virtually no sentiment expressed in Congress for repeal of the tax or even lowering exemptions to prewar levels. This suggests the extent to which the income tax, in only a few decades, had become ingrained within the structure of the American state.

Tax Policy Between the World Wars

Following the Republican landslide in 1920, the opportunity to reduce the rates for the income tax arose. President Warren G. Harding left tax policy mostly to his treasury secretary, Andrew W. Mellon, who led the well-known campaign for a return to "tax normalcy." In a speech before a joint session of Congress on April 12, 1921, Harding set the tone for the rest of the decade with respect to tax policy: "I know of no more pressing problem at home than to restrict our national expenditures within the limits of our national income, and at the same time measurably lift the burdens of war taxation from the shoulders of the American people."[87] Under Mellon's long reign at Treasury, a significant portion of the wartime debt was retired, and the wartime excess profits tax was abandoned in favor of a moderate corporate income tax. In November 1923, Mellon proposed a 25 percent reduction in the tax on earned income, reducing the "normal" tax from 4 percent to 3 percent at the lower income brackets and from 8 percent to 6 percent at the higher levels.[88] Mellon favored reducing marginal rates, because he felt that the wealthy were simply moving their assets into tax-exempt state bonds to avoid the excessive 65 percent surtax, thereby reducing federal revenue collected

---

86. Curtis, "Federal Deficits and the Boundaries of Democratic Politics," 11.

87. Warren G. Harding, "Special Address to Congress," in *Messages and Papers of the Presidents* (New York: Bureau of National Literature, n.d.), 8937.

88. Mellon's theories on taxation were set out in his popular book, *Taxation: The People's Business* (New York: Macmillan, 1924).

from the higher income brackets from 1918 to 1920.[89] While tax rates were lowered throughout the 1920s, budget surpluses were actually generated – and the relative contribution of the income tax to total federal revenue actually increased. This trend continued until the end of the decade, when budget surpluses ceased. By that time, tax rates and federal expenditures had been returned to prewar levels. At the close of the decade, the federal income tax was pretty much what it had been in 1913, with only slight modifications and some judicial fine-tuning to show for the two decades of experience. Indeed, the overall structure of the federal government described by reference to its activities and fiscal organization had changed remarkably little from that of the post–Civil War decades. As Makin and Ornstein have noted, by the close of the 1920s "the federal government resembled what it had been in 1800 more than the institution that it would become by 1948."[90]

With the collapse of the financial markets in 1929, the onset of the Great Depression, and the end of Republican control of the White House following the 1932 elections, one would have expected radical departures in tax policy. The New Deal was a significant event in the history of the American state. However, the New Deal had surprisingly little lasting impact upon the structure of the federal income tax. During the first few months of 1933, the new administration of Franklin D. Roosevelt pursued a policy aimed at balancing the federal budget through reduced federal expenditures. At the same time, federal receipts from the corporate and individual income tax decreased sharply on account of the economic downturn. By 1934, revenue from these taxes declined to less than one-third of total federal revenues, down from 67 percent as late as 1931.[91] There was no grand effort to use the income tax to redistribute wealth or resolve the economic crisis. As has been widely observed, Roosevelt's initial response to the Great Depression simply did not comport with what is now known as classic Keynesian fiscal policy. In

89. For a recent analysis of the Mellon tax cuts of the 1920s, see Gene Smiley and Richard H. Keehn, "Federal Personal Income Tax Policy in the 1920s," 55 *J. Econ. Hist.* 285, 332 (1995): "Federal personal income tax rates were reduced in 1921 as a result of the general belief that the wartime levels could not be justified and the recognition that widespread tax avoidance by high-income taxpayers had effectively shifted more of the tax burden to lower-income taxpayers."

90. Makin and Ornstein, *Debt and Taxes*, 92.

91. Figures from U.S. Census, *Historical Statistics*, cited by Mark H. Leff, *The Limits of Symbolic Reform: The New Deal and Taxation, 1933–1939* (New York: Cambridge University Press, 1984), 12–13.

fact, the main effort to raise revenue during the first two years of the first Roosevelt administration came from increases in excise taxes, following the pattern of Republicans pursuant to the Revenue Act of 1932. Later, this offered Republican members of the House Ways and Means Committee the opportunity to exploit the situation, joining unanimously to denounce the New Deal excise taxes as "discriminatory" taxes that "fall most heavily on the poor and those least able to pay."[92] And of course, one of the main public policies of the early New Deal, the Social Security Act of 1935, was funded through a "regressive" payroll tax, apparently at Roosevelt's personal insistence.[93]

By 1934, "soak-the-rich" rhetoric began to penetrate the New Deal.[94] The Revenue Act of 1934[95] reflected the administration's concessions to the emerging egalitarian sentiment among congressional Populists and Progressives. Under the 1934 act, rates for the individual income tax were raised, the progressivity of the tax was enhanced, capital gains rates were graduated, the deduction for net capital losses was limited to $2,000 per year, and the disallowance rule for sales of property between "related parties" was introduced to the tax code, as was the "personal holding company" penalty provisions. Under pressure from Senate Progressives led by Robert La Follette of Wisconsin, the federal estate tax was increased to 60 percent on taxable estates above $10 million. Nevertheless, the final bill was relatively tame, and attempts by Progressives on the Senate floor to introduce more extreme measures were fought back. Senator La Follette and Senator Huey Long of Louisiana lobbied to increase tax rates further, but these efforts were opposed by the Roosevelt administration and ultimately failed to gain support in Congress as well. Even still, the 1934 act "confirmed the administration's fear that a rise in corporate or upper-bracket individual taxes

92. Testimony of Republican members of the House Committee on Ways and Means, "Extension of Certain Excise Taxes and Postage Rates," H. Rept. 935 to accompany H.J. Res. 375, 75th Cong., 1st sess. (1937), 21.

93. This is the conclusion of Mark H. Leff, "Taxing the 'Forgotten Man': The Politics of Social Security Finance in the New Deal," 70 *J. Am. Hist.* 359 (1983).

94. William Safire traces the first written citation of the slogan "soak the rich" to James P. Warburg, *Hell Bent for Election* (Garden City, N.Y.: Doubleday, Doren, 1935), in which the author charged Franklin D. Roosevelt with trying to steal the "thunder on the Left" from Huey Long by coming out with his own "soak-the-rich" message. The phrase was used previously in a speech on the House floor by Congressman Fiorello La Guardia. See William Safire, "On Language," *N.Y. Times Mag.*, November 11, 1990, 22, and December 9, 1990, 26.

95. Pub. L. No. 216, 48 Stat. 680.

would antagonize the economic elite."[96]

By 1935, proponents of soak-the-rich sentiment gained in strength and ardor. Roosevelt eventually was pushed toward a more aggressive tax policy, in part because Long's agrarian populist movement was swelling. In addition, pressure was constantly exerted from the La Follette Progressives. In the mid-1930s, still no more than 5 percent of the population was required to file an income tax return. One of the central tenets of La Follette's tax program was to lower personal exemptions to bring the middle classes under the income tax. The La Follette tax plan would have cut the personal exemption by one-fifth, increased tax rates, and used the graduated rates to redistribute wealth from the rich *and* middle classes to the poor.[97] In response, the president in June 1935 presented a new tax policy to Congress in a message on tax reform. Roosevelt proposed three reform measures. First, he called for a federal inheritance tax on the transfer of great wealth: "[I]nherited economic power is inconsistent with the ideals of this generation as inherited political power was inconsistent with the ideals of the generation which established our Government." Second, Roosevelt asked Congress for an increase of the surtax on income above $1 million: "Social unrest and a deepening sense of unfairness are dangers to our national life which we must minimize by rigorous methods. . . . Therefore, the duty rests upon the Government to restrict such incomes by very high taxes." And third, he wanted a graduated corporate income tax to replace the flat 13.75 percent rate then in effect.[98]

On August 30, 1935, Roosevelt's proposals bore fruit in a new tax bill, the Revenue Act of 1935.[99] The 1935 tax act increased the surtax rates on higher levels of income – beginning at 31 percent on income over $50,000 and rising to 75 percent on income over $5 million. The corporate income tax also was increased from the 13.75 percent flat rate to a graduated-rate structure that rose from 12.5 percent on net income up to $2,000 to 15 percent on income in excess of $40,000. There were increases to the penalty tax imposed on personal holding companies.

96. Leff, *Limits of Symbolic Reform*, 65.

97. La Follette's tax program is discussed in much greater detail in ibid., 103–19. Much of this discussion draws upon Leff's interesting account of tax policy during the New Deal.

98. The text of Roosevelt's tax proposal is found in "A Message to the Congress on Tax Revisions," in *The Public Papers and Addresses of Franklin D. Roosevelt* (New York: Random House, 1938), 4:270.

99. Pub. L. No. 407, 49 Stat. 1014.

These provisions (which in some cases were actually less than Roosevelt had asked for) failed to satisfy radicals on the Left, such as La Follette, but nevertheless provoked intense negative reaction among conservatives. This tax act alone accounted for much of the dread and loathing of Roosevelt among conservatives, Republicans, and the "wealthy" in general. The incident helps to explain why Roosevelt was generally forced to take the middle ground in New Deal tax policies.

In April 1838, a congressional tax bill passed without Roosevelt's support. Under the Revenue Act of 1938,[100] congressional conservatives were able to lift the tax burden imposed on corporations somewhat. Specifically, the tax on undistributed corporate earnings was reduced. The taxation of capital gains for individuals was changed to the system that survives largely intact to this day. The 1938 bill provided for an eighteen-month holding period for long-term capital gains. For gain recognized on the sale of capital assets held more than eighteen months but less than twenty-four months, one-third of such gain was excluded from taxation; for assets held more than twenty-four months, the exclusion was 50 percent. The 1938 tax act was followed by the Revenue Act of 1939,[101] which was even more notable for what it gave back to business and the wealthy.

Thus, for all the ideological sound and fury of the New Deal, only the Revenue Act of 1935 "made any pretense of using personal income taxation to redistribute wealth."[102] Despite the ideological pretensions of the New Deal and its importance in the development of the American administrative state, its long-term impact on the structure of the federal income tax was negligible. For this reason, the tax policy of the New Deal has been described as more political rhetoric and "symbolic reform" than genuine redistributive policy.[103] What most conspicuously distinguishes the tax policy pursued by Democratic New Dealers during the 1930s from that pursued by their Republican predecessors during the 1920s was that tax rates drifted upward throughout the decade. On the other hand, the New Deal generally left the overall structure of the federal income tax intact.

Perhaps the greatest achievement of the 1930s was the codification and collation of the tax laws under the Internal Revenue Code of 1939.

100. Pub. L. No. 554, 52 Stat. 447.

101. Pub. L. No. 155, 53 Stat. 862.

102. Leff, *Limits of Symbolic Reform*, 91.

103. This is the general theme of Leff's excellent account of tax policy during the New Deal. Ibid.

This great work was a product of the joint efforts of the administration and Treasury, with significant assistance from the Joint Committee on Internal Revenue Taxation. Notwithstanding this impressive legislative effort, the new tax code was mostly a restatement (and simplification) of existing law and did not effect major changes to the tax regime. But soon enough, the fiscal demands imposed by the great worldwide military conflagration of the 1940s would inflict genuine and radical changes to the federal income tax.

World War II and the Transformation of the Income Tax

It is commonly said that World War II transformed the federal income tax from a "class" tax into a "mass" tax. This phrase neatly captures what was in essence the most radical expansion of the fiscal powers of the American state. Before the war, only a few wealthy citizens were subject to the income tax. By the end of the war, the vast majority of U.S. citizens had become taxpayers. Secretary of Treasury Henry Morgenthau Jr. tried to put a good face on this when he announced to Congress that "for the first time in our history, the income tax is becoming a people's tax."[104] This transformation of the income tax into a "people's tax" was a landmark event in the development of the modern American state.

The first reaction to the outbreak of war in Europe was similar to that experienced in 1916–17.[105] In response to an estimated deficit of $2.876 billion for fiscal year 1941, President Roosevelt requested new legislation to raise an additional $500 million in revenue. This produced the first Revenue Act of 1940 (enacted in June), pursuant to which personal exemptions were slightly reduced, a minor surtax was imposed on personal income over $6,000, and corporate tax rates were increased. Treasury estimated that the number of tax returns filed under this new provision would be more than double. Then on July 1, Roosevelt requested of Congress a "steeply graduated excess profits tax, to be applied to all individuals and all corporate organizations without discrimination."[106] After considerable debate over the issue throughout the

---

104. Senate Committee on Finance, Hearings on H.R. 7378, vol. 1, 77th Cong., 2d sess. (1942), 3.

105. For a more comprehensive account of the initial reaction to World War II, an account on which this analysis draws, see Roy G. Blakely and Gladys C. Blakely, "The Two Federal Revenue Acts of 1940," 30 *Am. Econ. Rev.* 724 (1940).

106. *The Public Papers and Addresses of Franklin D. Roosevelt: 1940 Volume* (New York: Macmillan, 1941), 276.

summer, Congress enacted the excess profits tax pursuant to a second Revenue Act of 1940. The excess profits tax was designed to tax profits attributable solely to the defense buildup.[107] After his landslide victory in the 1940 election, Roosevelt continued to pursue a "flexible finance program" consisting in increasing borrowing, raising the debt limit, reducing personal exemptions and raising rates for the individual income tax, and expanding the excess profits tax.[108] This approach was implemented under the Revenue Act of 1941, the largest federal revenue measure enacted to that date. But even this proved inadequate as federal spending rose dramatically after 1941, climbing from $20 billion for that year to almost $100 billion by 1944. Federal expenditures for the period July 1940 to August 1945 amounted to $337 billion, of which $304 billion was devoted to the war effort.[109] The Revenue Act of 1942 followed the president's objective of significantly raising taxes to lessen the need of the federal government to borrow. Enacted in November, the 1942 act raised the normal personal income tax from 4 percent to 6 percent and added a progressive surtax ranging from 13 percent on income over $6,000 to 82 percent on income over $200,000. Personal exemptions were lowered to only $500 for an individual and $1,200 for a married couple. It was this lowering of the personal exemptions that so greatly expanded the application of the tax to the vast majority of the working public.

Over the course of the revenue crisis of World War II, tax rates and the volume of revenue collected under the income tax increased dramatically. By 1944 the maximum tax rate rose to 94 percent for individuals (on income in excess of $2,000,000) and 40 percent for corporations (in addition to the excess profits tax). Total federal receipts from the income tax rose sevenfold. The expansion of the tax base was evidenced by the number of tax returns filed by individuals, which increased nearly eightfold from 1940 to 1945.[110] The number of individuals subject to the income tax increased over the course of World War II, eventually reaching over 74 percent of the population.

107. For a discussion of the workings of the excess profits tax, see Carl Shoup, "Taxation of Excess Profits III," 56 *Pol. Sci. Q.* 226, 246 (1941): "The tax is designed primarily to reach profits that are due to the defense program."

108. The president's plan is explained in great detail in Ratner, *American Taxation*, 501–5.

109. Ibid., 516.

110. The number of tax returns filed by individuals increased from four million in 1939 to forty million by 1943. Figures cited in King, *Money, Time, and Politics*, 121.

The administration of the federal tax laws also was radically transformed during World War II. This was largely effected through the introduction of "withholding at the source,"[111] which had been considered and favored when the income tax was originally enacted in 1913, in particular by Cordell Hull of Tennessee, Democratic chairman of the House Ways and Means Committee. Proponents had viewed with favor the British system, which imposed a flat rate on prescribed payments and was indifferent to the income or financial status of the recipient—and thus was highly administrable.[112] Despite initial support for the concept, withholding at the source was not put into effect until 1943, pursuant to the Current Tax Payment Act of 1943.[113] Until that time, the individual income tax was paid solely through quarterly payments of estimated tax for the current year.[114] The Roosevelt administration recommended withholding requirements in order to speed up the collection of the badly needed revenue to which the national government now laid claim. The new legislation created a new obligation for "payers" of compensation, interest, and dividends, requiring them to withhold a prescribed amount of income tax from the payment itself.[115] Decades later, "information reporting" requirements were also imposed upon these categories of payers.[116]

Thus, the important impact of World War II on the structure and functional role of the federal income tax can be summarized as follows: tax rates increased, personal exemptions were lowered, and a great majority of the population became subject to the tax; administrative

111. For a discussion of the politics behind the enactment of the first withholding requirements, see Paul, *Taxation in the United States*, 333-34.

112. See Blakely and Blakely, *The Federal Income Tax*, 75, 511-20. Proponents of withholding at the source also looked to the English experience with envy, since it raised significant revenue through this device.

113. Pub. L. No. 78-68, 57 Stat. 126.

114. This is still the method of payment of tax with respect to "self-earned" income. See IRC secs. 6315 and 6654. Technically, there is no requirement to pay such estimated taxes. However, there are penalties for failure to make adequate quarterly payments of one's annual income tax liability. Absent these provisions, individuals would not need to make any income tax payments until April 15 of the following year—the due date for their income tax return.

115. The withholding requirements, expanded greatly since they were introduced in 1943, are now found in the Internal Revenue Code at sections 3401-3406.

116. Subsequent legislation requires payers of compensation, interest, and dividends to report such payments to the IRS on an annual basis. Information-reporting requirements are found at IRC sections 6041-6050N.

powers were greatly expanded, and the federal government became even more addicted to the revenue produced from the income tax. Most significantly, the changes made to the tax code to finance World War II were not withdrawn after the wartime crisis ended, as had been the case following both the Civil War and World War I. The higher rates and the expanded scope of the tax were retained, and the expansionist trend continued into the immediate postwar decades, albeit at a slowed pace. In 1950, 59 percent of the population was subject to the individual income tax; the figure increased to 81 percent by 1970. Likewise, revenue from the federal income tax rose to 45 percent of all federal tax receipts by 1950; by 1985, the figure was 73 percent. After World War II, the federal income tax would emerge as the most wide-ranging and all-encompassing fiscal tool, relied upon by politicians to finance the activities of an expanded federal government as well as to implement social and economic policies impinging upon virtually every aspect of American life.

3

Tax Policy in the Postwar Era

A possible danger to the successful and permanent operation of an income-tax law, as is true of all tax laws, is the disposition even of its friends to insert additional exemptions here and there and to add liberal qualifications, thereby opening many doors to those who would evade or avoid their full share of taxes.
— Rep. Cordell Hull (1918)

It's time for a complete overhaul of our income tax system. I feel it's a disgrace to the human race.
— Jimmy Carter (1976)

Tax Policy After World War II

The basic structure of the post–World War II income tax was largely a product of the wartime experience. This was most evident in the high marginal rates, low personal exemptions, and graduated-rate structure of the tax. Indeed, the single most pressing tax issue in 1945 was how and when to roll back the extraordinary 94 percent maximum individual tax rate still in effect. That wartime rate included an excess profits tax that was soon repealed. However, the maximum individual rate continued to hover at or above the 90 percent mark for nearly two decades after the war. The issue of rate reduction dominated the politics of the income tax into the 1980s, when the extraordinary wartime rates were finally withdrawn during the ascendancy of Republican tax policy in the first Reagan administration.

In the decades following World War II, tax policy was made within the context of the post–New Deal party system in which the Democratic Party generally dominated Congress. However, at the close of 1945, with the Great Depression and the war finally over, the Republican Party and its business constituency found a far more hospitable political environment, especially with respect to tax policy. Republicans gained control of both houses following the 1946 elections after securing a 51-to-45 majority in the Senate and a 242-to-188 majority in the House. This marked the first time since 1930 that the Republican Party controlled Congress. Budget cutting and tax reduction were the dominant Republican themes in the 1946 elections. Representative Harold Knudsen, who became chairman of the House Ways and Means Committee following the Republican victory, had campaigned in 1946 for a 20 percent overall cut in income tax rates. Immediately following the election, Republican leaders jointly announced their intention to "return to conservative fiscal policy, with a balanced budget and lower taxes."[1] Party leaders prevailed in the House in introducing legislation that would have implemented broad tax cuts for individuals. However, splits emerged within the ranks of congressional Republicans, especially between Senate Republicans and their brethren in the House, who generally favored much more radical tax cuts.[2] The Democratic Truman administration, as well as the House minority Democrats, strongly and persistently opposed any such tax cuts.[3]

Compromise legislation was proposed by the new Republican Speaker of the House, Joseph Martin of Massachusetts. The compromise bill reported out of Knudsen's committee (H.R. 1) provided for a 30 percent cut for low-income tax brackets and a 10.5 percent tax cut at the higher income brackets. With minor modifications, the conferees as well as the Senate accepted the bill, which passed on June 1, 1947. Backing the bill was a "conservative coalition" of Republicans and Southern Democrats, supported by major business interests;[4] opposing the bill were liberal Northern Democrats and the Democratic administration. Truman vetoed the bill, which was then reenacted in substantially similar form only a month later—and again vetoed by the president. In early 1948, with wartime tax rates actually generating a budget surplus, Republicans and Democratic sympathizers put together another compromise bill that included graduated rate reductions somewhat less than those

1. "GOP Plan: Cut Taxes, Balance Budget, Remove Controls from Business," *Wall St. J.*, November 7, 1946, A1.
2. "GOP Senators Set to Balk 20 Percent Tax Slash Advocated by Republicans in House," *Wall St. J.*, January 2, 1947, A1.
3. Republican politics in general during this period is the subject of David W. Reinhard, *The Republican Right Since 1945* (Lexington: University Press of Kentucky, 1983), 15–36.
4. The postwar voting record of this conservative coalition of Republicans and Southern Democrats is more fully analyzed in Thomas J. Reese, *The Politics of Taxation* (Westport, Conn.: Quorum Books, 1980), 130–35.

proposed in 1947, along with additional tax benefits for taxpayers in all tax brackets.[5] This bill gained broad bipartisan support, with the same conservative coalition supporting the bill. The bill passed the House by a 297-to-120 vote, with all Senate Republicans and thirty Democrats (mostly from the South) voting in favor of the bill. This time there were enough votes to override Truman's veto.[6]

The tax bill that became law, the Revenue Act of 1948,[7] lowered the maximum individual income tax rate to 77 percent. Consensus for the bill was achieved through a wide dispersal of benefits to create a majoritarian coalition of convenience. A nonpartisan pattern of trading votes for tax benefits (logrolling) made passage of the 1948 bill possible. This practice became the norm for postwar tax legislation, much as it had characterized the politics of the tariff earlier in the century.[8] In addition, the partisan split between Republicans and Democrats, which was expressed throughout the 1920s and 1930s but suppressed during the war years, emerged once again after 1945 as the dominant division in Congress over tax policy. For the next forty years, the parties would disagree over how progressive the tax should be (with Democrats generally favoring a steeper, more graduated rate structure) and how to implement rate reductions (with Republicans preferring across-the-board tax cuts). Since World War II, Republicans have been on the whole less favorably inclined toward "tax reform" than Democrats, although considerable care must be exercised in drawing such a conclusion, since expediency often dictates how that term is used in political discourse.[9]

In the 1948 elections, Democrats regained control of both houses of Congress. Pressure for revenue increased as the Cold War deepened, and prevented the dismantling of the American military. After 1950, the

5. H.R. 4790 implemented tax rate reductions of 20 to 30 percent for taxpayers with income below $4,000 and 10 percent for taxpayers with taxable income over $4,000. See "Report of House Ways and Means Committee," 80th Cong., 2d sess. (January 27, 1948), H. Rept. 1274.

6. In his veto message, Truman expressed his objections to reducing government revenue by $5 billion in the face of challenges to peace by the "forces of dissension and chaos." See "Message from the President of the United States," 80th Cong., 2d sess. (April 2, 1948), H. Doc. 589.

7. Pub. L. No. 80-471, 62 Stat. 110.

8. This politics of logrolling and vote trading over the tariff was observed by E. E. Schattschneider during the 1920s and 1930s. See E. E. Schattschneider, *Politics, Pressures, and the Tariff* (New York: Prentice-Hall, 1935).

9. "There is a high correlation between liberal Democrats and tax reform, and between opponents of tax reform and conservatives (both Republicans and Democrats)." Reese, *Politics of Taxation*, xxi; see also 141–42.

outbreak of overt military hostilities during the Korean conflict necessitated a tax increase. This was implemented through the Revenue Act of 1951,[10] signed by Truman in October 1951. The bill raised individual tax rates by 11 percent and the corporate tax by 5 percentage points, increased military expenditures, and offered some new special-interest provisions as well. For instance, the now sacred exclusion for gain realized on the sale of a principal residence was added to the tax code under the 1951 act, and the tax-free treatment of corporate reorganizations was clarified and expanded.[11] Since Republicans had lost control of both houses in the 1948 elections, the 1951 tax act was mostly the product of a Democratic administration supported by Democratic leadership in the Congress.

In the wake of the Eisenhower landslide in 1952, Republicans again regained control of both the Senate and House. During the first Eisenhower administration, the politics of the income tax continued to revolve around the familiar issue of rate reduction. However, this time it was the Republican administration that resisted the already scheduled cuts now supported broadly in the Republican-controlled Congress. This conflict was attributable in part to the divergence of interests between the executive and legislative branches, and in part to the division in ranks within the Republican Party itself between fiscal conservatives and proponents of tax cuts, a split that reemerged in the 1980s during the Reagan and Bush administrations. In 1954, Republican support for tax rate reduction was stronger in Congress than in the White House.[12]

In 1954, the Republican Party suffered losses that once again gave the Democrats control of both houses of Congress. In early 1955, House Republicans relinquished their majority committee seats for what would turn out to be a forty-year hiatus. In his 1954 State of the Union message to Congress, President Eisenhower proposed postponing all remaining tax cuts scheduled under the 1948 bill; he also proposed a major effort to rewrite and codify the income tax laws. The later proposal culminated in what was then the most significant tax legislation ever enacted, the Revenue Act of 1954.[13] This massive bill codified decades of prior tax legislation and judicial "glosses" on the statutes under what became

10. Pub. L. No. 82-183, 65 Stat. 452.
11. Conference Report on the Revenue Act of 1951, 82nd Cong., 1st sess. (October 15, 1951), H. Doc. 1179.
12. For an account of the split within Republican ranks during the early 1950s, see Reinhard, *The Republican Right*, 75–114.
13. Pub. L. No. 83-591, 68A Stat. 3.

known as the Internal Revenue Code of 1954. After 1954, the most significant tax legislation of the decade created a new tax entity, the so-called Subchapter S corporation, a state-law corporation treated for purposes of federal income tax essentially like a partnership.[14]

The Revenue Act of 1954 evidenced the politics of the federal income tax that would characterize the entire postwar period: steeply progressive tax rates were preserved through logrolling and trade-offs granting special exclusions for business, investment, and a wide variety of special interests. Ronald King has described the policymaking for the 1954 bill and the resulting consequences for the tax code as follows: "The new bill [the Revenue Act of 1954] . . . taught that narrowly written provisions could be approved somewhat more easily. The nominal rate schedule would be scaled sharply upward as a matter of conscious policy, yet its progressive impact would be tempered via a number of categorical exemptions and dispensations. The tax system would continue to give the appearance of egalitarianism while actually reducing burdens for those engaged in specific practices, notably owner expenditures for new productive facilities."[15] In this way, the income tax would function as a tool of the state in *both* alleviating class antagonisms and accumulating capital.

The debate over rate reduction during the immediate postwar years reflected the conflicting imperatives that would continue to drive tax policymaking over the next half century. Pressure for increased revenue remained constant, even during the periods of relative peace between overt military engagements. At the same time, the ideological commitment to tax rate reduction that first emerged during Secretary Mellon's long tenure in Treasury in the 1920s remained strong within the Republican Party, especially within Congress. On account of the relatively even balance of power within both houses (especially taking into account conservative Southern Democrats, who often voted with Republicans beginning in the late 1950s), compromise was always necessary to secure passage of any significant tax legislation. Likewise, where any tax bill

14. Subchapter S was added to the Internal Revenue Code under the Technical Amendments Act of 1958, Pub. L. No. 85-866, 72 Stat. 1606, Title 1.

15. Ronald F. King, *Money, Time, and Politics: Investment Tax Subsidies and American Democracy* (New Haven: Yale University Press, 1993), 138. This theme invokes an observation by F. A. Hayek: "[T]he illusion that by means of progressive taxation the burden can be shifted substantially onto the shoulders of the wealthy has been the chief reason why . . . the masses have come to accept a much heavier load than they would have done otherwise." Friedrich A. Hayek, *The Constitution of Liberty* (Chicago: University of Chicago Press, 1960, 311).

adversely affected any significant discrete interest or constituency (something nearly impossible to avoid in major tax legislation), trade-offs and logrolling were required to put together a winning coalition, which by necessity had to include members of the opposition party.

> When new tax legislation was desired, whether by the president or the congressional leadership, the Republicans or Democrats, tax benefits had to be yielded *to both sides* if the tax legislation was to have a chance of getting through the system of checks and balances. . . . No one has been able to pass tax legislation without literally buying off opposition from representatives interested in protecting their constituents. The result of this political stale-mate has been that the politics of taxation has degenerated into the micro politics of special interest wrangling.[16]

The logrolling and vote trading would "continue to the point where no one [was] satisfied but few [could] afford to see the bill defeated."[17] This is the essence of the "normal" politics that has dominated federal income tax policymaking since the 1940s.

Reform and Consensus: Tax Policy in the 1960s

In the 1960s, federal policymakers came under the sway of Keynesian principles of economics and fiscal policy, which embraced the notion that the tax code should be an integral tool of fiscal policy. From this perspec-tive, progressive rates are justified not so much on grounds of egalitaria-nism or the redistribution of wealth, but rather based upon their worth as a countercyclical stabilizer for the economy. Likewise, the tax code came to be viewed increasingly as a neutral vehicle for implementing social and economic policy. These important principles took shape dur-ing the Kennedy administration.

In his 1962 economic message, President Kennedy presented what would become the agenda for tax policy for the next three decades. Kennedy paid tribute to the need for "tax reform" but, at the same time,

---

16. Sven Steinmo, *Taxation and Democracy: Swedish, British, and American Ap-proaches to Financing the Modern State* (New Haven: Yale University Press, 1993), 137.

17. John F. Witte, *The Politics and Development of the Federal Income Tax* (Madison: University of Wisconsin Press, 1985), 144. In the discussion herein, I am greatly indebted to Witte's survey of postwar tax policy.

insisted upon a pragmatic use of the tax code for implementing economic and social policy—a schizophrenic vision of the income tax that still prevails among policymakers: "Later this year, I shall present to Congress a major program of tax reform. This broad program will reexamine tax rates and the definition of the income tax base. It will be aimed at simplification of our tax structure, the equal treatment of equally situated persons, and the strengthening of incentives for individual effort and productive investment."[18] Kennedy's pronouncement, as much as any single expression of political rhetoric, reflects the many disparate uses of tax policy: the mandatory emphasis on tax-reform themes, the politician's pragmatic impulse to use the tax code to implement public policy, and the Keynesian vision of the income tax as a macroeconomic tool for managing the national economy.[19] These conflicting notions of tax policy have infused and thereby undermined the coherence of contemporary tax legislation ever since.

With the appointment of Stanley S. Surrey of Harvard Law School as assistant secretary of the treasury for tax policy, the movement for tax reform found an untiring academic proponent in the highest tax-policymaking position in the executive branch. Yet, the tax legislation enacted during the brief Kennedy administration was hardly what one would expect from a Treasury dominated by Surrey, an activist for tax reform and an outspoken critic of excessive use of tax preferences and expenditures. Practical political considerations, rather than the principles of tax reform, dominated the White House. Kennedy himself continued to pay lip service to tax reform in his 1963 State of the Union address: "I am convinced that the enactment this year of tax reductions and tax reform overshadows all other domestic problems in this Congress."[20]Yet, declining economic conditions pushed the administration to propose, not tax reform, but rather an investment tax credit to be funded in part by

18. John F. Kennedy, "January 1962 Economic Message," in *Public Papers of the Presidents, John F. Kennedy, 1962* (Washington, D.C.: Government Printing Office, 1963), 58.

19. Kennedy framed his message in what Ronald King has referred to as an ideology of "growthsmanship," in which labor's interests are linked to the success of business. Kennedy expressed this sentiment in the same January 1962 economic report to Congress: "Among both businessmen and workers, there is a growing recognition that the road to higher real profits and higher real wages is the road to increased productivity." Ibid., 51.

20. John F. Kennedy, "Annual Message to the Congress on the State of the Union," (January 1963), in *Public Papers of the Presidents: John F. Kennedy, 1963* (Washington, D.C.: Government Printing Office, 1964), 13.

new withholding requirements on dividends and interest. The initial proposal for the investment tax credit had its origins in the Treasury Department and provided for a complicated graduated rate structure; the Kennedy administration settled for a flat 7 percent tax credit for the sake of simplicity.[21]

In markup, the House Ways and Means and Senate Finance Committees dropped most of the revenue-raising provisions from the administration's bill, adopting only the tax-reduction provisions. The result was the Revenue Act of 1962,[22] a bill supported by a coalition built by offering tax benefits to many diverse interests, following no coherent plan or pattern other than to spread around the tax pork barrel. This mode of politics was again prominent behind the tax bill introduced by the Kennedy administration in January 1963 and subsequently enacted during the Johnson administration, following Kennedy's death. As Cathie Martin has put it: "The [political] lessons of 1962 motivated the administration to develop the coalition strategy in 1964."[23]

The Revenue Act of 1964 implemented significant tax reductions that cut the maximum marginal tax rate from 91 percent to 70 percent

21. The most comprehensive discussion of the Kennedy proposal for the investment tax credit is found in King, *Money, Time, and Politics*, 163–77, 265–91, 318–19. King describes the initial opposition of business to an investment tax credit and its preference for accelerated depreciation. Later, business (with the acquiescence of labor) came to regard the credit as fundamental to the formation of capital – a goal not necessarily of uniform value to all sectors of business. King traces the academic origins of the investment tax credit to an article by E. Cary Brown, "The New Depreciation Policy Under the Income Tax: An Economic Analysis," 8 *Nat. Tax J.* 93 (1955), written as a criticism of the new accelerated depreciation enacted under the Revenue Act of 1954.

22. Pub. L. No. 87-834, 76 Stat. 960.

23. Cathie J. Martin, *Shifting the Burden: The Struggle over Growth and Corporate Taxation* (Chicago: University of Chicago Press, 1991), 61. A central theme of Martin's insightful account of the Kennedy tax bills is that policymakers learned to pull together a selective coalition of private-sector pro-business interests that would lobby in favor of the administration's bill. In this way, state actors in the executive branch were able to orchestrate private societal interests in pursuit of a mutually beneficial tax and fiscal policy: "Organized by the administration and oriented toward a larger policy vision, the movement [business lobbying for the 1964 act] was of political benefit to both the executive branch activists and their business allies." Ibid. at 79. As such, executive officials used outside private interests for support vis-à-vis congressional policymakers: "[P]residential mobilization of business was a strategy for side-stepping the autonomous authority of other political figures. . . . Both administrations [Kennedy and Johnson] mobilized business interests to discipline a reluctant [Wilbur] Mills and his fellow conservative legislators." Ibid. at 197.

(where it remained until 1981).[24] Tax rates in the lower brackets were reduced as well, but in somewhat lesser proportions.[25] This significant reduction in marginal tax rates, amounting to a 23 percent rate reduction, would inspire a later generation of supply-side economists.[26] However, the legislation also bestowed generous "tax reductions and scattered those reductions across the entire income spectrum."[27] In addition, the bill included many provisions that created new and expanded existing tax preferences.

During the final year of the Johnson administration, tax-reform proponents in the Treasury Department fashioned a collection of reform and revenue proposals. Budget shortfalls forced Johnson, and later Nixon, reluctantly to take up the bill. The need to secure additional revenue to finance the prolonged military conflict in Vietnam forced Congress and the executive to embrace a conception of "tax reform" consisting in closing revenue "leaks" and reversing the "erosion" of the tax base concomitant to the many preferences that had crept into the tax code. This political impulse was essentially motivated by revenue concerns. In the first year of the new Republican administration of Richard Nixon, these reform proposals were presented to Congress. Nixon expressed much the same mixed message on tax policy/tax reform as Kennedy had: "Reform of our Federal income tax is long overdue. Special preferences in the law permit far too many Americans to pay less than their fair share of taxes. Too many other Americans bear too much of this tax burden. . . . We must reform our tax structure to make it more equitable and efficient; we must redirect our tax policy to make it more conducive to stable economic growth and responsive to urgent social needs."[28] The administration's bill was enacted as the Tax Reform Act of

24. Pub. L. No. 88-272, 78 Stat. 19.

25. For an overall assessment of the so-called Kennedy tax reductions, see Lawrence B. Lindsey, *The Growth Experiment: How the New Tax Policy Is Transforming the U.S. Economy* (New York: Basic Books, 1990), 28–40.

26. To be accurate, the origin of supply-side sentiments ought to be traced back to Secretary of Treasury Mellon, who expressly argued that tax reductions would result in increased revenue – which in fact was the case throughout the 1920s.

27. Witte, *Politics,* 161 (describing the Ways and Means bill). For a detailed account of the politics behind the Revenue Act of 1964, see John Manley, *The Politics of Finance: The House Committee on Ways and Means* (Boston: Brown, Little, 1970), 359–74.

28. House Committee on Ways and Means, 91st Cong., 1st sess. (April 22, 1969), Tax Reform Proposals, 1–4 (Washington, D.C.: Government Printing Office, 1969).

1969,[29] which was notable in that more revenue was actually raised than was given away in new or expanded tax preferences. Several aspects of the politics behind this major tax bill warrant specific attention.

First, the bill was a massive revision of a good deal of existing tax law. The now familiar tendency to rewrite the entire tax code every few years was already evidenced in the 1969 act, which included so many provisions amending so many sections of the tax code that no single individual, even those directly in control of the legislative process, could possibly comprehend the bill as a whole. Taking on so much all at once and under the short deadlines imposed by the legislative process has contributed to an increase in tax legislation that is poorly thought out, poorly written, inconsistent with other sections of the tax code, and often internally incoherent. The increased need to enact technical corrections legislation points out the shortcomings of this approach. In 1986, this phenomenon reached new heights as the overwhelming burden of crafting such a massive tax bill in such a short time resulted in an extraordinary number of flawed statutory provisions.[30]

Second, the legislative process for the Tax Reform Act of 1969 was securely in the hands of Wilbur Mills, who from his position as chair of the Ways and Means Committee exerted more control over the postwar tax legislative agenda than any other individual (including a succession of presidents). Mill presided over the tax legislative process from 1958 to 1974, at which time he was forced to resign from the House for a combination of personal and political reasons.[31] On account of Mills's

---

29. Pub. L. No. 91-172, 83 Stat. 487, Titles 1-9.

30. Charles McLure refers to such legislation as policymaking "under the gun." Charles A. McLure Jr., "The Budget Process and Tax Simplification/Complication," 45 *Tax L. Rev.* 25, 79-81 (1989). One saving grace may be that such massive tax bills keep lobbyists and interest groups off guard, providing policymakers with greater independence in a floor vote. Many otherwise well-organized interest groups were simply unable to keep up with the fast pace or fully appreciate the import of many of the provisions on the tax-reform agenda in 1986.

31. For a discussion of Mills's powerful role as chairman of the Ways and Means Committee, see John F. Manley, "Wilbur D. Mills: A Study in Congressional Influence," 63 *Am. Pol. Sci. Rev.* 442 (1969); idem, *The Politics of Finance,* 98-150; Catherine E. Rudder, "Tax Policy: Structure and Choice," in *Making Economic Policy in Congress,* ed. Allen Schick (Washington, D.C.: American Enterprise Institute, 1983), 196-201. For a more recent perspective on the Mills era in light of the post-Watergate congressional reforms, see Randall Strahan, *New Ways and Means: Reform and Change in a Congressional Committee* (Chapel Hill: University of North Carolina Press, 1990), 44-46.

domination of the tax-policymaking process on the House side, this bill exhibited what became a traditional pattern of tax legislation: the House bill was far less generous in giving away tax benefits than was the Senate markup. This trend persisted after the departure of Mills from the House, and even now the Senate tends to provide more generous tax reductions to favored interests than the House.[32]

Third, the Tax Reform Act of 1969 introduced certain familiar tax-reform proposals that have been repeatedly on and off the policy agenda in the decades since. For instance, a proposal emerged in the House (later dropped in the Senate) for repeal of the long-standing and much criticized exemption for interest paid on state and municipal debt obligations.[33] This issue was revisited, again unsuccessfully, during the tax-reform efforts of 1985–86. The House also sought unsuccessfully to introduce provisions to govern the deduction of losses attributable to investments in real estate transactions designed to produce artificial tax benefits. In retrospect, this was the origin of the tax shelter industry that ran wild in the late 1970s. Pursuant to its tax-reform initiatives in 1969, the Nixon administration proposed the outright repeal, rather than suspension, of the investment tax credit first introduced by President Kennedy in 1962.[34] That measure was reluctantly supported by a skeptical Mills, and later survived a challenge by the Finance Committee. Thus, the investment tax credit was unexpectedly (but, as it turned out, temporarily) repealed in 1969.

---

32. This trend was best illustrated by the markups of the 1986 bill in the respective houses of Congress. Compared with even the worst version of the House bill, let alone the final draft that had emerged from the House for consideration by the Senate, the first version of the Senate bill to emerge, dubbed "Packwood I" by cynics, was a wholesale surrender to special-interest lobbyists. In 1995, Senate Republicans bucked the trend and attempted to reduce the magnitude of the tax benefits bestowed by their brethren in the House upon constituent elements of the Republican Party. Whether this becomes a long-term trend remains to be seen.

33. IRC sec. 103.

34. In his tax-reform proposals, Nixon linked repeal of the 7 percent investment tax credit to a phaseout of the 10 percent surcharge. Ronald King has noted the irony of Nixon's recommending the repeal of the investment tax credit and also proposing to share federal revenue with state programs designed to encourage investment and job creation in distressed urban areas: "Oddly, a Republican president with conservative beliefs and a business constituency explicitly proposed to withdraw a lucrative corporation tax preference in exchange for lower burdens on average citizens and the promise of future funding for the welfare state." King, *Money, Time, and Politics*, 332.

In another revealing episode during consideration of the 1969 initiative, the Senate Finance Committee included a reform provision for the alternative minimum tax (or AMT). The alternative minimum tax is typical of the kind of reforms that emerge from incremental policymaking operating within democratic electoral institutions and motivated by a liberal politics premised upon the appeasement of capital. Rather than simply eliminate tax preferences and expenditures determined to have insufficient economic justification, policymakers succumbed to the temptation to have their pork and eat it too. Congress created a whole new parallel tax system, the AMT, in which such preferences are disallowed. However, the AMT was simply grafted onto the "regular" federal income tax regime, permitting legislators to retain existing tax preferences under the regular income tax, while simultaneously cultivating the appearance that they were preventing "tax abuse" by disallowing the same preferences under the AMT. The inability of tax policymakers to choose a definitive direction for tax policy predictably yielded further complexity and incoherence in the income tax.

Tax Policy in the 1970s

Persistent inflation and economic stagnation undermined the U.S. economy throughout the 1970s and was reflected in the tax and fiscal policy of the Nixon administration. Increasingly under the influence of Treasury secretary John Connally, the Nixon administration presented a wide range of proposals to Congress—from the infamous "closing of the gold window," which freed up the price of gold,[35] to the unexpected introduction of wage and price controls by a Republican administration.[36] The many tax proposals of the administration included the reintroduction of an investment tax credit (with a stepped rate of 10 percent for the first year and 5 percent in the second) and a new accelerated depreciation schedule known as the asset depreciation range (ADR) intended to stimulate the economy and economic productivity.

35. For a discussion of this important political and economic event, see Joanne Gowa, *Closing the Gold Window: Domestic Politics and the End of Bretton Woods* (Ithaca, N.Y.: Cornell University Press, 1983).

36. Economist Herbert Stein, who served on President Nixon's Council of Economic Advisers in 1971 when wage and price controls were introduced, has recently referred to that economic experiment as "one of the greatest vanities of recent experience." Herbert Stein, "Here We Go Again," *Wall St. J.*, April 29, 1993, A14.

Still firmly under the control of Wilbur Mills, the Ways and Means Committee generally accepted the Nixon administration's proposals, adding only a few modifications, such as returning the investment tax credit to a flat 7 percent. The Senate Finance Committee added some of its own provisions, including additional tax benefits that would have greatly reduced revenue from the bill, but most were withdrawn by the conferees.[37] One of the few provisions added by the Senate that survived was a deduction for dependent-care expenses, still found in the tax code. The final bill that emerged from the Conference Committee was virtually identical to the House bill and was signed by President Nixon as the Revenue Act of 1971.[38] The combined annual revenue loss from the new ADR depreciation schedules, the new Domestic International Sales Corporation (DISC) provision intended to aid U.S. exports, and the resurrected investment tax credit was estimated to be $24.8 billion.[39] The costly DISC provision was so hated by economists in Treasury, uniformly strong supporters of tax reform, that some reportedly refused to work on it.[40] Indeed, on this basis Stanley Surrey – by then back at his teaching position at Harvard Law School – called the 1971 act itself the "worst measure in many a decade from the standpoint of the integrity and fairness of the tax system."[41]

Tax policy was generally neglected during the balance of the Nixon administration; the White House's attention was increasingly diverted by and obsessed with the constitutional crisis that ultimately led to the president's resignation. After Nixon's climactic departure from office on August 9, 1974, a tax bill became a pressing concern of the new Ford administration. The initiative for a bill came from the "new" Ways and

37. Witte, *Politics,* 178.

38. Pub. L. No. 92-178, 85 Stat. 497.

39. Joint Committee on Internal Revenue Taxation, *Summary of the Revenue Act of 1971, As Passed by the House of Representative,* October 7, 1971 (Washington, D.C.: Government Printing Office, 1971).

40. This story is recounted by Reese, *Politics of Taxation,* 55.

41. Stanley S. Surrey, *Pathways to Tax Reform: The Concept of Tax Expenditures* (Cambridge: Harvard University Press, 1973), 175. The *New York Times* had similar disdain for the 1971 tax act: "By any reasonable standard of responsible legislating, Congress has put on a classic demonstration of how not to write a major bill. . . . This tax bill is in many ways a bad bill, seriously eroding the nation's tax base when social needs are unmet and providing more incentives to business to expand capital expenditures when existing capacity is underused . . . . [T]he legislative process has been brought perilously close to parody." *N.Y. Times,* December 7, 1971, 46, col. 1.

Means Committee, which emerged from the post-Watergate congressional reforms implemented in the wake of Nixon's resignation and Wilbur Mills's own downfall later in 1974.[42] In 1975, the committee introduced the earned income tax credit (EITC) for the "working poor" with low incomes and supported the outright repeal of the oil depletion allowance. The latter proposal did not survive long in the Finance Committee, where it was quickly "modified" out of existence by Chairman Long. The final bill, the Tax Reduction Act of 1975,[43] generally followed the House version except for repeal of the oil depletion allowance and expansion of the investment tax credit (which was raised to 10 percent). The 1975 act also included the EITC provision.[44]

During debates over the 1975 tax bill, proposals were already in the works for the decade's most important tax legislation. A new initiative by the administration was defined by Treasury secretary William Simon, who emerged as a strong proponent of tax-deferred accounts (to encourage savings) and integration of the corporate and individual income taxes. The latter is a perennial favorite of economists and Republicans opposed to the disincentives resulting from the "double taxation" of corporate income imposed under the present tax regime.[45] Integration was one of the major themes of the 1977 Treasury report, "Blueprints for Basic Tax Reform."[46] The debates on this bill were particularly intense

42. The effect of the post-Watergate reforms on the House Ways and Means Committee is discussed further in Chapter 6.

43. Pub. L. No. 94-12, 89 Stat. 26.

44. Recently, the EITC has come under strong criticism both for being overly complicated (thereby preventing many from claiming the refundable credits due to them) and for probably being ineffective in achieving its purported goal. See General Accounting Office, "Earned Income Tax Credit: Design and Effectiveness Could Be Improved" (GAO/GGD-93-145) (September 24, 1993); see also Barbara Kirchheimer, "The EITC: Where Policy and Practicality Collide," 65 *Tax Notes* 15 (October 3, 1994).

45. For a discussion of the arguments in favor of integration, see George F. Break, "Corporate Integration: Radical Revisionism or Common Sense?" in *Federal Tax Reform: Myths and Realities,* ed. Michael J. Boskin (San Francisco: Institute of Contemporary Studies, 1978); Alvin Warren, "The Relation and Integration of Individual and Corporate Income Taxes," 94 *Harv. L. Rev.* 717 (1981); idem, "Colloquium on Corporate Integration," 47 *Tax L. Rev.* 427 (1992).

46. Department of Treasury, *Blueprints for Basic Tax Reform* (Washington, D.C.: Government Printing Office, 1977). The Treasury Department report outlined two very different versions of tax reform. The first envisioned an integrated, broad-based income tax with indexed capital gains taxed at the same rate as ordinary income. The second was essentially a "cash flow" consumption tax. In 1992, the Treasury Department reignited the

as Senate liberals, led by Senator Edward Kennedy, Democrat of Massachusetts, challenged the pattern of Senate tax legislating that had emerged during the previous fifteen years, which consisted in reducing taxes and bestowing tax preferences on favored interests or industries. Kennedy denounced the Senate bill for violating the sacred principles of tax reform and equity: "From the standpoint of tax equity, the bill as it comes to the Senate floor is a travesty of tax reform – more tax privileges and benefits for rich and powerful individuals and corporations who are already traveling first class in our society, while continuing the excessive tax burden and inequities for ordinary citizens."[47] However, Senator Long and the "traditional" politics in the Senate maintained firm control over the committee, and in the end the liberal Democrats had little impact on the final bill.

The politics behind the final bill, the Tax Reform Act of 1976,[48] generally followed the legislative pattern established by the early 1960s. The initiative for the bill came from the White House, but its contents were defined almost exclusively by Congress, in particular by Ways and Means. This was true even as the new chairman of the Ways and Means Committee, Al Ullman, exerted considerably less political clout than Mills in directing the committee's bills on the floor. The House bill that passed in December of 1975 was at the core of the final legislation. The Senate Finance Committee's most significant contribution was to strip out a provision intended to limit the deduction of artificial losses (the so-called limitation on artificial losses, or LAL, provision) in favor of the considerably less effective "at-risk" provisions of the tax code (which limit an investor's deduction of tax losses to his economic investment at risk of loss).[49] The Senate bill quietly passed in August 1976, and Conference Committee deliberations were quickly concluded.

---

debate over integration when it issued its *Report on Integration of the Individual and Corporate Tax Systems: Taxing Business Income Once* (Washington, D.C., 1992) and *A Recommendation for Integration of the Individual and Corporate Tax Systems* (Washington, D.C., 1992). The Congressional Research Service published its own study – Jane Gravelle, *Corporate Tax Integration: Issues and Option* (Washington, D.C.: Congressional Research Service, 1991) – and the American Law Institute published a proposal for integration in 1993. These more recent proposals are examined in Matthew P. Haskins, "The Theory and Politics of Integration," 67 *Tax Notes* 401 (April 17, 1995).

47. *Congressional Record*, 94th Cong., 2d sess. (June 16, 1994), 122, pt. 15, 18560.

48. Pub. L. No. 94-455, 90 Stat. 1520.

49. The "at-risk" rules are found at IRC section 465.

The 1976 Tax Reform Act was, at the time, the most massive tax bill ever enacted, implementing tax-reform proposals that had been brewing in the Treasury Department for years. It also implemented significant tax cuts, with much of the revenue loss attributable to a four-year extension of the 10 percent investment tax credit ("temporarily" raised from 7 percent in 1975).[50] Although the 1976 legislation was massive, it had no particular defining principles or philosophy – again, characteristics typical of legislation produced by logrolling and incremental policymaking.

One of the most controversial provisions of the 1976 Tax Reform Act was introduced in the Conference Committee. This was a provision for repeal of the long-standing statutory exception from taxation of built-in gain that would otherwise be recognized on death. The statutory exception allows heirs to "step up" the tax basis of assets received from the decedent, thus eliminating taxation of any built-in capital gain inherent in such assets. This exception allows the built-in gain to escape taxation altogether and had long irked tax reformers, who would close all such "loopholes." This particular loophole became an integral part of tax planning for wealthy individuals, and its correction had long been sought by proponents of a comprehensive income tax base. However, the success of tax reformers in 1976 proved to be short-lived, since the statutory mandate for repeal of the loophole was reversed before ever taking effect.[51]

The presidency of Jimmy Carter commenced in January 1977 with tax reform already high on the policy agenda.[52] Carter had championed tax reform throughout the 1976 electoral campaign, repeatedly referring to the U.S. tax system as a "disgrace to the human race."[53] In his acceptance speech before the Democratic National Convention, Carter declared, "It's time for a complete overhaul of our income tax system.

---

50. Staff of the Joint Committee on Taxation, *General Explanation of the Tax Reform Act of 1976* (Washington, D.C.: Government Printing Office, 1976), 165–66 (estimating revenue losses of $1,300 million in fiscal year 1977, $3,306 million in fiscal year 1978, and $2,444 million in fiscal year 1981).

51. The effective date of IRC section 1023 was first delayed pursuant to the Revenue Act of 1978 and then repealed altogether by the Crude Oil Windfall Profits Tax Act of 1980. Oddly enough, reversal of this reform measure was supported by most Senate liberals on the Finance Committee.

52. The most comprehensive account of the ill-fated Carter tax-reform efforts is found in King, *Money, Time, and Politics,* 387–429. For an assessment of the Carter tax-reform initiatives, see Edward R. Kantowicz, "The Limits of Incrementalism: Carter's Efforts at Tax Reform," 4 *J. Pol'y Analysis & Mgmt.* 217 (1985).

53. Quoted in the *N.Y. Times,* September 14, 1976, A28.

I feel it's a disgrace to the human race."[54] The new administration wasted no time and early in 1977 put a proposal to the Ways and Means Committee. The package was notable for its $50 rebate scheme for all taxpayers, coupled with increased credits for business (permitting businesses to chose between a 4 percent credit based on payroll or a 12 percent investment credit on equipment). Most provisions of the president's ill-fated package were heavily modified, if not dropped altogether, by the Democratic Congress. The final bill, the Tax Reduction and Simplification Act, though signed by Carter in May 1977, was mostly a congressional bill.[55]

Notwithstanding his failure in 1977, Carter again committed himself to tax-reform legislation in his 1978 State of the Union speech, and his Treasury Department completed a comprehensive bill early in 1978. This legislative package pulled together many "classic" tax-reform proposals that had been formulated in and floating about Treasury over the past decade. In many respects, Treasury was pitted against White House staff, since each held a fundamentally contrary view of tax reform – with Treasury obsessed with integration and White House operatives pursuing traditional liberal notions of progressivity and committed to the traditional post–New Deal constituency of the Democratic Party.

The bill ran into trouble as soon as the Ways and Means Committee began its markup. There proved to be little support for the Carter proposals even among Democratic committee members, and the House implemented its own proposals after essentially dropping those of the administration. The Finance Committee was even less kind to the president's tax-reform proposals, following its usual path toward increasing the revenue losses to be derived from the legislative effort; the Senate as a whole was even more generous with tax reductions and less hospitable toward Carter's vision of tax reform. Likewise, the Conference Committee bill "was a complete renunciation of the Carter tax reform proposals and any notion of tax reform."[56] The 1978 Revenue Act marked the triumph of congressional policymaking over the tax reformer's vision of the tax code.[57] Much of the failure of tax reform in the 1970s can be traced

54. Jimmy Carter, "Acceptance Speech Before the Democratic Party," July 15, 1976, reprinted in the *N.Y. Times,* July 16, 1976, A10.

55. The Tax Reduction and Simplification Act "bore almost no resemblance to the legislation proposed by Jimmy Carter." Witte, *Politics,* 199.

56. Ibid., 213.

57. Edward Kantowicz believes that the Carter reform proposals failed because the president acted "too much like a conventional, mainstream liberal" and the tax-reform

to the joint effort of Republicans and Southern Democrats who opposed liberal Democrats on most such tax-reform measures.[58]

As a final note, it must be recognized that the 1950s and 1960s were a unique period for tax policymaking. These were decades of sustained and unprecedented prosperity and economic growth, which supported unique patterns of tax policymaking that ultimately persisted beyond the economic conditions. The period has been aptly described as an era of "easy financing," when even "mistakes in fiscal policy would be unlikely to place much pressure on the budget or increase deficits more than temporarily."[59] Economic growth, and the inflationary effects associated with it, were responsible for the postwar phenomenon known as bracket creep, wherein taxpayers are forced into higher marginal tax brackets simply on account of the effect of inflation on wages. From the perspective of congressional policymakers, bracket creep is akin to constant, automatic tax increases, providing a ready source of revenue for Congress, whose members are thereby spared the political costs and electoral fallout associated with legislated tax increases. The political windfall derived from bracket creep allowed congressional policymakers to rely upon the federal income tax for an abundant and easy source of revenue to finance new domestic-policy programs and generally expand the post–New Deal administrative state. These revenues also allowed Congress the luxury of granting tax rate reductions to constituents through tax expenditures and preferences added to the tax code. The result was an income tax that, though formally progressive in structure (especially before the 1980s), was only mildly, if at all, effec-

---

proposals were not "radical enough." Somehow Kantowicz interprets all this as demonstrating the "limits of incrementalism" and the need for a "bold, comprehensive approach" to tax reform. Kantowicz, "Limits of Incrementalism," 29–31.

58. A survey of partisan voting on tax issues was conducted by the public-interest group Taxation with Representation. Focusing upon the Ninety-fourth and Ninety-fifth Congresses, this study found that Democrats voted much more often for tax reform than did Republicans. See "Comprehensive Tax Reform Voting Scale, 94th Congress," published by Taxation with Representation, October 20, 1976, reprinted in 4 *Tax Notes* 3 (October 25, 1976), and "95th Congress Rated on Tax Reform," published by Taxation with Representation, October 15, 1978. The results of these surveys are summarized in Reese, *Politics of Taxation,* 141–42.

59. C. Eugene Steuerle, *The Tax Decade: How Taxes Came to Dominate the Public Agenda* (Washington, D.C.: Urban Institute Press, 1992), 3.

tive in redistributing income from the top quintile of the population to the lowest.[60]

The period of easy financing came to an end by the late 1970s. One recent study has determined that from 1870 to 1972, the American economy grew at an annual rate of 3.4 percent after inflation; during the twenty-year period after 1973, the economy grew at only 2.3 percent a year after inflation.[61] The cumulative effect of this 1 percent loss in annual economic growth has been severe, especially with respect to federal receipts under the income tax.

> During these twenty years, the loss of goods and services produced by the economy as a result of the 1 percent a year reduction in the growth rate has amounted to roughly $12 trillion (in 1987 dollars). . . . As for the federal budget deficit, not only would it have disappeared entirely had the country grown at its historic rate, but by the early 1990s the U.S. would have run a substantial budget surplus. This would have happened because, with no change in tax rates, tax revenues would have been about $2.5

60. This has been true for all periods of the income tax. For instance, the federal income tax during the 1980s lacked progressive incidence. See, e.g., ibid., 196–97; see also Joseph A. Pechman and Benjamin A. Okner, *Who Bears the Tax Burden?* (Washington, D.C.: Brookings Institution, 1974) (analysis of progressivity of the federal income tax based upon data from 1966, concluding that progressive taxation reduces income inequality by less than 5 percent under the most progressive set of incidence assumptions, and only 0.25 percent under the least progressive assumptions), and Joseph A. Pechman, *Who Pays the Taxes?* (Washington, D.C.: Brookings Institution, 1985) (concluding that the 1981 individual federal income tax cuts, together with rate increases in employment taxes, corporate income tax, as well as state and local taxes, made the tax system as a whole less progressive than it was in the early to mid-1970s). A more recent study of this issue is Joel Slemrod, *Tax Progressivity and Income Inequality* (New York: Cambridge University Press, 1994). Economist Laurence J. Kotlikoff, by employing a broader analysis (taking into account all taxes and benefits) and focusing upon the individual's lifetime (so-called generational accounting), has attempted to redefine the question of how taxes redistribute wealth: "Since the proper base for measuring progressivity in the analysis of distribution policy is lifetime income, not current income, and since such analysis would consider all taxes paid (as well as benefits received), not just federal income taxes, a proper distribution analysis may well yield a view of the fairness of the U.S. fiscal system dramatically different from that based on current annual income." Laurence J. Kotlikoff, *Generational Accounting: Knowing Who Pays, and When, for What We Spend* (New York: Free Press, 1992), 102.

61. Angus Maddison, *Dynamic Forces in Capitalist Development* (New York: Oxford University Press, 1991), 50–53. This represents the worst performance during any twenty-year period since 1870.

trillion higher as personal income rose, and we would have avoided over half of the more than $4 trillion in federal debt we currently have.[62]

In the 1970s, double-digit inflation and a weakening economy created new fiscal pressures on the federal budget. Economist Barry Bosworth has described the adverse effect of inflation on the tax system as follows: "Sustained high inflation during the 1970s increased effective rates of taxation, particularly those reported from capital. The income tax system, with its particular definition of taxable income and a graduated tax rate structure, had been designed for an economy of relative stability."[63] Coupled with the adverse effect of inflation was the trend toward two-earner families filing joint returns, which filing practice pushes a family's marginal income into the higher tax brackets.[64] By the close of the 1970s, the growth rate for real income was frozen at zero, and unemployment had increased to over 7.5 percent. During the same period, the budget process came to be dominated by apparently irresistible increases in federal expenditures, mostly attributable to so-called entitlement payments such as Social Security benefits and military pensions that are outside the reach of budget controls.[65] The pressures for increased expenditures, coupled with the erosion of the tax base by the many tax preferences already enacted, set the stage for the dramatic changes in federal tax policy that came in the 1980s.

62. Jeff Madrick, "The End of Affluence," *N.Y. Rev. Books,* September 21, 1995, 13.

63. Barry P. Bosworth, *Tax Incentives and Economic Growth* (Washington, D.C.: Brookings Institution, 1984), 7.

64. Ibid., 133–38.

65. Entitlements as a percentage of total federal outlays has increased significantly during the postwar period. See Aaron B. Wildavsky and Carolyn Webber, *A History of Taxation and Expenditure in the Western World* (New York: Simon & Schuster, 1986), 5: "Entitlement spending rose from 35.5 percent of federal outlays in fiscal 1967 to 53.6 percent in 1974 to 55.7 percent in 1980." This trend has created a distinct and significant problem for the budgetary process as the discretion of policymakers is even further limited. The Office of Management and Budget estimated that over 50 percent of the federal budget for fiscal year 1994 was attributable to nondiscretionary entitlement expenditures that are not subject to annual review. See "Administration Sets Four-Year Targets for Mandatory Spending," *Daily Tax Rep.* (Bureau of National Affairs), no. 174, September 10, 1993, G-1.

4

The 1980s: Perpetual Tax Legislation

Tax legislation has become a catch–as–catch–can affair that produces complexities, unfairness, conflicting moves in all directions, almost mindless provisions.
— Stanley S. Surrey, "Our Troubled Tax Policy" (1981)

Just as China in the 1960s has perpetual revolution, so the United States in the 1980s has perpetual income tax legislation.
— Daniel Shaviro, "Beyond Public Choice and Public Interest" (1990)

The 1980s have been appropriately characterized as the "tax decade."[1] During the decade, there was a virtual explosion in tax legislation, inflicting radical changes on the Internal Revenue Code. The Tax Reform Act of 1986 (TRA)[2] is the most significant tax bill in the history of the federal income tax. However, no less than six other major tax bills were passed during the 1980s, and the onslaught continued unabated into the 1990s. The glut of tax legislation threatened to undermine the ability of the American state to administer the income tax laws.[3] Likewise, the capacity of the federal courts to adjudicate the increasing number of disputes litigated between the government and taxpayers was

1. C. Eugene Steuerle, *The Tax Decade: How Taxes Came to Dominate the Public Agenda* (Washington, D.C.: Urban Institute Press, 1992), 1.
2. Pub. L. No. 99-514, 100 Stat. 2085.
3. To date, the Internal Revenue Service has been unable to draft all the regulations mandated by Congress to implement the new tax statutes enacted during the 1980s. The enormous backlog numbers some 330 regulations projects in progress as of January 31, 1996. IRS Office of Chief Counsel, "Report on Regulations Projects Status and Disposition as of January 31, 1996" (January 31, 1996).

severely strained during the 1980s.[4] For its part, the private tax bar struggled just to keep up with all the new and increasingly complex tax statutes and regulations.

Tax policy was also particularly unstable during the 1980s, shifting suddenly from supply-side economics to tax reform in a matter of only a few years. During the decade, tax policy seemed at one time or another to express, accommodate, and offend nearly every significant ideological perspective and economic interest.

The Economic Recovery Tax Act of 1981

The decade began with a significant political battle over ideologically driven tax policy. During the 1980 presidential campaign, Ronald Reagan had endorsed in principle a tax-rate-reduction proposal first introduced in 1977 by Senator William Roth and Representative Jack Kemp. The "Kemp-Roth I" proposal called for a 33 percent reduction in the tax rate for individuals and a reduction in the corporate rate of 3 percentage points. In the spring of 1981, newly elected President Reagan introduced his own legislative proposal for somewhat more modest tax rate reductions styled on Kemp-Roth.[5]

Reagan's proposal ran into stiff opposition in Congress, notwithstanding his having just won a clear and convincing electoral victory over Democratic presidential incumbent Jimmy Carter. But by midsummer 1981, Reagan was able to bring together a bipartisan conservative congressional coalition to pass the Economic Recovery Tax Act of 1981 (ERTA).[6] While the ERTA tax cuts were less than those under Kemp-Roth, as well as less than what the president originally proposed, they

4. As of July 31, 1994, the U.S. Tax Court still faced a backlog of 30,591 cases, down considerably from 54,135 four years before, but considerable nonetheless. Many of these cases are leftover tax shelter disputes. "Dwindling Backlog," *Wall St. J.*, August 31, 1994, A1.

5. The Reagan proposal called for 10 percent rate reductions in each of three successive years, retroactive to January 1, 1981. That would have amounted to an overall 27 percent reduction in the tax rate for individuals.

6. Pub. L. No. 97-34, 95 Stat. 172. The final bill passed the House easily with 303 members voting in favor and 107 against. All but one Republican in the House voted for the bill, and Democrats were almost evenly split.

still constituted the most significant tax rate reductions in the history of the federal income tax.[7]

The 1981 tax bill had its intellectual origins in the "supply-side" economics that held sway over conservative Republican economic thought during the late 1970s and throughout the 1980s, especially over White House advisers during the Reagan years.[8] The revisions to the tax code enacted by ERTA reflected Republican tax theory as it had evolved since Secretary Mellon's long tenure in Treasury during the 1920s; the overriding principle was that economic investment and capital formation would be stimulated through incentives resulting from lower marginal income tax rates. The Kennedy tax cuts enacted in 1964 were commonly invoked by supply-siders to support their case. This "new" Republican tax policy contrasted sharply with the monetary and fiscal policy of economists who had dominated tax policymaking during prior Republican administrations of the postwar period, most of whom had little faith in or attachment to supply-side theory.[9]

7. ERTA provided rate reductions of 5 percent, 10 percent, and 10 percent over three successive years, effective beginning October 1, 1981. This amounted to a 23 percent rate reduction; however, the full effect of ERTA rate reductions was offset by subsequent legislation. ERTA implemented a three-year budget cut in expenditures of $130.5 billion and a tax cut of $787 billion over the same period. The tax rate cuts proposed in 1963 by President John F. Kennedy and enacted after his death in March 1964 reduced the top marginal tax rate from 91 to 70 percent–a 23 percent reduction. The lowest tax rate was reduced from 20 to 14 percent; middle-income rates were reduced somewhat less.

8. During the Reagan years, perhaps the most ardent supply-side proponent was Paul Craig Roberts, who was economic adviser to Representative Jack Kemp in 1975 and, later, assistant secretary of treasury under Reagan. His own account of the "rise" of the supply-sider cause is found in Paul Craig Roberts, *The Supply-Side Revolution* (Cambridge: Harvard University Press, 1984). Other supply-side advocates in Treasury during this period included Donald Regan and Norman Ture.

9. On the President's Council of Economic Advisers, Alan Greenspan was the chief proponent of "neoclassical" economic policy, while Paul Volcker at the Federal Reserve Board pursued traditional Republican monetarism. Supply-side economics has been openly criticized by Herbert Stein, former chairman of the Council of Economic Advisers under Presidents Nixon and Ford, in *Washington Bedtime Stories: The Politics of Money and Jobs* (New York: Free Press, 1986), 120–25; see also idem, "Here We Go Again," *Wall St. J.*, April 29, 1993, A14: "[T]here are still people who believe that the supply-side prescription worked, or would have worked if followed more rigorously. . . . In any case, after 1981 the deficit grew, saving declined and there was no significant revival of long-run output and productivity."

Traditional Republican fiscal and monetary policy had been pursued almost exclusively through executive action, albeit with the necessary cooperation of the Federal Reserve Board. However, supply-side economics had to be enacted through amendments to the tax laws approved by the legislature. This proved to be problematic for Republicans because, though they occupied the White House throughout the 1980s, they had considerably less influence in Congress. To the extent that the tax code became the vehicle for enacting the new conservative policy agenda, White House Republicans were rendered dependent upon a largely unsympathetic Democratic Congress. In the end, this proved fatal to the cause.

Although the Reagan administration started the legislative ball rolling, the final 1981 tax bill displayed as much the nonpartisan handicraft of congressional committees as supply-side economics. Indeed, the legislative process took on a perverse dynamics all its own in favor of tax reduction, with each branch of government, each house in Congress, and each political party seemingly intent on upping the ante at every round. Much has been written about this unusual competition and the resulting "bidding war" to grant the most tax benefits.[10] On this account, ERTA has often been cited as one of the worst examples of congressional pork-barrel politics and "antireform" tax legislation.[11]

The proposals added to the bill at each of the various stages of the legislative process were mostly revenue losers, including provisions for expanding the eligibility requirements of individual retirement accounts (IRAs) to include virtually every taxpayer (rather than just those who are not covered by a qualified pension plan); increased tax credits for

---

10. "[W]ith each successive round of bargaining, the bill widened in scope." John F. Witte, *The Politics and Development of the Federal Income Tax* (Madison: University of Wisconsin Press, 1985), 224; see also Timothy J. Conlan, Margaret T. Wrightson, and David R. Beam, *Taxing Choices: The Politics of Tax Reform* (Washington, D.C.: Congressional Quarterly Press, 1990), 33–35. Cathie Martin offers the most insightful explanation of the respective motivations of Democrats and Republicans in entering into this odd bidding war. See Cathie J. Martin, *Shifting the Burden: The Struggle over Growth and Corporate Taxation* (Chicago: University of Chicago Press, 1991), 123–31.

11. See, e.g., John F. Witte, "The Tax Reform Act of 1986: A New Era in Tax Politics?" 19 *Am. Pol. Q.* 438, 443 (1991): "The 1981 Economic Recovery Act (ERTA) stands as the most strident *anti-reform* bill"; Daniel Shaviro, "Beyond Public Choice and Public Interest: A Study of the Legislative Process As Illustrated by Tax Legislation in the 1980s," 139 *U. Pa. L. Rev.* 1, 108 (1990): "[M]ost supporters of tax reform would agree [that ERTA] was almost pathologically bad special interest legislation."

research and development; an expanded child-care credit; a new low-income housing credit; an election to expense $10,000 of business property annually in lieu of capitalization; liberalized depreciation schedules under the new Accelerated Cost Recovery System (ACRS); and the so-called safe harbor lease.

The safe harbor lease was strictly a statutory creation.[12] The rationale behind the provision was to enable "loss corporations" (i.e., corporations with no net taxable income) to use the tax benefits attributable to the ownership or acquisition of business property that would otherwise qualify for tax preferences intended to stimulate investment, such as the investment tax credit and accelerated depreciation deductions under ACRS. Such qualified property included plants, equipment, machinery, and even railroad cars. Pursuant to a safe harbor lease, a loss corporation could enter into a sale-leaseback of the qualified depreciable property to a corporation with taxable income. The underlying purpose of the transaction was to allow the loss corporation to "sell" the tax benefits attributable to the property—benefits that otherwise would go unused on account of the loss corporation's not having taxable income.[13]

The effect of the more generous accelerated depreciation schedule provided under ERTA, combined with the investment tax credit and tax deductions for interest expenses incurred in borrowing to purchase property eligible for both tax benefits, could actually create a "negative" tax rate with respect to such an investment. With a negative tax rate, an investor could be economically better off making an entirely worthless investment solely on account of the tax benefits. In effect, a positive subsidy was paid out of the federal Treasury to support the taxpayer's investment. Today, scores of nearly empty office buildings in cities across the United States bear testimony to the folly of such misallocations of capital through tax subsidies.

---

12. The provision was found at section 167(f)(8) of the 1954 Internal Revenue Code.

13. In a safe harbor lease, possession and use of the relevant property would remain with the original owner (the loss corporation). The terms of the lease could easily be crafted to mirror the terms of the financing agreement for the "sale" of the same property. This would result in no net cash payments between the parties—other than compensation to the loss corporation from the buyer/lessor corporation (the profitable corporation) for the tax benefits derived from taking legal title to the subject property. For a more detailed illustration of how losses are "sold" under a leveraged lease, see Marvin A. Chirelstein, *Federal Income Taxation*, 4th ed. (Mineola, N.Y.: Foundation Press, 1985), ¶ 6.08(b).

Before 1981, the Internal Revenue Service in federal court had successfully challenged many of the most "abusive" sale-leaseback transactions as lacking "economic substance" and motivated solely by tax considerations. Suddenly in 1981, sale-leaseback transactions were sanctioned by Congress.[14] As was anticipated at the time, the provision resulted in massive sell-offs of tax benefits by loss corporations at an enormous cost to the U.S. Treasury.[15] A number of major safe harbor lease transactions received considerable attention by the media. For instance, Global Marine Corporation was reported to have "sold" to Hilton Hotels some $135 million of tax benefits derived from oil rigs, and Ford Motor Company reportedly transferred to IBM some $1 billion of tax benefits for a price estimated to range from $100 to $200 million. Popular accounts suggested at the time that many other corporations were entering into similar transactions, albeit of lesser magnitude.[16] Several public-interest groups publicized the most dramatic incidents of safe harbor leasing. These reports stimulated a strong negative public reaction, something Congress had not anticipated. This led to the quick repeal of the safe harbor lease provision in 1982. Nevertheless, the experience left many with the general impression that Congress was under the influence of "big business," and thus may have contributed to the success of the political movement for tax reform in 1986.

Finally, beyond those provisions that attracted most of the popular attention at the time, ERTA may very well be remembered most for its indexing of the income tax brackets. As previously noted, bracket creep had been a general trend throughout the postwar period, but was particularly severe during the 1970s, when the inflation rate reached double digits. The staff of the Joint Committee on Taxation innocently suggested that indexing was adopted because "[t]he Congress believed that 'automatic' tax increases resulting from the effects of inflation were unfair to taxpayers, since their tax burden as a percentage of income

14. John Witte describes in great detail a meeting on June 7 and 8, 1981, between a group of business leaders and Treasury and White House officials, a meeting resulting in agreement that Treasury tax experts should explore "ways to aid businesses that would not benefit from tax reductions because they were losing money or had past losses that would offset future tax liability." Witte, *Politics*, 225.

15. See Staff of the Joint Committee on Taxation, *General Explanation of the Economic Recovery Act of 1981* (Washington, D.C.: Government Printing Office, 1981), 102–7.

16. These transactions are recounted in Jeffrey H. Birnbaum and Alan S. Murray, *Showdown at Gucci Gulch: Lawmakers, Lobbyists, and the Unlikely Triumph of Tax Reform* (New York: Vintage, 1988), 11.

could increase. . . . Indexing [would] prevent inflation from increasing that percentage and thus [would] avoid the past pattern of inequitable, unlegislated tax increases and induced spending."[17] Indexing was really a much more partisan "reform" of the tax-policymaking process than the committee report suggested. Conservative Republicans had long favored indexing specifically as a means to deny Congress access to such easy financing for its expenditures. Given that so much of the rest of the 1981 bill was repealed by the end of the decade, indexing may turn out to be ERTA's greatest legacy.

Changing Course in Midstream: TEFRA and DEFRA

Almost as soon as ERTA was enacted in 1981, congressional tax policy-makers began to shift course in the wake of new and gloomy forecasts of increased budget deficits attributed to the ERTA tax rate cuts. The problem was that the administration had not reduced spending to counteract the impact of the ERTA tax cuts. As economist Barry Bosworth has described the outcome, the fiscal stimulus from the current and anticipated budget deficits, coupled with the "large capital borrowing that it entailed, collided with a monetary policy intent on restricting the supply of credit and economic activity to reduce inflation. The result was a sharp increase in interest rates that overwhelmed the investment incentives of the tax cut."[18]

Notwithstanding President Reagan's personal commitment to lower tax rates,[19] many members of Congress, including important Republicans such as Senator Robert Dole, then chairman of the Finance Com-

17. Staff of the Joint Committee on Taxation, *General Explanation of the Economic Recovery Tax Act of 1981*, 38.
18. Barry P. Bosworth, *Tax Incentives and Economic Growth* (Washington, D.C.: Brookings Institution, 1984), 187.
19. Reagan's commitment to lower tax rates is often attributed to his unpleasant experience with the 90 percent top marginal tax rate imposed upon earnings from his career as a movie actor – an experience allegedly shared by Senator Bill Bradley, who paid the top tax rate on his salary as a professional basketball player. See, e.g., Birnbaum and Murphy, *Showdown at Gucci Gulch*, 25–26. David Stockman has suggested that Reagan's commitment to lower marginal tax rates was "one of the few things Ronald Reagan deeply wanted." See David A. Stockman, *The Triumph of Politics: Why the Reagan Revolution Failed* (New York: Harper & Row, 1986), 229.

mittee, lacked comparable faith in supply-side principles. Indeed, the White House itself was severely divided over how to respond to projected budget deficits.[20] By late 1981, proposals dealing with the need for additional revenues began to emerge in Congress. Early in 1982, the administration introduced "revenue-enhancement" proposals, including a minimum corporate tax and a cutback on the use of the "completed contract method" of tax accounting for long-term construction contracts. The latter was enacted in similar form in 1986, with additional cutbacks made in subsequent years until nothing was left of the tax preference. However, the Reagan administration did not push very hard for any of these proposals, and consequently, none were adopted by Congress at the time.

Spurred on by the failure of the administration to take more decisive action with respect to the budget deficit, and motivated by a general rejection of supply-side economics, Congress responded with its own deficit-reduction legislation. Perhaps the most interesting aspect of this legislative initiative was that it was advanced by Dole from his helm at the Finance Committee. Representing the traditional wing of the Republican Party and raised on principles of fiscal conservatism, Dole balked at the supply-side notion of reducing taxes in order to raise revenue. He became increasingly concerned about the budget-deficit crisis that loomed on the horizon. On the floor of the Senate, defending the revenue-raising provisions of the bill, Dole declared that "the roots of this evening's debate actually go back to February [1982], when the President [Reagan] released a budget calling for deficits in excess of $700 billion over the next 3 years. Those deficits were unacceptable by any criteria."[21] Rebuking those who opposed the tax increases included in the measure, Dole scolded, "Do we want to reduce the deficit, do we want to continue the downward trend of interest rates, or do we want to signal to the financial markets and the people in our States that we really do not care, that we really have not quite enough courage to take this step, because some tax might affect someone in our constituency?"[22] The irony of Senate Republicans acting to repudiate and reverse the Reagan tax policy enacted just the prior year was not lost on either Speaker of the

---

20. The considerable dissension and conflict within the White House and Treasury Department over supply-side principles is recounted in great detail by one of the strongest supply-side protagonists, Paul Craig Roberts, *The Supply-Side Revolution.*

21. *Congressional Record,* 97th Cong., 2d sess. (August 19, 1982), 128, pt. 16, 22408.

22. Ibid., 22407.

House Tip O'Neill or Ways and Means Committee chairman Rosten-kowski, both of whom were delighted with the prospect of a Republican civil war.

Dole played the crucial leadership role in securing passage of the 1982 tax legislation. The high esteem afforded Dole by his colleagues in the Senate, both Democrats and Republicans alike, provided a basis for his leadership in the tax legislative arena. Catherine Rudder has linked Dole's successful role in securing passage of the 1982 bill to a combination of his stature among his peers in the legislature, the pressures induced by the deficits created by the 1981 act, and the budget procedure imposed under the Budget Act of 1974: "Senate Finance Committee Chairman Dole was able to produce legislation that meshed with fiscal policy and improved the integrity and equity of the tax code. He did so, however, only under extra-ordinary pressure stemming from the economy and with the aid of a new source of responsibility, the congressional budget process, which was established in 1974. But even with the help of the reconciliation procedures . . . the process that produced the 1982 tax bill was far from a model of deliberation."[23] Assisted by the professional staff of the Finance Committee, as well as that of the Joint Committee on Taxation, the Office of Management and Budget (OMB), and the Office of Tax Policy in Treasury, Dole and Republican members reported out of the Finance Committee a $100 billion revenue bill in late June 1982. Dole was instrumental in shepherding the legislation through the Senate, where it passed on July 23. Voting for the bill followed strict partisan lines—with Republicans voting *for* the tax increase.

In August, the Senate's tax bill emerged largely intact from Conference Committee, and the House adopted the bill soon after, with both Republicans and Democrats in the House divided. In the Senate, Dole defended the measure in terms of deficit reduction to be achieved through cutting expenditures, this despite the fact that 70 percent of the deficit reduction was attributable to tax increases. By a final vote of 52 to 47, the measure passed the Senate. Reagan was apparently persuaded to sign the bill by his own aides, notwithstanding that it contradicted many of the principles at the core of his 1981 tax bill.[24]

23. Catherine E. Rudder, "Tax Policy: Structure and Choice," in *Making Economic Policy in Congress*, ed. Allen Schick (Washington, D.C.: American Enterprise Institute, 1983), 214.

24. The strange politics behind the 1982 tax bill is recounted in Roberts, *Supply-Side Revolution*, 226–45. Roberts portrays Reagan as manipulated and duped by those on his

The final bill, the Tax Equity and Fiscal Responsibility Act of 1982 (TEFRA),[25] included some of the administration's proposals from 1981 and early 1982, but added the Senate's revenue-raising provisions, most notably with respect to strengthening the compliance provisions of the tax code. These provisions included expanded information reporting on interest, dividends, and even on the gross receipts from the sale of securities, this last incumbent upon brokers. Among tax practitioners TEFRA is less than fondly remembered for its expanded penalty provisions and major revisions to the audit procedures for partnerships and Subchapter S corporations. TEFRA also reduced the investment tax credit and cut back on the accelerated depreciation granted in ERTA. Arguably, this emphasis on cutbacks of overly generous tax preferences marked a reversal in position by President Reagan himself, thereby setting the stage for the tax-reform effort that began in 1985.

It also should be noted that an impending shortfall in the Social Security trust fund pushed Congress to enact the Social Security Amendments of 1983.[26] This bill followed the typical pattern of Social Security tax policy in the postwar era—carefully avoiding benefit reductions by imposing tax increases. The bill raised the payroll tax rates and tax base, and it also imposed income tax on one-half of Social Security benefits in excess of certain income thresholds (such benefits having previously been treated as wholly exempt from income taxation). In addition, the bill postponed the retirement age for Social Security recipients from 65 to 67 (with a gradual phase-in scheduled to begin in the next century). These increases in Social Security taxes amounted to $85 billion per year, representing the largest tax increase of the decade.[27]

With its 1984 budget submission, the Reagan administration introduced some modest proposals that evidenced a continued movement away from supply-side tax policy. These included restrictions on tax-exempt leasing and tax-exempt bond issues by state and municipal governments, as well as a cap on tax-free employer medical benefits.

---

staff who were not "true" disciples of Reaganomics, and presents himself as virtually alone in the White House in carrying the banner of supply-side principles.

25. Pub. L. No. 97-248, 96 Stat. 324.

26. Pub. L. No. 98-21, 97 Stat. 65.

27. An excellent account of the turbulent politics behind Social Security taxes during this period is found in Aaron B. Wildavsky and Joseph White, *The Deficit and the Public Interest: The Search for Responsible Budgeting in the 1980s* (Berkeley and Los Angeles: University of California Press, 1989), 310–30.

Versions of the first two of these proposals found their way into legislation that year, although in modified form. Yet, once again the tax legislation actually enacted was more the product of congressional initiatives, particularly those of Senator Dole, than of the White House.

The omnibus revenue bill, known as the Deficit Reduction Act of 1984 (DEFRA), included significant income tax provisions.[28] Some DEFRA tax-reform provisions, like those contained in TEFRA, tightened information reporting; other DEFRA reforms were later more fully developed in 1986, such as restrictions upon "tax straddles"[29] and volume caps on tax-exempt private activity bonds.[30] Revenue-raising provisions included new rules imputing interest on "below-market"-interest loans[31] and preventing premature accruals of tax deductions.[32] DEFRA also included revenue losers: the bill reduced the holding period for long-term capital gains from twelve months to six months[33] and provided a statutory exclusion for income from employee fringe benefits.[34] One particularly curious provision of the 1984 act granted Alaskan companies owned by Eskimos (so-called Alaska Native Corporations) the special privilege of trafficking in tax losses. This provision created tax benefits both for Eskimos with tax losses (not a particularly big voting block) and the profitable non-Eskimo corporations that were permitted to purchase such losses (clearly a much more significant constituency within the Republican Party).[35] Mercifully, this tax boondoggle was repealed in 1988.[36]

The overall effect of TEFRA and DEFRA was to raise modest amounts of new revenue, mostly through tax increases, with few cuts to

---

28. The DEFRA tax provisions were enacted as the Tax Reform Act of 1984. Pub. L. No. 98-369, 98 Stat. 494. Division A of the Deficit Reduction Act of 1984 is the Tax Reform Act of 1984, while Division B is the Spending Reduction Act of 1984.

29. IRC sec. 1092.

30. IRC sec. 141.

31. New IRC sec. 7872.

32. New IRC sec. 461(h).

33. Amending IRC sec. 1222.

34. New IRC sec. 132.

35. The story of how one particularly well situated group of Washington insiders made a financial killing (estimated in the range of $10–20 million) by introducing Eskimos with tax losses to profitable American corporations is recounted in Michael Lewis, "The Access Capitalists," *New Republic*, October 18, 1993, 20–29.

36. Technical and Miscellaneous Revenue Act of 1988, Pub. L. No. 100-647, 102 Stat. 3342, sec. 5021, repealing rules permitting loss transfers by Alaska Native Corporations.

expenditures.[37] These two tax bills also collectively "reformed" a good many of the supply-side economic policies of ERTA right out of the tax code. While the deficit crisis was hardly resolved by TEFRA and DE-FRA, these bills generally reversed the worst trends established by ERTA, although hardly to the satisfaction of either those who demanded more serious expenditure cuts or those who supported the tax cuts as a means for altering individual and business incentives in favor of savings and the investment of capital. The politics behind these tax bills reflected the struggle of congressional policymakers to balance ideology with conflicting revenue demands.

The Tax Reform Act of 1986

During the second Reagan administration, tax policy made an unpredicted change in course as the ideological movement for tax reform supplanted supply-side economics as the driving force behind tax legislation. General calls for tax reform had been "in the air" for decades. As recounted in Chapter 3, John F. Kennedy had proclaimed tax reform the highest domestic-policy priority of his administration. However, it was not until the mid-1980s that the movement for tax reform successfully shaped tax policy to any great extent.

Ironically, the campaign for tax reform in the 1980s was instigated by a president hardly known for his interest in reform politics. Reagan initiated the campaign when, in his 1984 State of the Union address, he called upon the Treasury Department to study the feasibility of tax reform and simplification.[38] This was a little like telling lions to eat meat. Treasury had been working on significant tax-reform proposals for decades, and little encouragement was needed to stimulate further efforts. Reagan ended up unintentionally setting in motion a two-year

37. It was estimated by the staff of the Conference Committee that TEFRA would close the deficit by $115.8 billion over three years. The 1984 act was projected to raise $50.7 billion over five fiscal years, 1984–87. *General Explanation of the Revenue Provisions of the Deficit Reduction Act of 1984* (Washington, D.C.: Government Printing Office, 1985), 1256.

38. "Let us go forward with an historic reform for fairness, simplicity and incentives for growth. I am asking [Treasury] Secretary Don Regan for a plan for action to simplify the entire tax code, so all taxpayers, big and small, are treated more fairly." Ronald Reagan, "Address Before a Joint Session of the Congress on the State of the Union" (January 25, 1984), in *Public Papers of the Presidents: Ronald Reagan, 1984* (Washington, D.C.: Government Printing Office, 1986), 87.

struggle for reform of the tax laws, culminating in the enactment of TRA. Contrary to all expectations, tax reform became the centerpiece of domestic policy in the second Reagan administration.

The substance of tax policy changed dramatically as tax reform emerged as the dominant policy goal. Responding in part to the fear that Democrats would appropriate and capitalize on the issue of tax reform during the forthcoming presidential election in November 1984, Republican strategists decided to seize the initiative themselves.[39] Reagan issued his vague and perhaps somewhat unconvincing call for tax reform in the January 1984 State of the Union address to the joint houses of Congress. It is doubtful whether any of the members of Congress who heard the president's speech would ever have predicted the eventual outcome.[40] Much the same could be said of Reagan himself. Presidents have the power to bring ideas and policies to the fore of the political agenda; however, such policies commonly take on a life all of their own.[41] In this case, Reagan's noncommittal initiative marked the beginning of a reform effort that would have a significant impact upon the income tax.

In response to the president's call for a study on tax reform, Treasury and the White House generated a series of proposals that served to highlight the great divergence of opinion regarding what constitutes "reform" of the tax laws. The various initiatives that emerged out of the executive branch in 1984 and early 1985 forced the hand of Congress toward some version of tax reform. And as the political movement for reform gained in momentum, Congress reluctantly took up the challenge in earnest. Eventually, the White House and the tax committees were occupied for nearly two years with the campaign for tax reform. Even more surprising, the movement bore fruit in the fall of 1986 with

---

39. The evolution of this Republican strategy is discussed in Birnbaum and Murray, *Showdown at Gucci Gulch*, 33–39.

40. It has been reported that several members of Congress actually laughed openly at the president's call for Treasury to prepare a postelection report on tax reform. Apparently, these congressmen were skeptical of the president's commitment to the cause of tax reform, given the timing of the report – that is, *after* the election. The incident is recounted in ibid., 41.

41. "[O]utcomes . . . can be unpredictable. An administration proposes a bill, then is unable to control subsequent happenings." John W. Kingdon, *Agendas, Alternatives, and Public Policies* (New York: Harper Collins, 1984), 186. For a presentation of the general theme of presidents losing control of policy initiatives once set in motion, see Stephen Skowronek, *The Politics Presidents Make: Leadership from John Adams to George Bush* (Cambridge: Harvard University Press, 1993), 414–29 (applying this theme to the Reagan tax and economic policies).

the enactment of the Tax Reform Act of 1986. This bill took aim at income tax policy as it had evolved over the past eight decades.[42]

TRA has been widely hailed as the most significant tax-reform legislation in the history of the federal income tax.[43] By virtue of the sheer volume of the revisions and amendments to the tax laws that it implemented, the 1986 act was the most massive restructuring in the eighty-year history of the federal income tax, dwarfing by far its last major overhaul in 1954. Perhaps more significant, TRA came closer to codifying the reformist's vision of the ideal tax code than had any other tax bill ever to emerge from the congressional tax committees (purportedly, the bastion of special interests).

The intense political maneuvering attending any major tax bill in the House Ways and Means and Senate Finance Committees determines whether, and in what form, tax legislation will be enacted. This was particularly true in 1986, when the political leadership of Chairman Dan Rostenkowski, and to a lesser extent Senate Finance Committee chairman Robert Packwood, made the passage of TRA a reality. They were the final arbiters who determined that tax reform would carry over into the final bill: "Dan Rostenkowski became a reformer because the president's endorsement of reform represented a challenge and a threat to both him and his party. . . . Bob Packwood became a reformer out of desperation: With Reagan and Rostenkowski moving together, he had no choice but to produce a bill or be branded a sellout to special interests."[44] The irony is that the "traditional" political institutions and

42. The best journalistic account of the political events leading up to the passage of the 1986 act is Birnbaum and Murray, *Showdown at Gucci Gulch*. The best scholarly analysis of TRA is the study by Conlan, Wrightson, and Beam, *Taxing Choices*. Of the many articles on the tax-reform process, among the best are Joseph J. Minarik, "How Tax Reform Came About," 37 *Tax Notes* 1359 (December 28, 1987); Alvin Rabushka, "The Tax Reform Act of 1986: Concentrated Costs, Diffuse Benefits—An Inversion of Public Choice," 9 *Contemp. Pol'y Issues* 50 (1988); Henry J. Aaron, "The Impossible Dream Comes True," in *Tax Reform and the U.S. Economy*, ed. Joseph A. Pechman (Washington, D.C.: Brookings Institution, 1987). A less insightful account from the former chief of staff of the Joint Committee on Taxation is David Brockway, "The Process Behind Success ful Tax Reform," 31 *Vill. L. Rev.* 1803 (1986).

43. See, e.g., Witte, "The Tax Reform Act of 1986," 4: "TRA can only be viewed as a remarkable legislative accomplishment and by far the most radical example of peacetime tax reform in history"; Shaviro, "Beyond Public Choice and Public Interest," 5: "[T]he 1986 Act was the all-time leading example of tax reform."

44. Birnbaum and Murray, *Showdown at Gucci Gulch*, 287.

actors (namely, the president and the chairmen of the tax committees) mattered most in the struggle for tax reform.

The importance of leadership in congressional politics, especially on the House Ways and Means Committee, lies in determining not only whether particular legislation is enacted, but also what form it will take. The different leadership styles of Wilbur Mills, Al Ullman, and Dan Rostenkowski are an important factor in explaining the behavior of the Ways and Means Committee during the years of their respective chairmanships, as well as in explaining the success or failure of individual tax policy initiatives. In addition, the origin and success of many recent proposals can be traced to "policy entrepreneurs" such as Bill Bradley and Jack Kemp, the halls of academia, or the policy papers of some Washington think tank, rather than to the dictates and demands of the congressional leadership. (This recent development in the tax legislative process is discussed further in Chapter 6.)

Nevertheless, the role of policy entrepreneurs and think tanks in initiating policy and shaping the political agenda must be kept in perspective. If the policy entrepreneurs "kicked the ball off" for tax reform, in the end they "orchestrated little of what followed."[45] Likewise, if the ideas of some academics, such as Stanley Surrey or Joseph Pechman, eventually became the favorite policy issues of policy entrepreneurs, it must be recognized that these ideas had been "in the air" for a considerable period of time—in some cases, since the 1940s and 1950s. Thus, the crucial question remains, Why did the traditional leader-ship at that moment come to accept the "ideas" peddled by the policy entrepreneurs?[46]

Chairman Rostenkowski and Speaker O'Neill ultimately came to accept and even embrace tax reform in 1986 because they correctly

---

45. Conlan, Wrightson, and Beam, *Taxing Choices*, 249.

46. For instance, the recent attack upon tax expenditures has been motivated less by the sudden conversion to Stanley Surrey's views than by economic considerations making such revenue losers unattractive in today's deficit-conscious political climate. See Rob Bennett, "From Ivory Towers to the Halls of Power," 50 *Tax Notes* 1301, 1301 (March 18, 1991). The new economic reality has contributed to institutionalized changes in the tax committees. See, e.g., Randall Strahan, *New Ways and Means: Reform and Change in a Congressional Committee* (Chapel Hill: University of North Carolina Press, 1990), 136: "Under Rostenkowski's leadership and the fiscal and political pressures created by massive budget deficits, by 1984 politics on the committee appeared in some respects to have come almost full circle since the [1974] reforms—back to the moderate partisanship, attention to fiscal responsibility, and consensual decisionmaking style of the Mills years."

perceived that the political benefits to them, their party, and the House (the political institution most dear to them) outweighed whatever countervailing pressures would be exerted by the lobbyists representing those interest groups most adversely affected by the pending proposals for tax reform. This is the beneficial side of an electoral politics that subjects political elites to the constraints of the electorate and, accordingly, forces them to weigh the various interests and reach viable compromises capable of aggregating enough support to give them effect. Institutional and party "leaders" in Congress often must take the high road, acting on principle and in favor of broader constituencies than are typical with nonleaders. According to Derthick and Quirk: "Leaders on an issue will be more prone to act on their conceptions of the public interest. . . . Compared with other congressmen, leaders will have diminished regard for the wishes of organized interest groups."[47]

The traditional congressional leadership fully took control of the reform bill in Conference Committee. This was nowhere more evident than in the blatant efforts to protect specific narrow interests–some even targeted to specific individuals–and key interest groups, such as labor and oil and gas, from reform initiatives by providing them with overly generous transition rules.[48] Many objected to this "corrupt" use of transition rules to benefit special interests located in the districts of committee members. However, by granting special favors through the transition rules, Rostenkowski was able skillfully to hold together a voting coalition to secure passage of a purer "reform" package than what would otherwise have been possible.[49] On the whole, securing support

47. Martha Derthick and Paul J. Quirk, *The Politics of Deregulation* (Washington, D.C.: Brookings Institution, 1985), 103.

48. The journalists Donald L. Barlett and James B. Steele won a Pulitzer Prize in 1989 for a lengthy investigative report, "The Great Tax Giveaway," detailing the use of transition rules used to protect narrow, special interests from the reforms of the 1986 act. *Phila. Inquirer*, April 10–16, 1988. Perhaps the best-known and most blatant example of a transition rule designed to benefit individual taxpayers was the infamous "Gallo" amendment (to the sole benefit of the families of Ernest and Julio Gallo of the California winery that bears their name). This transition rule effectively exempted the Gallo family from the new tax on generation-skipping transfers enacted under the 1986 act. For a discussion of the politics behind the Gallo amendment, as well as the use of transition rules in general with respect to the 1986 act, see Birnbaum and Murray, *Showdown at Gucci Gulch*, 140, 146–47, 240–43.

49. "Thus, a great many provisions in the Ways and Means bill took care of the needs of supportive members and key constituencies. . . . Many more won additional favors in the form of transition rules. . . . Rostenkowski skillfully blended the old distributive

for a tax bill by offering generous transition rules (which permit certain industries or even individuals to retain more favorable tax treatment under prior law) was preferable to offering new special tax provisions or expenditures that would become a permanent fixture in the code.

Regardless of the source of the tax-reform proposals, the bill that was finally adopted in 1986 was largely the handiwork of White House staff and the traditional leadership of Congress. And that legislation was finally implemented through the technical regulations drafted by tax experts in the Treasury Department. This reflects the complicated dynamic process through which tax legislation is made.

In some respects, the final version of TRA can be seen as a conservative tax bill—for instance, in greatly reducing marginal tax rates. However, in many other important respects, the final bill was outside the conservative/Republican agenda, notwithstanding its historical linkage to the initial Reagan initiative. Once the White House political staff and the congressional tax committees redefined the initial reform proposal produced by the professional tax experts in Treasury ("Treasury I"),[50] little was left to satisfy supply-siders. For example, supply-side economist Paul Craig Roberts (assistant secretary of the treasury for economic policy from 1981 to 1982) has attributed the downfall of the Bush presidency to the "economic dominoes toppled by the Tax Reform Act of 1986." He puts the blame for "this disastrous legislation" on Bush advisers James Baker and Richard Darman, who in 1986 were high-level policymakers in Treasury.[51] Nor for that matter were many of the original proponents of tax reform in Treasury very satisfied with the way the White House rewrote Treasury I. One of the chief architects of Treasury I, economist Charles E. McLure Jr., resigned his position in Treasury and returned to the Hoover Institution at Stanford University as a result

---

politics of tax expenditures with the new politics of reform. By preserving tax provisions of greatest value to key members in the process of enacting reform legislation, the committee retained its all-important power to influence the tax code in beneficial ways." Conlan, Wrightson, and Beam, *Taxing Choices,* 117–18.

50. The formal appellation of Treasury I was *Tax Reform for Fairness, Simplicity, and Economic Growth: The Treasury Department Report to the President* (Washington, D.C.: Government Printing Office, 1984).

51. The 1986 act is also blamed by Roberts for destroying the value of real estate and "thereby collapsing savings & loan associations and commercial banks." Paul Craig Roberts, "Economic Dominoes," *Nat. Rev.,* November 30, 1992, 37.

of his dissatisfaction with Treasury II, largely the handiwork of the consummate politico, James Baker.

In 1985, the political movement for tax reform was the single most cohesive force aggregating a wide array of political interests into the coalition behind TRA. Tax reformers have long argued that the tax laws have been distorted by the many narrow special-interest provisions enacted over the decades. Special-interest provisions, as well as the increasingly sophisticated and bold schemes put forth by the tax shelter industry, became the object and focus of the reformists' wrath in the mid-1980s. However, contrary to prior experience in the 1960s and 1970s, reformists were actually effective in 1986 in securing passage of legislation that eliminated or limited many of the most time-honored "abuses" of the tax laws.

Special interests so often succeed in the political arena of tax policy by exerting intense pressures on those issues most significant to them. It is generally difficult to mobilize the "public" or any broad interest with regard to policies that have only marginal and dispersed effects, whereas narrow interests are easily mobilized and quite willing to act at great expense when issues of most concern to them are at stake. The impact of the academic vision of tax reform on the tax-policymaking process, however, is generally less understood. What distinguished tax legislation in 1986 from the incremental policymaking that otherwise dominates during periods of politics-as-usual was the strong reformist ideology behind the legislation.

Among the more infamous abuses upon which reformists focused their attention was the real estate tax shelter[52] and the business deduction for the so-called three-martini lunch.[53] TRA also curtailed a number of less notorious provisions, such as the completed contract method of tax accounting.[54] Most surprisingly, TRA eliminated or severely re-

---

52. The chief provision attacking tax shelters is IRC section 469, which limits deductions for passive activities.

53. IRC sec. 274(n) (deduction limited to 80 percent of business expense for food). See Treasury Department, "The President's 1978 Tax Program" (1978), 195–202. Pursuant to the Revenue Reconciliation Act of 1993, the food-and-entertainment deduction was reduced to 50 percent.

54. Due to perceived abuses in the defense industries, Congress limited, and later prohibited, the use of the completed contract method. Staff of the Joint Committee on Taxation, *General Explanation of the Tax Reform Act of 1986* (Washington, D.C.: Government Printing Office, 1987), 524–30. However, this method of tax accounting was also used widely by other industries, most notably the home-construction business, which was caught completely off guard by this reform. It is questionable whether any of the members

stricted some of the most popular tax "loopholes" for individuals, such as the deduction for personal interest,[55] the deduction for state and local sales taxes,[56] contributions to individual retirement accounts,[57] and deductions for miscellaneous itemized deductions.[58] Caught up in the zeal for tax reform, policymakers even attacked one of the most sacrosanct of exemptions recognized in the tax laws—that of the rental value of a parsonage provided to clergy by their congregation.[59] Treasury secretary Donald Regan presented the reason for stripping this "sacred cow" from the tax code: "[W]e've mugged everybody else—why should the clergy escape?"[60]

These and a host of other special tax provisions, while often portrayed by the popular media as abusive tools of the rich used to avoid their fair share of taxation, in actuality provided tax benefits to a wide spectrum of taxpayers, including—perhaps disproportionately—the middle class. The widespread availability of many of these provisions helps to explain their popularity and resilience in the face of prior reformist efforts to eliminate them. These provisions, as well as many other narrow tax breaks that had crept into the tax code with little economic justification beyond lowering taxes for the specific interest groups that benefited from their passage, were either severely limited or entirely eliminated in the crusade for reform that so unexpectedly found political success in 1986.

The tax policymaking generally associated with interest-group politics must be contrasted with the dramatic tax policies enacted pursuant

---

of the tax committees had any idea of the meaning of new IRC section 460 (the provision that imposed such restrictions on use of the completed contract method). For a discussion of the technical application of this provision, see Sheldon D. Pollack, "IRC Section 460: Long-Term Construction Contract Issues," 68 *Taxes* 30 (1990).

55. Pub. L. No. 99-514, sec. 511, 100 Stat. 2244 (adding new IRC sec. 163(h)).

56. Ibid. at sec. 134(a), 100 Stat. 2116.

57. Ibid. at secs. 1201–1203, 100 Stat. 2520.

58. Certain objects of the reformists' wrath were able to survive the onslaught of reform, essentially due to political considerations holding together the coalition for reform. These items include the deduction for state and local income and property taxes as well as the host of provisions favoring labor's vested interest in tax-free fringe benefits, long a favorite preference of Senator Robert Packwood, then chairman of the Senate Finance Committee.

59. This exemption is found at IRC section 107.

60. Quoted in Conlan, Wrightson, and Beam, *Taxing Choices*, 59. Ironically, the exemption was one of the few tax loopholes that survived the onslaught of tax reform in 1986.

to TRA. The 1986 act is distinct from other major tax legislation (even those which Congress self-servingly refers to as "tax reform") to the extent that it attacked those special interests that have long been assumed to "control" the tax committees. "In tax reform [in 1986], winners were those who retained some tax benefits instead of losing them altogether."[61] Tax reform in 1986 was guided by an abstract vision of the federal income tax long advocated by academic tax experts. That vision of tax reform (explored further in Chapter 8) unexpectedly became the basis for a viable political coalition that prevailed against the typically stronger, more focused special interests. The peculiar dynamics of the tax-policymaking process surrounding the 1986 act is discussed in greater detail in Chapter 6.

Throughout the remainder of the Reagan years and those of the Bush administration, supply-side economics never regained the importance that it had in 1981. A core group of White House conservatives continued to pursue a supply-side tax policy agenda, but it was a futile effort; proposals from the executive branch seldom even emerged from the congressional committees that were controlled largely by unsympathetic Democrats.

Tax Legislation: 1987–1989

In the years immediately following the enactment of TRA, tax lawyers and taxpayers were left to digest the massive, radical changes that had been implemented. Legislation of the magnitude of TRA simply could not have been a practical possibility again for years to come, even if the political will had been there. Indeed, tax legislation for the rest of the decade consisted mostly of a mix of budget-reduction proposals and technical corrections to the many provisions enacted under TRA.

In response to the deficit, and in order to avoid an automatic sequester of funds imposed under the Balanced Budget and Emergency Deficit Control Act of 1985 (so-called Gramm-Rudman-Hollings),[62] tax experts in the Treasury Department under the direction of economist Eugene Steuerle (then deputy assistant secretary of the treasury for tax analysis) formulated a deficit-reduction package that included some tax

61. Conlan, Wrightson, and Beam, *Taxing Choices*, 232.
62. Pub. L. No. 99-171, 99 Stat. 1037, sec. 200 et seq.

increases and some cuts to expenditures.[63] This proposal stalled within Treasury itself, generally out of concern for the Reagan administration's adamant opposition to any tax increases. However, the significant crash of the stock market on October 19, 1987, forced the administration to accept the notion that some deficit reduction was in order.

The tax legislation that was ultimately enacted, the Revenue Act of 1987,[64] was relatively modest in scope from the perspective of the revenue involved. The legislative process through which this bill was hammered out has been described by Steuerle himself as a "chaotic bargaining session involving numerous members of congressional leadership, heads of committees, and members of the administration."[65] In other words, no one was really in charge, and behind the legislation were no guiding principles other than the need to squeeze some additional revenue out of the tax laws somehow without giving the impression that taxes had been raised. Additional revenues from employment taxes were raised through the sleight of hand of increasing the annual wage base. The effort that began in 1986 to tighten and restrict the use by taxpayers of favorable tax-accounting rules for long-term construction contracts, particularly of value to defense contractors, was advanced one step further. Overall, the 1987 bill raised no more than $14 to $16 billion in each subsequent fiscal year through 1992, and even less success was achieved in curbing expenditures.

Tax legislation in 1988 was relatively minor; the Technical and Miscellaneous Revenue Act of 1988 consisted mostly of technical corrections to glitches and errors in the complicated provisions of TRA.[66] These drafting errors would seem to be inevitable where such a massive tax bill is enacted under overly tight time constraints. The 1988 bill also included two rather minor reforms, one aimed at the sale of single-premium life insurance, the other offering tax-free interest income for the purchase of series EE U.S. savings bonds as an inducement for taxpayers to save for educational expenses.[67] The latter provision was typical of tax preferences enacted in the post-1986 tax world; the middle class was targeted as the beneficiary of the provision. Tax benefits were

63. Steuerle identifies himself as the "instigator and principal designer" of this deficit-reduction package. Steuerle, *Tax Decade*, 165. For a discussion of the workings of Gramm-Rudman-Hollings, see Wildavsky and White, *The Deficit and the Public Interest*, chap. 19.

64. Titles 9 and 10 of the Omnibus Budget Reconciliation Act of 1987, Pub. L. No. 100-203, 101 Stat. 1330-282.

65. Steuerle, *Tax Decade*, 166.

66. Pub. L. No. 100-647, 102 Stat. 3342.

67. Sec. 6009, adding new IRC sec. 135.

"phased out" for upper-income taxpayers, and the "poor" (as well as the so-called working poor) were left out altogether, since they lacked sufficient taxable income ever to make use of such tax credits and deductions. The revenue raised by denying the "rich" the benefit of such tax expenditures is generally marginal, but such phaseouts permit tax policymakers to appear committed to the middle class (the real winners) and at the same time hostile to the wealthy.

The final legislative venture from 1988 is also worthy of note. In response to a minor proposal by the administration to amend Medicare benefits, Congress took hold of the initiative and added a provision for expansive new coverage for catastrophic medical care for the elderly, the Medicare Catastrophic Coverage Act of 1988.[68] This new legislation would have cost the Treasury some $7 billion in lost revenue the first year, with substantial cost increases built into the provision. But the expanded coverage was funded through a new progressive surtax imposed upon the federal income tax liability of the elderly beneficiaries, subject to a cap on the maximum tax that would be imposed. In effect the tax was imposed in direct proportion to the taxable income of the recipients of the coverage—a clear departure from the typical approach of taxing the wages of younger workers to finance benefits provided to elderly recipients without regard to their income level.[69]

This new approach to financing Social Security entitlements might have introduced a measure of fiscal responsibility and set a precedent for the whole Social Security program. Congress apparently saw the cost of the program as too high for all but the wealthy to bear, yet, motivated by political instinct, sought to provide even more medical coverage to the elderly—an active and vocal political constituency of all members of Congress.[70] The result was a scheme whereby the wealthiest among the elderly would end up bearing most of the cost of the program, with their

68. Pub. L. No. 100-360, 102 Stat. 683, repealed by Pub. L. No. 101-234, 103 Stat. 1979.

69. Among the best studies on the Social Security program are Martha Derthick, *Agency Under Stress: The Social Security Administration in American Government* (Washington, D.C.: Brookings Institution, 1990); idem, *Policymaking for Social Security* (Washington, D.C.: Brookings Institution, 1979); C. Eugene Steuerle and Jon M. Bakija, *Retooling Social Security for the Twenty-first Century: Right and Wrong Approaches to Reform* (Washington, D.C.: Urban Institute Press, 1994).

70. Eugene Steuerle has described Congress's position as follows: "Congress was in a bind: average costs were considered too high to impose on the average person in a group that had above-average wealth and average incomes." Steuerle, *Tax Decade*, 169.

costs exceeding the value of the coverage they would receive.

The new surtax was especially forbidding to the elderly who would have had to confront the tax annually. Because the surtax was imposed on the participant's income tax liability, the liability could not be computed until after the close of the taxable year. Undoubtedly, the calculation of the surtax liability would have been more complicated for many elderly than the calculation of their income tax liability in the first place.[71] In this respect, the design of the Medicare surtax and its connection to the federal income tax was poorly thought out and overly complicated. Furthermore, the surtax would have created an undesirable connection between the Medicare trust fund and the federal income tax; any decline in income tax revenue would reduce revenues for the Medicare trust fund. This would have introduced one more complication into a policy program in many ways already beyond the control of congressional policymakers. The outcry from the well-organized senior citizens' lobby was predictably harsh and swift. In the face of strong opposition to the program, and with a good deal of embarrassment, Congress repealed the act prior to its effective date.

The final tax bill of the 1980s, the Revenue Reconciliation Act of 1989,[72] was passed during the first year of the new Bush administration. The politics behind this bill reflected the indecision that gripped the tax-policymaking and budget processes. There was no major initiative from either the White House or Congress to either raise revenues or cut expenditures, but tax policymakers were forced to accommodate budget-deficit reduction. Included in the bill were slight increases in employment taxes, further restrictions on long-term construction contracts, and reductions in the tax benefits of employee stock ownership plans (ESOPs).

The political story behind ESOPs is particularly revealing. Originally recognized as a qualified stock bonus plan under the Employee Retirement Income Security Act of 1974 (ERISA),[73] ESOPs were subsequently expanded in 1976, 1984, and again in 1986 (pursuant to TRA). The tax benefit afforded to ESOPs was originally provided in the form of a tax credit, but was changed to a tax preference for lenders and owners

71. For an explanation of the catastrophic medical coverage and how the complicated surtax was to be imposed, see B. D. Schobel, "New Tax Surcharge Supplements Medicare Premiums," 70 *J. Tax'n* 284 (1989).

72. Pub. L. No. 101-239, 103 Stat. 2301, Title 7.

73. Pub. L. No. 93-406, 88 Stat 829.

associated with the funding of an ESOP. This had the effect of greatly increasing the attractiveness of the entity from a tax perspective. From his chairmanship of the Senate Finance Committee, Senator Russell B. Long (Democrat of Louisiana) led the crusade for ESOPs, touting them as a means for furthering "worker control" of domestic business enterprises, and virtually as a cure for all the ills of capitalism:

> I've been spending a great deal of my time advocating the idea of employee stock ownership. . . . I think that it's a great idea for employees to own stock in the company for which they work. . . . I say bring on those tired, labor-plagued companies, ESOP will breathe new life into them. It will revitalize what is wrong with capitalism. It will increase productivity. It will improve labor relations. It will promote economic justice. It will save the economic system. It will make our form of government and our concept of freedom prevail over those who don't agree with it.[74]

Through the perseverance and exaggerations of Senator Long and considerable support from organized labor, ESOPs became an entrenched public policy through preferences offered in the tax laws.

But the tax benefits attributable to establishing and funding ESOPs mostly go to the owners of the business/sponsor of the plan. The banks that lend funds to ESOPs (to acquire stock) also benefit from an exclusion for a portion of the interest income received on such loans.[75] Management benefits from ESOPs insofar as they are commonly used as a tool to defeat hostile takeover bids (with management voting the ESOPs shares as directed by employee shareholders—who tend not to favor hostile takeovers in which many workers commonly lose their jobs). The corporate employers benefit from a deduction for dividends paid on ESOP-owned stock, and many such employees are able to defer the recognition of gain on appreciated employer stock sold to their ESOP until benefits are actually withdrawn from their ESOP account. However, that ESOPs actually increase worker control of business enterprises and further improve labor-management relations is much less certain. In other words, the public policy underlying ESOPs entered the tax code through the initiatives of one well-placed member of Congress based upon unfounded speculations on economics and labor-

74. Speech by Senator Russell B. Long, *Congressional Record*, 94th Cong., 2d sess. (June 10, 1976), pt. 14, 17595–96.

75. IRC sec. 133.

management theory, and quickly became entrenched in both the tax code and the U.S. economy. In this respect, the history of the ESOP is sadly indicative of much contemporary tax policy in the postwar era.

George Bush and Tax Policy

After serving two terms as the vice-president of Ronald Reagan, George Bush finally took residence in the White House in January 1989. The presidency of George Bush will be remembered neither for its success in reforming the tax code nor for the coherence of its tax policy. One of the first and most important tax campaigns pursued by the Bush administration was for reinstatement of a preferential tax rate for capital gains.[76] Proposals for a preferential rate had begun to surface almost immediately after 1986 when tax rates were equalized for ordinary income and long-term capital gains. The tax shelter industry, which had been effectively shut down by TRA, supported any effort to reinstate even a modest preferential rate for capital gains. While the Republican Party generally supported a preferential rate as a means to stimulate the investment of capital, Bush became particularly attached to the cause. Later, the 1992 Republican Party platform reaffirmed the president's commitment: "Reducing the tax on investment will be the biggest possible boost for the new technologies, businesses, and jobs we need for the next century."[77]

The Republican case for a preferential rate has been broadly stated in terms of the need to amend the tax laws to implement specific national economic policies—namely, to encourage the formation of capital and encourage liquidity in the capital markets.[78] Alternatively, the preferential rate for capital gains has been justified in terms of the additional revenue that it would raise (purportedly to be derived from the increased volume in capital transactions in which gain is recognized), thereby echoing the supply-sider's theme that lower tax rates can result in

76. For an account of this campaign, see Sean Ford, "Bush Budget Kind and Gentle to Capital Gains and Savings," 46 *Tax Notes* 605 (February 5, 1990); Ian K. Louden, "No Tax Surprises in '91 Budget As Bush Seeks Capital Gains Cut, Family Savings Initiative," 46 *Tax Notes* 607 (February 5, 1990).

77. Republican National Committee, "The Republican Platform 1992," August 12, 1992, 28.

78. See, e.g., Charls E. Walker and Mark A. Bloomfield, "The Case for the Restoration of a Capital Gains Tax Differential," 43 *Tax Notes* 1019 (May 22, 1989), and Martin Feldstein, "Why Capital Gains Taxes Are Unfair," *Wall St. J.,* November 21, 1994, A16.

increased revenues by creating economic incentives for the formation of capital. This theme has been at the heart of Republican tax policy since the 1920s, when Secretary of Treasury Andrew Mellon admonished his critics: "It seems difficult for some to understand that high rates of taxation do not necessarily mean large revenue for the Government, and that more revenue may often be obtained by lower rates."[79] Supply-siders in the 1980s similarly argued that lower tax rates promote capital investment, fuel economic growth, and ultimately garner more revenue than higher tax rates. President Bush consistently adhered to a capital gains tax cut as an article of religious faith based upon the twin principles of raising revenue and stimulating the economy.[80] Conversely, key Democrats in Congress, especially those on the tax committees, consistently and just as religiously denied both assumptions.

The Democratic leadership of both the House and the Senate dug their heals in for a fight on the issue.[81] The largely Democratic opposition to the administration's proposals steadfastly maintained that a preferential tax rate for capital gains favored the "rich" at the expense of the middle class and the poor.[82] Congressional Democrats argued that any return to a lower rate of taxation for capital gains would breach the implicit bipartisan bargain that was central to the passage of TRA.[83] Purportedly, such a breach would lead to the unraveling of the whole reformist package as other special interests would show up at the tax committees' doorstep to plead their own case for an exception.

79. Andrew W. Mellon, *Taxation: The People's Business* (New York: Macmillian, 1924), 16.

80. See, e.g., "Capital Gains Tax Cut Would Lower Cost of S&L Bailout, U.S. Chamber Report Says," *Daily Tax Rep.* (Bureau of National Affairs), no. 181, September 18, 1990, G-7; David Wessell and Jackie Calmes, "Bush Still Seeks Capital-Gains Tax Cut As Negotiators Haggle over Trade-off," *Wall St. J.*, September 18, 1990, A32.

81. See Pat Jones and Lane Davenport, "Bush Tax Proposals Roughed Up Before House, Senate Tax Panels," 46 *Tax Notes* 1223 (March 12, 1990).

82. Pat Jones, "Depreciable Asset Exclusion Complicates Debate on Bush Capital Gains Plan," 42 *Tax Notes* 1288, 1288 (March 13, 1989); idem, "Taxwriters Look at Capital Gains; Brady Nixes Rate Trade," 42 *Tax Notes* 1407, 1407 (March 20, 1989); Richard L. Schmalbeck, "The Uneasy Case for a Lower Capital Gains Tax: Why Not the Second Best?" 48 *Tax Notes* 195 (July 9, 1990).

83. Eugene Steuerle, "Tax Reform and the Capital Gains Debate," 44 *Tax Notes* 719, 720 (August 7, 1989) (agreeing with the argument that "the issue of capital gains cannot be separated from the tax reform contract" but also acknowledging that equity requires "dealing with the taxation of inflationary gains"–that is, introducing some form of indexing to account for phantom gain attributable solely to inflation).

In 1981, the differential between the maximum rate of tax imposed on long-term capital gains and that on ordinary income had increased markedly. The former was reduced to a post-World War II low of 20 percent, while the latter was reduced from 70 percent to 50 percent (having previously been lowered from 91 percent in 1964).[84] As a result, the relative differential between the two rates for the period from 1981 to 1986 was as much as 30 percentage points for taxpayers in the highest marginal tax bracket.[85] The significant difference between the two tax rates was one of the most important forces behind the growth of the tax shelter industry in the 1960s. The imbalance between the two rates was eventually resolved by TRA, which equalized the tax rates for ordinary income and capital gains. This took considerable steam out of the tax shelter industry, since one of the basic elements of a shelter was to "convert" ordinary income into capital gains. Curiously enough, throughout the Bush administration's crusade for a preferential rate, the Democratic opposition largely ignored its contribution to the tax shelter industry. Likewise, Democrats failed to note the serious structural, functional, and administrative problems associated with the differential rate.[86] Instead, their response was to offer as an alternative the equally implausible and economically unproven path of stimulating investment through special tax-deferred savings plans—specifically, an expanded version of the individual retirement account.[87]

84. Economic Recovery Tax Act of 1981, Pub. L. No. 97-34, sec. 102, 95 Stat. 186 (setting a maximum rate of 20 percent on qualified net capital gain); IRC sec. 1 (prior to amendment in 1986, setting a maximum rate of 50 percent on ordinary income).

85. While a significant differential, this was by no means the historic high. For example, in 1938, net income over $1 million was taxed at a maximum rate of 79 percent, while the Revenue Act of 1938 lowered the tax on capital gain to 15 percent—a differential of a whopping 64 percentage points.

86. In a report issued in 1989, the Committee on Taxation of the Association of the Bar of the City of New York concluded that the elimination of the capital gains preference in 1986 resulted in significant simplification of transactions. Committee on Taxation of the Association of the Bar of the City of New York to Lloyd Bentsen, LEXIS, Fed. Tax Library, TNT (September 28, 1990). Surprisingly, the Democratic opposition to President Bush's proposals ignored this argument. Conversely, conservatives who otherwise would favor simplification of the taxation of economic transactions find it convenient to ignore this issue as they plead their case for special tax treatment of capital gains.

87. The so-called super IRA proposal was first introduced in early 1991 by Senate Finance Committee chairman Lloyd Bentsen (who remained a strong proponent of the proposal in his capacity as secretary of the treasury in the Clinton administration) and committee member William Roth. Different versions of the bill have been put forth over

Although the tax benefit derived from the lower rate applicable to long-term capital gains was denounced by political opponents as an unjustifiable special tax break for "wealthy" taxpayers, the view of economists is mixed, at best, regarding the impact of the preferential rate on the population as a whole.[88] Economist Herbert Stein has perfectly summarized the prevailing absence of consensus: "Economists have made numerous efforts to estimate the revenue effect of changes in the tax on realized capital gains. . . . What the studies do show is that no one knows."[89] The preferential rate has been proposed as a reform capable of stimulating a slumping economy (presumably starved by the misallocation of capital locked into existing investment assets as a result of excessively high tax rates imposed upon sales triggering a taxable gain). Others argue that a preferential rate will encourage stock investors to adopt a long-term perspective in holding their investments, rather than looking for short-term gains.[90] Whether a preferential rate for long-term capital gains actually encourages such a perspective is open to debate. The most recent word on the subject comes from the Treasury's Office of Tax Analysis (OTA), which concluded that the short-term effects of introducing a preferential rate could be significant, but that long-term permanent effects will likely be marginal.[91]

---

the years. See, e.g., S. 612, 102d Cong., 1st sess. (1991). "Back-loaded" IRAs (IRAs in which deposits are made in after-tax dollars, with interest accumulating free of tax) present considerable political difficulties in a world of revenue-neutral tax legislation, since they are by definition revenue losers. Ironically, proposals for a back-loaded IRA made a reappearance in 1994 pursuant to the Republican Contract with America. Once again, the sentiment of professional economists is that such a plan does little to encourage savings and much to reduce federal revenue. See, e.g., Jane G. Gravelle, "Individual Retirement Accounts and Related Proposals," Congressional Research Service (CRS) Report, Library of Congress, March 24, 1995.

88. Schmalbeck, "The Uneasy Case," 195; Alan J. Auerbach, "The Effect of Reducing the Capital Gains Tax," 43 *Tax Notes* 1009 (May 22, 1989); Staff of the Congressional Budget Office, "Capital Gains and Economic Growth," 49 *Tax Notes* 105 (October 1, 1990); Congressional Budget Office, "Indexing Capital Gains," 49 *Tax Notes* 103 (October 1, 1990); Ralph Estes, "Should Capital Gains Taxes Be Cut?" 60 *Tax Notes* 1755 (September 27, 1993); Randall P. Mariger, "Taxes, Capital Gains Realizations, and Revenues," 48 *Nat'l Tax J.* 447 (1995).

89. Herbert Stein, "The Taxation of Realized Capital Gains," 43 *Tax Notes* 1013, 1016 (May 22, 1989).

90. See, e.g., James R. Repetli, "Long-Term Capital Gains, the Long-Term Investment Perspective, and Corporate Productivity," 42 *Tax Notes* 85 (October 1, 1990).

91. Leonard E. Burman and William C. Randolph, "Measuring Permanent Re-

In response to the inability to push legislation through Congress to reintroduce preferential treatment of capital gains, Republicans turned to more circuitous routes during the waning days of the Bush administration. President Bush contemplated issuing an executive order to implement "indexing" of capital gains for inflation through Treasury regulations. However, the effort was abandoned when legal advisers in the Departments of Justice and Treasury concluded that the president lacked the legal authority to pursue such a route.[92]

Ironically, with Republicans taking control of Congress and the tax committees in January 1995, both of these items (indexing and a capital gains tax cut) from the Republican tax agenda of the 1980s reemerged as the salient political issues of the 1990s. In the world of Washington politics, it seems especially true that the more things change, the more tax policy remains the same.

---

sponses to Capital Gains Tax Changes in Panel Data," OTA Paper no. 68 (August 1994).

92. See "Bush Accepts DOJ's Rejection of Legality of Capital Gains Indexing; Seeks Legislation," *Daily Tax Rep.* (Bureau of National Affairs), no. 173, September 4, 1992, G-4. For a discussion of the legal arguments concerning this issue, see Lee A. Sheppard, "Some Other Reasons Why Treasury Cannot Index Gains," 56 *Tax Notes* 1249 (September 7, 1992).

5

The Deluge Continues

Nowadays the State of the Union and the state of the budget have become essentially equivalent.
— Aaron B. Wildavsky (1988)

The federal income tax code is un-American in spirit and wrong in principle.
— U.S. Senator Peter V. Domenici (1994)

I personally would like to tear the income tax out by its roots and throw it overboard.
— House Ways and Means chairman Bill Archer (1995)

While there was continual tax legislating in the latter half of the 1980s, much of it consisted of technical corrections to the massive Tax Reform Act of 1986. At the same time, the difficult issue of the budget deficit was never adequately addressed—neither on the revenue side nor with respect to cutting expenditures. Ironically, the framework of revenue neutrality adopted by policymakers during the battle for tax reform in 1986 may actually have hindered the effort to find an overall approach to closing the budget deficit. Under revenue neutrality, wherein any legislative provision that cuts revenue must be paired with another provision to offset it, every revenue raiser becomes a much treasured ticket for a tax preference, rather than a contributor to closing the gap between revenue and expenditures. And that gap was widening by the close of the decade.

The 1990 Budget-Deficit Reduction

By 1990, the economy was sliding toward recession, and concern over the federal deficit heightened. The deficit as a percentage of GNP had fallen from a peak of 6.3 percent in 1983 to some 3.4 percent in 1988. However, it then rose again to 4.1 percent for fiscal year 1990 and was estimated to be 5 percent by the close of the year.[1] Propelled by its inability to persuade Congress to impose further spending cuts on federal expenditures, the Bush administration entered into budget negotiations with Democratic congressional leadership in May 1990 in an effort to achieve reconciliation over budget cuts coupled with increases in tax rates. To a great extent, the Bush administration was pushed into these negotiations by the looming presence of a worsening economy and the threat of a sequester of government spending mandated under Gramm-Rudman-Hollings. The president's initial budget projections were for a $40 billion deficit, but that figure began to skyrocket as the economy declined.

The negotiators adopted a target of $40.1 billion in deficit reduction for fiscal year 1991 and a $500 billion deficit-reduction package spread over five years. However, there were few guiding principles or goals behind the negotiations. In many respects, this reflected the president's own lack of clear principles for tax policy, other than his pragmatic preference not to raise taxes. Much the same nonideological approach was shared by Bush's chief negotiator, OMB director Richard Darman. To conservatives, both the 1990 budget negotiations and Darman became symbols of the Bush administration's lack of commitment to "true" conservative principles. Arguably, the weakness of the administration permitted the congressional tax committees to maintain control over the negotiations, much to the detriment of the president's position. Pressure was also imposed upon the president, as well as reluctant members of Congress, by the threat of a sequester requiring the shutdown of the federal government. This pressure only increased as the October 1 deadline for a new budget approached. When the deadline came and went without agreement on a congressional resolution authorizing the government to continue to spend money, operations were effectively shut down after October 5 for the Columbus Day holiday weekend.

Much has been written of the political hay made by Democrats over the administration's many strategic blunders in the negotiations.[2] The

---

1. Congressional Budget Office, *The Economy and Budget Outlook: Fiscal Years 1991–1995* (Washington, D.C.: Government Printing Office, January 1990), app. E, table E-2.

2. See, e.g., Alan Murray and Jackie Calmes, "How the Democrats, with Rare Cunning, Won the Budget War," *Wall St. J.*, November 5, 1990, A1, and Donald F. Kettl, *Deficit Politics: Public Budgeting in Its Institutional and Historical Context* (New York: Macmillan, 1992), 3–12. An interesting assessment of the budget agreement is found in Aaron

administration interpreted the president's "no-new-taxes" pledge to apply only to income taxes, allowing agreement to be reached over increased user fees and a ten-cent increase in the gasoline tax. But eventually the White House gave in and accepted an increase in the top individual tax rate from 28 percent to 31 percent, with the tax on long-term capital gains capped at the 28 percent rate as a compromise. In addition, increases in the excise taxes on liquor and cigarettes were adopted. More controversial was a new 10 percent excise tax imposed on certain high-priced "luxury" commodities. The pretext for this tax was the need to raise revenue in conjunction with the spending cuts contemplated by the budget-reduction plan. In fact, the luxury tax was put forth largely at the instigation of the Democratic leadership of Congress pursuant to its campaign to reimpose the tax burden on the "wealthy," which allegedly had been shifted to the middle class during the Reagan years. The tax was imposed on the excess of purchase price above certain threshold limits on retail sales of automobiles, private planes and boats, jewelry, and furs.[3] In enacting the luxury tax, policymakers learned the limits inherent to raising revenues through a commodity-specific tax imposed on nonessential luxury items. Projected revenues failed to materialize, and the tax was soon dismissed by the administration as "counterproductive." OMB director Richard Darman announced support for repeal based upon recognition that the tax had raised only minimal revenue and arguably had led to plant closings and layoffs in the boat and aircraft industries.[4] By 1992, congressional Republicans and Democrats alike accepted repeal of the tax for all commodities other than luxury automobiles. However, the legislative initiative to repeal the luxury tax ended up a victim of Bush's veto of the entire 1992 revenue bill (discussed further below).

B. Wildavsky and Joseph White, *The Deficit and the Public Interest: The Search for Responsible Budgeting in the 1980s* (Berkeley and Los Angeles: University of California Press, 1989), 577–89; see also C. Eugene Steuerle, *The Tax Decade: How Taxes Came to Dominate the Public Agenda* (Washington, D.C.: Urban Institute Press, 1992), 173–84.

3. The original threshold limits were as follows: $30,000 for automobiles, $100,000 for boats, $250,000 for aircraft, and $10,000 for furs and jewelry. See IRC secs. 4001, 4002, 4003, 4006, and 4007.

4. Others have recognized that the plant closings in these construction industries were more likely attributable to the general economic recession that had already begun in 1990, and not to the luxury excise tax. See, e.g., "Luxury Tax May Be Permanent in 'Monopoly,' but Congress Plays Game with Vanishing Ink," *Wall St. J.*, April 7, 1993, A16.

Budget negotiators in 1990 also produced such ill-conceived revenue raisers as a "phaseout" of personal exemptions and the 15 percent tax bracket, as well as the reduction of certain miscellaneous deductions above thresholds of adjusted net income. These all represented little more than a sleight-of-hand attempt to disguise what were in fact increases in marginal tax rates.[5] This game had also been played in 1986 with the so-called bubble, a 5 percent surtax applicable to adjusted income within certain ranges, but thereafter inapplicable.[6] The bubble fooled no one into believing that the highest tax rate was anything other than 34 percent, although it did confuse many into believing that tax rates were lower for the wealthy (confusing effective or average tax rates with marginal tax rates).

The final tax bill to emerge from the negotiations, enacted as the Omnibus Budget Reconciliation Act of 1990,[7] reflected no clear principles or ideology, nor did it suggest any new, emerging trends in tax policymaking. Much to the dismay of conservative Republicans, the overall effort to reduce the deficit was based more upon tax increases than expenditure cuts. Approximately 45 percent of the total deficit reduction from the package was derived from tax or user-fee increases, as opposed to reductions in expenditures. The bill was projected to raise $137 million of additional revenue over the five fiscal years 1991 through 1995.[8]

With the 1990 act, a decade of intense tax legislating came to an end with policy adrift and no clear direction evident. Neither Democrats nor Republicans wished to claim credit for the final bill, which made only a modest contribution to closing the budget deficit. More important, the episode left the Bush administration in full retreat on tax policy.

The 1992 Tax Bill

Following the passage of the 1990 act, the Bush administration had no credible tax policy of its own to stand upon, having been thoroughly

---

5. Once a taxpayer had crossed the threshold for the "phaseout" of personal exemptions, which began at $100,000 for a single taxpayer, as well as the threshold for the phased-in reduction in the enumerated deductions, which began at $150,000 for the same single taxpayer, the *marginal* tax rate was really 34 percent, and not the statutory 31 percent.

6. Former IRC sec. 1(g), repealed by Pub. L. No. 101-508, sec. 11101(b)(1).

7. Pub. L. No. 101-508, 104 Stat. 1388.

8. Estimates of expenditure cuts and revenue effects are from Congressional Budget Office and Joint Committee on Taxation, "Budget Reconciliation (H.R. 5835)—Revenue Provisions As Reported by the Conferees," October 26, 1990 (JCX-45-90).

outmaneuvered by congressional Democrats. The political decision to repudiate the premises of the 1990 budget agreement (i.e., accepting higher taxes in exchange for modest budget cuts) left the administration internally divided and without direction for future tax policy initiatives. As a result, when agitation for a new tax bill commenced in Congress in the spring of 1992, the White House became more of an observer responding to congressional initiatives than a leader asserting control over the tax policy arena.

A tax bill was passed by the House on July 2, following all the same patterns that had led to the budget crisis in the first place. Imposing little in the way of budget cuts, the House offered up some $2.5 billion in additional federal funding for urban social programs (explicable in the wake of the recent disturbances in Los Angeles) as well as a 50 percent exclusion for capital gains on "urban enterprise zone assets" held for five years. The Senate passed its own modified version of this urban-aid tax package on September 29, 1992. In many ways, the bill signaled the formal abandonment of both the principles behind tax reform in 1986 and the supply-side tax policy that had prevailed in 1981 under the prior Republican administration. The bill represented a distinct retreat to the more comfortable tax policymaking of the 1960s – only this time without the luxury of sufficient revenue to fund such congressional excesses.

In the Conference Committee, Chairmen Rostenkowski and Bentsen attempted to strip down the bill so as to render it more palatable to President Bush. Even still, the Senate conferees persisted in retaining two revenue-raising provisions (tax increases in all but name) originating in the Senate amendments, making permanent the phaseout of personal exemptions and the limitations on itemized deductions enacted in 1990.[9] Estimates put the price tag on the Senate bill at $36.6 billion, $19.6 billion for the House version. In October, both the House and Senate passed the Conference Committee's bill (a $27 billion compromise), notwithstanding the president's open threat of a veto. The veto came on November 4, 1992, one day after Bush was defeated in his bid for reelection.

Lacking congressional will or support for a veto override, the 1992 tax bill was laid to final rest.[10] Following his stunning electoral defeat to Arkansas governor Bill Clinton, George Bush's legacy in tax policy

9. See "Tax Conferees to Meet Today; House Members to Oppose Senate Revenue Raisers," *Daily Tax Rep.* (Bureau of National Affairs), no. 191, October 1, 1992, G-7.

10. One consequence of the veto of the 1992 act was that a number of technical corrections and extensions of expiring tax credits were never enacted. Technical problems

remains his "no-new-taxes" pledge, the commitment to a preferential rate for capital gains, the reputed 1990 budget agreement, and his veto of the 1992 tax bill.

Tax Policy and the Clinton Administration

With the election of a Democratic president in November 1992, tax policy took a decided turn, although not necessarily for the better. Even before actually moving into the White House in January 1993, Clinton aides floated several unusual tax proposals–some perhaps more seriously than others. Of these proposals, only one was included in the president's economic program announced in February 1993–that providing for the reinstitution of the investment tax credit. The rest were never set out in concrete proposals. However, the very fact that they were raised at all said much about the "new" direction of tax policy under the Democratic administration.

Beginning with his 1992 presidential campaign, Clinton continually proclaimed his commitment to some form of investment tax credit– said to be needed to "jump-start" the stagnant economy. Of course, the first hints of the president-elect's preference for an investment tax credit had the undesirable effect of inducing businesses to delay scheduled purchases so as to reap the significant tax benefits to be derived from a future tax credit. Arguably, any benefits to be derived from the proposed investment tax credit were already negated by the distortions the proposal had inflicted on the capital markets as well as by the negative impact on the federal budget.[11]

In one short-lived trial balloon floated in early January 1993, the president expressed interest in eliminating the long-sacred doctrine of exempting from taxation the gains inherent in a taxpayer's property

---

resulted that were only partially resolved pursuant to the Clinton administration's 1993 tax initiative.

11. See, e.g., Brian W. Cashell and Jane B. Gravelle, "Investment Tax Credit: Using Macroeconomic Models to Assess Short Run Effects," CRS, Library of Congress, January 7, 1993 (concluding that the enactment of an investment tax credit would have no short-term effect on the economy and only modest gains in employment, but would likely cause a substantial increase in the budget deficit); see also Mortimer M. Caplin, "Drop Investment Tax Credits," *Wall St. J.*, March 29, 1993, A12.

that is recognized upon death.[12] The long-standing policy has been to forgive the recognition of any gain inherent in bequested property, giving the estate and beneficiaries a "stepped-up" tax basis equal to the fair market of the property on the date of death.[13] This tax preference, one of the last great tax loopholes remaining in the tax code, allows heavily appreciated assets to be transferred from one generation to the next without ever paying income tax on the built-in gain. This provision has irked tax reformers for years; it has also been a tempting source of additional revenue.[14]

As recounted in Chapter 3, under reforms enacted by the Tax Reform Act of 1976, property acquired from a decedent would have taken a "carryover" tax basis equal to the decedent's basis immediately prior to death. The provision still allowed for deferral of tax on the built-in gain, but would have prevented complete avoidance. However, that reform effort provoked such strong, organized resistance that the effective date of the provision was first delayed until 1978, and then repealed altogether before ever taking effect. The very hint of an attempt to close the loophole once again generated strong and dedicated opposition, and nothing more was ever heard from the Clinton administration on this issue.

In his 1992 campaign, Clinton had also promised that his administration would collect an additional $45 billion over a four-year period from foreign corporations doing business in the United States. It was asserted that additional revenue could be raised by limiting techniques used by foreign corporations to understate their U.S. income, thereby reducing their U.S. income tax liabilities. The problem pertains to foreign corporations inasmuch as domestic corporations are subject to U.S. income taxation on their worldwide income, with credits allowed for comparable income taxes paid to foreign governments. Even if a U.S.

12. See, e.g., "Clinton Suggestion of Possible Capital Gain Tax upon Death Stirs Ire Among Powerful Interests," *Wall St. J.*, January 5, 1993, A16.

13. IRC sec. 1014. The estate can elect to value the bequested property as of an alternate date (six months after death) if more favorable. IRC sec. 2032.

14. The revenue loss has been calculated to be as high as $46 billion a year. "Revenue Losses – Estimates for Selected 'Tax Expenditures' by Function: 1989–1993," in *Statistical Abstract of the United States 1992* (Washington, D.C.: Government Printing Office, 1993), table 497. Treasury calculated that repeal of this exclusion would raise $28 billion in additional revenue in 1993. The Congressional Budget Office concluded that repeal would yield $17 billion over five years. While estimates differ, all seem to agree that the Treasury loses significant revenues from this special treatment.

corporation is able to reduce its "U.S. source" income, its worldwide taxable income will remain the same, merely having been shifted to sources outside the United States. Conversely, if a foreign corporation is able to shift taxable income away from the United States and into a foreign jurisdiction with lower tax rates, its overall tax liability will be reduced, since the United States can only tax the U.S. source income of the foreign corporation. United States taxable income can be reduced through the manipulation of costs charged for various sales and exchanges between foreign and U.S. businesses owned and controlled by the same parent. Such techniques are commonly referred to as "transfer-pricing." The U.S. tax code requires that such prices between related entities be set at an arms-length standard, but discerning an arms-length price is no easy matter.[15] Despite the easy political target that foreign corporations made in the search for additional revenue during the budget crisis, no such initiatives emerged in the president's 1993 revenue proposals, most likely because of the difficulty in crafting and enacting such provisions, as well as the political fallout from foreign trading partners who would undoubtedly object to, and possibly retaliate against, such measures.

These proposals reveal much about the direction of tax policy in the 1990s. First, these reforms are merely reincarnations of proposals from prior decades. For instance, the investment tax credit was first introduced in 1962, suspended briefly in 1966,[16] terminated in 1969,[17] reinstated in 1971,[18] and finally repealed pursuant to the Tax Reform Act of 1986 as an "abuse" with no economic justification. Likewise, the attack on the exclusion of gain recognized at death was an old theme of tax reformers. This pattern of reintroducing the last decade's proposal as today's innovation is characteristic of the incremental tax-policymaking process discussed further in Chapter 9.

During the 1992 presidential campaign, candidate Bill Clinton had indicated numerous times that revival of the tax bill and dealing with the budget deficit would be among the highest priorities of his administration. During the months following his election and preceding his

15. IRC sec. 482. The broad language of section 482 authorizes the secretary of the treasury to "distribute, apportion, or allocate gross income" between certain related entities in order that income is clearly reflected and taxes are not evaded.

16. Pub. L. No. 89-800, 89th Cong., 2d sess. (1966).

17. Tax Reform Act of 1969, Pub. L. No. 91-172, 91st Cong., 1st sess. (1969).

18. Revenue Act of 1971, Pub. L. No. 92-178, 92d Cong., 1st sess. (1971).

inauguration, Clinton reiterated his campaign commitment to address the deficit, but also continued to assert that his administration would still lower taxes on the middle class.[19] However, economic realities soon caught up with campaign rhetoric as new projections of an increasing budget deficit forced the retraction of this pledge even before taking office.[20] By then, it was already evident that the dynamics of congressional politics would dictate that the deficit shortfall would be addressed by the new Democratic administration through tax increases, rather than through significant reductions in expenditures. The Republican administration just departing from the White House had been unable to advance the latter position through the congressional legislative process—partly because it was controlled by Democrats, but as much because Congress as a political institution is overwhelming oriented toward increasing spending, rather than reducing expenditures. Just as higher tax rates became the cornerstone of the 1990 budget agreement negotiated between President Bush and Congress, so too would tax increases dominate the proposals emanating from the White House in early 1993.

The Revenue Reconciliation Act of 1993

In his first State of the Union address on February 17, 1993, President Clinton formally presented his new economic program to Congress.[21] This hodgepodge collection of proposals set the stage for the political debate that continued for the next six months. As was the case during the Reagan and Bush administrations, tax policy emerged as one of the dominant themes of domestic policymaking, since a good deal of

19. See, e.g., "Bentsen Stresses the Importance of Deficit Cuts," *Wall St. J.*, January 13, 1993, A2.

20. See "Top Democrats Say Tax Cut Seems Doubtful," *Wall St. J.*, January 11, 1993, A2; "Clinton Suggests Deficit May Cancel a Tax Cut," *Wall St. J.*, January 14, 1993, A18; "Clinton Stresses Taxes over Spending Cuts in Attack on Deficit," *Wall St. J.*, January 18, 1993, A1.

21. The revenue proposals were stated by the Treasury Department in its "Summary of the Administration's Revenue Proposals," released on February 25, and by the Office of Management and Budget in "A Vision of Change for America," released on February 17. A more detailed description of the White House tax proposals is found in the study by the Joint Committee on Taxation, "Summary of the President's Revenue Proposals" (JCS-4-93), March 8, 1993.

Clinton's "economic policy" consisted of proposals to be implemented through the federal tax code.

In his address to Congress, Clinton revealed what was already obvious—that his economic agenda would include a significant increase in the highest marginal tax rate applicable to individuals, anticipated at the time to be somewhere in the range of 3 to 5 percent.[22] Clinton reiterated his support for a proposal that had been championed by congressional Democrats since 1990—a so-called millionaires surtax. In the president's proposal this was transformed into a 10 percent surtax imposed on taxable income in excess of $250,000. Clinton also persisted with his campaign pledge to reinstate some form of an investment tax credit.[23]

Beginning with this commitment to the investment tax credit, the Clinton revenue proposals exemplified little that was new—and a good deal that can only be seen as tinkering at the margins of the tax code. The administration also faced problems putting together its economic program, because most of the top tax positions in Treasury and the IRS had still not been filled—including assistant secretary for tax policy, deputy assistant secretary for tax policy, IRS commissioner, and IRS chief counsel. It has been asserted that, on account of this, the staff of the Senate Finance Committee played a leading role in formulating the proposals, while Treasury staff and that of the Joint Committee on Taxation were largely left out of the process.[24] The administration's proposals for "capital investment and economic growth" consisted in retroactively extending and making permanent the tax credits for research-and-development expenditures, employer-provided education assistance, low-income housing, and targeted jobs. Included also was a diluted version of a plan for fifty "enterprise zones" wherein would apply special tax-incentive credits.[25] A new capital gains exclusion for 50

22. "Clinton Stresses Taxes over Spending Cuts in Attack on Deficit," A1.

23. "Investment Tax Credit Planned for Stimulus," *Wall St. J.*, February 3, 1993, A1.

24. See remarks by N. Jerold Cohen, former IRS commissioner, in "Planning Opportunities and Pitfalls Under the 1993 Tax Act," 80 *Std. Fed. Tax Rep.*(Chicago, August 26, 1993), report 36, published by Commerce Clearing House.

25. Enacting new Subchapter U, found at new sections 1391 et seq. of the Internal Revenue Code. The provision provides for a general business tax credit for certain wages paid to "qualified zone employees." This new "empowerment zone employment credit" is considerably less than what was proposed by former HUD secretary Jack Kemp, and hence will surely be denounced as inadequate by such supporters, since it will inevitably fail to reverse the half-century decline of American cities and countless other social and economic problems.

percent of the gain recognized on the sale of certain "small business stock" was offered up by the administration as a stimulus for capital investment.[26]

Also introduced into the Clinton proposals with virtually no fanfare or public notice (and later enacted with little more attention) was a curious provision allowing for the deferral of gain on the sale of publicly traded securities where the proceeds are reinvested (or, in tax parlance, "rolled over") into a "specialized small business investment company."[27] Such a company is provided for under the Small Business Investment Act of 1958.[28] These specialized small business investment companies are firms that invest in businesses owned by "disadvantaged" individuals (minorities, disabled individuals, veterans, and women). Thus, this provision effectively inserted into the tax code specialized treatment of taxpayers based upon the usual "politically correct" classifications. Perhaps even more interesting, the proposal was apparently inserted into the Clinton tax bill entirely at the instigation of a single member of Congress, Representative William Jefferson (Democrat of Louisiana), through a successful personal lobbying crusade undertaken while sharing a fifteen-minute airplane ride with the president.[29]

The revenue-raising provisions of the bill added up to little more than increasing marginal tax brackets. Proposed rate increases included the following: a new maximum tax bracket of 36 percent for individuals with taxable income above $115,000 ($140,000 for married couples filing joint returns), with the aforementioned 10 percent surtax applicable to taxable income above $250,000 (resulting in a top rate of 39.6 percent); a maximum tax rate of 35 percent on corporate income over $10 million (representing a 1 percent increase); and preservation of the 55 percent maximum tax rate on gifts and estates (scheduled to decline to 50 percent under prior law).

26. New IRC sec. 1202. This provision returned to the repertoire of the tax lawyer tax planning for the conversion of ordinary income into capital gains.

27. New IRC sec. 1044.

28. Sec. 301(d) of the Small Business Investment Act of 1958, as in effect on May 13, 1993. 15 U.S.C. sec. 661 et seq. The Small Business Administration has announced that there are 103 specialized small business investment corporations that qualify for this new tax provision. "More Than 100 Firms Are Investment Vehicles Under Capital Gains Provision," *Daily Tax Rep.* (Bureau of National Affairs), no. 227, November 29, 1993, G-1.

29. The interesting story of how this provision was inserted into the Clinton economic package, with virtually no lobbying or support in either the Congress or White House, is recounted in Eugene Carlson, "How a Small-Business Group Found a Niche in Tax Bill," *Wall St. J.*, May 26, 1993, B-2.

Other provisions proposed limitations upon, or the outright elimination of, several long-standing business deductions. While ideologically motivated and largely directed at business, these proposals were essentially driven by a more pragmatic consideration – the search for revenue. For instance, the business deduction for meals and entertainment would be further reduced to 50 percent (having previously been reduced to 80 percent). The impact of this proposal was blunted by a new tax credit for restaurants for the payroll taxes they pay on employee tips. This provision explains the lack of organized opposition to the reduction of the deduction for meals and entertainment. The final bill was supposed to institute the credit for tax years beginning in 1994. However, due to sloppy drafting, the credit arguably applied for 1993. In a closed-door session, Ways and Means considered a technical correction supported by the Joint Committee on Taxation to rectify the error. However, the measure failed (partly through the efforts of Representative Don Sundquist of Tennessee, who himself has investments in restaurants), giving the restaurant industry an even more significant benefit than originally intended.[30] Employee deductions for moving expenses were also cut back, and other provisions eliminated altogether business deductions for dues paid for membership in any social or athletic club and lobbying expenses. Most provocatively, under the bill deductions for nonperformance-based executive compensation in excess of $1 million were disallowed to publicly traded corporations.[31]

One of the most controversial proposals in the president's program was a provision for a broad energy tax, the so-called Btu tax. As might be

30. For an account of this controversy, see Jackie Calmes, "Congressman Who Cooked Up Tax Break for Restaurants May Get Taste Himself," *Wall St. J.*, October 29, 1993, A3.

31. These provisions all reflect both the relentless search for revenue as well as a specific ideological perspective regarding who should bear the burden of additional taxes. In this case, these provisions are skewed against some vague group known as the "rich" – or, at least, highly compensated business executives. There is a long history of Congress using the tax code to impose salary limits, to determine what is "unreasonable" compensation paid to corporate executives. For instance, the Senate Finance Committee added to the Revenue Act of 1932, the most important tax bill of the early New Deal, a provision that taxed compensation in excess of $75,000 at a special 80 percent rate and denied the corporate taxpayer a deduction for such amounts. Senate Committee on Finance, Revenue Bill of 1932, S. Rept. 665 to accompany H.R. 10236, 72d Cong., 1st sess., 13–14: "[L]arge amounts of compensation, particularly in the form of bonuses, emoluments, and rewards frequently paid to the officials of corporations are greatly in excess of reasonable compensation for the services actually performed."

expected, this new tax provoked immediate opposition from congressional delegations from the gas- and oil-producing states.[32] Equally controversial among revenue-raising provisions was the president's proposal to tax up to 85 percent of the Social Security benefits for those with income and benefits exceeding the current-law thresholds of $25,000 for single individuals and $32,000 for married couples filing jointly.

These proposals, many of which can be traced directly to campaign promises made during the 1992 election, served as the initiative for the debate over tax policy that dominated domestic politics over the first six months of the Clinton administration. Tax policy was the first serious political battle of the administration (as reform of the nation's health-care system was still on the back burner at that time). While the president started the ball rolling in 1993 for tax legislation, the executive branch played a largely secondary role in determining the specifics of what actually became law. After the initiative commenced, congressional politics took over in shaping the outcome with respect to particular issues. The president's initiative fell within the mold of traditional postwar tax policy and incremental policymaking, and it contained little (other than the Btu tax) to offend the traditional congressional politics. While the budget deficit continued to loom over tax policymaking, there simply was no "extraordinary" source of popular will or countervailing political force in 1993 to overcome the congressionally based politics that took hold of the executive's initiative.

Beginning in early 1993, the House Ways and Means Committee took up consideration of the president's proposals.[33] Even while facing serious personal political problems (which eventually led to his resignation from the House), committee chairman Rostenkowski remained firmly in control of tax policymaking in the House.[34] In a display of

32. Senator David Boren, Democrat of Oklahoma, led the opposition to this proposal that eventually was its demise. See, e.g., "President Clinton, Sen. Boren to Meet on Tax Bill," *Daily Tax Rep.* (Bureau of National Affairs), no. 105, June 6, 1993, G-9, and "Senate Democrats Close to Compromise on Clinton Tax Plan As House Vote Nears," *Daily Tax Rep.* (Bureau of National Affairs), no. 100, May 26, 1993, G-6.

33. The president's tax proposals were introduced in the House as H.R. 1960 on May 4, 1993, and thereafter, subject to a markup by the Ways and Means Committee. The legislation was later passed by the House on May 27, 1993, as part of the Budget Reconciliation Bill of 1993, H.R. 2264.

34. For an interesting account of the chairman's legal problems as well as his political strengths, see "Rostenkowski's Woes Spotlight the Decline of House's Old School," *Wall St. J.*, July 23, 1993, A1.

remarkable party coherence, Republicans opposed the entire package, ironically leaving it to Democrats on Ways and Means to direct the course of markup. Clinton was accused by members of his own party of too quickly abandoning such provisions as the investment tax credit and the Btu tax, as well as accepting a lower corporate tax rate—leaving those Democrats on the Ways and Means Committee who had supported his proposals bitter over his apparent willingness to compromise on "fundamental" principles with all interested parties.[35] In the end, the executive initiative was strongly influenced by pressures from important regional interests, as well as the institutional and political interests that dominate congressional policymaking.

Much the same dynamics were evidenced in the Senate's consideration of the 1993 tax bill. The tendencies uniquely characteristic of the Senate since the 1960s were exerted in markup by the Senate Finance Committee. However, in the end, the Senate followed the House bill, but with several notable departures. For example, the Senate accepted the president's proposal for a 36 percent maximum tax rate for individuals, but broke with the president and House in applying the 10 percent surtax to net capital gains only. The Finance Committee also took the position that the rate increase should apply only as of the effective date of the tax bill (to be achieved through a blended annual rate), and *not* retroactively to January 1, 1993, as the House version had it. Few original initiatives came out of the Senate markup, the exceptions being a proposal for the repeal of the so-called stock-for-debt exception for the recognition of income on the cancellation of indebtedness for companies in a bankruptcy proceeding, and a new Indian Investment and Employment Tax Credit. The repeal of the stock-for-debt exception (estimated by the Joint Committee on Taxation to bring in some $100 million a year, or $622 million over five years) was slipped in during the closing hours of negotiations, without public hearings or debate. For this reason, it received little notice before its effective date of December 31, 1994. At that time, significant lobbying efforts commenced to return the exception to the tax code.[36]

Also notable was the strength of Senate resistance to the Btu tax. An alternative proposal emerged from the Senate in favor of a 4.3-cents-per-gallon increase in the federal gasoline tax, which provision ultimately

35. See, e.g., "White House Concedes to Pressure to Drop ITC, Curb Corporate Rate Hike," *Daily Tax Rep.* (Bureau of National Affairs), no. 90, May 12, 1993, G-5.

36. For an account of these lobbying efforts, see Milo Geyelin, "Revival of Sick Firms' Tax Break Is Sought," *Wall St. J.*, December 23, 1994, B-6.

prevailed in the final bill. Finally, both the Senate and the House (as well as the Clinton administration) again supported repeal of the 1990 luxury tax as applied to boats, aircraft, jewelry, and furs (retaining the tax only for luxury automobiles). Because overall revenue from the tax had declined every year since 1990, repeal was projected to cost the Treasury only $270 million over five years.[37] By contrast, the excise tax on luxury automobiles was a revenue raiser and, hence, was retained. No public policy—only the pressure for revenue—justified retaining the tax on automobiles while repealing it for the other items previously taxed. The auto excise tax (presently imposed on the purchase price exceeding $32,000) brought in some $400 million to the Treasury in fiscal year 1993. On this basis alone, continual efforts by lobbyists of the automobile industry to have the tax repealed have been unsuccessful.[38]

Once the Senate passed its bill, negotiations shifted to the Conference Committee. Agreement was quickly reached with respect to tax rate increases, with incremental increases acceptable to Democrats in both houses. Disagreement continued over the effective date of such tax increases, the Btu tax, the viability of the enterprise zone initiative as originally proposed by Clinton, and the House's proposed expansion of the earned income tax credit.[39] Conference Committee negotiations were notable in that the leadership of the Finance Committee had devolved upon Senator Daniel Patrick Moynihan upon Senator Lloyd Bentsen's "promotion" to the executive branch as secretary of treasury. This probably gave some greater control over the legislative process at this stage to Rostenkowski, the more experienced Ways and Means chairman, although the senator from New York could hardly be said to be lacking in political savvy. On most key points the House version prevailed. For example, Moynihan publicly swore that individual tax rate increases would not be retroactive to January 1, 1993; nevertheless, they were. In addition, the House and Rostenkowski prevailed in placing limitations on the IRC section 936 "possessions" tax credit (which is

37. Revenue projections for fiscal years 1994–98, as prepared by the Staff of the Joint Committee on Taxation, *Summary of the Revenue Provisions of the Omnibus Budget Reconciliation Act of 1993* (Washington, D.C.: Government Printing Office, 1993), 38.

38. See "Auto Lobbyists Try to Get Congress to Kill or Phase Out a Luxury Tax," *Wall St. J.*, August 30, 1995, A1.

39. "Tax Conferees Face Resolution of Most Issues This Week," *Daily Tax Rep.* (Bureau of National Affairs), no. 142, July 27, 1993, G-5; "Few Surprises Found in Revenue Provisions of Budget Reconciliation Compromise," *Daily Tax Rep.* (Bureau of National Affairs), no. 148, August 4, 1993, G-9.

relatively important to Moynihan's New York constituency, with its strong ties to Puerto Rico, the main beneficiary of the development resulting from the credit) and the amortization of acquired intangibles. While it might be too strong to conclude that the House was the "winner" in Conference Committee or that Rostenkowski's seniority was the significant difference in determining the outcome over any particular issues, the House prevailed on most significant issues.

As was the case with the House and Senate versions of the bill, floor voting on the bill that emerged after weeks of compromise in the Conference Committee followed unusually strict party lines (with Senate Republicans held firmly in line on floor votes by Senate minority leader Robert Dole and in the Finance Committee by ranking minority member Robert Packwood). The final vote in the Senate ultimately was decided by Vice-President Gore in his capacity as president of the Senate. The Senate vote came on August 6, 1993 – one day after the House had passed the bill by the narrow margin of 218 to 216. The president signed the Revenue Reconciliation Act of 1993 into law on August 10, 1993.[40] The Joint Committee on Taxation predicted that the final bill would raise $240 billion of additional revenue over the first five fiscal years.[41]

In many ways, the politics surrounding the enactment of the 1993 tax bill exemplified the same trends that had characterized the 1986 and 1990 bills. The enduring budget crisis continued to play a crucial role in orienting tax policymaking in 1993.[42] Likewise, while executive initiatives served as the basis for tax legislation, congressional politics and interests dominated the tax-policymaking process, much as it had in 1990. But in its most significant aspects, the 1993 act marked a distinct retreat from the principles of tax reform that had shaped TRA, reversing the movement for lower tax rates and broadening of the tax base that

40. Pub. L. No. 103-66, 107 Stat. 312.

41. Joint Committee on Taxation, "Estimated Budget Effects of the Revenue Provisions of H.R. 2264 (The Omnibus Budget Reconciliation Act of 1993) As Agreed to by the Conferees" (JCX-11-94), August 4, 1994.

42. Soon after the enactment of the 1993 act, the White House budget office issued predictions that the deficit would decline to $180 billion by fiscal year 1996. These predictions were, as is typical, based upon somewhat more optimistic economic forecasts that those used by the Congressional Budget Office in its estimates. See "White House Sees '96 Deficit of $180 Billion," *Wall St. J.*, September 2, 1993, A2, and "White House Projects $504.8 Billion in Deficit Reduction over Five Years," *Daily Tax Rep.* (Bureau of National Affairs), no. 169, September 2, 1993, G9–10.

had distinguished the 1986 act. The politics of tax reform was nowhere to be found in 1993.

The "New" Republican Tax Agenda

In November 1994, the Republican Party gained eight seats in the U.S. Senate and 52 in the House, providing it with majorities in both chambers at once for the first time since January 1955 – the Senate alone being controlled by Republicans from 1980 through 1986. During the 1994 elections, House Republicans promoted their platform by committing themselves to a set of campaign promises laid out in the so-called Contract with America, a considerable portion of which consisted of policies to be implemented through the tax code. Of the ten or so major proposals contained in the Contract, the following provided for amendments to the income tax: an exclusion of 50 percent of net long-term capital gains, the indexing of capital assets, an allowance for capital losses recognized on the sale of a principal residence, certain modifications of the Accelerated Cost Recovery System (ACRS), increasing the $600,000 unified estate and gift tax life-time credit to $750,000, increasing the annual expensing allowance under IRC section 179 to $25,000, expanding the availability of deductions (and tax-free withdrawals) for IRA contributions, eliminating the so-called marriage penalty, and a new $500-per-child tax credit for families with income up to $200,000.

The Treasury Department estimated that the tax cuts included in the Contract would cost $197.2 billion over the first five years and $514.8 billion more over the five subsequent years.[43] (The significant costs during the second five-year period would be attributable to long-term revenue loss from modifications to IRAs, the cost-recovery system, and capital gains rates, which would kick in only after the first five years.) Of course, these Treasury revenue estimates assumed that preferences such as the capital gains tax cut would *cost* the Treasury revenue – an

---

43. The Treasury revenue estimates were first made public in a December 17, 1994, press release, reprinted in 65 *Tax Notes* 1609 (December 26, 1994). Later, the Joint Committee on Taxation estimated that the Contract would cost $196.3 billion over five years and $704.4 billion over ten years. Joint Committee on Taxation, "Estimated Revenue Effects of the Tax Provisions Contained in the 'Contract with America' " (JCX-4-95), February 6, 1995.

assumption that itself became the focus of considerable political controversy as congressional Republicans raised questions over the method of "scoring" revenue estimates used by the professional staff in the tax bureaucracy. Beginning soon after the fall elections, the Republicans exerted pressure on the Congressional Budget Office (CBO) and Joint Committee on Taxation (JCT) to employ "dynamic" rather than "static" scoring techniques to predict the impact of tax provisions on revenue raised under the income tax. The Office of Tax Policy in Treasury and the Congressional Budget Office use somewhat different scoring techniques, but neither uses the kind of dynamic scoring that assumes macroeconomic results attributable to the very changes to the tax laws then under consideration. For example, an assumption that the economy will prosper on account of a lower tax imposed on capital gains can lead to the conclusion that such tax cuts will actually result in greater revenue collected by the Treasury. This was the basis for the Bush administration's prediction that its proposed capital gains tax cuts would increase revenue over the long run. After the Republican leadership replaced the chief of staff of the JCT and the director of the CBO, dynamic scoring looked like it might become political, if not economic, reality.[44] Nevertheless, Republicans eventually backed off from their position after they took control of the 104th Congress, with House Ways and Means Committee chairman Bill Archer of Texas acknowledging that it was perhaps undesirable to turn the revenue-estimating process into a "political football."[45]

44. The politics of the issue is recounted in Sean Ford, "Battle over Revenue Estimates Takes Back Seat to GOP Contract," 65 *Tax Notes* 1172 (December 5, 1994); Paul A. Gigot, "GOP Team Rethinks Its Enemies List," *Wall St. J.*, December 23, 1994, A10; Barbara Kirchheimer, "Republicans Accuse Treasury of 'Political' Revenue Estimating," 65 *Tax Notes* 1583 (December 26, 1994); Lucinda Harper and David Wessel, "A Primer: What Congress Will Face in Debate over Taxes and Revenue," *Wall St. J.*, December 27, 1994, A2. The best discussion of the technical issues is found in the "Written Testimony of the Staff of the Joint Committee on Taxation Regarding the Revenue Estimating Process," presented to the Joint Hearing of the House and Senate Budget Committees of the 104th Congress on January 10, 1995 (JCX-1-95), January 9, 1995, reprinted in *Daily Tax Rep.* (Bureau of National Affairs), no. 7, January 11, 1995, L-18 through L-32. See also Jane G. Gravelle, "Behavioral Feedback Effects and the Revenue-Estimating Process," 48 *Nat'l Tax J.* 463 (1995).

45. Archer made his statement to reporters in a press conference on January 4, 1995, available on LEXIS or Dialogue at 95 TNT 3-2 (January 5, 1995). Senate Budget Committee chairman Pete Domenici had already pronounced that changing the current budget-estimating methodology had been "laid to rest as a scoring issue." Quoted in *Daily Tax Rep.* (Bureau of National Affairs), no. 7, January 11, 1995, G-10.

Following the success of Republicans in the 1994 elections, the odds of a return to a preferential tax rate for capital gains increased dramatically. Chairman Archer expressed his support for this proposal immediately after the November elections.[46] By January 1995, business leaders were already testifying before Congress to praise the benefits they anticipated from a return of the preferential rate for capital gains.[47] In fact, the capital gains tax cut was the *only* provision on the Republican tax agenda that business leaders actively supported. For instance, the president of the National Association of Manufacturers admitted that while industry leaders had "substantial enthusiasm" for the capital gains provision, the rest of the House's tax-cutting measures generated little ardor among business.[48] The revenue loss attributable solely to the capital gains preference (which under the initial Contract proposal would have applied to corporate taxpayers as well as individuals) was calculated by the JCT to be $36.8 billion over five years and $103 billion over ten years.[49]

In March and April, the Contract tax package breezed through the House as promised by Speaker Gingrich. All of the tax policies included in the Contract emerged fully intact in the final bill (H.R. 1215). House Republicans held firm and, as promised, repealed an amendment (added to the tax code by the 1993 Clinton tax legislation) that increased the taxable portion of Social Security benefits, held fast for the indexing of basis in capital assets and 50 percent exclusion for capital gains (although, to reduce the revenue loss, the corporate preference was cut

46. Barbara Kirchheimer, "Republicans Eager to Push Their Tax Agenda in New Congress," 65 *Tax Notes* 799 (November 14, 1994).

47. Representatives of the National Association of Manufacturers, the National Federation of Independent Business, and the U.S. Chamber of Commerce appeared before the House Ways and Means Committee on January 12, 1995, to endorse the proposed capital gains tax cut in the House Republicans' Contract with America. See "Business Leaders Strongly Endorse Capital Gains Tax Cut," *Daily Tax Rep.* (Bureau of National Affairs), no. 9, January 13, 1995, G-6.

48. Jerry Jasinowski, president of the National Association of Manufacturers (NAM), quoted in "Capital Gains Tax Cut Only Proposal with Support of Manufacturers, Says NAM," *Daily Tax Rep.* (Bureau of National Affairs), no. 33, February 17, 1995, G-7.

49. Joint Committee on Taxation, "Estimated Revenue Effects of the Tax Provisions Contained in the 'Contract with America'" (JCX-4-95), February 6, 1995. The Republican proposal was analyzed in great detail by the JCT in its study, "Tax Treatment of Capital Gains and Losses" (JCS-4-95), February 13, 1995.

back to a 25 percent maximum rate rather than a 50 percent exclusion), and retained the $500-per-child credit even for higher income-level taxpayers. Even more remarkable, for tax years beginning after the year 2000 the House bill repealed the corporate alternative minimum tax (AMT), a measure particularly adverse to certain capital-intensive industries. In a separate measure, the House also voted to repeal a special tax provision granting deferral of gain realized on the sale of an FCC-licensed broadcasting station to a "minority" purchaser.[50] Originally proposed as the revenue raiser to support the permanent extension of the 25 percent deduction for the medical expenses of self-employed persons (which had already expired as of January 1, 1994), repeal of this provision looked as if it might herald some new debate over minority set-asides and federal affirmative action programs. However, that debate never materialized in 1995 as cutting taxes and balancing the budget dominated the Republican agenda for the rest of the year.

As was entirely predictable, each of these provisions produced a strong partisan reaction among Democrats, although the 50 percent exclusion, the $500-per-child credit, and the repeal of the corporate AMT brought the sharpest partisan rebukes. The main argument of Democrats was the familiar refrain about such a tax policy favoring the "rich." The House's effort to repeal the corporate AMT led to sharp and immediate opposition from Citizens for Tax Fairness, which public-interest group had actively promoted the original adoption of the AMT as a "backstop" reform to prevent "profitable" corporations from avoiding paying any income tax. Conversely, the AMT was intensely hated by businesses that incurred considerable costs just to comply with the tax. The Joint Committee on Taxation produced its own study, which concluded that the AMT was paid by relatively few corporations (ranging from 0.7 percent to 1.5 percent of all corporate taxpayers, these being the

---

50. The special tax treatment was provided under IRC section 1071, originally enacted under the Revenue Act of 1943, granting the Federal Communications Commission authority to issue "tax certificates" to implement certain of its programs (for example, FCC prohibitions against ownership of multiple stations in the same market). In 1978, the FCC amended its program to include issuing tax certificates to station owners who sell their licensed facilities to "minorities" (defined by the FCC to include "Blacks, Hispanics, American Indians, Alaskan Natives, Asians and Pacific Islanders"). For a history and explanation of the social policy implemented by this tax provision, see Joint Committee on Taxation, "Background and Issues Relating to the Application of Code Section 1071 Under the Federal Communications Commission's Tax Certificate Program" (JCX-8-95), March 6, 1995.

most capital-intensive businesses), raised relatively little revenue (only about $2.6 billion per year, or 2.6 percent of corporate income tax revenue), imposed significant compliance costs (since even corporations that do not actually incur any tax liability under the AMT still must prepare AMT returns), and was a likely source of inefficiencies and misallocations of resources within the economy as a whole.[51]

Not until late in the spring of 1995 did the Senate even turn to the tax preferences contained in the House bill. Even then, the Senate proceeded at its own pace. Having neither signed a contract nor made any promises to cut taxes, Senate leadership felt itself in no way bound by the same frantic hundred-day schedule adhered to by House Republicans. Indeed, the House tax cuts were put on hold as the Senate took up consideration of budget-reduction plans. Finance Committee chairman Packwood and other Senate Republican leaders viewed the tax-cut measures as secondary to deficit reduction, and negotiations between Senate and House Republicans stalled.[52] But by the end of June, Senate Republicans agreed to accept as much as $245 billion of tax cuts spread over seven years (up from their initial commitment to $170 billion contingent upon fiscal savings realized through expenditure cuts). A nonbinding budget resolution (H. Con. Res. 67) adopted by both chambers on June 29 assumed that the $245 billion of tax cuts would be paid for with a $170 billion "fiscal dividend" (purportedly to be derived from interest savings attributable to a balanced budget itself) and $75 billion of additional spending cuts to be determined at a later date. It was agreed that $270 billion of the $894 billion in projected spending cuts would come from cuts to Medicare, $182 billion from Medicaid, $190 billion from nondefense spending, and $175 billion from various entitlement programs, such as welfare. House Republicans stuck to their own plan for a $500-per-child tax credit for taxpayers with income up to $200,000, provoking a split with Senate Republicans who wanted a much lower cap on the credit.

The outcome on these issues, as with all other Contract tax provisions, remained up in the air throughout the summer of 1995 as congressional Republicans struggled to reach agreement among themselves on

51. Joint Committee on Taxation, "Present Law and Issues Relating to the Corporate and Individual Alternative Minimum Tax (AMT)" (JCX-22-95), May 2, 1995.

52. See Jackie Calmes and Rick Wartzman, "GOP Weighs $245 Billion Tax-Cut Compromise," *Wall St. J.*, June 22, 1995, A6; Christopher Georges and David Rogers, "House and Senate Republicans Split over Details of $245 Billion Tax Cut," *Wall St. J.*, June 27, 1995, A18.

a course for tax policy in the new Congress they controlled. With Packwood's September 7 announcement of his resignation from the Senate, William Roth (Republican of Delaware) was appointed chairman of the Finance Committee by a unanimous vote of the Senate GOP Caucus on September 12. Even while more strongly committed to tax reduction than Packwood, Roth's advanced age and questionable legislative skills initially raised doubts about the ability of Republicans to shepherd their conservative tax policy agenda through the Senate. But Roth fooled his critics and turned out to be surprisingly adept in leading the Finance Committee and in avoiding being dominated by his more aggressive partisan counterparts in the House, as well as his more powerful and influential fellow Republican on the Finance Committee, Robert Dole.

Within the framework of the previously agreed figure of $245 billion in total net tax reductions over seven years, the House and Senate tax committees began the task of drafting a new tax bill. However, there were significant differences in the specifics favored by the respective chambers. Furthermore, tax reduction itself was only one element in the broader ideological initiative advanced by the Republican majority in the House. Cast within a balanced-budget reconciliation bill, tax cuts would be funded by spending reductions to be implemented over seven years. The most significant reductions were earmarked for the increasingly expensive "entitlement" social programs dating back to the New Deal and greatly expanded during the 1960s. Under the House budget plan, Medicare would be cut $270 billion and Medicaid $170 billion over the seven-year period from 1996 to 2002; welfare would be turned over to the state governments under a block-grant formula; agricultural income subsidies and price-support programs would be reduced by as much as $13.8 billion; the earned income tax credit (EITC)–the subject of much criticism by conservative Republicans throughout the year–would be scaled back in scope; and the Commerce Department would be eliminated altogether. With the budget committees controlling the overall balanced-budget initiative, the tax committees faced the difficult task of forging an agreement between House and Senate Republicans on a tax bill.

The starting point for the new House tax bill was the original Contract tax bill (H.R. 1215) adopted in January during the first days of the 104th Congress. The largest single item in the new House tax bill (H.R. 2491) was the Contract provision for the new nonrefundable $500-per-child tax credit. This "pro-family" credit was a nonnegotiable item on the platform propounded by the aggressive, highly partisan, and unified block of freshmen House Republicans. Also included in the

House bill was a refundable credit of $5,000 for expenses relating to the adoption of a child and a nonrefundable credit of $1,000 for care of a dependent parent. The Senate was lukewarm toward the $500 credit, with moderate Republicans opposed to enacting such a significant revenue loser in the midst of the effort to balance the budget. The $500 credit was scored by the Joint Committee on Tax as costing the Treasury some $147 billion over seven years.[53] This amounted to 60 percent of the total $245 billion in proposed tax cuts. Finance Committee chairman Roth's markup of the House bill included the $500 credit, but provided for a phaseout for taxpayers in the income range of $75,000 to $95,000. The House adhered to a phaseout in the range of $200,000 to $250,000. In addition, the House credit was retroactive to January 1, 1995, whereas the Senate version provided that the credit would not become effective until January 1, 1996.

The second most significant item in the House tax bill was the much ballyhooed tax preference for long-term capital gains. Republican supporters made great (and generally unsubstantiated) claims for this preference, predicting millions of new jobs and a burst of investment and economic growth attributable to a reduction in the tax on the return from capital investment.[54] For individual taxpayers, there would be an exclusion for 50 percent of long-term capitals gains (other than gain realized on "collectibles" such as artwork and jewels); the maximum tax on capital gains for corporate taxpayers would be capped at 25 percent. This preference was scored by the Joint Committee on Taxation as costing the Treasury $35 billion in revenue over seven years. With respect to capital gains, the Senate generally followed the House, except the top corporate rate was fixed at 28 percent and indexing of capital assets was left out altogether. Likewise, a House provision allowing a deduction for losses realized on the sale or exchange of a principal

53. Joint Committee on Taxation, "Estimated Budget Effects of Revenue Reconciliation and Tax Simplification Provision of H.R. 2491" (JCX-53-95), November 16, 1995.

54. While there is no empirical proof that a reduced tax on capital gains leads to such economic growth and job creation, it is quite true that taxing the return on capital (which is after-tax savings in an income tax regime) amounts to double taxation, reduces the after-tax rate of return on investment, and hence creates disincentives to saving (i.e., investment). But the question is, How much does that matter in a world economy where the overall rate of taxation in the United States compares rather favorably with the higher rates imposed by Japan and Western European nations? Prior experience with a capital gains differential tax does not indicate the kind of economic benefits touted by Republican supporters.

residence (an otherwise nondeductible personal loss) was dropped by the Finance Committee. These changes in the House capital gains provisions made by the Senate taxwriters reduced the seven-year revenue loss by over $12 billion.

The bill that emerged from the Finance Committee also deleted several much publicized provisions from the House bill. One was the repeal of the 1993 increase (from 50 percent to 85 percent) in the portion of social security benefits subject to tax (at least for high-income recipients). Another was a House provision intended to allow employer/sponsors of qualified retirement plans to withdraw "excess" contributions earmarked to fund future pension commitments to employees. The Senate taxwriters also opposed the outright repeal of the corporate alternative minimum tax included in the House bill, proposing instead an incremental reform—eliminating the onerous requirement that corporate taxpayers use a different depreciation schedule for purposes of computing tentative taxable income under the corporate AMT. Senate modifications to the House bill included an even more generous expansion of the eligibility requirements for existing IRAs, including new allowances for tax-free withdrawals for qualified expenses. Both the House and Senate bills provided for new "medical-spending accounts" modeled on IRA accounts. Senator Roth had championed IRAs throughout his tenure in the Senate; in each Congress since 1986, Roth had introduced legislation that would ease the eligibility rules for tax-free IRAs and allow for penalty-free withdrawals. Roth now used the occasion of his elevation to the chairmanship of the Finance Committee to advance his cause.

Senate majority leader Dole remained an active member of the Finance Committee even while leading his party's budget initiative and seeking its nomination for the presidency. Dole was largely responsible for adding a provision granting a new $1.5 million exemption from estate tax for family-owned businesses and farms. This exemption was on top of the House's proposal for a gradual increase in the lifetime gift and estate tax exemption to $750,000 from its current level of $600,000. Dole also sponsored a provision to classify newspaper carriers as independent contractors, as opposed to employees of the newspapers for whom they perform services—much to the advantage of the newspaper companies.

Other Republicans on the Finance Committee and Ways and Means Committee were similarly rewarded with the usual assortment of special-interest provisions tacked on revenue measures merely to satisfy the personal and professional commitments of congressional policymakers. For example, included in the House draft were three provisions targeted at helping the funeral industry. While all three provisions were quite minor and had limited revenue impact (collectively losing only $500,000 in annual revenue), the only justification for including them in the House tax bill seemed to be that four members had particularly close ties to family-run funeral businesses.[55] Provisions granting Medicare recipients the option to purchase private medical insurance, tax incentives to encourage the purchase of long-term contracts for medical care, and incentives to insurance companies to offer policies providing "accelerated death benefits" had the insurance industry all "excited."[56]

Senate Republicans had their own list of special-interest provisions buried in the massive tax bill. As Democratic senator Bill Bradley put it, if the $500-per-child credit and capital gains preference were the proclaimed "Crown Jewels" of the Republican tax plan, there was no shortage of "little baubles and bangles" for special interests. Indeed, every Republican on the Finance Committee, save for conservative presidential candidate Phil Gramm of Texas, had some special-interest provision inserted in the Senate bill. It was almost as if Bob Packwood had never left the Senate. Beneficiaries (and their respective supporters on the Finance Committee) included the aforementioned newspaper companies (Robert Dole of Kansas), small gas and electric companies (William Roth of Delaware, the home of the Delmarva Power & Light Co.), water utilities and real estate developers (Charles Grassley of Iowa), college football coaches (Orrin Hatch of Utah, a close friend of Brigham Young University's football coach), life insurance companies (Alfonse D'Amato of New York), and independent gasoline marketers (Don Nickles of Oklahoma).[57]

Both tax committees finished their work late in the month. On October 26, the House passed the Ways and Means Committee bill by a 227-to-203 margin, with voting following partisan divisions. The Finance Committee approved the chairman's bill by a 11-to-9 vote that followed strict party lines. The full Senate passed the Finance Committee bill on

55. For an account of how these provisions made their way into the House tax bill, see Glenn R. Simpson, "Budget-Cutting Bill Calls for Breaks That Would Aid Funeral Industry," *Wall St. J.*, December 7, 1995, A16, col. 1.

56. The insurance-industry provisions are the subject of Christina Duff, "Insurance Industry's Lobbying and Donations Pay Off Handsomely in Balanced-Budget Bill," *Wall St. J.*, December 18, 1995, A16, col. 1. A spokesman for the American Council of Life Insurance was quoted as saying in reference to these new pro-industry provisions: "We're excited about this."

57. See Jackie Calmes, "GOP Tax Plan Is Cheered by Football Coaches, Convenience Stores and Various Other Interests," *Wall St. J.*, October 24, 1995, A24, col. 1. Calmes provides an excellent account of how the special-interest provisions were inserted into the tax bill by Senate Finance Committee members.

October 28 by a 52-to-47 vote, with all Democrats voting against the bill and all Republicans save for William Cohen of Maine voting in favor. Immediately before the Senate vote, majority leader Dole agreed to include amendments proposed by moderate Senate Republicans intended to soften the blow of the Medicare spending cuts. Dole also supported an amendment to the Finance Committee bill that raised the deduction for medical insurance for self-employed persons to 55 percent from 30 percent.

Only days after the two chambers adopted their respective tax bills, House and Senate tax conferees convened to commence the delicate process of crafting a compromise bill suitable to Republicans in both chambers. They were successful in working up a compromise bill by mid-November. The conferees largely followed the House on key issues, although on several important matters the Senate prevailed. For example, the Conference Committee's bill included the $500-per-child credit, but it was retroactive only to October 1, 1995 (as Senate conferees urged and revenue constraints dictated). The Senate conferees also prevailed in lowering the phaseout threshold for the $500 credit and in retaining the corporate AMT (giving up only the depreciation-simplification provision to appease corporate taxpayers). The final bill included a provision that had originated on the Senate side providing for the repeal of the 50 percent exclusion for interest received by banks and insurance companies from loans used to leverage corporate ESOPs. Repeal of this exclusion had first been proposed by Ways and Means Committee chairman Rostenkowski in 1989, but was defeated by lobbyists for major corporations that benefited from management-dominated ESOPs in fending off hostile takeovers by corporate raiders.

On most other significant issues, the House had its way. This was especially true with respect to the campaign to reinstate a preferential tax rate for capital gains. The 50 percent deduction was adopted in conformance with the original Contract provision. The preference would be retroactive to December 31, 1994, and indexing of capital assets would be phased in by the year 2002. Other Contract tax provisions that were adopted in the final bill included the deduction for capital losses realized on the sale of a principal residence,[58] increasing the $600,000 gift and estate tax exemption to $750,000, increasing the annual expensing allowance for small businesses, expanding the coverage of IRAs, and

58. For a discussion of this and other provisions in the bill pertaining to the taxation of gain realized on the sale or exchange of a principal residence, see Sheldon D. Pollack, "Technical Corrections to IRC Sections 1034 and 121: Victims of the Balanced Budget," 70 *Tax Notes* 589 (January 29, 1995).

reducing the so-called marriage penalty. The final bill also included a major effort to simplify provisions governing pension plans and the taxation of Subchapter S corporations. The Subchapter-S-simplification package had originally appeared in the ill-fated 1992 tax bill vetoed by President Bush, and subsequently was the object of considerable lobbying in its behalf by the American Institute of Certified Public Accountants (AICPA), which strongly favored relaxing the complex rules governing the taxation of Subchapter S corporations.

Conferees also inserted into the tax bill a separate bill, previously enacted by the House (H.R. 2494), introducing changes to the tax treatment of bad debt reserves by thrift financial institutions. The provision, which was also previously approved by a "sense of the Senate" resolution, would require thrifts to use the same method of accounting for their bad debts as commercial banks, but would also reduce the tax cost of such conversion to soften the impact. The overall measure was projected to bring in some $1 billion of revenue in its first year.

The Conference Committee's tax bill was included in, and in many respects was submerged by, the Republicans' massive legislative effort to "reform" Medicaid and Medicare and balance the federal budget by the year 2002. The omnibus revenue and budget bill reported out by the budget committees, known as the Seven-Year Balanced Budget Reconciliation Act of 1995, passed the House by a vote of 237 to 189 on November 17, 1995. The Senate followed suit later that same day, adding to the Medicare provisions a minor amendment that was thereafter agreed to by the House on November 20, 1995. Senate Democrats, led by Senator Daniel Patrick Moynihan, ranking minority member of the Finance Committee, argued that the seven-year balanced budget was a sham, since the true impact of the tax cuts would not be felt for at least ten years. In remarks on the floor of the Senate on November 27, Moynihan declared that "the explosion in the long-term revenue costs of these tax cuts results from the attempt to hide their true impact" by intentionally drafting them to fall outside the seven-year period covered by the bill.[59] This was true enough and substantiated by the revenue estimates of the CBO and JCT, but nevertheless it was entirely beside

---

59. Quoted in Lauren Darling, "10-Year Cost of Tax-Plan 'Astounding,' Sen Moynihan Says," *Daily Tax Rep.* (Bureau of National Affairs), no. 230, November 30, 1995, G-3. Moynihan pointed to three provisions in the Republican bill that would lead to much increased revenue losses in the years after the seven-year plan: the capital gains preference for individual taxpayers, the expansion of IRAs, and the increased exemptions for estate taxation.

the point. The Seven-Year Balanced Budget Reconciliation Act expressed the partisan ideology of congressional Republicans and was not to be denied by such minor trifles as economic facts.

On November 30, 1995, soon after it was approved by the GOP majorities in both chambers, the Seven-Year Balanced Budget Reconciliation Act was presented to President Clinton, who followed through with his oft-repeated promise and vetoed the legislation on December 6. The president specifically attributed his action to the $270 billion reduction in Medicare spending and $163 billion reduction in Medicaid spending over seven years. In his veto message, Clinton declared: "I am returning herewith without my approval H.R. 2491, the budget reconciliation bill adopted by the Republican majority, which seeks to make extreme cuts and other unacceptable changes in Medicare and Medicaid, and to raise taxes on millions of working Americans. . . . While making such devastating cuts in Medicare, Medicaid, and other vital programs, this bill would provide huge tax cuts for those who are already the most well-off."[60]

Anticipating the president's veto of the Republican budget plan, economic advisers within the administration (Laura Tyson, assistant to the president for economic policy; Gene Sperling, deputy assistant to the president for economic policy; and OMB director Alice Rivlin) had already been busy drafting the outline for a new White House budget—the third offered by the White House for the year. Clinton expressed willingness to compromise on at least some of the major issues included in the Republican bill. Specifically, the president accepted the idea of a balanced budget to be achieved over seven years (down from his prior commitment to a ten-year timetable), some form of a child credit (in the White House's version starting at $300 for each child under age 13, rising to $500 in 1999, with a phaseout for taxpayers earning between $65,000 and $70,000 a year), a new $5,000 deduction for educational tuition, acceptance of a higher income phaseout range for existing IRA saving accounts, and new IRA-styled savings accounts with penalty-free "back-end" withdrawals for qualified expenses.

The White House benefited from the assistance of Senator Moynihan in redrafting three proposals the Democrats had been touting all year. These provided a tax on gain inherent in the property of expatriating U.S. citizens, modifications to the tax treatment of foreign grantor trusts, and some minor adjustments to the EITC. The Democratic president now also accepted in principle deeper cuts in discretionary spending than he previously had. The White House plan called for reducing Medicare spending by $124 billion over seven years (although still authorizing $1.5 trillion in expenditures over seven years) instead of the $270 billion reduction called for by Republicans (who themselves authorized spending $1.42 trillion during the same period—hardly amounting to "decimating" the program, as Democrats charged).

Overall, the president's plan was projected to provide $105 billion in gross tax cuts over seven years, offset by $35 billion in additional revenues to be raised over the same period. This demonstrated just how far House Republicans had come in shifting the framework for the political debate. Still, the White House held firm on some issues, leaving out entirely any preference for capital gains, increases in estate tax exemptions, and changes to the corporate AMT—perhaps to gain some additional bargaining room in the forthcoming negotiations. The White House plan embraced several GOP revenue raisers from H.R. 2491, including the disallowance of interest deductions on corporate-owned life insurance (COLI) policy loans, the legislation designed to encourage thrifts to convert to chartered banks, and a provision designed to reverse the favorable tax result achieved by Seagram Co. in a well-publicized and much-criticized transaction in April 1995 in which Dupont Co. paid an extraordinary stock "dividend" on its stock held by Seagram.[61] The administration also proposed several new provisions aimed at corporate taxpayers that would raise $20 billion over seven years. These included limiting the carryback of net operating losses to one year (down from the current three), restricting the use of so-called captive insurance companies, reducing the "dividends-received" deduction (available to corporations owning less than 20 percent of the stock of another corporation) from 70 percent to 50 percent, and phasing out one major component of the section 936 "possessions" tax credit.[62] Another provision announced separately by the Treasury Department proposed eliminating a deduction by corporations for interest paid on bonds with a maturity date of

61. For a description and analysis of this transaction, see Lee A. Sheppard, "Can Seagram Bail Out of Dupont Without Capital Gains Tax?" 67 *Tax Notes* 325 (April 17, 1995); see also Allan Sloan, "For Seagram and Dupont, a Tax Deal That No One Wants to Bandy About," *Wash. Post*, April 11, 1995.

62. For a description of the White House tax proposals, see Lauren Darling, "Clinton's Budget Plan Takes Aim At 'Abusive' Corporate Loopholes," *Daily Tax Rep.* (Bureau of National Affairs), no. 236, December 8, 1995, G-10.

more than forty years. The mere announcement of Treasury's intentions put an immediate halt to several planned issues of hundred-year bonds, which had become the rage on Wall Street because they provided corporate issuers with all the tax benefits of debt instruments but otherwise offered the preferable features of equity on a corporate balance sheet.[63]

The disagreement between the White House and congressional Republicans extended to the economic assumptions that supported the parties' respective plans for balancing the budget. Congressional Republicans relied upon the relatively conservative economic forecast of the Congressional Budget Office (now in Republican control under Director June O'Neill), which predicted a slightly lower rate of annual growth for the economy than did the Office of Management and Budget (OMB), which itself was more conservative than most Wall Street economists. At the time, private economists on Wall Street were predicting annual growth (adjusted for inflation) somewhere in the range of 2.8 to 3.0 percent. The White House used OMB projections forecasting a 2.5 percent annual growth rate, while congressional Republicans relied upon the 2.3 percent rate that CBO had projected in April 1995. This seemingly minor 0.2 percent difference between the CBO and OMB economic forecasts required $400 billion in extra cuts under the congressional plan in order to bring the budget into balance by the year 2002. The impasse was bridged to some extent when CBO revised its economic assumptions in a new December report.[64] In its new report, CBO anticipated greater corporate profits over seven years (resulting in increased revenues from corporate taxes), based upon lower interest rates attributable to the balanced budget itself. The April 1995 CBO report had assumed that pretax corporate profits as a percentage of gross domestic product (GDP) would be 6.7 percent in 2002; the revised CBO report restated this figure upward to 8.0 percent.

CBO's more rosy economic forecast meant that there would be an extra $135 billion in revenue to play with, thereby closing the gap

---

63. The impact of the Treasury announcement on Wall Street practices is the subject of Christina Duff, "Tax Provisions Would Hurt Wall Street," *Wall St. J.*, December 8, 1995, A3, col. 1; see also Stephanie Strom, "Citing Tax Proposal, Monsanto Drops Plan for 100-Year Bonds," *N.Y. Times*, December 9, 1995, 37.

64. CBO memorandum, "The Economic and Budget Outlook: December 1995 Update," released December 11, 1995. For a discussion of the political implications of the economic assumptions in the CBO report, see Christopher Georges, "New Estimates Help Shrink Deficit Gap, but Budget Gap Talks Still Have Far to Go," *Wall St. J.*, December 12, 1995, A2, A8.

between congressional Republicans and the Democratic White House to only $300 billion over seven years. Furthermore, bipartisan agreement was reached for a technical modification to the apparently overstated cost-of-living adjustments (COLA) provided to social security recipients under the 1983 amendments. This modification (supported by a host of reputable economists) would result in a 0.2 percent annual reduction in the consumer price index (CPI) as determined by the Bureau of Labor Statistics, and free up an additional $31 billion of revenue over seven years. This extra revenue would help achieve a balanced budget, even accepting the reduced cuts to Medicaid and Medicare spending demanded by Democrats. Based upon the new economic assumptions released by CBO, Medicare savings under the Republican plan dropped to $226 billion (down from the original projection of $270 billion) and Medicaid savings to $133 billion (down from $163 billion) over seven years.[65]

Attempts to reach agreement between Congress and the White House on an overall balanced-budget plan continued throughout the second week of December. The federal government had already been partially shutdown for six days starting November 14, with some 800,000 "nonessential" federal workers kept off the job. A temporary spending measure had been adopted by Democrats and Republicans to bring federal employees back on the job and avert a default on federal debt obligations, but this authorization lasted only until December 15.[66] In the end, even the threat of another shutdown could not push the parties to compromise. Negotiations ended abruptly, and the federal government again shut down following the expiration of the temporary spending measure at midnight on December 15.

The December shutdown was more limited than that in November, since nine of the thirteen required appropriations bills were actually in place. This was no "train wreck," just a slight derailment. Still, a number of cabinet departments (including Interior, Labor, and Health

65. The revised revenue estimates based on the new December 1995 CBO baseline were included in Joint Committee on Taxation, "Estimated Budget Effects of Revenue Reconciliation and Tax Simplification Provisions of H.R. 2491" (JCX-55-95), December 12, 1995.

66. H.R. 2586, approved by the House Ways and Means Committee on November 7, 1995, increased the statutory limit on the public debt to $4.95 trillion for debt outstanding before December 13, 1995. This was less than the increase to $5.5 trillion included in the Republican's budget reconciliation bill (H.R. 2491), but provided a few weeks breathing room for negotiations between the White House and Congress.

and Human Services) and independent agencies (such as the Environmental Protection Agency and the National Aeronautics and Space Administration) were unfunded and, hence, forced to close down operations. The impact was mostly felt by foreign tourists who were denied access to federal parks and monuments. Negotiations peaked and ebbed the week before Christmas. But in the wake of a threatened revolt by House Republican freshmen against their more "moderate" leadership, positions hardened. Republicans declared that budget talks could not continue until the president negotiated in "good faith"—meaning on their terms.[67] Negotiations reached deadlock. The December recess came, the government remained shut down, and the first session of the 104th Congress ended with neither a budget in place for fiscal year 1996 nor *any* tax-reduction legislation.

Despite the express intention of all parties to "deal," House Republicans and the White House dug their respective heels in and resisted compromise. After much concession, the president finally refused to concede anything more. And why not? One poll taken in early December indicated that 44 percent of the public supported the president's budget stance, whereas only 41 percent favored the budget proposed by congressional Republicans. The same poll found that less than one in ten respondents saw "lowering taxes on the middle class" as the top domestic-policy goal.[68] Rather than lead a ground swell of popular discontent with taxes, congressional Republicans seemed intent upon creating one themselves—to say nothing of beating the incumbent Democratic president into submission.

What, then, went wrong for Republican tax policy in 1995? First, House Republicans refused to follow the most basic rule of postwar tax policymaking: When you actually want to pass a tax bill, rather than just grandstand, you must provide some benefits to *everyone*. Logrolling is the essence of the politics of the federal income tax; it is not sufficient to offer benefits only to those among the party faithful. This strategy works fine in game theory, which holds that a "minimum-maximum" winning coalition will offer the slimmest majority the greatest "spoils" to share among themselves. But it is a risky strategy in tax policymaking. With an apparently secure majority behind him in the House,

67. Senate majority leader Dole called the president's position "garbage." Quoted in David E. Rosenbaum, "With No Budget, Clinton and Republicans Pass the Blame," *N.Y. Times*, December 17, 1995, 40.

68. The result of this *Wall Street Journal*/NBC News poll were reported in the *Wall St. J.*, December 8, 1995, A1, col. 5.

Speaker Gingrich was in a reasonable position to restrict the benefits of the tax bill to his own "mini-max" coalition. But that would not work in the Senate, where moderate Republicans made it impossible to hold together a strictly conservative coalition. And even in the House, Democratic support ultimately would be needed to have any chance in overriding the inevitable presidential veto. But with every provision in the tax bill targeted at either the conservative Republicans or their pro-business, pro-family constituents, there was simply nothing in it for the Democrats. In the short run, moderate Republicans had no place to go, and so they stayed (for the moment, at least) with their more conservative GOP leadership. But with no inducements for Democrats to join the coalition, the highly partisan House tax bill went as far as it could go—to a losing showdown with the Democratic president, who felt that he could be pushed no further. With little offered to the White House by the way of compromise, anything short of a presidential veto would have thoroughly alienated the president from the rank and file of his own party.

The special-interest provisions of 1995 tax bill were, however, consistent with modern tax policymaking. Any tax bill of the enormous magnitude of the 1995 effort is sure to include a host of such provisions buried deep in the mire. No single legislator can maintain control over the tax-legislative process where the bill touches upon so many sections of the tax code and amends so much of current tax law. With the tax bill itself submerged within a massive budget bill that would abolish entire cabinet departments and rewrite programs such as Medicare and Medicaid all at once, it was impossible to comprehend all aspects of the legislative effort. This allowed members of the tax committees, as well as party leadership (be it Republican or Democrat), to slip in provisions that would aid their own favored constituents. Likewise, it meant that when it came time for individual legislators to vote on the single omnibus bill, they were forced to do so without very much knowledge of what was in the package. For better or worse, this forced them to rely upon party leadership for signals regarding how they should vote.

On the other hand, as in 1986, policymakers have somewhat more freedom to take on special-interest groups in such a massive tax bill, especially where the driving force behind the bill is ideology. In 1986, lobbyists for special interests were caught off guard by the sheer magnitude of the tax-reform enterprise. Likewise, in 1995, even the American Medical Association (AMA) and the American Association of Retired Persons (AARP) were unable to resist the Republican initiative to reverse the half century of steady expansion in spending for the New Deal social welfare programs. In the end, it was the president's veto, and not the lobbyists cajoling, that prevented their effort from succeeding.

Why then did Republican congressional leaders spurn compromise with the White House, at least to enact what would have amounted to a fair share of their program? Perhaps they believed that they could orchestrate a replay of 1948, when Republicans took control of the House and Senate for the first time in decades, battled a Democratic president, and ultimately succeeded in overriding President Truman's third veto of their tax-reduction bill (which became the Revenue Act of 1948). But in 1948, Republicans had substantial support from Southern conservative Democrats. No such bipartisan coalition was crafted in 1995. As a result, there was no Republican tax bill at all in 1995. Still, the political battle lines had been drawn and partisan positions carefully staked out, assuring that the GOP's initiative to cut taxes and reduce entitlement spending would dominate the policy agenda during the second session of the 104th Congress and define the debate in the forthcoming 1996 presidential contest.

Alternatives to the Income Tax

In the final months of 1994, a number of tax proposals other than those included in the Contract with America also began working their way onto the policy agenda. Perhaps the most significant were proposals to abandon the income tax altogether and replace it with some form of a flat consumption-based tax. Proponents of the various forms of consumption taxes have been preaching the gospel in Washington for decades. In the 1980s, a flat consumption tax was the subject of a highly influential study by two academics at Stanford's Hoover Institution, economist Robert Hall and political scientist Alvin Rabushka.[69] Hall and Rabushka were the original "policy entrepreneurs" behind the flat tax, and though largely ignored in the late 1980s, their plan reappeared with a vengeance on the tax policy agenda in the 1990s. Interest in the flat con-

---

69. Hall and Rabushka first proposed their flat consumption tax in a 1981 article in the *Wall Street Journal* and later developed it into a full proposal in Alvin Rabushka and Robert E. Hall, *Low Tax, Simple Tax, Flat Tax* (New York: McGraw-Hill, 1983). The argument was subsequently refined in *The Flat Tax* (Stanford, Calif.: Hoover Institution Press, 1985), an updated edition of which was reissued in 1995.

sumption taxes was renewed, and proponents saw their first serious opportunity for success in the political arena.

As the legitimacy and revenue-raising capacity of the federal income tax came to be increasingly questioned, all sorts of radical statements in favor of abandoning it became common fare. This sentiment was reflected in the many legislative proposals, as well as academic articles, devoted to the consumption tax. Actually, there are several different types of consumption taxes, and scholars have their own cottage industry generating a considerable literature covering all the possibilities.[70] The main examples of "direct" consumption taxes include excise taxes, sales taxes, and the value-added tax (VAT). Excise taxes are essentially consumption taxes imposed upon particular commodities (e.g., cigarettes, alcohol, gasoline, or such luxury items as yachts or furs). Sales taxes are imposed upon sales of broad categories of commodities or services. The VAT is a variation on a sales tax most common in Europe and recently adopted by New Zealand and Canada. In the case of Canada, the national sales tax took the form of the much abhorred Goods and Services Tax, adopted in 1991, much to the delight of cigarette smugglers. The VAT is imposed upon the value added to a particular commodity by businesses engaged in the various stages of the manufacturing process (i.e., the tax is essentially imposed upon the difference between a business's gross income from sales and services and its outlays for raw materials). Ultimately, the "cost" of the tax is borne by the final consumer of the good. The basic feature common to all of these taxes (sales, excise, and VAT) is that they are imposed upon the consumption of goods and services, rather than on savings. This feature is shared in common with a so-called expenditure tax, which is a consumption tax imposed upon individuals, rather than on the sellers or manufacturers of goods. An expenditure tax may be structured following a "cash-flow"

---

70. For a broad discussion of the various forms of consumption taxes, see Joseph A. Pechman, *Federal Tax Policy,* 5th ed. (Washington, D.C.: Brookings Institution, 1987), chap. 6 ("Consumption Taxes"); see also Nicholas Kaldor, *An Expenditure Tax* (London: Allen & Unwin, 1955); Alice Rivlin, ed., *Economic Choices 1984* (Washington, D.C.: Brookings Institution, 1981); David G. Davies, *United States Taxes and Tax Policy* (New York: Cambridge University Press, 1986), 77–90; Peter Mieszkowski, "The Choice of Tax Base: Consumption Versus Income Taxation," in *Federal Tax Reform: Myths and Realities,* ed. Michael J. Boskin (San Francisco: Institute of Contemporary Studies, 1978), 27–54; David F. Bradford, *Untangling the Income Tax* (Cambridge: Harvard University Press, 1986), 59–99.

model, with taxation imposed upon the net consumption of the individual over the year.[71]

Other forms of consumption taxes also began to attract serious attention in the early 1990s. A national sales tax was raised during the first months of the Clinton presidency as a means for raising new revenue to finance the administration's ill-fated health-care reforms. Although that particular justification expired with the Clinton health-care initiative itself, strong interest in a sales tax or a European-style value-added tax persists. For example, Representative Sam Gibbons of Florida, ranking Democrat on the Ways and Means Committee, has been a long-time supporter of some form of VAT. Senator Richard G. Lugar (Republican of Indiana), would-be Republican presidential candidate for 1996, became an ardent supporter of a national sales tax to replace the income tax. A sales tax is one form of a consumption tax in that it is imposed on the sale (and presumably consumption) of goods and commodities, and if imposed only on sales at retail (but not the various intermediate stages of production or manufacture), it should have economic effects similar to a VAT. Lugar proposed a flat 17 percent sales tax on all goods and services (excepting food and medicine, to mitigate the overall "regressive" impact of a sales tax). But some economists figure that to raise the same level of revenue as the current income tax, at least a 21 percent rate would need be imposed if food and medicine were exempted, and something in the order of 27 percent would be needed if housing were also exempted.[72]

71. For a description of such a tax, see William D. Andrews, "A Consumption-Type or Cash Flow Personal Income Tax," 87 *Harv. L. Rev.* 1113 (1974). A recent defense is found in Laurence S. Seidman, "A Better Way to Tax," 114 *Pub. Interest* 65 (1994).

72. See William Gale, "Building a Better Tax System: Can a Consumption Tax Deliver the Goods?" 69 *Tax Notes* 781 (November 6, 1995); see also Bruce Bartlett, "Replacing Federal Taxes with a Sales Tax," 68 *Tax Notes* 997 (August 21, 1995). The Joint Economic Committee calculated that a tax rate of 27.7 percent would be needed to replace the revenue from current federal taxes collected by the IRS; a rate of 32 to 65 percent would be needed if personal services and personal-care goods (such as food, clothing, and medical supplies) were excluded from the tax base. Joint Economic Committee, "Consequences of Replacing Federal Taxes with a Sales Tax," August 18, 1995. Federal Reserve governor Lawrence Lindsey, himself a noted Republican supply-side economist, expressed caution and warned that the central bank would run into difficulties in adjusting monetary policy if the income tax was replaced with a national sales tax. See "Switch to a Sales Tax Would Present Challenge to Fed," *Daily Tax Rep.* (Bureau of National Affairs), no. 206, October 25, 1995, G-7.

Perhaps all this reflects the depth of dissatisfaction with the income tax as much as the pressures now felt by federal policymakers to find new sources of revenue. The commitment to the flat tax among Republicans certainly reflects the persistent rejection of the progressive income tax among the party faithful. Unexpectedly strong support for a consumption tax or value-added tax or both was expressed in the fall of 1994 by members of the Bipartisan Commission on Entitlement and Tax Reform, which expired on December 15 without reaching any consensus on either cutting entitlements or reforming the income tax. Nevertheless, a surprising number of prominent commission members seemed to favor junking the income tax for a consumption tax. For instance, Sam Gibbons, then acting chairman of the House Ways and Means Committee (following Dan Rostenkowski's resignation), used the commission as a platform from which to announce his support for a broad-based value-added tax to replace the individual and corporate income taxes, as well as payroll taxes. Co-chairman of the commission, Senator J. Robert Kerry (Democrat of Nebraska), simply declared that "Americans are fed up with the current tax system, [and] they do not want us to merely tinker around the edges."[73] Senator Boren similarly took the opportunity to express his interest in a consumption tax, based upon his belief (undoubtedly erroneous) that such a tax would be more "simple" and administrable compared with the current income tax.

Several serious legislative proposals for consumption-like taxes surfaced in the waning days of the 103d Congress, and these had considerable appeal within both political parties. Senators David L. Boren (Democrat of Oklahoma) and John C. Danforth (Republican of Missouri), both of whom retired with the close of the 103d Congress, sponsored a proposal for a "business activity tax" (BAT).[74] In 1994, Senators Sam Nunn (Democrat of Georgia) and Pete Domenici (Republican of New Mexico) sponsored a proposal for a so-called Universal Savings Allowance, which has features similar to a consumption tax.[75] The latter

73. Quoted in John Godfrey, "Bipartisan Commission Members Favor a Consumption Tax," 65 *Tax Notes* 154 (October 10, 1994).

74. The Boren-Danforth proposal is examined in great detail in Oliver Oldman and Alan Schenk, "The BAT: Is It a Better Value Added Tax?" 65 *Tax Notes* 1547 (December 19, 1994).

75. Senator Domenici presented a convincing and detailed defense of his proposal in "The Unamerican Spirit of the Federal Income Tax," 31 *Harv. J. on Legis.* 273 (1994). The chief intellectual force behind the plan was Ernest Christian, former deputy assistant

was reintroduced in the Senate by Nunn and Domenici in April 1995 as the USA Tax Act of 1995 – a full-blown replacement for the individual and corporate income taxes. The central features of the Nunn-Domenici proposal included a flat 11 percent tax on the "gross profit" of all businesses (both corporate and unincorporated alike); a credit for both businesses and individuals for Social Security (FICA) taxes; an exclusion for income earned from sales outside the United States; and a progressive consumption-like tax on individuals. The latter would be imposed at rates ranging from 19 percent to 40 percent on the taxable income of individuals (wages and capital gains, with a family allowance and personal exemptions, and deductions allowed for savings, mortgage interest, charitable contributions, and alimony). This tax as it applies to individuals would have characteristics of both a consumption tax (on account of the unlimited deduction for savings) and an income tax. While well respected for its thoroughness and comprehensive approach, the Nunn-Domenici plan is neither simpler nor more attractive politically than the present income tax regime. Hence, it has generally been viewed more as a creative exercise than as a viable political alternative. That is not the case with some of the other proposals for consumption taxes given consideration by the 104th Congress.

The most important proposal for a flat consumption tax surfaced even before the 1994 elections. Representative Richard K. Armey (Republican of Texas) introduced a proposal for a flat 17 percent tax the prior summer.[76] Armey's bill (H.R. 4585), the Freedom and Fairness Restoration Act of 1994, received only minor notice before the November elections. However, for obvious reasons, the plan attracted much more attention following the 1994 elections once Armey emerged as the heir apparent House majority leader. Armey's proposal would phase in a 17 percent flat tax imposed on the wages (and pension distributions) of an individual in excess of relatively high standard deductions ($13,100 for a single taxpayer and $26,200 for a married couple filing jointly) and generous dependent allowances of $5,300. None of the traditional deductions of the current income tax system would be allowed. Business

---

secretary (tax policy) of the Treasury Department in the early 1980s. Christian defends the hybrid tax in "Good Intentions Do Not a Tax System Make," 69 *Tax Notes* 1041 (November 20, 1995), and "The Tax Restructuring Phenomenon," 48 *Nat'l Tax J.* 373 (1995).

76. Armey described his flat tax proposal (introduced as H.R. 4585) in an article in *Commonsense*, a Republican policy journal published by GOP chairman Haley Barbour's National Policy Forum. Richard K. Armey, "The Flat Tax: Restoring Freedom and Fairness," 1 *Commonsense* 48 (1994).

activity would likewise be taxed at the same 17 percent rate, with the tax imposed on the businesses's "gross active income," which would *not* include investment income. Thus, the tax on individuals would be "progressive" to the extent that average tax rates rise in proportion to the individual's income, and the overall tax base would be consumption (rather than income) because the return on capital investment would not be taxed. Overall, the intent of the bill was to integrate the taxation of individuals with that of business (by allowing a deduction to businesses for wages paid) and to tax earned income only once at the same flat rate (with individuals benefiting from the standard deduction and personal exemptions). That the flat tax is in substance a broad-based consumption tax should be no surprise, since the Armey plan was expressly modeled on the Hall-Rabushka flat tax plan.

Following the success of Armey's proposal in attracting considerable and unexpectedly favorable attention, Republican presidential hopeful Senator Arlen Specter of Pennsylvania introduced his own flat tax proposal substantially similar to that of Armey—the key differences being a flat 20 percent rate, lower personal exemptions, and limited deductions for charitable contributions and home mortgage interest.[77] In January 1995, House minority leader Richard A. Gephardt (Democrat of Missouri) proposed a plan for a flat (or flatter) income tax to be imposed at a 10 to 11 percent rate on all but the wealthiest 20 percent of American taxpayers.[78] Thereafter, on July 6, 1995, Gephardt did an about-face, putting forth a new proposal, this time for an income tax reform bill that would lower the top marginal rates and virtually eliminate all deductions except for home mortgage interest.[79] Under the Gephardt plan, no deduction would be allowed for state or local taxes or for charitable contributions. The tax credits for child care would be repealed, while the earned income and foreign tax credits would be retained. Capital gains would be taxed at the same rates as ordinary income, while fringe benefits and employer-provided health insurance would all be taxable. Employer contributions to pension plans would be taxed (and deducted) when contributed. The Gephardt plan was the only

77. Specter's flat tax proposal (S. 488) and a detailed defense can be found at *Congressional Record*, 104th Cong., 1st sess. (May 2, 1995), 141, no. 39, S3416.

78. Gephardt's proposal, a complete about-face on his position stated before the November 1994 elections, was made on January 10, 1995, as reported in R. A. Zaldivar, "In Shift, Gephardt Calls for a Flat Tax," *Phila. Inquirer*, January 11, 1995, A1, col 1.

79. Gephardt further elaborated on his tax plan in "The 10% Solution," *N.Y. Times*, July 13, 1995, A23.

Democratic alternative to the various Republican proposals because the Clinton administration resisted joining the chorus for repeal of the income tax or even for any significant tax reform. White House aides apparently advised the president to stay out of the fray, fearing the popular backlash from any attempt to repeal such popular individual tax preferences as the deductions for interest on a home mortgage and charitable contributions, as well as the exemptions for fringe benefits and health insurance.[80] Treasury secretary Robert E. Rubin repeatedly expressed the administration's opposition to proposals for replacing the income tax with a flat tax, as well as "deep misgivings about the potential economic risks of comprehensive tax reform."[81]

The success of the Armey and Specter proposals in attracting media attention was enhanced considerably by the fact that Ways and Means Committee chairman Archer emerged as one of the most ardent antagonists of the current income tax.[82] Following the November landslide, Archer declared, "I firmly believe that we've got to look at a new way of raising revenue than the income tax."[83] Later, Archer was appointed chairman of the House Ways and Means Committee and expressed his utter contempt for the federal income tax: "I personally would like to tear the income tax out by its roots and throw it overboard."[84] Archer continued his campaign against the income tax even while markup on the Contract tax preferences proceeded through Ways and Means.

Senate Finance Committee chairman Packwood was considerably more cautious in endorsing any of these flat tax proposals. Nevertheless, Packwood held well-publicized hearings on the topic and eventually expressed sympathy for the general concept of switching to a consumption-based tax, although he included so many qualifications (such as

80. Clay Chandler, "Clinton Aides See Risks in Tax Reform," *Wash. Post*, July 11, 1995, D1.

81. "Rubin Criticizes Flat Tax; Other Reform Proposals," 68 *Tax Notes* 787 (August 14, 1995). Later, Treasury assistant secretary (tax policy) Leslie B. Samuels would advance the administration's case against the flat tax. See Fred Stokeld, "Samuels Says Flat Tax Would Help the Rich and Hurt the Middle Class," 69 *Tax Notes* 7 (October 2, 1995).

82. Archer's rise to the top of the House tax committee is recounted in Alissa J. Rubin, "Archer: A Quiet Conservative with an Explosive Agenda," *Cong. Q.*, August 12, 1995, 2426; see also Jackie Calmes, "Rep. Bill Archer Is Stepping into the Limelight As New GOP Catches Up with His Conservatism," *Wall St. J.*, September 18, 1995, A20.

83. Quoted in *Daily Tax Rep.* (Bureau of National Affairs), no. 218, November 15, 1994, G-6.

84. Quoted in Barbara Kirchheimer, "Archer Addresses Contract Compromises and Reform," 66 *Tax Notes* 1083 (February 20, 1995).

preserving the current treatment of interest income and employee bene-fits) as to leave in doubt his commitment.[85] For his part, Senate majority leader Dole expressed much the same message in the midst of his presidential campaign. Dole occasionally threw sharp arrows at the income tax, going so far as to urge the elimination of the Internal Revenue Service[86] and on occasion the demise of the income tax.[87] But on the whole, Dole seemed content to have his more radical Republican brethren lead the battle against the income tax.

Pressure from Dole's right was exerted by another Republican presi-dential contender, Senator Phil Gramm of Texas. Gramm, who filled the seat on the Finance Committee left open by Packwood's resignation from the Senate, campaigned on a platform of a balanced budget, a flat tax, and repeal of all federal estate taxes.[88] But the strongest antitax rhetoric came from long-shot Republican candidate Steve Forbes, who entered the race in September with a simple and persistent message, urging voters to "[scrap] the income tax. Don't fiddle with it. Junk it. Throw it out. Bury it. Replace it with a pro-growth, pro-family tax cut that lowers tax rates to 17 percent across the board."[89] Beyond such rhetoric, Forbes offered few specifics in his antitax campaign.

Both the Armey and Specter plans for a flat tax presuppose that all the many "special-interest" provisions will be stripped out of the tax code. Ironically, this is the stuff that liberal economists at the Brookings Insti-tution have been dreaming of for decades but never would have believed politically feasible. In fact, the flat tax may not be *economically* feasible. The Treasury Department quickly put something of a damper on Armey's plan; it estimated that a 17 percent flat tax would cost $244 billion in lost revenue a year. Treasury initially calculated that a 25.8 percent flat tax would be needed to achieve "revenue neutrality."[90] Later, the Joint Committee on Taxation issued its own highly critical analysis of the flat

85. See, e.g., "Packwood Supports a Flat Tax," 68 *Tax Notes* 521 (July 31, 1995).

86. See "Dole Pushes For Elimination of Internal Revenue Service," *Daily Tax Rep.* (Bureau of National Affairs), no. 206, October 25, 1995, G-12.

87. John Harwood, "Dole Proposes 'Radical Tax Simplification,' " *Wall St. J.*, Septem-ber 6, 1995, A3, col. 4.

88. See "Gramm Promises End to Estate Tax, Calls for Balanced Budget and Flat Tax," *Daily Tax Rep.* (Bureau of National Affairs), no. 201, October 18, 1995, G-3.

89. Steve Forbes, "Presidential Announcement Speech," National Press Club, Sep-tember 22, 1995.

90. Reported in Barbara Kirchheimer, "Armey Flat Tax Panned by Treasury," 65 *Tax Notes* 655 (November 7, 1994).

tax proposals–specifically focusing on the Specter plan.[91] Notwithstanding such criticism, the flat tax has considerable support, especially within the business community. Furthermore, the pro-business lobbying group Citizens for a Sound Economy (CSE) launched an aggressive $500,000 national campaign to drum up support within the business community for the Armey flat tax proposal. Direct mailings of CSE proclaimed the simplicity and "fairness" of the flat tax and also stressed that the new tax would "reduce the individual income taxes of virtually all Americans." This is true in that a good deal of the individual income tax is shifted to business under the Armey plan and in that the overall plan, compared to the current tax system, comes up about $200 billion short annually.

To help Republicans sift through the various proposals on the table, Senate majority leader Dole and Speaker Gingrich appointed former housing secretary and member of the House Jack Kemp to chair the National Commission on Economic Growth and Tax Reform. The appointment of the commission was timed so that its recommendations would be issued right before the 1996 presidential campaign kicked into full swing–assuring that the flat tax issue would be on the policy agenda for the foreseeable future. By the close of 1995, it already was apparent that the so-called Kemp Commission would recommend a version of the flat tax and support a full-fledged, comprehensive tax-reform plan.[92]

The primary argument advanced by economists in favor of consumption taxation rests upon the assertion that there are significant advantages to be gained from adopting a tax base other than "income." One of the purported advantages of so taxing an individual's "consumption" is said to be greater "equity."[93] The argument is that an individual's consumption presents a fairer base for taxation than income. Conversely, others argue that consumption taxes are necessarily "regressive," since the consumption of lower-income individuals represents a higher percentage of their income

91. Joint Committee on Taxation, "Discussion of Issues Relating to Flat Tax Rate Proposals" (JCS-7-95), April 3, 1995; see also Joint Committee on Taxation, "Description and Analysis of Proposals to Replace the Federal Income Tax" (JCS-18-95), June 5, 1995.

92. The Kemp Commission made public its report on January 17, 1996. Taking a moderate and cautious approach, the commission recommended a flatter rate and broader base for the current income tax–something well short of an endorsement of the Armey flat/consumption tax. National Commission on Economic Growth and Tax Reform, "Unleashing America's Potential: A Pro-Growth, Pro-Family Tax System of the Twenty-first Century," January 1996.

93. See, e.g., Alvin Warren, "Would a Consumption Tax Be Fairer Than an Income Tax?" 89 *Yale L. J.* 1081 (1980).

than it does for wealthy individuals. This is true; however, generous personal exemptions can make the tax structure progressive to the extent that lower-income taxpayers are exempt from tax altogether (thus effectively introducing a zero tax bracket to the rate structure). Likewise, a cash-flow expenditure tax can include a progressive tax rate structure, although that negates some of the benefits often attributed to a flat consumption tax—for example, simplicity and enhanced administrability.

It is also argued that consumption taxes are more "efficient" with respect to avoiding distortions in the formation of capital—an argument also commonly advanced by economists.[94] On this basis, supply-side economists likewise favor consumption taxes as an alternative to income taxation. The notion is that in taxing income, which includes the return on investment capital, the present tax regime creates economic disincentives to savings and incentives in favor of consumption. The taxation of savings, it is argued, is deleterious to an economy that depends upon capital formation from investment derived from savings. This is hardly a new observation. Thomas Hobbes expressed the same sentiments in favor of a consumption tax in *Leviathan* (1651). Hobbes asked loquaciously, "For what reason is there, that he which laboreth much, and sparing the fruits of his labor, consumeth little, should be charged, more then he that living idley, getteth little, and spendeth all he gets; seeing the one hath no more protection from the Commonwealth then the other?"[95] The logic of Hobbes's inquiry remains compelling in light of the U.S. economy's failure to achieve satisfactory levels of savings and investment in recent decades. Whether a consumption tax will actually achieve this desired goal is another question.[96]

Ultimately, the most significant political obstacle to adopting an expenditure-styled consumption tax is the great difficulty in phasing out the present income tax and phasing in the consumption tax. The problem arises because savings previously taxed under the old tax regime (savings in "after-tax" dollars) must be identified and provided with some form of exemption under the new regime; otherwise, these amounts will be taxed

94. This perspective is reflected in Joseph A. Pechman, ed., *What Should Be Taxed: Income or Expenditure?* (Washington, D.C.: Brookings Institution, 1980); see also Joseph Bankman and Thomas Griffith, "Is the Debate Between an Income Tax and a Consumption Tax a Debate About Risk? Does It Matter?" 47 *Tax L. Rev.* 377 (1992).

95. See, e.g., Thomas Hobbes, *Leviathan*, pt. 2, chap. 30.

96. For a discussion of some of the reasons why a consumption tax may *not* produce the increase in savings that proponents often claim, see Gale, "Building a Better Tax System," 784–85.

a second time if they are subsequently consumed. Proponents recognize such problems, but generally dismiss them as "solvable." However, if there is some extended period wherein the new tax is phased in while the income tax is phased out, there will be two tax regimes that taxpayers must confront and plan around. A truly radical break with the past is impossible, and the transition period promises to be even more complex, since two tax systems will be in place – three if the alternative minimum tax is counted. The problem of introducing a consumption tax into an economy already geared to an income tax is much greater than what would be experienced by an emerging nation with a developing economy. In such cases, the choice of a consumption tax as opposed to an income tax is considerably more appealing.[97] However, because of the difficulty in implementing an expenditure-type consumption tax within the context of a long experience with an income tax, excise taxes have more commonly been used in recent decades as mere revenue enhancers for the income tax. Even this also does not always turn out as expected – witness the disappointing 1990 luxury excise tax.

Despite all the political rhetoric and braggadocio in favor of such reforms of the income tax, it is unlikely that any of the proposals for a flat tax will be enacted in the foreseeable future – certainly not during the 104th Congress. Such proposals provide excellent opportunities for grandstanding before constituents, and indeed, both tax committees have held well-publicized hearings on the flat tax proposals since the spring of 1995. But there is considerable institutional resistance to such a wholesale assault upon the federal income tax. The income tax has become so deeply entrenched and intertwined with the development of the American state over the last eight decades that any threat to the $700 billion or so of revenue it raises should be looked at skeptically. The flat tax threatens so many political interests and runs counter to so much of what motivates American policymakers that such a reform is unlikely to succeed politically (even if the merits are genuine). On the other hand, with tax policy set in flux during the first session of the 104th Congress, legislative proposals that seemed entirely beyond the realm of political reality only months ago are now prominently on the policy agenda. So it may be presumptuous to dismiss outright the viability of the flat tax initiative. One thing is certain: Radical tax reform is sure to be a central theme of the 1996 presidential campaign.

97. See, e.g., Charles A. McLure Jr. and George R. Zodrow, "Implementing Direct Consumption Taxes in Developing Countries," 46 *Tax L. Rev.* 405 (1991).

6

A New Dynamics of Tax Policy?

[P]rospects for structural tax reform have been dimmed by recent "reforms" in congressional practices; public pressure to enact income tax reforms seems nonexistent; political leadership on tax matters has become increasingly diffuse. . . . In short, for those who would urge massive tax reforms, there is more than ample cause for despair.

— Michael J. Graetz (1984)

[T]he principal problem is that *no one* controls tax policy.

— John F. Witte (1985)

All the diverse forces that motivate tax policymakers at various times— the revenue imperative, ideology, party politics, and nonpartisan instrumentalism—were especially intense during the 1980s. Accordingly, the inherent weaknesses of federal income tax policy were exaggerated beyond the norm.

On the surface, the legislative process through which tax law was made in the 1980s was little different from that which had prevailed for decades. However, there were several important structural changes in American politics that had an impact upon the tax-policymaking process. Perhaps the most significant of these were the post-Watergate reforms of the congressional committee system, the looming presence of significant budget deficits, and the continued weakening of the American party system (although not necessarily partisanship per se). At the same time, the institutional conflict attributable to tensions between a Democratic Congress and a conservative Republican White House exacerbated the usual interparty conflict that characterizes the tax-policymaking process.

These conditions permitted a number of new players to intrude into the tax-policymaking arena. These included so-called policy entrepreneurs, tax experts, journalists, the media, policy promoters in Washington think tanks, and public-interest groups. This "opening" of the tax-policymaking process was reflected in the tax policy of the 1980s—of which the enactment of the Tax Reform Act of 1986 (TRA) stands out as the major event in a decade of intense policymaking. There is a strong temptation to treat TRA as some kind of aberration from the prevailing patterns of "politics-as-usual" that otherwise have dominated the tax-policymaking process during the postwar period or, alternatively, as heralding the beginning of some "new era" of tax reform. Neither description is fully adequate or completely wrong; at the same time, neither adequately locates TRA within the context of a decade of turbulent tax policymaking.

Looking back on the success of proponents of tax reform in 1986, one of the more observant commentators on the politics of the federal income tax pointed out that there have been no structural changes that would necessarily lead to any new era of tax reform: "Without changes, the institutional framework that brought us both ERTA and TRA remains and it is difficult to see why actions in the future should necessarily tilt in the direction of tax reform rather than antireform."[1] The implication is that tax policy will probably lack direction and stability for the foreseeable future. Likewise, the conclusion here is that neither the passage of TRA nor the general instability of tax policy throughout the decade marked the beginning of any new era in tax policy—neither a new era of tax reform nor supply-side economics. Nor is there likely to be a period of Republican hegemony in the 1990s. Rather, the instability of tax policymaking in the 1980s was the culmination of a number of long-term political trends that began decades earlier and have produced an unstable structure for tax policymaking. This is likely to persist.

Some of those trends (for instance, the tendency of tax policymakers qua politicians to provide more public goods than the electorate is apparently willing to pay for through taxation) reflect the influence of a democratic electoral politics on the tax-policymaking process. The proliferation of tax policy entrepreneurs and public-interest groups reflects the decline of the party hierarchy in Congress and the weaknesses of the American party system. These developments in the political system began before the 1980s, but became more acute during the decade and exacerbated the existing deficiencies and weaknesses in the federal tax-policymaking process. In other words, the erratic course of tax policy during the 1980s was a product of the continuing changes in the political process by which tax policy is made. The unstable political framework

1. John F. Witte, "The Tax Reform Act of 1986: A New Era in Tax Politics?" 19 *Am. Pol. Q.* 438, 454 (1991).

and the lack of consensus over tax policy objectives resulted in an unusually turbulent decade of tax politics. This politics could produce tax legislation such as ERTA in one year and a tax-reform bill such as TRA only five years later. Tax policy in the early 1990s suggests that much the same problem continues to haunt federal income tax policymaking.

The sections below treat of those factors which were new to the tax policymaking process in the late 1970s and early 1980s. These factors were exacerbated by broader systemic trends—most particularly, the decline of the party system and the weakening of the congressional hierarchy. Whether the rise of a regenerate Republican Party in Congress will lead to a reversal of any of these trends, producing any greater coherence and stability in tax policy, remains to be seen. There is reason to be pessimistic.

The Tax Policy Agenda

Tax policy is made through a dynamic process reflecting the interplay of many different economic, political, and institutional interests. These various interests compete for influence and control over the policymaking process within Congress and its committees. They include the president, the national political parties, special-interest groups, individual congressmen, tax experts and professionals from within the legislative and executive branches, public-interest groups, policy promoters from Washington think tanks, as well as the journalists who report on politics and legislative events. In the struggle for influence over tax policy, the ultimate goal is to shape the outcomes of the legislative process, and the first step in exerting such influence is to affect what appears on the "political agenda."

Political scientist John Kingdon has contrasted the ability to influence the political agenda (defined as "the list of subjects or problems to which governmental officials, and people outside of government closely associated with those officials, are paying some serious attention at any given time") with the ability to define the policy alternatives from which policymakers choose. Kingdon concludes that while presidents generally have the power to influence and even in some cases set the agenda of Congress, experts often play a much greater role in defining the alternatives from which congressional decisionmakers ultimately must choose in deciding how to address a perceived problem of public policy. Conversely, the influence of interest groups in defining the political agenda is more significant in "negative blocking" than in putting issues on the agenda.[2]

Kingdon's distinction between setting the policy agenda and defining the policy alternatives is particularly relevant to the tax-policy-making process. Constitutionally, enacting the tax policy agenda is a legislative function; for all practical purposes, the preferences of key members of the tax committees and the majority party's leadership are paramount. The president (and in some cases congressional leadership) possesses the ability to put proposals on the tax policy agenda. But a great many other offices, groups, and interests compete to influence which political issues are given the most serious consideration by congressional tax policymakers, who themselves must rely upon tax experts on their staffs to frame the policy alternatives for them. Once tax policies are actually adopted in the form of specific legislation, tax professionals in the bureaucracy inherit the difficult task of translating what are often little more than broad policy directives into coherent and consistent tax laws. Before the 1970s, the president and congressional committees did fairly well in maintaining control over the tax policy agenda and the tax-policymaking process. However, since the 1960s and 1970s, interest groups and various new players outside the formal legislative process have played an increasingly important role in setting the agenda in the area of tax policy, defining and promoting policy alternatives and, in many cases, determining legislative outcomes. These "extraconstitutional" players in the tax game, located outside the formal legislative process, are discussed below, as are the reasons behind their success in penetrating the previously "closed" tax-policymaking process.

Post-Watergate Reforms of the Legislative Process

Before the 1970s, members of the House Ways and Means Committee were on the whole more insulated from electoral and interest-group pressures than other members of Congress.[3] This was largely attributable to the tight institutional grip exerted over the tax-policymaking process in the House by Wilbur Mills, chairman of the Ways and Means Committee, as well as the control exercised by the

---

2. John W. Kingdon, *Agendas, Alternatives, and Public Policies* (New York: Harper Collins, 1984), 3, 52–53.

3. See Richard F. Fenno Jr., *Congressmen in Committees* (Boston: Little, Brown, 1973), 2–5, 51–57.

Rules Committee over the tax legislative agenda.[4] The seniority system, which originally was seen as a progressive reform following the 1910 revolt against the Speaker and the party hierarchy in the House, served to reinforce the power and autonomy of committee chairmen such as Mills.[5]

This institutional/party control over the congressional tax-policy-making process weakened significantly in the mid-1970s in the wake of the post-Watergate reforms of congressional hierarchy and procedures. Following the constitutional crisis triggered by the Nixon White House, reformers seized the opportunity to cleanse the entire legislative process, especially the tax-policymaking process controlled by the House Ways and Means Committee and its powerful chairman, Wilbur Mills. The post-Watergate congressional reformers condemned such committees as personal fiefdoms of their committee chairmen. Ironically, reformers also viewed committees as overly susceptible to interest-group pressures and committee members as too prone to follow their own electoral interests in enacting pork-barrel tax policies solely for the benefit of constituents—or, even worse, for the benefit of powerful economic interests that dominate their districts and political campaigns.

One effect of the reforms of the 1970s was to undermine the organizational structures of Congress—most particularly the Ways and Means Committee and the seniority system. The reform innovations exacerbated a half-century decline in the control of committees over the congressional legislative agenda. While the role of Congress remains predominant in tax policymaking, no committee chair is likely again to exert the kind of control over the tax policy agenda exerted by Wilbur Mills. Although predictions of the decline of Congress in the post–New Deal party system may be premature, congressional committees and the seniority system were seriously weakened by the reforms of the 1970s. In this way, the post-Watergate reforms had the effect of weakening the once dominant role of the chairmen of the House Ways and Means and

---

4. The classic description of Wilbur Mills's control over tax policy and the Ways and Means Committee is John F. Manley, *The Politics of Finance: The House Committee on Ways and Means* (Boston: Little, Brown, 1970); see also idem, "Wilbur D. Mills: A Study in Congressional Influence," 63 *Am. Pol. Sci. Rev.* 442 (1969).

5. For a discussion of how members use, and are restrained by, the committee system in the quest to maximize their own personal power within Congress, see Lawrence C. Dodd, "Congress and the Quest for Power," in *Congress Reconsidered*, ed. Lawrence C. Dodd and Bruce I. Oppenheimer (New York: Praeger, 1977).

Senate Finance Committees in directing the tax-policymaking process.[6]
These reforms loosened the hold of senior majority members over
committee chair assignments insofar as the power to ratify those assignments was transferred to the Democratic steering committee. Likewise, whereas Mills had abolished subcommittees in Ways and Means,
thereby strengthening his own control over virtually all revenue measures passing through the committee, Democratic reformers reinsti-
tuted them soon after Mills's fall from grace. The closed markup
sessions under which Ways and Means operated under Mills were also
abandoned in favor of open sessions. In 1973 the House adopted a rule
stating that "each meeting for the transaction of business, including the
markup of legislation, of each standing committee or subcommittee
thereof shall be open to the public except when the committee or subcommittee, in open session and with a quorum present, determines by
rollcall vote that all or part of the remainder of the meeting on that day
shall be closed to the public."[7] This rule applied to the Ways and Means
Committee as well. However, contrary to the intentions of reformers,
who saw themselves prescribing greater "openness" for tax committees,
the result of open markup sessions has generally been adverse to their
goals. Critics have characterized this particular reform as evidence of
the naïve and utopian reformist politics that flourished in the post–
Watergate climate.[8]

---

6. A detailed account of the new directions taken by the House Ways and Means
Committee after the reforms of the 1970s is Randall Strahan, *New Ways and Means:
Reform and Change in a Congressional Committee* (Chapel Hill: University of North
Carolina Press, 1990).

7. H.R. Res. 259, 93d Cong., 1st sess. (1973).

8. Strahan has concluded that "[c]ontrary to the hopes of reformers, according to
most committee members the change to open committee markups in the mid-1970s
tended to strengthen the pull of the electoral connection as members often felt pressured to stake out uncompromising positions when working under the watchful eye of
representatives of local interests or groups who were electoral allies (or potential
enemies)." Strahan, *New Ways and Means,* 173; see also 38, 53–90. Former chairman of
the House Ways and Means Committee Dan Rostenkowski recently stated in reference
to the closed sessions behind TRA: "I think if there was anything critical that we
convinced Members of the Ways and Means Committee that we do, it was to go into the
executive session [closed-door hearings]. It's not that you want to ignore the public. It's
just that the lobbyists, the pressure groups, the trade associations–they have all their
pet projects. If you put together something in public, the Members are looking over at
the lobbyists, and the lobbyists are giving the 'yes' and 'no' signs." "Interview with the
Hon. Dan Rostenkowski," 15 *Newsletter (ABA Section of Taxation)* 11, 12 (1996). For a

Under the chairmanship of Mills, the Ways and Means Committee invariably asked for and received a closed rule from the Rules Committee. But after 1975, major tax bills were generally reported under an open rule. Initially, tax reformers believed that this would be to their advantage, but that has not necessarily been the case. There may be disagreement over the exact effect of open rules, but clear "losers" have been the party leadership and the chair of Ways and Means, whose tight control over the tax process was weakened by open rules.[9] This loss of control over the tax policy agenda was also evidenced in the rise of committee defeats on the House floor—a phenomenon virtually unheard of during Mills's tenure.[10] Mills operated through a system of "consensual" decisionmaking in which he built a secure coalition before taking a tax bill to the floor of the House. Hence, he seldom lost a floor vote, enhancing his image as an invincible power broker. Mills's successors in Ways and Means have been unable to exert similar influence over the legislative process.

All these changes occurred within the context of the century-long decline of the national political parties into loose coalitions of locally elected political elites, in many respects beyond the control of the central party leadership in Congress.[11] As a result of these post–Watergate reforms, legislators became further immune from institutional and partisan constraints exerted within Congress.[12] Ironically, the effect of

---

these reforms, see Rob Bennett, "The Open and Shut Case of Tax Bill Markups," 49 *Tax Notes* 1375 (December 17, 1990).

9. For a summary of the various arguments for and against a closed rule for tax bills, see Thomas J. Reese, *The Politics of Taxation* (Westport, Conn.: Quorum Books, 1980), 120–24.

10. The increase in failures of the chairman in floor votes is described in ibid., 124–30, and Strahan, *New Ways and Means,* 80–82.

11. The general decline of the national political parties is described in James L. Sundquist, *Dynamics of the Party System* (Washington, D.C.: Brookings Institution, 1973), and David S. Broder, *The Party's Over: The Failure of Politics in America* (New York: Harper & Row, 1972); cf. Larry J. Sabato, *The Party's Just Begun: Shaping Political Parties for America's Future* (Glenview, Ill.: Scott, Foresman, 1988). The best account of the ties of congressional representatives to their local districts is Richard Fenno Jr., *Home Style: House Members in Their Districts* (Boston: Little, Brown, 1978).

12. For instance, the weakness of congressional party leadership vis-à-vis the individual member of Congress helps to explain why the October 1990 budget-summit compromise was defeated on the floor of the House despite the support of the House leadership. See Tim Gray, "Budget Agreement Mired in Political Brinkmanship," 49 *Tax Notes* 127 (October 8, 1990).

these institutional reforms on tax policy, and perhaps public policy in general, was to expose policymakers to greater interest-group pressures in the absence of any strong countervailing majoritarian forces. When political parties are weak and no clear majorities control the legislative agenda, the impact of interest groups can be magnified.[13] Likewise, the same breakdown of institutional control over the tax committees that opened the door to interest groups also created an increased opportunity for the success of tax-reform politics pursued by political entrepreneurs—both those operating from outside government as well as members within Congress (but outside the confines of party discipline and platforms) intent upon promoting themselves or their personal principles. As is discussed further below, less senior committee members became adept at playing the role of the political entrepreneur in the absence of party cohesion and powerful committee chairmen.

As a result of the congressional reforms implemented in the 1970s, the door was left open to interest groups (both public and private), political entrepreneurs (including proponents of "tax reform") and the media—allowing them all to play a greater role in shaping the tax policy agenda. As a result, the problem is not that special-interest groups "control" tax policy, but rather that "*no one* controls tax policy."[14] This is simply because so many groups and interests have access to the decision-making process. With the weakening of congressional authority and control over the legislative process, those outside who would influence what issues appear on the tax policy agenda became bona fide players in the tax-policymaking process.

Tax Policy Entrepreneurs

Beginning in the 1970s, students of public policy noticed a new phenomenon—policy entrepreneurs acting outside the committee-system hierarchy began to play an increasingly significant role in setting the policy

13. This was found to be the case by Kingdon in his study of how issues are brought to the political agenda: "[T]he lower the partisanship, ideological cast, and campaign visibility of the issues in a policy domain, the greater the importance of interest groups." Kingdon, *Agendas, Alternatives, and Public Policies,* 49.

14. John F. Witte, *The Politics and Development of the Federal Income Tax* (Madison: University of Wisconsin Press, 1985), 21.

agenda.[15] Acting both within and without the formal institutions of the legislative process, individuals who promote special causes (rather than the issues favored by organized political parties) increasingly began to shape public policy. Such individuals were members of Congress, academics, and policy activists from within the broader "Washington community."

In a 1980 study, James Q. Wilson described such a policy promoter as a "skilled entrepreneur" who is a "vicarious representative" mobilizing "latent public sentiment."[16] Policy entrepreneurs adopt certain issues in order to promote their own interests, gain favors and obligations for future bargaining, or simply because they personally favor particular policies.[17] The policy entrepreneur peddles ideas – often ideas that have been in the air for decades but that find a place on the policy agenda because some political figure finds it convenient and useful to promote such issues at that particular time. Academic policy institutes and think tanks also play an important role in providing policy entrepreneurs with an arsenal of well-defined and researched ideas to promote, as illustrated by the persistence and recent success of the "fathers" of the flat consumption tax proposal, Robert Hall and Alvin Rabushka of Stanford University's Hoover Institution (as discussed in Chapter 5).

The notion that ideas "matter," and hence influence political outcomes, emerged as a common theme in the public-policy literature in the 1970s and 1980s.[18] It became commonplace to argue that ideas matter

15. See, e.g., Nelson Polsby, *Political Innovation in America: The Politics of Policy Initiation* (New Haven: Yale University Press, 1984), and Nancy C. Roberts, "Public Entrepreneurship and Innovation," 11 *Pol'y Stud. Rev.* 55 (1992); see also Daniel P. Moynihan, *Maximum Feasible Misunderstanding* (New York: Free Press, 1969), 21–37, and Jack L. Walker, "Setting the Agenda in the U.S. Senate: A Theory of Problem Selection," 7 *Brit. J. Pol. Sci.* 423 (1977).

16. James Q. Wilson, "The Politics of Regulation," in *The Politics of Regulation,* ed. James Q. Wilson (New York: Basic Books, 1980), 370–71.

17. See, e.g., Kingdon, *Agendas, Alternatives, and Public Policies,* 129–30, 214–15.

18. See, e.g., Robert Reich, ed., *The Power of Public Ideas* (Cambridge: Harvard University Press, 1988), especially the essays by Steven Kelman, "Why Public Ideas Matter," and Gary R. Orren, "Beyond Self-Interest"; Timothy J. Conlan, Margaret T. Wrightson, and David R. Beam, *Taxing Choices: The Politics of Tax Reform* (Washington, D.C.: Congressional Quarterly Press, 1990), 240–42 (discussing this recent political science literature and examining this "ideational model"); Mark V. Nadel, "Making Regulatory Policy," in *Making Economic Policy in Congress,* ed. Allen Schick (Washington, D.C.: American Enterprise Institute, 1983), 221–56; see also the essay by John W. Kingdon, "Politicians, Self-Interest, and Ideas," in *Reconsidering the Democratic Public,*

more than partisan interests and traditional political coalitions in many policy areas. For instance, the drive to deregulate the trucking industry in the 1970s was supported by a most unlikely figure, Democratic senator Kennedy, as well as elements within the trucking industry itself. Such an unusual alliance of liberal politics and regulated industry was not uncommon in the 1970s and 1980s.[19] Such political unions contradict the conventional wisdom that a particular pattern of politics emerges out of the interlocking and common political interests of congressional committees, bureaucratic regulators, and interest groups – the so-called iron triangles of interest-group politics.[20] Congressional policy entrepreneurs found the issue of deregulation convenient and useful in furthering their own personal ambitions as well as their vision of politics. Most important, satisfying these goals contributed to their personal and professional success within Congress itself.

The peculiar pattern of politics evidenced with respect to deregulation was also witnessed in tax policymaking during the late 1970s and 1980s. Key political actors, beholden to neither special interests nor the traditional partisan politics that otherwise dominates the tax-policymaking process, were able to influence the debate over tax policy. In many respects, these individuals – outsiders to the hierarchy of leadership in Congress – realized the potential appeal and effectiveness of playing to reformist impulses and speaking in the reformist's rhetoric to mobilize political support for their domestic-policy agenda. Divisions

---

ed. George E. Marcus and Russell L. Hanson (University Park: Pennsylvania State University Press, 1993).

19. See, generally, Martha Derthick and Paul J. Quirk, *The Politics of Deregulation* (Washington, D.C.: Brookings Institution, 1985) (a study of the deregulation of three industries – trucking, railroads, and aviation – cases wherein Congress took positions apparently contrary to those favored by entrenched economic interests).

20. In the 1960s, it was common in the political science literature to write of the "iron triangle" and the "capture" of agencies by the very interest groups they were set up to regulate. However, new bureaucratic structures characterized the regulatory agencies of the 1970s – OSHA and the EPA, for example. These agencies took very different approaches and displayed different styles in regulating interest groups. As John Kingdon has put it, "[T]he triangles between bureaucrats, congressional committees, and clienteles that used to dominate policy are not so iron as they once were." Kingdon, *Agendas, Alternatives, and Public Policies,* 51 (paraphrasing Hugh Heclo, "Issue Networks and the Executive Establishment," in *The New American Political System,* ed. Anthony King [Washington, D.C.: American Enterprise Institute, 1978], chap. 3). See also Wilson, "The Politics of Regulation," especially 384–90.

within the business community regarding which tax policies are most beneficial also give policy entrepreneurs a good deal of extra autonomy in the pursuit of their own tax policy agenda. According to Cathie Martin: "[T]he inconsistency of tax initiatives reflects contradictory business pulls. Outcomes become to a large extent dependent on the particular political coalitions put together by policy entrepreneurs."[21]

Those who first recognized the potential for successfully aggregating a broad bipartisan coalition in favor of tax reform were Senator Bill Bradley and Representative Jack Kemp, with sympathy from Representative Richard Gephardt. President Reagan only belatedly joined the ranks of the converted. Bradley and Kemp deserve most of the credit for bringing tax reform to the public's attention in the early 1980s: "Entrepreneurs like Kemp and Bradley seized upon professional concepts like horizontal equity and investment neutrality and converted them into powerful populist themes like fairness and economic growth."[22] Bradley is widely regarded as most committed to tax reform out of personal principle; he was instrumental in bringing tax reform to the fore of the policy agenda by the sheer force of such convictions. Kemp was also a relentless policy entrepreneur motivated by personal commitment to tax reform, albeit a version quite different from that which motivated Bradley.

Bradley and Kemp were sophisticated promoters who relied upon their advisers for the technical expertise that allowed them to codify their broad notions of tax reform into formal legislative proposals. In the 1980s economist Joseph Minarik (previously of the Treasury Department and the Joint Committee on Taxation) served as Bradley's chief tax adviser during the campaign for lower tax rates and tax reform.[23] By giving substance to the notions of "fairness" and "reform," experts enabled the policy entrepreneurs to bring the issue to a wider political audience.

Subsequent congressional proponents of tax reform (such as Ways and Means chairman Dan Rostenkowski, Senate Finance Committee

21. Cathie J. Martin, *Shifting the Burden: The Struggle over Growth and Corporate Taxation* (Chicago: University of Chicago Press, 1991), 200.

22. Timothy J. Conlan, David R. Beam, and Margaret T. Wrightson, "Tax Reform Legislation and the New Politics of Reform" (paper delivered at the annual meeting of the American Political Science Association, Washington, D.C., 1988), 27.

23. Minarik is the associate director for economic policy in the Office of Management and Budget in the Clinton administration.

chairman Robert Packwood, former OMB director and assistant secretary for tax policy in Treasury Richard Darman, and President Reagan himself) jumped on the bandwagon out of fear of being left behind—or, worse yet, being cast in the role of opponents of fairness, equity, and reform. The political entrepreneurs were the catalyst behind the initial movement in favor of tax reform, but ironically, it was the traditional political leadership that actually brought tax reform to fruition—shepherding the preliminary initiatives through the legislative process, where it was subjected to all the conflicting parochial interests that prevail in Congress. Without skillful political leadership, tax reform never would have made it off the tax policy agenda and into the tax code in 1986. Of course, what was new and most interesting about the campaign for tax reform was how policy entrepreneurs placed the issue on the tax policy agenda in the first place, contrary to all that was predicted by reference to prior patterns of incrementalist tax decisionmaking. Thereafter, pressure from public-interest groups and publicity generated by journalists and the popular media helped prod the traditional leadership in Congress to bring home the final tax bill.

Public-Interest Groups, Think Tanks, and Tax Policy

In recent decades, interests outside the formal institutions of government have increasingly intruded into and influenced the tax policy agenda. This includes so-called public-interest groups as well as the private special interests given so much attention in media accounts of tax policymaking. Beginning in the 1960s and 1970s, groups purporting to represent the "public," the "environment," and even "taxpayers" as some broadly defined class began to use the federal courts and the media to exert influence over the policymaking process.[24] As late as 1972, the U.S. Supreme Court still insisted that "standing" was required to bring a suit against an agency of the federal government, thereby denying interest groups access to the federal courts to litigate on behalf of the

---

24. The newly emerging role of public-interest-group lobbying is discussed in Jeffrey Berry, *Lobbying for the People* (Princeton: Princeton University Press, 1977); Mark V. Nadel, *The Politics of Consumer Protection* (Indianapolis, Ind.: Bobbs-Merrill, 1971); Andrew McFarland, *Public Interest Lobbies* (Washington, D.C.: American Enterprise Institute, 1976); Jeffrey H. Birnbaum, *The Lobbyists: How Influence Peddlers Get Their Way in Washington* (New York: Random House, 1992).

public interest.[25] However, in a trend-setting case in 1971, the Supreme Court permitted a challenge to a governmental decision to put a highway through a park under the Federal Aid-Highways Act of 1968, notwithstanding that there was no statutory authority providing for a "citizens suit."[26] By the mid-1970s, the floodgate was opened, and public-interest groups were commonly participating in the policymaking process through the access granted to them by the federal courts.

For example, by using cooperative federal courts, civil rights groups exerted considerable influence over the policymaking process within the Office for Civil Rights, leaving the agency in disarray from the nearly constant litigation over the definition of its purpose and mission.[27] Other comparable cases involved the Occupational Safety and Health Administration (OSHA), the Food and Drug Administration (FDA), and the Environmental Protection Agency (EPA).[28] All these agencies were subjected to a high level of pressure and litigation from public-interest groups during the 1970s. Notwithstanding the election of conservative Republican administrations in 1980 and 1984, the trend toward greater access to policymaking in administrative agencies continued unabated into the 1980s.

Public-interest groups generally did not challenge the tax-policy-making process in the federal courts with the same intensity that they challenged other policy processes.[29] Nevertheless, such groups played a new role in the 1980s in influencing the tax policy agenda. For

25. *Sierra Club v. Morton,* 405 U.S. 727 (1972). The Sierra Club had brought a legal action in federal court challenging a ruling by the Interior Department. As the litigant, the Sierra Club asserted that it had standing based upon its "long-standing" interest in environmental matters, supposedly thereby establishing a legitimate interest in intervening in policymaking in this area. However, the Supreme Court refused to allow a private interest group, in its own name, to assert a right to bring such an action against the government in order to litigate the "issue," rather than a "case" or "controversy," as is required under the U.S. Constitution, art. 3, sec. 2.

26. *Citizens to Preserve Overton Park v. Volpe,* 401 U.S. 402 (1971).

27. See Jeremy Rabkin, *Judicial Compulsions: How Public Law Distorts Public Policy* (New York: Basic Books, 1989).

28. Ibid., chap. 7 (OSHA); R. Shep Melnick, *Regulation and the Courts* (Washington, D.C.: Brookings Institution, 1983) (interest-group access to EPA policymaking); Paul J. Quirk, "The Food and Drug Administration," in *The Politics of Regulation,* ed. Wilson.

29. But see *Bob Jones Univ. v. United States,* 461 U.S. 574 (1983). In this unusual case, the U.S. Supreme Court on its own initiative appointed a private advocate to challenge an IRS administrative determination that this religious educational institution was entitled to tax-exempt status under IRC section 501(c). The Court sided with the advocate, withdrawing tax-exempt status.

instance, it has been argued that one of the most important stimulants for tax reform was the publication in October 1984 of a study prepared by public-interest lawyer Robert McIntyre of Citizens for Tax Justice, an activist public-interest group largely funded by labor and affiliated with Ralph Nader's umbrella organization, Public Citizen.[30] McIntyre's study showed that 128 large U.S. corporations had paid no federal income tax in at least one of the years from 1981 to 1983 – and seventeen had paid no taxes at all during these three years – notwithstanding that such corporations purportedly had made billions of dollars in "profit."[31] This study was given wide exposure by the media and allegedly stimulated committee action in favor of a tax-reform bill.[32] On the opening day of the Conference Committee for the 1986 bill, Citizens for Tax Justice issued an update of McIntyre's report, widely circulated among the conferees, showing that forty-two major American corporations had paid no income tax at all from 1982 to 1985.[33] Again, the popular press seized hold of this report, helping to propagate the notion that corporations did not pay their "fair share" of taxes, thereby creating an atmosphere in which the interests of corporations could be successfully challenged by the tax committees.

In general, public-interest groups function as classic muckrakers, challenging the Washington "establishment" regardless of partisan affiliation. For instance, McIntyre's Citizens for Tax Justice, a group generally associated with a liberal partisan perspective, has been vocal in denouncing Democrats for various positions they have taken in contradiction to the group's policy positions.[34] But the liberal pro-reform public-interest groups such as Citizens for Tax Justice, the Tax Reform Research Group (another Nader public-interest group), and Taxation

---

30. The importance of McIntyre's report is emphasized in Jeffrey H. Birnbaum and Alan S. Murray, *Showdown at Gucci Gulch: Lawmakers, Lobbyists, and the Unlikely Triumph of Tax Reform* (New York: Vintage, 1987), 12; Conlan, Wrightson, and Beam, *Tax Choices*, 202.

31. Robert S. McIntyre, *Corporate Income Taxes in the Reagan Years* (Washington, D.C.: Citizens for Tax Justice, 1984), 65–68.

32. See Birnbaum and Murray, *Showdown at Gucci Gulch*, 12.

33. This incident is described in Conlan, Wrightson, and Beam, *Tax Choices*, 202.

34. For instance, McIntyre more recently criticized President Clinton's appointment of Senator Lloyd Bentsen to be secretary of the treasury, on the grounds that Bentsen was an "insider" and, hence, beholden to special interests (e.g., Texas oil and gas). See Jill Abramson and John Harwood, "Some Say Likely Choice of Bentsen, the Insider, for Treasury Post Could Send the Wrong Signal," *Wall St. J.*, December 9, 1992, A26.

with Representation do not have a corner on the market for lobbying on behalf of tax policy. The Tax Foundation, a conservative public-interest group, has played an extremely active role in the tax policy debate, continually lobbying against any form of tax increase, including those supported by Republican presidents. Each year, the Tax Foundation announces "Freedom Day"–which is determined by reference to the number of days in the year that the average taxpayer must "work" for the federal government to satisfy one's annual tax liabilities.[35] Ironically, Citizens for Tax Justice, Common Cause, and the Tax Foundation all favored the tax reforms included in Treasury I. The liberal public-interest groups supported TRA because it eliminated a significant number of tax preferences from the code, and the conservative groups supported the bill based upon their preference for lower tax rates. This was the same common denominator that brought together supply-side Republicans and reform-minded liberal Democrats in Congress to support the 1986 tax bill.

Washington think tanks have also played a role, similar to that of the public-interest groups, in championing specific tax policies and lobbying against others.[36] Think tanks are instrumental in supplying policy entrepreneurs with academic studies and all sorts of "reports" that support their respective policy positions. One of the most notable examples of a successful campaign on behalf of public policy was the publication of the thousand-page *Mandate for Leadership* by the Heritage Foundation. Presented to Ronald Reagan soon after his election in November 1980, this report collected together various studies defining a policy agenda for the new conservative Republican administration.[37] Included in the *Mandate for Leadership* was considerable ammunition

35. Just for the record, the Tax Foundation's calculation for 1996 was that the average American taxpayer must work 127 days (or until May 7–one day later than for 1995) to satisfy all liabilities under federal, state, and local taxes. Tax Foundation, "Special Report," April 1996.

36. Two recent and comprehensive accounts of the rise of "think tanks" are David M. Ricci, *The Transformation of American Politics: The New Washington and the Rise of Think Tanks* (New Haven: Yale University Press, 1993), and James A. Smith, *The Idea Brokers: Think Tanks and the Rise of the New Policy Elite* (New York: Free Press, 1991).

37. Charles L. Heatherly, ed., *Mandate for Leadership: Policy Management in a Conservative Administration* (Washington, D.C.: Heritage Foundation, 1981). The success of the *Mandate for Leadership* in shaping the policy agenda during the Reagan administration, as well as promoting the Heritage Foundation itself, is recounted in Smith, *The Idea Brokers*, 194–202; see also Paul Light, *The President's Agenda: Domestic Policy Choice from Kennedy to Carter* (Baltimore: Johns Hopkins University Press, 1982).

supporting significant reductions in federal income tax rates.[38] Many of these proposals found their way into ERTA in 1981.

Public-interest groups and think tanks also played an important role in stimulating the movement for tax reform in 1986. The economists at the most prestigious Washington think tank, the Brookings Institution, published literally dozens of studies over the past thirty years promoting the issue of tax reform. Of late, the issue of tax rate reduction has again been promoted by conservative think tanks. The visibility and influence of conservative public-interest groups such as the Tax Foundation and the Institute for Research on the Economics of Taxation, and think tanks such as the Heritage Foundation, the Hoover Institution, the Manhattan Institute, the Hudson Institute, and the American Enterprise Institute, were greatly enhanced by the ascendancy of the Republican Party in Congress in 1994.[39] These organizations have been pressing for tax rate reductions for years, but they are likely to play an even more important role in advising policymakers and in cultivating public support for the traditional Republican tax issues: lower marginal tax rates, a preferential rate for capital gains, and tax credits for investment and savings – tax policies long favored by conservatives.

The success of such public-interest groups and think tanks in influencing the tax policy agenda is inextricably linked to their access to the media. While the media takes a more neutral stance, rather than promote particular tax policies, journalists often rely upon information (and "sound bites") provided by public-interest groups and think tanks. In this way, the media can function so as to advance certain policy preferences, cultivating popular support for, or stimulating public indignation against, specific policies. Thus, the role of the media in shaping the tax policy agenda must also be considered.

The Media and the Tax Policy Agenda

The importance of public-interest groups in the tax-policymaking process is directly connected to the rise of the popular media as a force in its

38. See Norman B. Ture, "The Department of the Treasury," in *Mandate for Leadership,* 647–64.

39. The trend toward an enhanced role for conservative think tanks has already begun. See David Rogers and John Harwood, "Conservative, Pro-Business Think Tanks Take Center Stage Before House Panel," *Wall St. J.,* January 12, 1995, A16, and Christopher George, "Conservative Heritage Foundation Finds Recipe for Influence," *Wall St. J.,* August 10, 1995, A10.

own right. The general role of the media, especially television, in influencing the political process has been much observed and discussed by political scientists.[40] Whether and how the media influences the tax policy agenda is less certain or clear.

The very fact that in recent years the media has focused on tax policy at all is itself surprising. This phenomenon has been associated with the "new politics" of the income tax witnessed in the 1980s.[41] Because the substance of tax policymaking is highly technical and arcane, it usually does not attract much attention by the popular media. However, during the mid-1980s, the media was suddenly in the vanguard in orchestrating public opinion in favor of tax reform – and with considerable effect. It has been calculated that stories on tax reform were featured on the front page of the *Washington Post* twelve times in 1984, fifty-four in 1985, and forty-six in 1986.[42]

Journalists tend to view the policymaking process through a somewhat crude and particularly narrow interest-group model of politics.[43]

40. See, e.g., Richard Josyln, *Mass Media and Elections* (Reading, Mass.: Addison-Wesley, 1984); Benjamin Ginsberg, *The Captive Public: How Mass Opinion Promotes State Power* (New York: Basic Books, 1986); Martin Linsky, "The Media and Public Deliberation," in *The Power of Public Ideas*, ed. Reich. John Kingdon concludes that the media plays a minimal role in putting issues on the policy agenda. However, he also concedes that the media is instrumental in affecting "public opinion," thereby playing an important role in indirectly shaping policy. Kingdon, *Agendas, Alternatives, and Public Policies*, 71–72; see also Donald R. Kinder and Shanto Iyengar, *News That Matters: Television and American Opinion* (Chicago: University of Chicago Press, 1989).

41. Conlan, Beam, and Wrightson, "Tax Reform Legislation and the New Politics of Reform," 28–30.

42. Conlan, Wrightson, and Beam, *Taxing Choices*, 250. The authors also determined that the *New York Times* featured on its front page fifteen stories in 1984, fifty-three in 1985, and forty-six in 1986. These figures far exceed the coverage given to tax reform during prior periods.

43. Typical of the approach of journalists is Morton Mintz and Jerry S. Cohen, *America, Inc.: Who Owns and Operates the United States* (New York: Dell, 1971); Philip M. Stern, *The Rape of the Taxpayer* (New York: Vintage, 1974); Jeffrey H. Birnbaum, *The Lobbyists: How Influence Peddlers Get Their Way in Washington* (New York: Random House, 1992). Perhaps the worst offender (and greatest seller of books) is Martin L. Gross, who every year or so writes a new (really the same) book harping on the same extravagant and entirely unproven claims. See, e.g., *The Government Racket: Washington Waste from A to Z* (New York: Bantam Books, 1992), 5: "Much of government spending is dictated by the needs of special-interest groups"; *The Tax Racket: Government Extortion from A to Z* (New York: Ballantine Books, 1995), 11: "The reality is that for the last quarter century, Congress and the presidents have betrayed us by concocting tax laws that are insincere, unfair, and convoluted. We're just learning that when it comes to taxes, Washington speaks with an accomplished forked tongue." Perhaps more than any other single

In many respects, this is one more manifestation of the long tradition of muckraking in American journalism. In a particularly apt description, journalists have been portrayed as "having received the views of the academic professions and reinforced them with a cynicism of their own about the relations among economic interests, government agencies, and congressional committees."[44] This pessimistic assessment of the capacity of journalists to comprehend the tax policymaking process is well illustrated by a 1991 account of U.S. tax policy, "America: What Went Wrong?" published by reporters Donald L. Barlett and James B. Steele in the *Philadelphia Inquirer*, a highly respected newspaper that has won numerous awards for the quality of its investigative reporting.[45] These same authors had previously won a Pulitzer Prize in 1989 for a widely praised seven-part exposé of the "special tax breaks" embodied in the Tax Reform Act of 1986 – in particular, the transition rules used to protect special interests from the reforms otherwise enacted by the 1986 act.[46] In the 1991 series, Barlett and Steele investigated the impact of special interests on tax policymaking. The series was extremely well received by the newspaper's readers, was awarded the George Polk award for economic reporting, and soon after was republished as a paperback book, *America: What Went Wrong?* – which immediately became a national best-seller.[47] This series catalogues nearly every imaginable negative economic trend of the 1980s and blames them all on an evil conspiracy of "special interests" and the "powerful and influential" ruling elite, who, along with their "lackeys in Congress," "write the complex tangle of [tax] rules" for their own express benefit.

Not content with the success of this series, Barlett and Steele pretty much rewrote the same polemic in 1994 – this time under the title

---

individual, Gross has contributed to lowering and distorting the public debate on issues relating to federal taxation.

44. Derthick and Quirk, *The Politics of Deregulation*, 12.

45. Donald L. Barlett and James B. Steele, "America: What Went Wrong?" *Phila. Inquirer*, October 20–28, 1991

46. "The Great Tax Giveaway," *Phila. Inquirer*, April 10–16, 1988. Barlett and Steele also won a Pulitzer Prize in 1975 for a series of articles titled "Auditing the IRS," which reported on inequities in IRS audits.

47. Donald L. Barlett and James B. Steele, *America: What Went Wrong?* (Kansas City: Andrews & McMeel, 1992). The book was on the *New York Times* paperback bestseller list for several months in 1992.

America: Who Really Pays the Taxes?[48] Once again, their account of tax policy emerged as a "literary" success, as evidenced by the widespread attention given to the book by the television news media and by the authors' appearances on all the right television talk shows. These two massive polemics by Barlett and Steele, which contain unsubstantiated claims too numerous to recount here, add up to little more than the same unproven assertion that Congress passes every tax statute, bankruptcy law, and labor law for the sole purpose of benefiting "the privileged, the powerful and the influential . . . at the expense of everyone else."[49] To experience the full flavor of this journalistic account, the reader is referred to the third part of the series, which is based upon the singular premise that "Congress has stood for the rich" and thus has enacted "laws and regulations crafted for the benefit of special interests."[50]

These journalistic accounts are not aberrational. Many journalists adopt a similar interest-group model, although it is seldom as crudely and directly expressed as by Barlett and Steele. For instance, a recent investigative report also published by the *Philadelphia Inquirer* linked the tax code to abuses perpetrated by the rich and powerful through "charities."[51] The series took the form of an exposé, showing how non-profit, tax-exempt entities (generally and inaccurately lumped together under the category of "charities") have grown wealthy, expanding their activities beyond traditional notions of charity. In another example, a December 1992 investigative series in the *Philadelphia Inquirer* focused upon the "predatory" pricing policies of the U.S. pharmaceutical industry.[52] A major theme of the series was that pharmaceutical companies have exploited the tax credit provided under section 936 of the tax code, which credit was enacted by Congress to strengthen the economies of U.S. commonwealth nations, most particularly Puerto Rico.[53] The

48. Donald L. Barlett and James B. Steele, *America: Who Really Pays the Taxes?* (New York: Simon & Schuster, 1994).

49. Barlett and Steele, "America: What Went Wrong?" *Phila. Inquirer,* October 20, 1991, A1.

50. "Big Business Hits the Jackpot with Billions in Tax Breaks," *Phila. Inquirer,* October 22, 1991, A1, A18.

51. Gilbert M. Gaul and Neill A. Borowski, "Warehouse of Wealth: The Tax-Free Economy," *Phila. Inquirer,* April 18–24, 1993.

52. Donald C. Drake and Marian Uhlman, "Making Medicine, Making Money," *Phila. Inquirer,* December 13–16, 1992.

53. "Nothing better illustrates the industry's profitmaking ingenuity than the way drug companies have taken advantage of Section 936 of the U.S. tax code." Ibid., December 16, 1992, A17.

authors were apparently dismayed to learn that U.S. drug companies actually relocated some of their drug-manufacturing facilities to Puerto Rico in order to take advantage of the section 936 tax credit.

While there is a real critique to be made of the misguided attempt by Congress to "create" jobs through such tax credits, journalists uniformly misunderstand this, focusing instead upon the profits of those who make use of such tax benefits. Politicians responded to the increasingly shrill outcry–spearheaded by such journalistic accounts as that which appeared in the *Philadelphia Inquirer*–against the section 936 credit. In early 1993 strong political sentiment emanated from the White House and floated about Congress for its outright repeal. A political compromise was ultimately reached pursuant to the Revenue Reconciliation Act of 1993, which imposed relatively minor limitations on the amount of the credit that could be claimed.[54] This was a much less radical approach than that found in the more severe proposals bandied about by members of Congress engaged in public grandstanding before their constituents.[55]

The obsession of journalists with interest-group politics has contributed to the widespread popular cynicism about policymaking, and tax policy in particular. The underlying interest-group model through which journalists view tax policymaking fails to explain why some groups are successful in achieving their goals through tax legislation, while others are not. If certain industries and economic sectors are protected by the tax laws, it is not just because they are big and powerful, hired the right lobbyist, or contributed to the right political action committee. Particular interests can succeed–even without lobbying, logrolling, and other political devices characteristic of interest-group politics–because ideas, movements, and political entrepreneurs set the agenda for debate. As Wildavsky and White put it: "Interest groups are ubiquitous, but are they dominant?"[56] And one can add: Are they necessarily pro-business? These are the tougher questions that are not even addressed by the simplistic interest-group

54. Pub. L. No. 103-66, 107 Stat. 312, sec. 13227, amending IRC sec. 936.

55. For an account of the drug industry's successful effort to moderate any congressional cutback to the section 936 tax credit, see Rick Wartzman and Jackie Calmes, "How Drug Firms Saved Puerto Rico Tax Break After Clinton Attack," *Wall St. J.*, December 21, 1993, A1.

56. Aaron B. Wildavsky and Joseph White, *The Deficit and the Public Interest: The Search for Responsible Budgeting in the 1980s* (Berkeley and Los Angeles: University of California Press, 1989), 532.

model applied to tax policymaking by journalists, as well as by certain academics.[57]

Journalists can mold popular perceptions about even such a dry and technical subject as the federal income tax. Such reports as those of Citizens for Tax Justice exert greater pressure when publicized by the media than when privately circulated among the members of the tax committees. Likewise, policy entrepreneurs such as Bradley and Kemp found that the media provided convenient and direct access to the public, and thereby to the tax policy agenda, something otherwise difficult of access for "loners" outside the inner circle of party leadership.

Like the public-interest groups, the media by nature adopts the muckraker's posture in attacking "corruption" and questioning the motives and integrity of lawmakers: "Since the content of tax policy is both complex and uninteresting to most readers, the press prefers to write about corruption and lobbying. The ideal story reports on a political campaign contribution to a member of the tax committee who has gotten a special interest amendment adopted for the contributor."[58] Indeed, some have argued that the media now constitutes a "fourth estate," challenging and checking the institutional powers of the presidency and Congress, and restraining the overweening ambition of political elites.[59] While this theme is often overstated, the media definitely played a significant role in aligning congressmen in favor of tax reform in the mid-1980s.[60] In general, the media portrayed the

---

57. I am thinking of those law school professors who adhere to what is generally referred to as the "economic theory of regulation"—a branch of so-called public-choice theory. Some of the worst examples of this school of thought are Richard L. Doernberg and Fred S. McChesney, "On the Accelerating Rate and Decreasing Durability of Tax Reform," 71 *Minn. L. Rev.* 913 (1987); idem, "Doing Good or Doing Well? Congress and the Tax Reform Act of 1986," 62 *N.Y.U. L. Rev.* 891 (1987); Fred S. McChesney, "Rent Extraction and Rent Creation in the Economic Theory of Regulation," *J. Legal Stud.* 101 (1987). For a devastating critique of the economic theory of regulation as applied to tax policy, see Daniel Shaviro, "Beyond Public Choice and Public Interest: A Study of the Legislative Process As Illustrated by Tax Legislation in the 1980s," 139 *U. Pa. L. Rev.* 1 (1990).

58. Reese, *The Politics of Taxation,* 56.

59. S. Robert Lichter, Stanley Rothman, and Linda S. Lichter, *The Media Elite: America's New Power Brokers* (Bethesda, Md.: Adler & Adler, 1986).

60. Birnbaum and Murray concluded that the media's favorable response to tax reform during the initial bargaining suggested to committee members that if they "allowed tax reform to die, they would take a beating in the press, and probably in public opinion." Jeffrey H. Birnbaum and Alan S. Murray, "Tax Reform: The Bill Nobody Wanted," *Pub. Opinion,* March/April 1987, 43.

politics of tax reform as a battle between reformers intent on cleansing the tax laws on one side and lobbyists representing "special interests" on the other. Daniel Shaviro has described the media as having "simplistically portrayed each tax reform proposal as the outcome of a struggle between 'good' reformers serving the public interest and 'bad' lobbyists serving the special interests."[61] Early news stories targeting opponents of tax-reform initiatives made clear which way the wind was blowing on this issue, although hard evidence of popular sentiment in favor of tax reform would not have turned a weathercock. Later, highly critical accounts of Chairmen Rostenkowski and Packwood's initial opposition or indifference to tax reform are credited with moving them in the other direction.[62]

In the end, the media certainly did not dictate that tax reform would become a reality in 1986. However, the sympathies of reporters and journalists were clearly in favor of tax reform, and the unusual interest in tax policy that was stimulated by the publication and promotion of Treasury I in 1985 can be credited with pushing committee members toward support of tax-reform proposals they otherwise would likely have opposed. How the media will affect the success or failure of Republican tax policy in the 1990s is less clear. It may very well turn out that conservatives too are capable of using the media (for instance, the *Wall Street Journal*) for their own purposes, as was evident when House Republicans employed a successful media campaign to publicize their Contract with America. What is clear is that the success or failure of tax policy initiatives often hinges upon how well proponents use media coverage for their own purposes. That has always been the case with politics in general, but was much less so with respect to tax policy before the 1970s and 1980s.

---

61. Shaviro, "Beyond Public Choice and Public Interest"; see also Conlan, Wrightson, and Beam, *Tax Choices*, 251: "[I]t is clear that populist rhetoric, bright lights, and the casting of tax reform as something legislators could only be 'for' or 'against' converted many who would not have sympathized with the cause under other circumstances."

62. An infamous story in the *New Republic* portrayed Senator Packwood in most unflattering terms as "Senator Hackwood" on account of his perceived opposition to tax reform and his stated preference for protecting the favored treatment of certain special-interest groups in the tax code. See Fred Barnes, "Senator Hackwood," *New Republic*, May 5, 1986, 12–14. Senator Packwood was once quoted as having said: "I kind of like the tax code the way it is." Quoted in Timothy B. Clark, "Real Estate Industry, Other Corporate Losers Open Fire on Tax Proposals," *Nat'l J.*, December 8, 1984, 2333.

Tax Experts and the Policy Agenda

On account of the highly technical nature of tax law, tax professionals play a more significant role in defining the alternatives than in other policy areas.[63] This trend only increased as the tax laws became ever more complicated and specialized in the postwar decades. However, rather than merely define the policy alternatives available to congressional policymakers, tax professionals in the 1980s also played an increasingly important role in setting the tax policy agenda. Later in the tax-policymaking process, other tax experts in the executive bureaucracy take on the difficult task of translating into concrete rules and regulations what are often only broad policy initiatives expressed in tax statutes. This process has not yet been completed even with respect to the Tax Reform Act of 1986.

The role of tax experts in shaping the tax policy agenda was most prominent during the two-year period preceding enactment of the Tax Reform Act of 1986. Tax professionals in Treasury along with academic proponents had been campaigning for tax reform for decades. Although the issue became politically viable only after the president and congressional leadership were prodded into action by congressional policy entrepreneurs, it was tax experts who gave tax reform substance in Treasury I. This document served as the starting point for all subsequent "political" revisions of the tax bill.

In many technical matters, tax experts may be the only ones in the federal government who are fully aware of and comprehend the intricacies (and abuses) of the tax laws. Likewise, many of the more technical and arcane provisions enacted in the tax code in the past decade found their way onto the tax agenda, and then into law, as a result of the persistence of tax professionals in the Treasury Department and on the staffs of the congressional tax committees. For instance, the staff of tax professionals on the Joint Committee on Taxation (which plays its most important role during the initial drafting stage of a tax bill) exerts considerable influence during markup, when experts prepare so-called

---

63. "As the complexity of the decision facing legislators increases so too does the likelihood that the staff will exert influence on the outcomes. Tax policy, infinitely complex, maximizes the importance of expertise." John F. Manley, "Congressional Staff and Public Policy-Making: The Joint Committee on Internal Revenue," 30 *J. Pol.* 1046, 1066 (1968).

staff pamphlets explaining the various options to committee members.[64] The influence of the staff on committee members and on their choice of problems to consider varies with the personalities of the staff and committee members and the importance of the particular issues to the members themselves.[65] Nevertheless, the expertise of the professional staff is always important in determining the options available to the tax committees, whose members are seldom tax experts themselves.

The role of experts in the tax-policymaking process increased in the postwar era. The staffs of the House Ways and Means Committee and the Senate Finance Committee became an institutional niche for tax experts. Much the same can be said for the Congressional Budget Office, which was created by Congress in 1974 to provide it with technical expertise to counterbalance the impact of the Office of Management and Budget (OMB) and the Treasury Department, with its great expertise and resources, in the tax legislative process. The Joint Committee on Taxation (JCT), however, is arguably the most important source of tax expertise for the Congress. Originally known as the Joint Committee on Internal Revenue Taxation, this committee was created pursuant to the Revenue Act of 1926 upon the recommendation of the Ways and Means Committee, which sought to improve the administration of the Bureau of Internal Revenue and promote the simplification of the tax laws.[66] Initially made up of five members from the Senate, five from the House, and five from the general public, the committee later evolved into a nonpartisan research tool, advising Congress on complex tax issues. The committee perhaps reached its zenith under the long tenure of Laurence N. Woodworth, who headed the staff for over ten years before joining the Carter administration as assistant treasury secretary for tax policy. After Woodworth's departure (and subsequent death in December 1977), the stature and prestige of the JCT declined somewhat, arguably because it has been perceived as playing a more partisan role in recent years.[67]

64. For a description of how staff pamphlets can influence the contents of a bill, see Reese, *Politics of Taxation*, 75–79, and Michael J. Graetz, "Reflections on the Tax Legislative Process: Prelude to Reform," 58 *Va. L. Rev.* 1389, 1429–31 (1972).

65. Manley concluded that "[t]he more salient the issue to a large number of participants the less likely the judgment of the staff will direct the decision." Manley, "Congressional Staff and Public Policy-Making," 1067.

66. The authorization for the committee and its activities is now found at IRC section 8001 et seq. The most comprehensive description of the workings of the JCT is found in Reese, *Politics of Taxation*, 62–86.

67. The charge of partisanship was often leveled by Republicans at the appointees of the Democratic Congresses of the 1980s who served as chiefs of staff. With the tables now

The role of congressional staff in defining and drafting legislative proposals is pervasive in all policy areas, but it is particularly decisive in the area of tax policy.[68] By defining the alternatives for presidential and congressional decisionmakers, tax experts exert considerable influence in determining what ultimately ends up as public law. Furthermore, among tax experts there is a strong consensus regarding what kinds of proposals constitute "good" tax policy. This is generally expressed in terms of a vision for tax reform (discussed further in Chapter 8). The reform proposals of tax experts often become the start of legislative efforts—for instance, Treasury I, the tax experts' dream reform bill. Notwithstanding the great influence of such political figures as James Baker (in the White House) and Chairman Rostenkowski (in the House) in redefining that bill, the initial proposal laid out by the tax experts in the Treasury Department set in motion and informed the political debate over tax policy for the next two years. The 1986 act was qualitatively distinguishable from prior tax legislation by the extraordinary influence of tax experts in raising the very issue of tax reform. The success of tax-reform legislative measures demonstrates how major policy initiatives, especially tax reform initiatives, can have their origins within the tax bureaucracy. Of course, tax professionals are still ultimately responsible to committee members, and thus are limited in how far they can go in placing reform issues that they personally favor on the policy agenda of the tax committees: "[T]he staff cannot very often afford to ignore the wishes of its employers, the tax committees and their chairmen."[69] Nevertheless, tax experts can be rather successful in giving specific substance and content to the "wishes" of the committee members.

Beyond defining the policy alternatives and influencing what tax issues emerge on the tax policy agenda in the first place, tax experts also play a significant role in determining how legislation is translated into

---

turned, liberal Democrats have made similar charges against the Republican-controlled JCT. For example, the editors of the *New York Times* recently denounced the committee staff as "appallingly slanted" and as having "discarded professionally responsible procedures in favor of ideologically driven reports that can only mislead Congress." "Tax Analysts Turn Partisan," *N.Y. Times*, October 19, 1995, 12E, col. 1.

68. For a general discussion (and perhaps overestimation) of the importance of congressional staff in the legislative process, see Michael J. Malbin, *Unelected Representatives* (New York: Basic Books, 1980); see also Harrison W. Fox and Susan W. Hammond, *Congressional Staffs* (New York: Free Press, 1977), and Samuel C. Patterson, "Professional Staffs of Congressional Committee," 15 *Admin. Sci. Q.* 22 (1970).

69. Reese, *Politics of Taxation*, 86.

concrete, administrable public policy. This is accomplished through so-called interpretive regulations drafted by the tax experts in the Treasury Department and the Internal Revenue Service.[70] In the world of highly arcane and technical tax law, policies can be created, and not just implemented, through these regulations. Whereas a generation ago it was the judiciary that provided the gloss upon the bare-bones statutes and thereby added the real substance to the code, the regulations and public pronouncements (i.e., revenue rulings and revenue procedures) of tax experts now give the tax laws much of their content and meaning. Tax professionals also draft committee reports that are subsequently relied upon by courts in interpreting the congressional "intention" behind the legislation and by the Treasury in drafting its regulations. In this way, the "legislative history" of a tax bill is influenced and even, on occasion, created out of thin air by committee staff.[71] Courts grant bureaucrats extraordinary deference and leeway in administering the tax laws, seldom overturn the Internal Revenue Service's interpretation of the tax code, and even more rarely overturn a regulation as contrary to the intention of Congress. Thus, tax experts enjoy considerable autonomy in implementing their interpretation of the often vague statutory commandments of Congress—more so than in most other areas of public administration.

Notwithstanding experts' influence on the tax policy agenda in 1985, tax experts have generally played a lesser role in setting the tax policy agenda since 1986. This raises the question why reform proposals appeared on the policy agenda in 1985 but were successful neither in prior years nor in the years subsequent to TRA. Or more precisely, one must ask why reform politics has fizzled in more recent years, contrary to what one would expect if tax experts played such a significant a role in tax policymaking. Particular and peculiar political circumstances seem to have temporarily opened the door to tax experts, allowing them to place reform on the tax policy agenda in 1985. That door has apparently been closed again—at least with respect to the particular vision of tax reform that dominated in the mid-1980s. Congressional Republicans in the 104th Congress have notions of "tax reform" that turn out to be very different from those which prevailed in

70. Section 7805 of the Internal Revenue Code authorizes the secretary of treasury to issue rules and interpretive regulations.

71. For a frank admission by a former staff member regarding his own role in "creating" some legislative history in a Senate Finance Committee report, see James B. Lewis, "The Natures and Role of Tax Legislative History," 68 *Taxes* 442, 445 (1990).

1986. Even still, the important role of tax experts in translating broad tax policy initiatives into specific bills and in implementing those through tax regulations has not been diminished.

What, then, permitted tax experts and reformers to influence what appeared on the tax policy agenda in the mid-1980s? First, the weakening of control over the tax legislative agenda once exerted by House Ways and Means chairman Wilbur Mills afforded a new opportunity to professional tax reformers. The rules of the game were changed dramatically by the post-Watergate reforms, thereby opening the door to those who would shape the tax policy agenda – tax experts, political reformers, and the many special interests outside the formal legislative arena. In addition, a new opportunity was provided to those within Congress itself who stood to gain from the loosening of the reins of party leadership and the weakening of the seniority system. Finally, the odd alliance of supply-side conservatives and liberal Democratic reformers provided an unusual opportunity to cut tax rates *and* broaden the tax base at once. That alliance has not come together again, leaving the tax-reform agenda of the professional tax experts in policy limbo.

Revenue Neutrality, Deficits, and Tax Policymaking

The impact of the national deficit on the policymaking process has received considerable attention of late.[72] In particular, the significant budget deficits that followed in the wake of the 1981 ERTA tax reductions have been identified as instrumental in forcing policymakers into an unusual and extreme posture for the rest of the decade and beyond. "The revenue reductions contained in the 1981 Act [ERTA], coupled with Reagan's immense defense buildup and the bipartisan opposition to substantial domestic budget cuts, established a dominant political framework for the 1980s."[73] This new political framework for tax policymaking demanded "distributional neutrality" – meaning that tax burdens could no longer be shifted between income classes, as had become

---

72. The impact of budget deficits on the political process is discussed in Wildavsky and White, *The Deficit and the Public Interest*; John H. Makin and Norman J. Ornstein, *Debt and Taxes* (New York: Random House, 1994); James D. Savage, *Balanced Budgets and American Politics* (Ithaca, N.Y.: Cornell University Press, 1988); Allen Schick, *The Federal Budget: Politics, Policy, Process* (Washington, D.C.: Brookings Institution, 1995).

73. Shaviro, "Beyond Public Choice and Public Interest," 21.

the norm in postwar tax policymaking.[74] The principle of revenue neutrality was fixed into a hard rule by amendments to the Congressional Budget Act of 1974 made by the Budget Enforcement Act of 1990. These created the so-called pay-as-you-go (or PAYGO) rule.[75] The PAYGO rule requires that annual net revenue losses from all new legislation must be offset by revenue enhancement or direct spending cuts.[76] If there is a revenue loss for the fiscal year as a whole (determined by reference to the annual fiscal-year budget baseline set by the Office of Management and Budget) sequestration of discretionary spending is imposed automatically. Under the 1990 budget act, the Budget Committee is authorized to report a "pay-as-you-go reconciliation directive" in the form of a concurrent resolution whenever any legislation creates a net revenue reduction for any fiscal year—in other words, when there is no revenue offset "within the same measure."[77] The PAYGO rule for annual offsets of revenue was translated by Chairmen Rostenkowski and Bentsen into a practice within both tax committees whereby any legislative proposal that costs revenue must be coupled with an offsetting revenue raiser *in the same bill*. This procedure is still followed in the 104th Congress, even with both Rostenkowski and Bentsen no longer members.[78]

Operating within such a strict framework of "revenue neutrality," members of Congress have been forced to weigh the respective equities between various preferences for special classes of taxpayers, rather than just offer preferences without regard to the consequences for the deficit. This rule for revenue neutrality limits the options available to policymakers: "[R]evenue neutrality altered the tax-writing process. Prior revenue bills were often constructed through political logrolling, whereby special interest provisions were added one to the next, until a

---

74. C. Eugene Steuerle, "Tax Reform and the Capital Gains Debate," 44 *Tax Notes* 719 (August 7, 1989) (noting that in 1986 it was accepted that the tax-reform process "would be basically neutral with respect to both revenues and the distribution of tax liabilities, that is, aimed less at the distribution of the tax burden among income classes than at efficiency and equity within income classes").

75. 2 U.S.C.A. sec. 601 et seq. (Title 6, "Budget Agreement Enforcement Provision").

76. 2 U.S.C.A. secs. 633(c), (f), and 902.

77. 2 U.S.C.A. sec. 604(a).

78. In the Senate, the so-called Byrd rule applies, in addition to the requirement for revenue neutrality. This rule, devised by West Virginia senator Robert Byrd, requires that any "extraneous" provision in a budget bill (one not having a significant revenue or spending impact) be stricken unless sixty senators vote on the floor of the Senate in favor of retaining such provision. The Byrd rule is found at 2 U.S.C.A. sec. 313. See also Schick, *The Federal Budget*, 85; Christopher Georges, "Byrd Procedural Rule Is Threatening to Derail Substantial Portions of the Republican Agenda," *Wall St. J.*, November 8, 1995, A22.

winning coalition was achieved. As intended, revenue neutrality converted this process into a 'zero-sum game:' each interest was in competition with all others."[79] Thus, the traditional mode of tax policymaking was altered as "the constraints of producing a revenue-neutral bill forced the distributive politics of taxation into a redistributive mold."[80] This in turn imposed a new set of constraints and a new pattern for policymaking that, at least in 1986, "effectively prevented many of these [special] interests from uniting against reform."[81]

The odd balancing act that is mandated of congressional policymakers by revenue neutrality remains a precondition for tax policymaking. This neutrality was illustrated in 1994 when Congress amended the treatment of domestic workers for purposes of Social Security taxes – the so-called nanny tax reform bill.[82] The revenue loss attributable to this reform was funded by limiting the payment of Social Security benefits to incarcerated criminals and the criminally insane confined to mental institutions by court order. Enacting more costly policies inevitably requires that policymakers target more powerful and influential "revenue sources" than prisoners and the criminally insane – perhaps one day even senior citizens and middle-class taxpayers.

The indexing of tax brackets pursuant to the enactment of ERTA in 1981 has also been linked to a new fiscal restraint imposed on the congressional tax-policymaking process. Before indexing, inflation caused continual "bracket creep" that in effect resulted in automatic, nonlegislated tax increases. Indexing tax brackets stripped Congress of these revenue increases, thereby altering the framework for decisionmaking. Former Treasury Department economist Eugene Steuerle has emphasized the impact of indexing on the tax-policymaking process:

> The major individual reform instituted in 1981 was not the direct reduction in tax rates, but the establishment of indexing of tax brackets. . . . [T]his provision was not even part of the original Reagan proposals, but it has dramatically altered the nature of

79. Conlan, Wrightson, and Beam, *Taxing Choices,* 101.

80. Ibid., 234.

81. C. Eugene Steuerle, *The Tax Decade: How Taxes Came to Dominate the Public Agenda* (Washington, D.C.: Urban Institute Press, 1992), 107.

82. The Social Security Domestic Employment Reform Act of 1994, H.R. 4278, Pub. L. No. 103-387, 108 Stat. 407. The bill raised the threshold for employer withholding from $50 per quarter to $1,000 and exempted altogether from Social Security taxation and coverage household workers under the age of eighteen whose primary occupation is not household employment.

tax legislation ever since. No longer could Congress follow the pattern of providing tax reductions that merely offset tax increases due to inflation. By 1990, the adjustment for inflation alone was estimated to have reduced receipts by over $57 billion relative to an unindexed tax code. . . . Eventually the indexing provision will dominate all other provisions of the 1981 Act.[83]

According to Steuerle, tax policymaking could no longer continue as purely distributive pork-barrel politics.

The gist of the argument concerning revenue neutrality and indexing seems to be that tax policymaking was suddenly transformed by experiences with severe revenue shortfalls. However, it is not entirely obvious that revenue neutrality and the budget deficits that followed ERTA changed the course or *substance* of tax policymaking. Policymakers always operate within the constraints imposed by the revenue imperative, and these fiscal constraints have been greater during prior periods (such as during the two world wars and the Great Depression). Furthermore, there are other responses to budget shortfalls that policymakers may opt for. The broad historical survey of U.S. tax policy in Chapters 2 through 5 suggests that federal policymakers will often elect to borrow or raise taxes when confronted by significant budget shortfalls. The particular choice seems to depend upon the particular political climate and economic circumstances. During periods of war and national crisis (when deficits have reached a higher percentage of gross domestic product than during the relative peace of the 1980s), increasing taxes coupled with cuts in domestic spending has been the most common response. Similarly, in 1982, 1984, and 1990, a Democratic Congress (with support from Republicans) elected to raise tax rates. This too was President Clinton's response in 1993 in the face of continuing budget shortfalls – taxes were raised in lieu of cutting expenditures.

Thus, the more appropriate question to ask is, why did members of Congress "choose" revenue neutrality as the framework for congressional tax policymaking beginning in 1986? Under what conditions will policymakers operating within the context of a highly distributive political arena impose constraints upon themselves such as revenue neutrality, which so clearly works to their own political disadvantage? When is the adoption of revenue neutrality a more compelling option for federal policymakers than raising taxes? These questions have not been

83. Steuerle, *Tax Decade,* 43. Steuerle, an economist and senior fellow at the Urban Institute, was deputy assistant secretary of the treasury for tax analysis from 1987 to 1989.

adequately addressed by those who emphasize the importance of revenue neutrality. The suggestion in Chapter 9 is that during periods of crisis policymakers will be more inclined to raise taxes and even cut domestic spending.[84] During periods of politics-as-usual, those options seem to be lie outside the realm of political possibilities. In some respects, revenue neutrality allows congressional policymakers to cultivate the illusion that they are making serious efforts to deal with budget deficits, without actually raising taxes or cutting previously authorized expenditures. Whether a Republican Congress will abandon or constitutionalize the principle of revenue neutrality (via a balanced-budget amendment) is uncertain.

In any event, while budget deficits and revenue neutrality have imposed a new framework on the tax policymaking process in the 1980s, neither explains very much about the *substance* of tax policy that is enacted. And hence, neither the end of budget deficits (highly unlikely in the foreseeable future) nor the abandonment of the framework of revenue neutrality (also unlikely) will have much impact upon the specific outcomes of contemporary tax policymaking.

Whither Tax Policy?

The intrusion of the media, public-interest groups, think tanks, policy entrepreneurs, and tax reformers into the tax-policymaking process in the late 1970s and early 1980s all reflected, rather than caused, the weakening of congressional institutions of tax policymaking – in particular, the House Ways and Means Committee. Because of declining national parties and weakened party leadership, there was little resistance to encroachments upon the tax-policymaking process by interests external to the formal institutions of government. It was not only private special interests that gained access to public decisionmaking through the tax committees; the media and lobbyists for public-interest groups did as well. Institutional boundaries weakened so as to permit

84. Sharkansky concluded that "[a] catastrophe of major proportions is likely to affect financial policy-makers. The Depression, the Second World War, the Korean Conflict, and postwar reconversions had impacts on economic resources and service demands that were sufficient to alter the allocation of spending to different types of agencies, to affect the total size of government budgets, to change tax policies and the distribution of governmental assistance, and to alter the relative financial responsibilities of federal, state, and local governments." Ira Sharkansky, *The Politics of Taxing and Spending* (Indianapolis, Ind.: Bobbs-Merrill, 1969), 202.

access to nearly every organized interest. As a result, tax policy has little direction and is overly susceptible to the influence of too many outside players.

Tax policy in the 1980s evidenced this pathological condition. In 1981, the Reagan conservative coalition was able to impose a distinct partisan perspective on tax policy. Even then, the distributive pork-barrel politics of the congressional tax committees prevailed at the last minute and changed the final bill. The "inability of the tax system to resist change" left the so-called Reagan Revolution only a fleeting memory within less than five years. In 1986, proponents of tax reform took advantage of the openness of the institutions of tax policymaking, capitalizing upon the opportunities arising from the unusual convergence of interests of supply-side conservatives in the White House and tax reformers to enact major tax-reform legislation. However, that too proved to be only a coalition of convenience, and its demise left the tax-policymaking arena open again to inroads by special interests, policy entrepreneurs, the media, and public-interest groups.

The long-term legacy of postwar American politics is that institutional and party control over the legislative process has been significantly weakened, resulting in compromises in the integrity of the tax-policymaking process. This was evidenced in the lack of consistency and stability in tax policy throughout the 1980s. The pattern has persisted into the 1990s.

7

Tax Complexity and the Illusions of Reform

[N]o one understands the Income Tax Law [the Revenue Act of 1913] except persons who have not sufficient intelligence to understand the questions that arise under it.
—Senator Elihu Root of New York (1913)

Simplicity in modern taxation is a problem of basic architectural design. Present legislation is insufferably complicated and nearly unintelligible. If it is not simplified, half of the population may have to become tax lawyers and tax accountants.
—Henry C. Simons, *Federal Tax Reform* (1950)

One consequence of the increased reliance by policymakers on the federal income tax as a vehicle to implement public policy has been an increase in the complexity of the tax laws. This increased complexity shows up in the various tax expenditures and special reform provisions that now pervade the tax code. Such provisions are typically drafted by tax professionals (generally those on the staffs of the tax committees) and enacted by Congress to effect their public policies. Later, tax professionals in Treasury (assisted by tax advisers in the Internal Revenue Service) add yet another layer of complexity through the regulations they draft to implement and interpret these statutes.

Tax professionals (especially tax lawyers) earn their livelihood from such complexities, and hence, many will be reluctant to acknowledge that there is even a "problem" at all. Because members of Congress can help secure their own reelection by railing against tax complexity, which ultimately is the product of their own labors, legislative proposals for tax simplification are not a very promising source for reform either.

The Increasing Complexity of the Tax Laws

Overall, the federal income tax has become ever more complicated through a process of gradual, evolutionary, and incremental adjustments to the original statute. However, beginning in the 1960s, the development of the federal income tax entered a new phase during which the volume and level of complexity of the tax code and Treasury regulations increased more dramatically. Thereafter, there was a virtual explosion in the complexity of the tax code. For instance, the Internal Revenue Code and Treasury regulations were published by Commerce Clearing House, Inc. (CCH) in a single volume before World War II. Presently, the code and regulations fill a total of twelve comparable volumes in the same series. The income tax provisions of the Internal Revenue Code of 1954 contained 103 sections; the Internal Revenue Code of 1986, including amendments from 1993, contains 698 sections. One report estimates that the volume of the income tax regulations increased 730 percent during the period from 1954 to 1994.[1] There has been a similar explosion in "law" in other tax-related policy areas as well. For instance, Title II of the Social Security Act of 1935 was only four pages long when enacted, grew to fifty pages by 1950, and two hundred pages by the 1970s. This did not even include new sections of the statute, such as medicare.[2] Tax practitioners have also experienced this explosion in tax law.[3] Most would agree with Alvin Rabushka and Robert E. Hall, who simply concluded that "[t]he current U.S. income tax system is a nightmare of complexity."[4]

In light of the increasing complexity of the income tax laws, tax simplification has emerged as one of the perennial themes in the aca-

1. Arthur P. Hall Jr., "Growth of Federal Government Tax 'Industry' Parallels Growth of Federal Tax Code," Special Report no. 39, Tax Foundation, September 1994.

2. See Martha Derthick, *Agency Under Stress: The Social Security Administration in American Government* (Washington, D.C.: Brookings Institution, 1990), 201.

3. In a 1992 interview, tax law professor Martin Ginsburg recounts that under the Internal Revenue Code of 1954 tax attorneys faced only a few statutory and regulatory "monsters." Under the 1986 code, the monsters now seem to dominate the playing field. Martin D. Ginsburg, "Interview with Professor Martin D. Ginsburg," 12 *Newsletter (ABA Section of Taxation)* 6 (1992).

4. Alvin Rabushka and Robert E. Hall, *The Flat Tax* (Stanford, Calif.: Hoover Institution Press, 1985), 5.

demic tax literature.[5] The U.S. Treasury Department, the staffs of the congressional tax committees, and the tax bar have all devoted considerable time and effort to the question of tax simplification.[6] Indeed, there is a widespread tendency to equate tax reform *per se* with "simplification."[7] Many of these reform proposals are blatant political efforts to appeal to constituents. This would apply to the 1991 tax-simplification proposals of House Ways and Means chairman Rostenkowski and Finance Committee chairman Bentsen,[8] as well as the earlier simplification efforts of then IRS commissioner Fred Goldberg.[9]

These kinds of proposals make for good press, but fail to address the fundamental causes behind the rise in tax complexity. Few reformers

5. See, e.g., Henry C. Simons, *Federal Tax Reform* (Chicago: University of Chicago Press, 1950), especially 28–30; Paul McDaniel, "Federal Income Tax Simplification: The Political Process," 34 *Tax L. Rev.* 27 (1978); Charles H. Gustafson, ed., *Federal Income Tax Simplification* (Philadelphia: American Law Institute, 1979); Sidney I. Roberts, "Simplification Symposium," 34 *Tax L. Rev.* 5 (1978); Boris I. Bittker, "Tax Reform and Tax Simplification," 29 *U. Miami L. Rev.* 1 (1974); Charles A. McLure Jr., "The Budget Process and Tax Simplification/Complication," 45 *Tax L. Rev.* 25 (1989); Stanley S. Surrey, "Complexity and the Internal Revenue Code: The Problem of the Management of Tax Detail," 34 *Law & Contemp. Probs.* 673 (1969); Sidney I. Roberts, Wilbur H. Friedman, Martin D. Ginsburg, Carter T. Louthan, Donald C. Lubick, Milton Young, and George E. Zeitlin, "A Report on Complexity and the Income Tax," 27 *Tax L. Rev.* 325 (1972); James S. Eustice, "Tax Complexity and the Tax Practitioner," 45 *Tax L. Rev.* 7 (1989).

6. See Department of Treasury, Office of Tax Analysis, "Tax Reform for Fairness, Simplicity, and Economic Growth: The Treasury Department Report to the President," reprinted in 25 *Tax Notes* 873 (December 3, 1984); Joint Committee on Taxation, 95th Cong., 1st sess., *Issues in Simplification of the Income Tax Laws,* Committee Print 1977; Sidney I. Roberts, Wilbur H. Friedman, Martin D. Ginsburg, Carter T. Louthan, Donald C. Lubick, Milton Young, and George E. Zeitlin, "A Report on Complexity and the Income Tax" (report prepared for the New York State Bar Association) 27 *Tax L. Rev.* 325 (1972).

7. See, e.g., David Brockway, "The Process Behind Successful Tax Reform," 31 *Vill. L. Rev.* 1803, 1803 (1986): "True tax reform will not be achieved unless there is significant simplification of code provisions."

8. Rostenkowski and Bentsen introduced the "Tax Simplification Act of 1991," S. 1394, H.R. 2777, 102d Cong., 1st sess. (1991). Subsequently, on November 1, 1993, Rostenkowski introduced another bill ("Tax Simplification and Technical Corrections Act of 1993," H.R. 3419) but neither was enacted by Congress.

9. See Lane Davenport, Marianne Evans, and Sean Ford, "Goldberg Still Beating Drum for Simplification; Says IRS Budget Is Way out of Balance," 45 *Tax Notes* 1398 (December 18, 1989). IRS commissioner Goldberg was once quoted as saying: "You don't want the tax-law pointy-heads running the world." *Wall St. J.,* December 20, 1989, A1, col. 5.

demanding simplification of the tax laws recognize the inherent difficulties in their positions. Excessive complexity is rooted in the very process by which U.S. tax policy is made. Some of the complexity is attributable to efforts by policymakers to accomplish too much through the tax laws, using the income tax code as the vehicle to implement too much public policy. Much of the complexity is attributable to prior reforms enacted in the pursuit of greater purity and equity in the tax laws. As Senator Russell Long once quipped: "The complexity of our code in the main is not there because of some mischief. Most of it is there in the effort to do more perfect justice."[10]

In other words, complexity does not enter the tax code so much out of malevolence as through overly zealous reform efforts and excessive demands made on the tax laws with respect to implementing public policies. The causes behind the excessive complexity of the tax laws are themselves a complex phenomenon that cannot be reduced to any single factor, and hence, open-ended calls for "simplification" invariably miss the mark. The underlying sources of tax complexity lie within the tax-policymaking process itself. In order to understand how and why the income tax laws became so much more complex over time, it is necessary first to consider the political process through which tax policy is produced. Finally, it is important to understand just what is the problem with excessive complexity in the tax laws.

The 1913 Income Tax: A Bare-Bones Statute

Tax complexity is not a new phenomenon, even if it has reached new heights in the past three decades. Since the first income tax statutes were adopted by the federal government, excessive complexity has been a constant complaint of taxpayers as well as a favorite theme of reformers. But to taxpayers and counsel who have grown accustomed to the statutory excesses and regulatory quagmires that seemed to become the norm in the 1980s, the first income tax laws appear relatively straightforward and uncomplicated—much like the "simple" flat tax touted by Republicans in the 104th Congress.

The tax return first used during the Civil War relied upon a simple conceptual framework. The 1865 return was a bit more sophisticated, but

10. Senator Russell B. Long, quoted in Senate Finance Committee Hearings, *Tax Reform Proposals,* vol. 3, 99th Cong., 2d sess., 53.

merely required the taxpayer to list separately each source of income (specifically, all "profits from any trade, business, or vocation," rental income from land or buildings, "profits realized" from the sale of real property, as well as interest and dividends) and allowed for "proper" deductions related to that source of income. Allowing for deductions for losses sustained on the sale of real estate, interest paid, rent actually paid for the taxpayer's "homestead," and an annual exemption for $600 of salary for military personnel, the tax was then imposed upon net income above the $600 personal exemption. Of course, many a sophisticated taxpayer struggled with that relatively "simple" income tax statute.[11]

The 1913 income tax merely resurrected the Civil War income tax statute, as well as the tax return used fifty years earlier. The original Form 1040 ("Return of Annual Net Income of Individuals") put in service by the Bureau of Internal Revenue in 1913 under the new income tax statute was in total only three pages long—including all schedules and the one-page instructions.[12] The return required taxpayers to compute and report just two separate items, "gross income" and total "general deductions," with relatively straightforward schedules provided for computing each. The tax was imposed on net income above the $3,000 exemption that was "received or accrued" during the calendar year, thereby employing a hybrid method of tax accounting that borrowed concepts from the cash and accrual methods of tax accounting now so familiar to tax professionals.[13]

Notwithstanding that the 1913 version of the federal income tax was rather basic and pristine by today's standards, it was already perceived by contemporaries as far too complicated to be understood by the average taxpayer. For instance, Senator Elihu Root of New York in 1913 wrote in response to a friend who had complained about the complexity of the Revenue Act of 1913: "I guess you will have to go to jail. If that is the result of not understanding the Income Tax Law I shall meet you

11. Indicative of the fact that even the rudimentary tax return used for the Civil War income tax was difficult for taxpayers to comprehend, Abraham Lincoln overpaid his taxes for 1864 by $1,250, a sizable amount by mid-nineteenth-century standards. The incident is recounted in David Burnham, *A Law Unto Itself: The IRS and the Abuse of Power* (New York: Vintage, 1989), 13.

12. The 1995 Form 1040 was just two pages long. However, a complicated return can include dozens of schedules and worksheets. There are now almost fifty pages of instructions and worksheets for Form 1040 alone.

13. See IRC sec. 446(c) (cash and accrual methods as "permissible" for computing taxable income).

there. . . . . [F]or no one understands the Income Tax Law except persons who have not sufficient intelligence to understand the questions that arise under it."[14] The impact and shock felt by those confronting the new federal income tax for the first time in 1913 must have been enormous. Part of the reason that the first income tax laws would have struck contemporaries as so complex and shocking was the sheer novelty of the idea of measuring an individual's "income," as the new tax required. Except for the brief experience with the Civil War income tax, U.S. citizens had never experienced such a "direct" form of taxation. While transactions and sales were subject to excise taxes and custom duties, the concept of treating an individual as a taxable economic unit was relatively new in 1913. Individuals were not yet accustomed to measuring their human endeavors in terms of "net income" and being treated as discreet economic units—"accounting" for their lives as so many living balance sheets. In this respect, the income tax was also instrumental in transforming the relationship between the individual citizen and the state. As Margaret Levi has put it: "The income tax reflected a major transformation in prevailing economic thought and fundamentally altered the individual's relationship to the central state."[15]

Oddly enough, the simplicity of the first "bare-bones" tax statutes may actually have contributed to the initial confusion, since they provided taxpayers with insufficient guidance regarding what was being measured and how to measure it. Successive decades of refinement of the statutes by lawmakers, as well as the issuance of interpretive regulations by the commissioner of Internal Revenue (under the authority of the 1913 income tax thereafter augmented by the Revenue Act of 1928[16]), contributed to clarifying the meaning of the basic concepts of the federal income tax, thereby bringing greater certainty and predictability of outcome to subsequent generations of taxpayers and attorneys, as well as the Treasury Department itself.

During the first decades of the federal income tax, the federal courts along with the Board of Tax Appeals added considerable flesh and blood to the original statute.[17] Indeed, on account of the broad, expansive

14. Quoted in Harold Dubroff, *The United States Tax Court: An Historical Analysis* (Chicago: Commerce Clearing House, 1979), 12.

15. Margaret Levi, *Of Rule and Revenue* (Berkeley and Los Angeles: University of California Press, 1988), 122.

16. Pub. L. No. 78-562, chap. 852, 45 Stat. 791.

17. The Board of Tax Appeals was established under the Revenue Act of 1924, chap. 234, sec. 900, 43 Stat. 336. The board was technically an "independent agency in the

language used by Congress in drafting the initial revenue laws, extensive litigation was inevitable. Accordingly, the federal courts were drawn into a process of articulating the meaning of the most basic and fundamental concepts of the income tax. For instance, the federal courts were immediately called upon to define the most basic concept – what is "income" for purposes of the new tax. The statutory definition of "income" provided in the Revenue Act of 1913 merely mirrored the language of the Civil War statute and the newly ratified Sixteenth Amendment, which sanctioned the imposition of a "direct" tax on "incomes, from whatever source derived." Since 1913, the statutory language has remained virtually identical. The present definition of income, found in section 61(a) of the Internal Revenue Code of 1986, simply states tautologically that "gross income means all income from whatever source derived."[18] Despite the broad net cast by the statute, there is still considerable room for debate and disagreement among reasonable persons over what constitutes income.

Given the minimal and somewhat cryptic statutory definition of income, the U.S. Supreme Court was soon called upon to clarify the concept. In a 1920 case, *Eisner v. Macomber*, the Court struggled with the problem, declaring that "income may be defined as the gain derived from labor, from capital, or from both combined."[19] Unfortunately, this overly restrictive definition implied that absent the contribution of labor or capital, gain would *not* be included in income – thereby leaving vast categories of "gain" out of the statutory scheme and, hence, out of the reach of the federal tax collector. In so refining the statutory definition, the Court actually introduced additional confusion into an already uncertain area.[20]

---

executive branch," rather than a judicial body. In fact, however, the board (which was renamed the Tax Court of the United States in 1942) functioned much as a federal trial court. In 1969, in recognition of this, Congress renamed the body the United States Tax Court and reclassified it as an "Article 1" federal court (i.e., a judicial entity created under the authority granted to Congress in Article 1 of the U.S. Constitution). Nevertheless, the hybrid nature of the Tax Court still raises problems. See, e.g., *Freytag v. Commissioner*, 111 S. Ct. 2631 (1991) (concerning the power and authority of the "special trial judges" of the Tax Court); see also "Note: Special Trial Judges, the Tax Court and the Appointments Clause: *Freytag v. Commissioner,*"45 *Tax Law.* 497 (1992). For a history of the Tax Court, see Dubroff, *The United States Tax Court.*

18. The 1939 Internal Revenue Code relied upon a somewhat more wordy definition of "gross income" in section 61(a), whereas the 1954 tax code returned to a definition closer to that first used in 1913.

19. *Eisner v. Macomber*, 252 U.S. 189, 207 (1920).

20. Marvin Chirelstein has aptly described the *Macomber* case as follows: "[C]ould it be asserted that 'labor' or 'capital' somehow inheres in every human activity? The *Macomber*

It was not until 1955, in *Commissioner v. Glenshaw Glass Co.,* that the Supreme Court finally cleared the air once and for all by embracing the broad language of the Sixteenth Amendment, including virtually everything in income – namely, all "accessions to wealth, clearly realized, and over which the taxpayers have complete dominion."[21] The statutory scheme that has prevailed ever since holds that every "accession" to wealth is presumptively included in income unless otherwise specifically excluded by statute or, in some limited circumstances, by judicial doctrine.[22] Indeed, this was the basic framework already adopted by the Bureau of Internal Revenue and, later, the Internal Revenue Service, even prior to the Court's acquiescence in *Glenshaw Glass.*

In these early cases, the federal courts crafted a practical and administrable concept of income for the new income tax. Even as the tax code otherwise has evolved to provide significantly greater details with regard to other statutory definitions, what specifically constitutes income

---

definition apparently possessed metaphysical properties which made it difficult to apply in an absolute fashion." Marvin A. Chirelstein, *Federal Income Taxation,* 4th ed. (Mineola, N.Y.: Foundation Press, 1985), 7.

21. *Commissioner v. Glenshaw Glass Co.,* 348 U.S. 426, 431 (1955).

22. Since the broad definition of income was adopted, there has been little room for judicial exceptions to the general rule that all "accessions to wealth" are included in income. However, during the years of the Great Depression, the courts commonly enunciated exceptions to the broadly inclusive definition of income. For instance, after outlining the rule for including income realized on the discharge of indebtedness – a common occurrence during the Great Depression, when the value of real property declined severely, leaving many mortgage lenders inadequately secured and willing to accept partial payoffs of loans – the courts carved out a number of rather dubious judicial exceptions that they have only recently been withdrawing (although the Treasury from the first never acquiesced in most of these decisions). See *Kirby Lumber Co. v. United States,* 284 U.S. 1 (1931) (in majority opinion, Justice Holmes holds that income was realized by corporation upon acquisition of its own debt instrument for less than face value); but see *Kerbaugh-Empire v. Bowers,* 271 U.S. 170 (1926) (where "overall transaction" was a loss, income not recognized on discharge of debt for less than face value). *Kerbaugh-Empire* has been severely criticized by courts and the IRS for years. See, e.g., *Vukasovcich, Inc. v. Commissioner,* 790 F.2d 1409, 1414 (9th Cir., 1986). Indeed, the whole debt-discharge area is still not supported on a firm theoretical foundation, as evidenced by the recent bizarre case of *Zarin v. Commissioner,* 92 T.C. 1084 (1989), rev'd, 916 F.2d 110 (3d Cir. 1990). For one of the better discussions of *Zarin,* see Daniel Shaviro, "The Man Who Lost Too Much: *Zarin v. Commissioner* and the Measurement of Taxable Consumption," 54 *Tax L. Rev.* 215 (1990).

has been determined by reference to these early judicial decisions. Of course, there still remains a sizable grey area concerning what is and is not income subject to the grasp of the federal income tax, even after decades of judicial construction. The courts also performed the essential task of drawing the boundaries of administrative power by reviewing administrative procedures and the government's own determinations of the meaning of the tax statutes. Although the courts paid all the usual deference to the expertise of the tax experts in the administrative agencies with respect to their interpretation of the tax laws, they would on occasion find in favor of taxpayers against the tax authorities. Through extensive litigation over the basic issues arising under the federal income tax, the courts enunciated the broad doctrine necessary to fill in the considerable gaps in the tax laws. In this respect, the federal courts played a fundamental role in the development of the tax.

During the first quarter of a century under the new federal income tax, its statutory framework was greatly clarified by the courts and Congress. In addition, Treasury offered administrative rulings refining and interpreting the tax laws. Furthermore, as the increasingly professionalized and specialized bar became more familiar with the meaning of the new tax laws through their experience representing clients, a new specialist was born – the tax lawyer.[23] Thus, the initial phase of the development of the income tax consisted in a gradual institutionalization of the tax system, a professionalization of roles played by the participants, and a specialization of functions within the administration of the tax system. During this period, the basic framework of the federal income tax was established and the participants in the administration of the tax laws came to understand the "rules" of the tax system. These refinements, along with judicial doctrine as it had evolved since 1913, were codified in the Internal Revenue Code of 1939.[24]

23. From 1905 to 1916, the American Bar Association maintained a Standing Committee on Taxation, which participated in the enactment of the Revenue Act of 1913. The ABA's Special Committee on Internal Revenue was instrumental in the creation of the Board of Tax Appeals. In 1939, the ABA approved the organization of the Section of Taxation, which today plays a prominent role in advising the Treasury and IRS on concerns of the tax bar. For a discussion of the role of the Tax Section, see Harry K. Mansfield, "A Brief Unofficial History of the Tax Section: 1939-1989," 44 *Tax Law.* 4 (1990).

24. Pub. L. No. 76-1. Simplification was a goal of Congress in establishing the Joint Committee on Internal Revenue Taxation in 1926. In 1939 this committee, along with legal experts in the Treasury and Justice Departments, completed the task of collecting and

The 1939 tax code included most of the basic features of the present income tax regime, since the "expansive" language of the first revenue statutes was pretty much filled in through almost three decades of statutory amendments, administrative pronouncements, and judicial review. Yet, even after more than a quarter century of experience with the federal income tax, the new tax code of 1939 seemed to contemporaries as forbidding and enigmatic as the Revenue Act of 1913. No less a distinguished figure than Judge Learned Hand expressed these sentiments with respect to the complexity of the 1939 tax code: "In my own case the words of such an act as the Income Tax, for example, merely dance before my eyes in a meaningless procession: cross-reference to cross-reference, exception upon exception – couched in abstract terms that offer no handle to seize hold of – leave in my mind only a confused sense of some vitally important, but successfully concealed, purport, which it is my duty to extract, but which is within my power, if at all, only after the most inordinate expenditure of time."[25] Judge Hand was not alone in his struggle with the income tax laws. Economist Henry Simons eloquently lamented the increasing complexity of the tax laws and could offer little hope for relief: "Simplicity in modern taxation is a problem of basic architectural design. Present legislation is insufferably complicated and nearly unintelligible. If it is not simplified, half of the population may have to become tax lawyers and tax accountants."[26]

Yet, rather than being simplified, the federal tax code grew much more complex in the decades following World War II. While the revenue derived from the income tax increased enormously during the war, the basic structure of the tax system remained essentially the same. The "transformation" of the federal income tax during the war really amounted to raising tax rates and lowering the personal exemption in pursuit of a broad-based tax and the great revenue it would bring into the Treasury. Conversely, most of the complexity that invaded the tax code in the postwar era can be traced to the use of the income tax for

---

codifying the various (and often contradictory) tax laws into a single coherent tax code. For an account of the 1939 codification process, see Roy G. Blakely and Gladys C. Blakely, *The Federal Income Tax* (New York: Longmans, Green & Co., 1940), 454–55.

25. Learned Hand, *The Spirit of Liberty: Papers and Addresses of Learned Hand,* ed. Irving Dilliard (New York: Knopf, 1952), 213.

26. Henry C. Simons, *Federal Tax Reform* (Chicago: University of Chicago Press, 1950), 28.

policy purposes. This resulted in the unprecedented rise in tax complexity that began in the 1950s and took off in the 1980s.

The Sources of Tax Complexity

The factor most often cited as responsible for the increased complexity in the tax laws is the perceived increase in the complexity of the "world" in general and of the "economy" in particular.[27] According to this common theme, the tax laws were necessarily expanded during the postwar period in response to, and in order to cope with, the increasingly sophisticated and complicated world of business, corporate finance, and international business. Purportedly, as business transactions became more complex, it became necessary for Congress to modify the income tax laws to keep up with the new practices of business.

There is a good deal of truth in this argument. For instance, the Treasury Department and IRS have struggled in recent years to keep up with the creativity of Wall Street investment bankers in crafting new so-called derivative, or hybrid, financial instruments, whose treatment for federal income tax purposes is quite baffling and, in some cases, quite costly to the government.[28] Since the 1950s, American businesses have progressively expanded into foreign markets, and foreign corporations have increasingly done more business in the United States. This change in the business environment has necessitated the expansion of the income tax laws to govern the taxation of multinational business transactions and corporations (both U.S. domestic as well as foreign) conducting business in multiple jurisdictions. Accordingly, the provisions of the tax code governing "international taxation" greatly expanded beginning in the 1960s.[29] Indeed, some of the most complicated provisions in

27. See, e.g., John F. Witte, *The Politics and Development of the Federal Income Tax* (Madison: University of Wisconsin Press, 1985), 149: "[T]he U.S. economy had become much more complex by the 1950's, and the rudimentary laws of the early income tax were no longer sufficient." Similarly, Wildavsky attributes the complexity of the budgeting process to "the complexity of modern life." Aaron B. Wildavsky, *The Politics of the Budgetary Process* (Boston: Little, Brown, 1964), 8.

28. For an interesting account of how the IRS has struggled to keep up with these new financial products, see Kathleen Matthews, "Officials Address Treatment of Hybrid Securities, Hedging Regulations," 65 *Tax Notes* 1592 (December 26, 1994).

29. Within the context of the U.S. income tax laws, "international taxation" has a somewhat misleading usage, referring to the taxation by the United States of domestic

the tax code were introduced during the 1980s in the area of international taxation. For instance, foreign corporations conducting business in the United States must now confront extremely complicated statutes and regulations to determine their "U.S. source" income,[30] their "effectively connected" U.S. income,[31] and their U.S. interest deductions.[32] They also must negotiate the "branch profits tax"[33] and complicated economic analysis required with respect to so-called intercompany transfer-pricing.[34] There is little doubt that in international taxation, tax complexity caught up to international business practices with a vengeance of its own.

Notwithstanding the initial appeal of this argument—that the tax laws increased in complexity in response to the increasing complexity of the world, the economy, or even life itself—it is not entirely satisfactory.

---

corporations and U.S. persons with foreign branches or income sources, or both, outside the United States, as well as foreign corporations and individuals with U.S. source income from conducting business and investment activities in the United States. For an excellent and comprehensive treatise covering all aspects of international taxation, see Joseph Isenbergh, *International Taxation: U.S. Taxation of Foreign Taxpayers and Foreign Income*, 3 vols. (Boston: Little, Brown, 1990).

30. See IRC secs. 861 and 862 (defining income from "U.S. sources" and income from sources outside the United States). Specific provisions of the tax code governing the taxation of foreign corporations and nonresident aliens are found in Subpart 2 of Subchapter N of the Internal Revenue Code.

31. For the definition of "effectively connected" income, see IRC sec. 864(c).

32. For example, the determination of the portion of a foreign corporation's U.S. debt allowable as a deduction under the U.S. income tax laws requires an allocation of world-wide debt based upon the location of the foreign corporation's assets. See Treas. Reg. sec. 1.882-5 (interest allocation rule) promulgated under the authority of IRC sec. 882(c)(1)(A). See also IRC sec. 863.

33. See generally IRC sec. 884.

34. Intercompany transfer-pricing is governed under IRC section 482. Spurred on by media accounts of foreign corporations grossly underpaying their U.S. income taxes, the Treasury Department began to pay serious attention to transfer-pricing in the 1960s. In 1988 Treasury issued a "White Paper" on the question of transfer-pricing: "A Study of Intercompany Pricing," Notice 88-123, 1988-2 C.B. 458. The White Paper was a radical departure from the usual attempt by Treasury to describe and cover every conceivable transaction and set of facts and circumstances in its regulations. However, after the publication of the White Paper, Treasury began the inevitable barrage of regulations. Many taxpayers objected to these regulations on various grounds. Treasury retreated somewhat and issued "simplified" regulations in January of 1993. Nevertheless, even these regulations impose highly technical standards that must be negotiated to avoid having the IRS recompute a corporation's U.S. income.

For example, the argument assumes that the use of new entities to conduct business led to the expansion of the tax laws to regulate such developments in business practice.[35] This is a peculiar reversal of the thesis that American law evolved and developed to accommodate the needs and interests of the dominant economic interests of civil society— that is, modern capitalism.[36]

Of course, it is relatively easy to find examples supporting both sides of the argument. For instance, in 1958 Congress created an entirely new tax entity, the so-called S corporation, for the express purpose of providing business with a new "pass-through" tax entity as an alternative to the traditional business corporation. The legislative intentions behind the creation of this new taxable entity have never been entirely clear, thus making it difficult to construe the many restrictions and rules governing Subchapter S corporations. However, there were definitive statements in the committee reports regarding the need to accommodate the interest of business by providing some sort of corporate pass-through entity.[37] The S corporation is strictly a creature of the federal tax code, and its adoption illustrates how the tax laws can develop to accommodate private economic interests. Yet, just as often it is the tax laws that produce changes in business practice, as well as in state corporate law.

The impact of the tax law on business practice and state law is illustrated by the creation of another entirely new legal entity for conducting business—the limited liability company. In 1977, Wyoming became the first state to enact a statute authorizing the organization of limited liability companies, and Florida followed suit in 1982. However, as late as 1988, there were only a handful of limited liability companies

35. "To match the complexity, the code needed to distinguish between corporations, corporations with income earned abroad, partnerships, holding companies, and a wide variety of tax-exempt and partially tax-exempt organizations. Complex organizations lead to complex sources and flows of income and costs, which in turn lead to demands for different treatment." John Witte, *Politics,* 149.

36. See, e.g., Morton J. Horwitz, *The Transformation of American Law: 1780–1860* (Cambridge: Harvard University Press, 1977), and idem, *The Transformation of American Law: 1870–1960* (New York: Cambridge University Press, 1992) (arguing generally that the evolution of American law has reflected the needs and dictates of private capital).

37. Subchapter S (found at sections 1361–1379 of the 1986 tax code) was first added to the tax code by the Technical Amendments Act of 1958, H.R. 8381, 85th Cong., 2d sess. The provisions were not in the original House bill, but rather were added by the Senate Finance Committee. S. Rept. No. 1983, 85th Cong., 2d sess., 1958 C.B. 1009.

actually organized under the laws of Wyoming and Florida. Then, in 1988, the Internal Revenue Service issued a favorable public ruling regarding the tax treatment of a Wyoming limited liability company.[38] Stimulated by the IRS's classification of the Wyoming limited liability company as a partnership for federal income tax purposes, this new business entity became "hot," and virtually every state has rushed to enact their own version of the statute.[39] As a result, changes in the tax law led directly to changes in corporate law and business practice. Consequently, the landscape for business and tax planning now includes yet one more legal/tax entity, with new rules and regulations presently being drafted by tax experts in the Treasury Department to govern the classification of the limited liability company and distinguish it from other pass-through tax entities—namely, S corporations and partnerships.[40]

Here, the development of state corporate law and business practice both accommodated the dictates of economic interests and responded to changes in federal tax law. Once the tax laws changed and the limited liability company became attractive on account of its favorable tax treatment, lobbying efforts quickly led to its adoption by most state legislatures.[41] Nevertheless, it would be a gross overstatement to say that in this case the federal tax laws developed to "serve" the needs or demands of private economic interests. Businesses and individual inves-

38. Rev. Rul. 88-76, 1988-2 C.B. 360.

39. By early 1996, a total of forty-eight states had enacted statutes providing for limited liability companies; the remaining two jurisdictions had bills pending. For a discussion of the benefits of a limited liability company as an entity for conducting business, see Sheldon D. Pollack, "Use of a Limited Liability Company for Conducting Business in Pennsylvania," 64 *Pa. Bar Ass'n Q.* 142 (1993).

40. The IRS has not yet revised the regulations to distinguish adequately between S corporations and partnerships, which are similar, but different in several important respects. This task has already begun with respect to limited liability companies. See, e.g., Rev. Proc. 92-35, 1992-1 C.B. 790; Rev. Proc. 92-33, 1992-1 C.B. 782 (addressing the question of free transferability); Rev. Proc. 94-1994, 1994-28 I.R.B. 129 (addressing the question of limited life); Rev. Proc. 95-10, 1995-3 I.R.B. 20 (procedure for ruling on requests for classification of a limited liability company as a partnership for federal income tax purposes). In early 1995, the IRS gave up and suddenly announced its intention to abandon the entire entity-classification enterprise and allow taxpayers to choose their preferred entity classification through a "check-the-box" system. IRS Notice 95-14, 1995-14 I.R.B. 7 (March 29, 1995). To date, the system has not yet been formally adopted.

41. State bar associations and the "Big 6" accounting firms led the lobbying efforts in most state legislatures. Law and accounting firms favor the limited liability company for the benefits it offers to both clients and themselves.

tors turned away from the traditional business corporation and began to use alternative business entities, such as partnerships and common-law creations (e.g., the Massachusetts business trust), precisely because of the more favorable tax results that could be achieved through such entities. As tax lawyers came to recognize the advantages to be gained by "restructuring" the traditional forms of business transactions through the use of partnerships, S corporations, and limited liability companies, business practices changed to accommodate the new federal income tax. Thereafter, the Treasury and IRS were forced to develop new regulations to govern the new transactions using these new entities.

This all suggests that the tax laws can play an independent role in shaping the development of business practices, rather than merely reflect and serve the needs of private capital. The expansion of the federal income tax had an impact upon how the economy developed, contributing in its own way to the increase in complexity of business practices. Obviously, the rise in complexity of the tax laws cannot be attributed solely to an increasingly complex economy and business world, although that surely contributed. Other factors were at work.

Tax Reform, Preferences, and Complexity

Many of the sources of the increased complexity in the tax laws can be found within the tax-policymaking process itself, rather than in the external environment (i.e., the "business world"). This is particularly true of high-minded tax-reform proposals, which have often ended up as nightmares of complexity.

Consider, for example, such reforms as the "passive activity loss" (PAL) rules, which were aimed at eliminating tax shelters; the original issue discount (OID) rules, which were aimed at preventing tax avoidance through deferral of the payment of tax; and the infamous regulations proposed under the authority of IRC section 89 for preventing discrimination in the use of pension plans and other tax-favored benefits by management to the exclusion of workers. The PAL rules and the OID rules are now a part of the regulatory landscape that every tax professional must navigate. The section 89 regulations would have imposed on employers even more complex and incomprehensible rules with respect to qualified retirement plans, but these were withdrawn by the Internal Revenue Service in direct response to the overwhelming outcry from the business and legal communities against this regulatory nightmare.[42] But rest assured, the IRS will get another try, since new regulations are scheduled to be promulgated in the near future. These and numerous other regulatory quagmires were originally conceived as "reforms" for preventing abuses of the tax laws. However, they ended up increasing the complexity of the tax laws to the point of where the laws nearly became dysfunctional—that point when taxpayers and the IRS could no longer understand or apply them.

In the last few years, Treasury officials adopted the position that future regulations would attempt to outline broad categories and general rules, rather than attempt to describe in examples every conceivable application of the prescribed legal standard, which attempt was sure to fail, since business transactions can be restructured in an almost infinite number of ways to avoid conformity with the precise facts and circumstances relied upon in the examples provided in the regulations. Of course, to the extent that regulations define legal standards in terms of simple, broad, and general rules, the legal standards are less clear and precise. Furthermore, the need to give substance to these broad rules will shift some power back to the courts, since the IRS must assert its position through successful litigation and favorable judicial decisions—something it has not always been able to achieve.

Beyond reform efforts to work "more perfect justice" through the tax laws, the other most important postwar contributor to complexity in tax policymaking was the tendency of Congress to implement more and more domestic policy through the tax code (e.g., tax expenditures). Paul McDaniel has written that "the use of tax expenditures constitutes the single biggest cause of complexity in our tax system."[43] This may be something of an overstatement, but it is hard to quarrel with the general assertion that tax expenditures significantly contribute to the overall complexity of the tax code. By the 1960s it was already common practice to use tax credits and preferences to implement social and economic policy. The effort to write so much of domestic policy into the tax code requires tax policymakers to draw ever more subtle distinctions between those taxpayers and transactions qualifying for the related tax benefits and those perceived to be abusing these provisions. These subtle distinc-

42. Pub. L. No. 101-140, section 203 (1989), repealed IRC section 89. See Elin Rosenthal, "Section 89 Foes Unimpressed by Treasury's Attempts at Compassion," 42 *Tax Notes* 528 (January 30, 1989), and idem, "Sobering Thoughts Intrude on Eulogy of Section 89," 45 *Tax Notes* 930 (November 20, 1989).

43. Paul McDaniel, "Federal Income Tax Simplification."

tions inevitably translate into increasingly complicated rules and regulations. Using the tax code to implement social policies as diverse as those reflected in the tax credits for "research and development" and low-income housing and in the tax deductions for contributions to universities and public charities contributes to increasing the complexity of the tax code.

While tax reformers have attacked the use of tax expenditures to implement policy, congressional policymakers find them highly effective in satisfying their own needs as elected officials. Even the wholesale assault on tax expenditures launched through the Tax Reform Act of 1986, as radical a departure from traditional tax policymaking as that represented, made only a dent in reducing the complexity resulting from these provisions. Since then, the use of tax expenditures to make policy has again been on the increase, thereby assuring that complexity will remain a salient feature of the federal income tax.

Economic Analysis in the Tax Code

The tax code has also grown in complexity as policymakers and the tax experts in the Treasury Department have become more and more sophisticated in perfecting the underlying concepts of the income tax. This is especially the case with respect to refining the statutory definition of income. The federal income tax rests upon the concept of taxing income received or accrued during the taxable year. As the tax experts have become more adept at defining taxable income in terms of "economic income," statutory provisions have become more complicated. Economic analysis has been introduced into the tax code in order to eradicate perceived abuses of the tax rules (i.e., avoidance of tax) by those taxpayers who themselves understand how to manipulate economic concepts to their own advantage.

The new "economic provisions" adopted in the 1980s introduced some of the most complicated rules and definitions to the tax code.[44] For instance, taxpayers once could purchase so-called zero-coupon bonds or other corporate debt obligations, thereby deferring the receipt and taxation of the "interest" payable on such obligations until the date of maturity (or redemption). Such deferral is viewed as unwarranted from

---

44. For example, there are now more than a half dozen different types of "interest" in the tax code, with various tracing rules designed to distinguish one form from another for tax purposes.

the perspective of the Haig-Simons definition of income (discussed further in Chapter 8) in that the debtholder's economic position has been enhanced over the course of the year just as if the interest had actually been paid, especially where the issuer is in sound financial condition and there is no reason to question the issuer's ability to satisfy its obligation to pay the accrued unpaid interest at maturity. Accordingly, the original issue discount rules were introduced in the 1980s, refining prior efforts to control this deferral of income recognition.[45] The OID rules impose taxation on the interest (and allow for a related deduction to the payer) based upon the economic accrual of the interest, rather than upon its receipt. This may be sound policy if the sole objective of the tax laws is to define taxable income so as to replicate economic (accrued) income. However, the OID rules introduced an extraordinary and unprecedented level of complexity into the tax laws, and if simplicity and administrability of the tax code are likewise to be respected when devising tax policy, statutes such as these must be considered a mixed blessing at best.[46]

Another example of how the intrusion of economic analysis into the tax code contributed to an increase in the complexity of the tax laws can be found in the campaign against "tax arbitrage" waged during the 1980s. Tax arbitrage involves taking advantage of the differential rate of return on investments arising solely from the unequal tax treatment of different sources of income.[47] The simplest example of tax arbitrage arises when an investor borrows in order to invest in tax-exempt municipal bonds. Under prior tax law, the investor could deduct all of the interest paid to carry such tax-preferred investment, while the interest income paid on the investment would be exempt from income tax. The result could be a profit derived solely from the differential created by the tax code itself. While this simple version of tax arbitrage is now disallowed under the tax code, other forms still remain part of standard tax planning.[48] For instance, investments in IRAs, Keogh plans, qualified

45. The original issue discount rules are found at IRC sections 1271–1275.

46. The Treasury regulations interpreting the OID rules are 441 pages long and use extremely complicated economic concepts. In some cases a computer must perform the computations required under the regulations to determine an "economic accrual" of interest under an OID debt instrument.

47. For a thorough discussion of tax arbitrage, see David J. Shakow, "Confronting the Problem of Tax Arbitrage," 43 *Tax L. Rev.* 1 (1987).

48. The simple version of tax arbitrage is disallowed by IRC section 265. Municipal governments used to engage in the reverse side of this transaction, borrowing at tax rates below market rates (on account of the interest-free treatment afforded such interest under

ERISA plans, and deductions for home mortgage interest involve tax-arbitrage opportunities available to most taxpayers.

Each of the provisions that create such arbitrage opportunities is really nothing more than a tax preference enacted by Congress to encourage taxpayers to move their capital into favored activities. Tax complexity results when reformers then introduce economic provisions to the tax laws in order to limit the ability of taxpayers to benefit from those tax preferences that create the arbitrage opportunities in the first place. The resulting tax code includes *both* the tax preference and the economic rules limiting the benefit thereof.

"Backstop" Tax Reform

As Congress has relied more and more on tax preferences to make public policy, it also has been forced to adopt other reform measures (such as those that govern tax arbitrage and original issue bond discounts) precisely to close the "leaks" in the tax base and prevent the "abuses" attributable to overuse of such tax preferences. In such instances, tax policymakers can be seen as rectifying their own poor judgment and overgenerosity in enacting too many tax preferences in the first place. Charles McLure has referred to measures designed to limit the use of tax preferences as "backstop" provisions intended to "prevent the abuse of tax preferences and/or the appearance of inequity."[49]

Through backstop reforms, the tax laws necessarily become even more complicated as new provisions are introduced to limit the applicability of yesterday's tax preferences. The incremental policymaking process that generates tax preferences is generally incapable of such a radical step as abandoning them altogether, even once they are denounced by the policymakers themselves as "abusive."[50] Incremental policymaking tends to produce only minor adjustments to existing tax

---

IRC section 103) and reinvesting the bond proceeds in higher-yielding markets, with the interest income exempt under IRC section 115 (exemption from federal income tax for "governmental entities"). This practice is now disallowed by IRC section 148.

49. McLure, "The Budget Process and Tax Simplification/Complication," 43.

50. To be somewhat more critical, such provisions reflect a certain lack of integrity: measures once considered favorable to the public interest are recharacterized as abuses when the tax benefits previously offered up by Congress are taken advantage of by taxpayers.

policies, and backstop reforms are highly compatible with such a strategy of policymaking.

Perhaps the alternative minimum tax (AMT) best illustrates how incremental policymaking is conducive to backstop reform.[51] Introduced in the Tax Reform Act of 1969, the alternative minimum tax is a tax system separate from and parallel to the "regular" federal income tax. The alternative minimum tax is an "add-on" tax intended to back up, or correct for, the inadequacies of the federal income tax itself. This parallel tax system begins with a comprehensive tax base in which deductions attributable to those tax preferences deemed to be most abusive are added back to adjusted net income. Under current law, "alternative minimum taxable income" is subject to a two-tier tax of 26 percent and 28 percent for individuals, having been originally introduced as a flat 10 percent rate and increased over the course of the next twenty-four years of incremental policymaking.[52]

As the many preferences appended to the tax code have accumulated over the years, wealthy taxpayers have used them more and more to reduce their overall tax liabilities. Not only is this all perfectly legal, but it is precisely what the statutes were *intended* to do—namely, induce individuals and corporations to engage in those economic activities or purchase those goods singled out by Congress as particularly worthy of subsidy. This does not make for good policymaking. However, the real problem is the lack of conviction evidenced by Congress when it heaps scorn upon those who use the tax preferences as Congress itself intended. The alternative minimum tax demonstrates how the tax law lends itself to incremental tax policymaking. It was easier for Congress to adopt this parallel tax regime, publicized as a reform, rather than to sweep the tax preferences out of the tax code altogether. After all, if use of the tax preferences to reduce tax liabilities was the problem, then reducing or eliminating them from the tax code would have been the logical solution.[53]

In the end, the alternative minimum tax reflects the worst tendency of incremental policymaking, tinkering with change at the margins and

51. The alternative minimum tax is found at IRC sections 55–58.

52. The latest rate increase, from a flat 24 percent to the aforementioned two-tier rate schedule, was implemented by the recently enacted Revenue Reconciliation Act of 1993. Pub. L. No. 103-66, 107 Stat. 312, sec. 1320.

53. Some have suggested that the problem is "piggishness" in overusing tax preferences to reduce one's tax liabilities. The alternative minimum tax is the kind of solution put forth to impose "selective limitations" on such abuse of tax preferences. See Daniel Shaviro, "Selective Limitations on Tax Benefits," 56 *U. Chi. L. Rev.* 1189 (1989).

thereby further complicating the tax laws, rather than abandoning an unwarranted tax preference altogether. And once a provision such as the alternative minimum tax finds its way into the tax code, it is possible to repeal it only when government is motivated as it was during the massive and rare tax reform effort in 1986. As described in Chapter 5, even the enthusiasm of House Republicans in 1995 was not sufficient to overcome the strong institutional support for the alternative minimum tax. House Republicans produced a bill (H.R. 1215) that would have repealed the corporate AMT altogether. Senate Republicans lacked the will to resist the inevitable backlash that such a move would have provoked among the Democratic opposition, liberal public-interest groups, and even some elements within the Republican Party itself. When the smoke cleared, the AMT remained intact.

Of course, even if repealed through the zeal of partisanship, such tax policies have a nasty habit of reappearing as the next generation's reform—as was the case with the investment tax credit, which resurfaced as a reform proposal of the Clinton administration only eight years after its most recent demise in 1986. Likewise, the tendency of incremental policymaking is to expand the scope of backup reform provisions, as has been the case with the add-on tax. On account of the expansion of this backup reform, more and more taxpayers now find themselves subject to the alternative minimum tax, although a high percentage remain unaware of the tax or their obligations and liabilities under it.

As a final note, it must be recognized that much of the complexity in the tax laws is introduced as policymakers attempt to draw increasingly subtle distinctions between the economic circumstances of different taxpayers. In other words, policymakers draft statutes that define ever more precise facts and circumstances under which the tax benefit is available, offering relief only to those taxpayers who genuinely qualify—that is, fall within a narrow and limited class of intended beneficiaries. But such efforts to achieve "equity" in the tax laws (by distinguishing between taxpayers that are not "similarly situated") are at odds with the goals of simplicity and administrability. A former high-level official in Treasury has recently observed that "[t]he tax law will always be an uneasy compromise between efforts to achieve equity and limit efficiency losses at a reasonable level of complexity."[54] When the impulse to achieve the highest level of

---

54. Daniel Halperin, "Are Anti-Abuse Rules Appropriate?" 48 *Tax Law.* 807, 811 (1995).

equity wins out, the result is the kind of overly complex tax provisions that distinguish between taxpayers but cannot be readily understood or applied by anyone but the most sophisticated tax professional – as is the case with the passive activity loss rules and the original issue discount rules.

On occasion, the interests of simplicity and administrability prevail, and Congress, the IRS, or both adopt a "brightline" test that draws few, if any, subtle distinctions. This is the case in many areas of corporate tax law, where brightline tests have been used. For instance, rather than attempt to define the elusive concept of "control" of a corporation, several statutes simply look to ownership of 50 percent or more of the voting stock of the corporation as conclusive evidence of control. Likewise, to be eligible for taxation as an S corporation, a corporate taxpayer may not own 80 percent or more of the stock of another corporation. This is an entirely arbitrary rule that employs a brightline test that any revenue agent in the field can readily apply.

Similarly, the IRS has long struggled to find a fair and efficient rule to govern the deductibility of costs relating to a so-called home office. Congress has provided that such costs are only deductible to the extent that the home office is the "principal place of business" for the taxpayer's relevant business.[55] Applying a nondiscriminatory standard, the IRS has resisted attempts by taxpayers to write off any portion of their personal residence as a business expense, and the U.S. Supreme Court has sanctioned its narrow interpretation of the statute.[56] This narrow standard has the effect of disallowing a good deal of the claims for home-office expenses – which of course is precisely the IRS's intention. Needless to say, congressional policymakers are considerably more responsive to the protests of disgruntled taxpayers who have been denied this deduction. In 1994, House Republicans included in their Contract with America tax bill (H.R. 1215) a provision to overturn the Supreme Court and permit a much broader category of taxpayers to claim the deduction for a home office. Such attempts to provide greater "equity" in the tax law inevitably cost the Treasury revenue and force the IRS to draft additional regulations to distinguish between the many different circumstances relating to home offices – lest every taxpayer with a business on the side write off a portion of his or her home as a "business" expense.

---

55. IRC sec. 280A.
56. *Commissioner v. Soliman*, 113 S. Ct. 701 (1993).

The "Tax Game"

One way to comprehend the dynamics behind the expanding complexity of the tax laws is to imagine the income tax laws as establishing a game—the "tax game."[57] The tax laws create a vast edifice, complete with rules and procedures that must be adhered to by those who, for better or worse, are required to play. The fact that taxpayers are forced to play the tax game does not affect the strategies or outcomes of play, nor is it particularly unusual for a game to be coercive. As with any game, there are different strategies that will produce superior outcomes, and in playing the game over time these strategies become evident to the players themselves, who adapt their play accordingly. The concern here is not so much the dynamics and logic of play—which is the immediate concern of tax lawyers and the IRS—but the development of the structures of the game and the impact of such on the rules of the game. Nevertheless, the interests and goals of the players shed light on how the rules develop.

The point of the tax game from the perspective of the taxpayer is to minimize one's tax liability (or that of one's client) while complying strictly and fully with all of the applicable rules.[58] Of course, since the "rules" are federal statutes buttressed by criminal sanctions, a failure to play by the rules can result in significant fines and imprisonment.[59] However, notwithstanding such penalties for failure to comply with the tax laws ("tax evasion"), there is no shortage of methods by which taxpayers can successfully (i.e., legally) minimize or avoid taxation ("tax avoidance"). Indeed, it becomes quite evident rather early in the career

57. Game theory can be traced to the seminal writings of Oskar Morgenstern and John Von Neumann in *The Theory of Games and Economic Behavior* (Princeton: Princeton University Press, 1944). Among the first applications of game theory to social science were William Riker, *The Theory of Political Coalitions* (New Haven: Yale University Press, 1962), and James M. Buchanan and Gordon Tullock, *The Calculus of Consent: Logical Foundations of Constitutional Democracy* (Ann Arbor: University of Michigan Press, 1962).

58. An alternative approach is to view the tax game as a "zero-sum" game played by various competing interests looking to secure benefits for themselves while imposing costs upon opposing interests. This perspective as applied to aspects of income tax policymaking is explored in Ronald F. King, *Money, Time, and Politics: Investment Tax Subsidies and American Democracy* (New Haven: Yale University Press, 1993).

59. See IRC secs. 7201, 7206, and 7343 (criminal sanctions for tax evasion and fraud). See also Sheldon D. Pollack, "The Penalty for Tax Fraud Against a Corporation," 72 *Tax Adviser* 464 (1992); Harry G. Balter, *Tax Fraud and Evasion* (Boston: Warren, Gorham & Lamont, 1983).

of every tax lawyer that any business transaction can be structured in a number of different ways, and different tax consequences can follow from these different structures for the deal, despite the Supreme Court doctrine holding that substance rather than form dictates the characterization and taxation of a particular economic arrangement or transaction.[60]

As successive generations of lawyers confronted the tax laws, the rules of the game became apparent, and the meaning, consequences, and outcomes of particular sets of tax rules were revealed. Much of this initial "learning stage" of the game was played out during the first decades of the federal income tax, from 1913 to 1939. In any new and complicated game, the level of play will rise to higher levels as players fully learn the range of moves possible under the rules.[61] However, in the tax game, as the players became more and more sophisticated in their play, the rules of the game were modified to counteract the increased level of players' skill. Thus, the tax game became more and more complex as it became more and more institutionalized.[62]

It is impossible to predict a priori who will benefit from such an increase in the level of complexity of a game. For instance, in chess, the beneficiaries of the enormous complexity of that game are those players with the greatest capacity to foresee the outcomes of the many possible successive moves of an opponent. In baseball, the progressive institutionalization of the game resulted in shifting the balance of power between the players. In the early stages of the game, before its rules and logic were fully revealed to players, hitters prospered. This was because players in the field had not yet fully "learned" their roles, meaning they

60. *CIR v. Court Holding Co.*, 324 U.S. 331, 334 (1945): "The incidence of taxation depends upon the substance of a transaction. . . . [T]he transaction must be viewed as a whole, and each step, from the commencement of negotiations to the consummation of the sale, is relevant."

61. As every child quickly learns, the range of possible outcomes for the game of tic-tac-toe is too limited, and hence, play soon becomes boring. Likewise, checkers soon bores most players, some of whom move on to more complex games such as chess. In fact, there are millions of possible outcomes in checkers (as opposed to tic-tac-toe). It is just that they all resemble each other, and thus, the game offers no great excitement.

62. This is not unusual. For instance, as the House of Representatives became increasingly institutionalized throughout the nineteenth century, the role of "representative" became more professional, decisionmaking became routinized and formal, leadership became hierarchical, and rules became more complex. See Nelson W. Polsby, "The Institutionalization of the U.S. House of Representatives," 62 *Am. Pol. Sci. Rev.* 144 (1968).

had not yet mastered their play. Accordingly, from 1900 through the 1940s hitters had what today would be considered improbably high batting averages. Thereafter, players became more proficient in their skills, especially pitchers, and rule changes were introduced with the express intention of restricting the success of hitters (such as raising the pitching mound). As a result, the batting averages of hitters declined in the postwar era of the 1950s.[63]

In the tax game, it is difficult to know with much certainty at any particular moment whether tax lawyers or the IRS is winning. The dynamics of the tax game are such that once some clever tax lawyer recognizes a new maneuver around a particular provision of the tax code, thereby successfully reducing the tax consequences attributable to a particular type of transaction, the maneuver becomes known within the tax bar, and eventually the IRS gets wind of it.[64] Thereafter, new regulations and perhaps even new statutes (the "rules" of the tax game) are adopted, giving the upper hand to the taxing authorities for the time being.[65] As such developments unfold, the rules of the game inevitably become a bit more complicated, and the tax lawyers must learn to play and devise new strategies under the new rules. The tax game is unusual insofar as one side (the IRS) also acts as the referee of the competition and is empowered to write new rules to favor its own side.[66] In such a game, one should not be surprised to discover that the rules grow ever

63. This interesting argument on the effect of institutionalization on baseball statistics (in particular, batting averages) was put forth by Stephen Jay Gould, "Losing the Edge," *Vanity Fair,* March 1983, 120.

64. Because the tax experts in the Treasury Department and the IRS generally come out of private tax practice, these techniques of tax avoidance eventually become known to the taxing authorities. This should be seen as one benefit of the so-called revolving door between business and governmental officials.

65. Recent examples of such new IRS regulations include the so-called May Stores transaction, which uses partnership distributions; the use of the section 754 election to step up basis in partnership assets in the context of a consolidated return; the taxation of new complex financial instruments designed to take advantage of the treatment of contingent interest under the OID rules; and the use of Subchapter K (partnership tax law) to avoid the adverse consequences of Subchapter F (taxing the undistributed income of controlled foreign corporations).

66. In this respect the tax game is analogous to what would result were gambling casinos permitted to amend the house rules in response to success by gamblers in beating the odds—for instance, by banning "card counting." Of course, state gaming officials can usually be persuaded to make such rule changes on behalf of the casinos.

more complex as the competitor/referee constantly rewrites the rules to its own advantage.[67]

Such increased levels of complexity in the tax laws (along with constant instability) eventually result in greater uncertainty, rather than less, in the outcomes decided under the tax laws. When the level of complexity reaches the point where players can no longer understand the rules, then players can no longer predict the outcomes. This has suggested to some that increased complexity is desirable from the perspective of both taxpayers and the taxing authorities, although not necessarily the tax bar.[68] According to this argument, higher levels of uncertainty increase the cost of litigation and, accordingly, increase the interest of taxpayers in pretrial settlements (which conversely reduce the tax lawyer's fees). Likewise, the IRS should generally favor higher levels of complexity, which make for greater uncertainty, pushing taxpayers in audits toward settling their disputes (thereby maximizing revenue for the government).[69] An interesting, albeit unproven, corollary of this argument is that congressional policymakers, the ultimate source of tax complexity, must introduce complexity into the tax code or, at a minimum, tolerate it, precisely to enhance the Treasury's collection of revenue under the income tax laws.[70]

This mode of analysis is useful in explaining the behavior of taxpayers, tax counsel, and the IRS in terms of their respective economic

---

67. A tax attorney in the film made from John Grisham's best-selling novel *The Firm* (New York: Dell Publishing, 1991; Paramount, 1993) neatly states this most cynical view: "It's a game. We teach the rich how to play it so they can stay rich—and the IRS keeps changing the rules so we can keep getting rich teaching them."

68. See, e.g., Michelle J. White, "Why Are Taxes So Complex and Who Benefits?" 47 *Tax Notes* 341 (April 16, 1990). According to White, accountants benefit most from a higher level of complexity, which forces taxpayers to seek professional advice in preparing their tax returns.

69. A recent study by the General Accounting Office (GAO) concludes that because of the great complexity and ambiguities of the tax laws, the IRS ends up litigating some of the same issues over and over. The GAO recommends legislative changes to rectify this, but obviously ignores the possibility that such continuous litigation maximizes revenue for the Treasury Department. General Accounting Office, "Tax Administration: Compliance Measures and Audits of Large Corporations" (GAO/GGD-94-70) (September 1, 1994).

70. The increased complexity and instability of the tax laws have been estimated to account for some $62 billion of the total $192 billion of costs attributable to complying with the income tax laws. A portion of this cost to taxpayers obviously shows up as additional revenue for the Treasury. See Arthur P. Hall, "The Cost of Unstable Tax Laws," 65 *Tax Notes* 759, 761 (November 7, 1994).

interests. It is assumed that the players of the game will make decisions based upon a rational assessment of their own self-interest narrowly defined in terms of the maximization of their economic position. However, when the same analysis is applied to the political elites who actually make the rules of the tax game, it breaks down. Congressional policymakers simply do not behave that way. "Rational-man" explanations take into account only pure economic motives such as revenue maximization, ignoring all of the personal and institutional motives and interests behind tax policymaking. Likewise, the impact of ideologies (such as tax reformism and the liberal political tradition itself) on the behavior of political elites is left out of game theory.

Ultimately, the political elites who are responsible for making the rules of the tax game (which account for the increased level of complexity) are driven by much more complicated and conflicting political motives and interests, rather than only by self-interest or the goal of maximizing revenue for the Treasury. Rather than a theory of decision-making based upon rational choice or the maximization of utility, the theory that more appropriately describes a political system that produces the great complexity pervading our tax laws is the so-called garbage can model of organizational behavior.[71] In describing the apparent anarchy of preferences motivating many large-scale complex organizations, such as the federal government, the originators of this theory have suggested that such an organization lacks a coherent structure and is best characterized as a "loose collection of ideas," discovering its "preferences through action more than it acts on the basis of preferences." The model applies to complex organizations in which participants have diverse goals and interests, and accordingly, preferences are left ill-defined precisely in order to avoid the conflict that will otherwise emerge under such circumstances. Nothing better describes the tax-policymaking process than this.

The Problem of Overly Complex Tax Laws

While there has been much concern of late with a tax code that is beyond the comprehension of the "average" taxpayer, little has been said to identify precisely what the problem is with such complex tax laws. In

---

71. Michael Cohen, James March, and Johan Olsen, "A Garbage Can Model of Organizational Choice," 17 *Admin. Sci. Q.* 1 (1972).

other words, it is generally assumed that because the tax code is complex, there must be a problem. One obvious solution to this formulation of the problem is to reduce the complexity of the tax code as confronted by the average taxpayer, who generally files a simple Form 1040 or, more likely, Form 1040-EZ (the "easy" version of the individual return for those in the unenviable position of having few deductions to claim). As such, tax complexity is left as a problem only affecting wealthy taxpayers and businesses, for whom professional tax advice is considered standard procedure.

This attitude has been expressed by the staff of the Joint Committee on Taxation, as well as by Congress: "[S]implification of the tax code itself is a form of tax reduction. . . . The [1986] Act reduces the complexity of the tax code for many Americans. . . . Taxpayers who will use the standard deduction rather than itemize their deductions will be freed from much of the recordkeeping, paperwork, and computations that were required under prior law."[72] According to this logic, the ultimate solution would be to tax gross income, rather than net income, thereby avoiding the difficult distinctions required to measure economic income. This approach, which was advocated by tax reformers in 1986, leads to the elimination of tax deductions and the imposition of threshold requirements (calculated, for instance, as a percentage of adjusted gross income) that most taxpayers will be unable to satisfy.[73] Such a notion of simplification will be of little comfort to those who lose the benefit of these deductions. This observation has not yet been grasped by those taxpayers who perceive some great benefit in filing a tax return on a postcard, as do proponents of the Hall-Rabushka flat tax. In that case, the size of the tax return reflects the absence of deductions available to, and hence distinctions to be made between, taxpayers at large.

To the extent that the computation of tax liabilities, the completion of forms, and the multitude of filing requirements can be simplified for a majority of individual taxpayers, administrative and revenue concerns of the government may be satisfied.[74] Furthermore the political expediencies of policymakers may be satisfied by simplifying the tax laws for

72. Staff of the Joint Committee on Taxation, *General Explanation of the Tax Reform Act of 1986* (Washington, D.C.: Government Printing Office, 1987), 11.

73. This is the underlying logic of IRC section 67, which limits certain "miscellaneous" deductions of individuals to the excess above 2 percent of the taxpayer's adjusted gross income. This provision was added to the tax code in 1986 under TRA.

74. See, e.g., Deborah H. Schenk, "Simplification for Individual Taxpayers: Problems and Proposals," 45 *Tax L. Rev.* 121, 166–67 (1989) (discussion of how complex recordkeeping requirements breed noncompliance among taxpayers generally).

the middle class, even while businesses and wealthy taxpayers confront increased complexity (as was the case with the 1986 act). In other words, dealing with tax complexity as it impinges upon the middle class may be sufficient to alleviate the political pressures exerted upon policymakers. Nevertheless, there is something rather cynical about treating tax complexity as a problem only to the extent that it is felt by the "average" (i.e., middle-class) taxpayer. This approach also ignores the enormous economic cost of compliance imposed upon businesses–estimated to be as much as $192 billion for tax year 1994.[75]

Recordkeeping is no doubt burdensome, but the real problem is that sound policy requires that the taxpayer qua citizen be able to understand the tax law. The reasons for tax simplification go beyond the difficulty of filling out tax returns and computing deductions. The present system of taxation has contributed much to the bureaucratization of modern life and the increased regulation of economic life, for both individuals as well as businesses. Those who are unsympathetic to the problem of governmental overregulation of business should recognize that an overly complex tax system also adversely affects individuals. As Moses Herzog once lamented in one of his great tirades against modernity: "Internal Revenue regulations will turn us into a nation of bookkeepers. The life of every citizen is becoming a business. This, it seems to me, is one of the worst interpretations of the meaning of human life history has ever seen. Man's life is not a business."[76]

The tax laws have a peculiar impact upon private behavior insofar as they do not strictly prohibit particular private action or conduct, but rather establish a broad framework of incentives and disincentives through which private activity is subtly altered. The tax laws impose a superstructure above and beyond the legal framework that prevails under the liberal political tradition. Certain activity may be entirely "legal" in the sense that no laws expressly prohibit the activity. However, under the tax laws, the activity may carry such a significant cost– namely, additional taxation–that it is effectively prohibited. Taxation discourages particular forms of business activities just as surely as if

75. Figure cited in Hall, "The Cost of Unstable Tax Laws," 761. Such cost estimates are notorious for their exaggeration. Two serious attempts to understand the costs associated with the individual income tax are found in Joel Slemrod and Nikki Sorum, "The Compliance Cost of the U.S. Individual Income Tax System," 37 *Nat'l Tax J.* 461 (1984), and Joel Slemrod and Marsha Blumenthal, "The Compliance Cost of the U.S. Individual Income Tax System: A Second Look After Tax Reform," 45 *Nat'l Tax J.* 185 (1992).

76. Saul Bellow, *Herzog* (New York: Viking Press, 1964), 11.

there was an outright legal prohibition against such conduct.[77] In this respect, the tax laws depart from the traditional principles of the liberal political tradition – in particular, the principle of the rule of law.

The rule of law assumes that clear legal standards are enunciated prior to taking effect, thereby providing citizens with notice of prohibited behavior and of the sanctions attached to violations of such prohibitions.[78] Fundamental to the concept of the rule of law is the notion that legal standards of public behavior be known, or at least knowable, by the citizenry. To the extent that the tax laws are public laws that similarly should be governed by the principles of the rule of law, their excessive complexity violates that principle, in that the legal standards enunciated under them cannot be comprehended by those subject to sanctions for a failure to comply. This case against overly complex and changing laws was best expressed by James Madison in *The Federalist Papers*: "It will be of little avail to the people, that the laws are made by men of their own choice, if the laws be so voluminous that they cannot be read, or so incoherent that they cannot be understood; if they be repealed or revised before they are promulgated, or undergo such incessant changes that no man, who knows what the law is today, can guess what it will be tomorrow. Law is defined to be a rule of action; but how can that be a rule, which is little known, and less fixed?"[79] In many respects, this has become the sad state of the tax laws. The tax code has become a massive and impenetrable edifice governing nearly all of economic life and business activity, as well as a good deal of private activity of the individual.

An alternative vision of tax policymaking, one favored here, was succinctly and eloquently expressed by an unusually insightful tax practitioner: "[T]he tax law should develop through judicial construction of general principles (in essence, as common law) rather than through ever more complicated prescriptive rules."[80] For decades, the tax laws have developed in entirely the opposite direction, and that is unfortunate for the American polity.

---

77. This theme echoes Chief Justice Marshall's oft-cited admonition: "An unlimited power to tax involves, necessarily, a power to destroy." *McCulloch v. Maryland,* 17 U.S. 316 (1819).

78. The classic statement of the rule of law is found in Fredrich A. Hayek, *The Constitution of Liberty* (Chicago: University of Chicago Press, 1960), 162–75.

79. James Madison, Paper No. 62, *The Federalist Papers* (New York: New American Library, 1961), 381.

80. Peter C. Canellos, "Acquisition of Issuer Securities by a Controlled Entity: Peter Pan Seafoods, May Department Stores, and McDermott," 45 *Tax Law.* 1, 14 (1991).

8

Tax Experts and Tax Reform

> The case for drastic progression in income taxation must be rested on the case against inequality—on the ethical or aesthetic judgment that the prevailing distribution of wealth and income reveals a degree (and/or kind) of inequality which is distinctly unlovely.
> —Henry C. Simons (1938)

> Fundamental reform almost always runs the risk of making things worse.
> —Rep. Dan Rostenkowski (1993)

In the vast literature on the federal income tax, considerable attention has been devoted to the issue of tax reform.[1] Tax experts (both economists and tax lawyers) generally agree on which policies constitute "reform" legislation. Ironically, this often means that commentators provide little justification why a particular tax bill (such as the Tax Reform Act of 1986) should be classified as "tax reform" rather than just one more proposal to shift the incidence of taxation from one group of taxpayers to another.[2] Because these tax experts play an important role

---

1. The numerous studies on this theme include Michael J. Boskin, ed., *Federal Tax Reform: Myths and Realities* (San Francisco: Institute of Contemporary Studies, 1978); George F. Break and Joseph A. Pechman, *Federal Tax Reform: The Impossible Dream?* (Washington, D.C.: Brookings Institution, 1975); Joseph A. Pechman, ed., *Options for Tax Reform* (Washington, D.C.: Brookings Institution, 1984); Boris I. Bittker, "Tax Reform and Tax Simplification," 29 *U. Miami L. Rev.* 1 (1974). See also notes 5 and 6 to Chapter 7.

2. On account of tax professionals' consensus regarding this agenda for tax reform, even one of the most observant scholars of the federal income tax could write an entire study on the topic of "tax reform" without expressly defining the concept or providing any

both in setting the agenda for tax policy and in defining the policy alternatives for congressional decisionmakers, the particular vision of tax reform that they embrace has been instrumental in shaping the course of U.S. tax policy.

The agenda for tax reform is very much at odds with the politics-as-usual that otherwise dominates congressional policymaking. For reasons discussed in Chapters 4 and 6, the politics of tax reform overwhelmed the traditional congressionally based tax politics in the mid-1980s. In 1986, tax reform *was* the politics of the federal income tax. The theoretical premises of tax professionals and their impact on the course of contemporary American tax policymaking are the subject of this chapter.

The Idea of Tax Reform

"Tax reform" has meant different things at various times in contemporary American political discourse. For instance, tax reform sometimes has been associated with perfecting the administration of the tax laws, preventing the "evasion" of taxation, or maximizing the revenue raised under the income tax. Tax reform has also been portrayed as the perfection of the tax laws so as more accurately to measure a taxpayer's "economic income" and, at other times, as the simplification of the tax laws—a goal that is likely to conflict directly with any effort to bring the definition of taxable income into closer harmony with an economic definition of income. Most recently, tax reform has been cast in terms of abandoning the income tax altogether—perhaps in favor of a flat consumption tax. All these diverse expressions of tax reform have been advanced at one time or another in the legislative arena. However, in the mid-1980s the politics of the income tax was informed by a very specific vision of tax reform and the ideal income tax.

That vision of tax reform behind the politics of TRA takes its intellectual bearings from a school of thought widely embraced by academics in American law schools, economists, and most tax professionals (especially those working for the tax committees on Capitol Hill and in the executive departments). Of course, any notion of tax reform assumes certain specific *normative* principles. Just as the decision to adopt a

---

criterion by which it should be judged. Joseph A. Pechman, *Tax Reform, the Rich and the Poor* (Washington, D.C.: Brookings Institution, 1989).

system of income taxation reflects a normative judgment, one that American policymakers confronted several times in the long history of the struggle over adoption of a federal income tax, so too does the decision to tax "income" rather than commodities, transactions, or the consumption of goods and services involve a normative determination. In this respect, a normative judgment is at the heart of the current debate over a consumption-based flat tax. Politicians tend to frame the debate in terms of "fairness" and "simplicity," while economists present the case in terms of "efficiency." But the fundamental *political* questions remain, Which economic groups and interests will benefit, and which lose, from the switch to a consumption-based tax from an income-based tax, and what is the justification for imposing such outcomes through governmental action? Tax reform invokes fundamental normative issues because sucha change constitutes a fundamental reconstitution of existing institutions, legislative procedures, and extant legal structures—which changes inevitably will benefit particular groups and interests while adversely affecting others. Specific interests and groups win or lose as the special protection of the U.S. tax code is withdrawn or extended under the cover of tax reform.

The main principles of tax reform advanced by most tax professionals can be traced to the writings and doctrines of particular economists and tax academics. From their positions in the top American universities and public-policy institutes, these academics have exerted considerable influence over the political debate and public discourse on federal tax policy. Furthermore, many of these same tax academics have at one time or another held important policymaking positions in the Treasury Department, thereby directly influencing the course of federal tax policy (for example, in contributing to the success of the movement for tax reform in 1986). In this way, theory has informed tax praxis.

Proponents of the tax experts' vision of tax reform make certain fundamental assumptions about the nature of the ideal income tax. The first of these is that an income tax must adopt the broadest, most inclusive definition of "income" as its theoretical foundation. Such a definition of income dictates in favor of adopting a broad tax base— commonly referred to as a "comprehensive tax base." A comprehensive tax base is one stripped of all tax loopholes, preferences, exclusions, exemptions, shelters, and expenditures. At the same time, many tax academics hold fast to certain principles of tax "equity"—specifically, the principles of "horizontal" and "vertical" equity. To the uninitiated, the principles of tax equity (examined further below) may be hard to distinguish from the subjective preferences of tax academics in favor of a very specific form and structure to the income tax. Furthermore, the case for tax reform is really an outgrowth of the preference for a comprehensive tax base and a commitment to the underlying values expressed by the principles of vertical and horizontal equity. This all constitutes the basis for a tax policy agenda shared by many tax academics and professionals, which in its turn has greatly influenced the ways in which tax lawyers, judges, members of Congress, as well as the general public, think about tax policy and the federal income tax.

The Definition of Taxable Income

The foundation and cornerstone of any system of taxation is its base— that commodity or conceptual construct upon which taxation is imposed. In the case of an income tax, the particular definition of "income" that is adopted will determine the tax base and, hence, the nature and scope of the tax system. Yet, arriving at such a definition is no simple matter. During the first decades of the U.S. income tax, policymakers and the courts struggled to find a conceptually coherent and workable definition of income.[3] In the ensuing decades, policymakers refined and expanded the initial definition in an effort to broaden the grasp of the income tax and thereby bring in greater revenue under the tax system.

As suggested in Chapter 2, the drafters of the original Civil War income tax had only a vague sense of the concept of income. Much the same uncertainty pervaded the 1913 income tax. As no statutory definition was even provided, these first income tax statutes did not so much resolve the crucial issue of defining income as sidestep it altogether. Over the next eight decades, the federal courts and the executive branch collectively crafted a practical and administrable basis for the income tax. Even as the tax code otherwise has evolved to provide significantly greater statutory details, what specifically constitutes taxable income is still often determined by reference to the early judicial decisions previously discussed in Chapter 7.

While the federal courts struggled with the difficult cases, making subtle distinctions in developing a workable formulation of taxable

---

3. An excellent account of the evolution of the concept of income during the first decades following the enactment of the federal income tax of 1913 is Roy G. Blakely and Gladys C. Blakely, *The Federal Income Tax* (New York: Longmans, Green & Co., 1940), chap. 21 ("Evolution of the Definition of Taxable Income").

income, tax academics embraced their own very specific conception, one that has greatly influenced subsequent discussions on the federal income tax. The initial formulation of what quickly became the accepted definition of economic income was advanced in 1921 by economist Robert Haig. Haig defined income as "the money value of the net accretion to one's economic power between two points of time."[4] Haig's definition still left open questions about the "economic power" of an individual and how that power is measured. In 1938, the eclectic economist Henry Simons of the University of Chicago built upon Haig's initial formulation and enunciated what for all practical purposes has become the standard definition of income in the tax literature: "Personal income may be defined as the algebraic sum of (1) the market value of rights exercised in consumption and (2) the change in the value of rights exercised in consumption between the beginning and end of the period in question."[5] This "economic" definition of income, generally referred to as the Haig-Simons definition of income in deference to Haig's original contribution, posits that economic income is the total accumulation of wealth and consumption over that period of time adopted for purposes of measurement. Economists often refer to the tax system grounded upon the Haig-Simons definition of income as an "accretion" or "accrual" income system.[6]

Under the Haig-Simons definition, income includes the monetary value of rights and consumption during the relevant period, as well as any net increase in the monetary value of the taxpayer's property and rights during the same period. Assuming that the taxpayer is an individual and that the relevant period of accrual is a calendar year,[7] then income will include the net increase in the value of all property and rights during the year, plus the dollar value of what was consumed by the individual during the same period. This economic/accrual definition

4. Robert M. Haig, "The Concept of Income," in *The Federal Income Tax* (New York: Columbia University Press, 1921), chap. 1.

5. Henry C. Simons, *Personal Income Taxation: The Definition of Income as a Problem of Fiscal Policy* (Chicago: University of Chicago Press, 1938), 50. For an interesting discussion of the Haig-Simons definition of income, see Richard Goode, "The Economic Definition of Income," in *Comprehensive Income Taxation*, ed. Joseph A. Pechman (Washington, D.C.: Brookings Institution, 1977), 1–36.

6. For a comprehensive description of a personal income tax system based on economic accretion, see David F. Bradford, *Untangling the Income Tax* (Cambridge: Harvard University Press, 1986), 32–55.

7. An individual's "taxable year" is a calendar year under the scheme adopted by the federal income tax. IRC sec. 441(g); Treasury Regulation sec. 1.441-1T.

of income is even more inclusive than the broad definition of gross income codified in section 61(a) of the Internal Revenue Code or that of the Supreme Court. For instance, the Haig-Simons definition includes unrealized gains—that is, the annual net increase in the market value of an individual's principal residence, land, and other investments such as stock and bonds, even if not sold during the year. It also includes "imputed income," such as that which is derived from an individual's ownership of his own home.[8] The concept of imputed income presupposes that one's home is an investment, and thus, the rent that would otherwise have been paid to a landlord ought to be imputed for the use of the property.[9] Even the Internal Revenue Service in its broadest definition of income has never dared to include "imputed income," for obvious reasons of practicality, administration, and, arguably, constitutionality.

The Haig-Simons definition of income has been the theoretical starting point for virtually all discussions of the U.S. income tax. Today, there is hardly a law school tax course or economics textbook on the income tax that does not at least pay lip service to the Haig-Simons definition.[10] The

8. See Simons, *Personal Income Taxation,* 51–55, 110–24 (recognizing the limitations of the concept and the inherent difficulty in distinguishing "consumption" from "expense").

9. This may be a difficult concept for the uninitiated. It is easier to understand in the situation where the house is owned by a corporation wholly owned by the taxpayer. In that case, a fair market rent would be paid by the individual to his corporation, such rent being a nondeductible personal expense of the individual and taxable income to the corporation as landlord. Of course, the corporate landlord would be entitled to depreciate the building and deduct all expenses related to this "investment." For a discussion of some of the implications of the concept of imputed income, see William F. Hellmuth, "Homeowner Preferences," in *Comprehensive Income Taxation,* ed. Pechman; see also Chirelstein, *Federal Income Taxation,* ¶ 1.03. Chirelstein points out that imputed income includes "[i]ncome derived from the use of 'household durables' such as a personal residence, car or television set, and from income from the performance of service's for one's own or one's family's benefit."

10. See, e.g., Joseph A. Pechman and Benjamin A. Okner, *Who Bears the Tax Burden?* (Washington, D.C.: Brookings Institution, 1974), 12; J. R. Hicks, *Value and Capital: An Inquiry into Some Fundamental Principles of Economic Theory* (London: Oxford University Press, 1939), 171–81; Richard A. Musgrave, *The Theory of Public Finance: A Study in Public Economy* (New York: McGraw-Hill, 1959), 164–73. Typical of the way textbooks on the federal income tax pay homage to the Haig-Simons definition of income is the treatment in John C. Chommie and Michael D. Rose, *Federal Income Taxation,* 2d ed. (St. Paul, Minn.: West Publishing Co., 1988), 17: "The most widely accepted definitions of income are those of Professors Haig and Simons. . . . [T]he Haig-Simons definitions of income and their many variants have contributed to current notions of the

Haig-Simons definition of income has had a singular impact upon, and virtual stranglehold over, the academic debate on income taxation and federal income tax policy. Only in recent years have academics (mostly economists) questioned the theoretical premises of an income-based system of taxation, and more recently, the political system has responded to these criticisms by considering alternatives such as a consumption-based system of taxation. Even still, any discussion of income taxation must begin with reference to the current system, which assumes the Haig-Simons definition of income as the basis for taxation.

A Comprehensive Income Tax

The Haig-Simons economic definition of income is all-inclusive, and hence, adopting it as the base for a system of taxation indicates a preference for a "comprehensive" tax base, one of the chief items on the policy agenda of tax reformers. "It is no exaggeration to say that a 'comprehensive tax base' . . . has come to be the major organizing concept in most serious discussions of our federal income tax structure."[11] A comprehensive tax base respects no tax preferences, exemptions, or exclusions from income and, at the extreme, becomes an almost Platonic ideal: "At the outer limits of economic income there is, in a region of some abstraction, what could be called the 'universal income tax base.' It includes *all* net enhancements of well-being. . . . If this were the base of taxation, much of the return to consumption that now escapes tax would in fact be reached. . . . A tax on the universal tax base would in fact satisfy simultaneously the elusive goals of efficiency and horizontal and vertical equity."[12] Imposing the federal income tax on this "universal income tax base" is the goal of tax reformers who begin with the Haig-Simons definition of income as the foundation for their tax system. The legacy of Henry Simons is found in the widespread adoption of his

---

economic concept of income"; and in William D. Andrews, "Personal Deductions in an Ideal Income Tax," 86 *Harv. L. Rev.* 313, 309 (1971): "[A]n ideal personal income tax is one in which tax burdens are accurately apportioned to a taxpayer's aggregate personal consumption and accumulation of real goods and services and claims thereto."

11. Boris I. Bittker, "A 'Comprehensive Tax Base' as a Goal of Income Tax Reform," 80 *Harv. L. Rev.* 925 (1967).

12. Joseph Isenbergh, "The End of Income Taxation," 45 *Tax L. Rev.* 283, 330 (1990).

definition of income and the concomitant adoption of the comprehensive tax base as the ideal for the federal income tax.[13] Simons himself expressed some initial misgivings about the practicalities of relying upon his definition of income as the basis for the U.S. income tax.[14] However, he later came to equate the effort to achieve a comprehensive tax base with "tax reform" per se.[15]

There have been remarkably few objections to constructing the entire edifice of the federal income tax upon the Haig-Simons definition of income and a comprehensive tax base. Even those economists who now question the choice of income as the base for the federal tax system are still ardent proponents of a *comprehensive* consumption tax base— namely, one that recognizes no tax preferences or exclusions. A rare exception is the insightful critique made a quarter century ago by Boris Bittker,[16] which challenged the prevailing orthodoxy that taxable income necessarily ought to equal economic income, as is implied by the Haig-Simons definition. Bittker's critique of the comprehensive tax base as the singular goal of tax reform is even more persuasive in light of the success of the reform movement in 1986.

The gist of Bittker's critique is that the adoption of a truly comprehensive tax base would effect radical departures from existing tax law—changes that might not even be desired by the opponents of tax preferences. Furthermore, even if such a comprehensive tax base were adopted, enormous conceptual difficulties would still remain in codifying the Haig-Simons notion of income. A truly "systematic elimination" of tax preferences to implement the Haig-Simons definition of income would require taxing such traditionally exempt sources as life insurance, governmental benefits furnished in cash payments or in kind (e.g., the monetary value of services provided to the poor), gifts and

13. The relevance of Henry Simons's writings to the current debate over tax policy is evidenced in a recent exchange in the editorial pages of the *Wall Street Journal* among economist Herbert Stein of the American Enterprise Institute, James M. Buchanan (a former recipient of the Nobel prize in economics), and Robert Bartley (editor of the *Wall Street Journal*) over the meaning and implications of Simons's 1938 book, *Personal Income Taxation. Wall St. J.*, January 30, 1996, A18.

14. "If one accepts our definition of income, one may be surprised that it has ever been proposed seriously as a basis for taxation." Simons, *Personal Income Taxation*, 103.

15. Henry C. Simons, *Federal Tax Reform* (Chicago: University of Chicago Press, 1950).

16. Bittker, "Comprehensive Tax Base." See also Boris I. Bittker, Charles O. Galvin, R. A. Musgrave, and Joseph A. Pechman, *A Comprehensive Income Tax Base? A Debate* (Branford, Conn.: Federal Tax Press, 1968).

inheritances, charitable contributions, recoveries for personal injuries and death, and the "imputed" income attributable to living in one's own home. In addition, the Haig-Simons definition would also include the market value of all rights and property consumed by the taxpayer during the taxable year, including not just the cash received from such governmental programs as Social Security, unemployment compensation, public welfare, and assistance from private charitable agencies, but also the market value of such noncash benefits as assistance from public and private social service agencies. To achieve a truly comprehensive tax base, the tax code would have to be stripped once and for all of such tax preferences as the investment tax credit and all the other tax credits (including those intended to benefit the working poor), deductions for the amortization of business assets, inventory pricing, and all the various provisions permitting tax-free exchanges for "policy" reasons.

Proponents of a comprehensive tax base acknowledge that some exceptions must be made to their principles, whether on the grounds of practicality and administrability or on the grounds of competing equities, which grounds would justify retention of personal exemptions and special exemptions for the aged, the blind, the poor, and others. Yet, as soon as any exception to the Haig-Simons definition of income is admitted, the horse is out of the barn. Once any exceptions are deemed justifiable, and once certain preferences are retained on the grounds that they promote some necessary and desirable social or economic goal, the comprehensive tax base becomes only a guiding principle. Thereafter, each preference must be evaluated on a case-by-case basis.

But as Bittker recognized, there are no objective or scientific standards for differentiating between those provisions which are "exceptions" and those which are the "rules" for defining income. "[T]he income tax structure cannot be discovered, but must be constructed; it is the final result of debatable judgments."[17] And such judgments are necessarily political judgments about what ought or ought not to be taxed. These are precisely the kind of judgments that are routinely imposed upon congressional policymakers by the structures of American political institutions. Indeed, this is the most important role for policymakers, who, as elected representatives, must judge and evaluate the constant flood of tax proposals and prioritize them under the constraints and demands imposed by the revenue imperative, partisan platforms,

17. Bittker, "Comprehensive Tax Base," 985.

and their constituencies. This is the *political* side of tax policymaking that tax reformers disdain and economists avoid discussing, but which reflects and serves the democratic/representative functions of congressional tax policymakers.

The most cautious and democratic ideal for tax policymaking is one in which preferences, exemptions, credits, and even tax-accounting rules are examined on a case-by-case basis and are retained if found justifiable on some satisfactory grounds and abandoned if found to reflect nothing more than a preference for some special interest. This "incremental" strategic approach can be contrasted with that of the tax reformer for whom no preference is sacred and no special privilege is politically defensible. Those who would abandon (or "throw overboard") the present income tax system, which has evolved over the past eighty years, in favor of an untested flat consumption tax would be well advised to proceed more cautiously. At risk is both the revenue raised by and the interests served through the present income tax regime.

The Principles of Tax "Equity"

Academic proponents of tax reform also commonly assert that the "fairness" of any system of income taxation must be evaluated by reference to the principles of "horizontal" and "vertical" equity. These principles have been expressed in classic textbook fashion as follows:

> One important goal of a good system of income taxation must be *fairness*. . . . The principle of horizontal equity is that people similarly situated should be taxed alike, which is translated under an income tax into the principle that people with the same income (properly defined) should pay the same tax. . . . Vertical equity refers to the relative amounts of taxes paid by people with different incomes. The rate structure of our income tax reflects the adoption of a principle of vertical equity called *progressivity*, which means that as one's income rises the *proportion* of income that one pays as a tax rises. . . . The philosophic underpinning of progressivity is the notion that . . . justice requires a more equal distribution of rewards than what we get with this [free-market] system.[18]

18. William A. Klein, Joseph Bankman, Boris I. Bittker, and Lawrence M. Stone, *Federal Income Taxation*, 8th ed. (Boston: Little, Brown, 1990), 19–20. Comparable state-

In other words, horizontal equity is said to dictate that all "similarly situated" taxpayers be treated equally. This premise is then translated into the maxim that all income, regardless of its source, must be treated comparably (i.e., taxed). Furthermore, vertical equity (or "justice") is said to "require" that those with greater income be taxed at higher marginal tax rates in order to effect a more equal distribution of wealth. "Progressive" tax reformers since Henry Simons have adopted this as the perspective from which to evaluate the income tax system.[19]

For example, the principle of horizontal equity is taken to mean that the income of similarly situated taxpayers must be treated equally in order that the tax system be deemed "fair."[20] The assumption is that individuals are similarly situated to the extent that they have similar levels of income (without respect to tax preferences). However, many special provisions in the tax code were adopted precisely in order to make distinctions between taxpayers with similar incomes, to take into account the special circumstances that affect their respective net disposable incomes. In other words, the tax preferences themselves attempt to compensate for the economic differences between taxpayers. For example, significant medical expenses can be deducted in recognition of the fact that the "situation" of the taxpayer who suffers such

---

ments are found in Timothy J. Conlan, Margaret T. Wrightson, and David R. Beam, *Taxing Choices: The Politics of Tax Reform* (Washington, D.C.: Congressional Quarterly Press, 1990), 26; Michael J. Graetz, *Federal Income Taxation: Principles and Policies,* 2d ed. (Westbury, N.Y.: Foundation Press, 1988), 17; Joseph J. Minarik, *Making Tax Choices* (Washington, D.C.: Urban Institute Press, 1985), 21.

19. See, e.g., John G. Head, "Tax-Fairness Principles: A Conceptual, Historical, and Practical Review," in *Fairness in Taxation: Exploring the Principles,* ed. Allan M. Maslove (Toronto: University of Toronto Press, 1993), 12: "The requirements of tax fairness have accordingly come to be understood, following Simons, in terms of the concepts of horizontal and vertical equity, interpreted more specifically as requiring progressive personal direct taxation on a broad income base designed in accordance with the Schanz-Haig-Simons net-accretions concept." Head goes on to point out that economists have more recently begun to stress "efficiency" over vertical equity and progressivity as the standard by which an income tax structure should be judged.

20. See, e.g., C. Eugene Steuerle, *The Tax Decade: How Taxes Came to Dominate the Public Agenda* (Washington, D.C.: Urban Institute Press, 1992), 9: "[A] fair tax system . . . is . . . one that taxes equally those with equal incomes"; and Martin Feldstein, "Why Capital Gains Taxes Are Unfair," *Wall St. J.,* November 21, 1994, A16: "Any fair system of income taxation should be based on the principle that two similar individuals with the same income should pay the same tax."

severe expenditures is not really "similar" to that of a taxpayer with the same income but few or no medical expenses.[21] Likewise, a family of four with the same gross income as a single taxpayer is not similarly situated, and thus, the tax code makes some attempt to balance these inequalities through personal exemptions.[22] Whether these are unjustifiable tax preferences or definitional provisions enacting horizontal equity is not so easy to determine a priori. In the end, the slogan of horizontal equity offers no specific direction or guidance in making any of the hard decisions or drawing the subtle distinctions that must be made when devising a fair and accurate system of taxation.

As noted above, the principle of vertical equity is commonly taken to imply that tax rates *ought* to be progressive (or graduated).[23] In other words, taxpayers ought to pay a greater percentage of their income in taxes as their income increases. This proposition may very well be a precondition for raising revenue, but it also assumes a specific theory of equality and justice, which must be defended beyond simplistic appeals to "equity." Unfortunately, there is seldom any justification offered for a graduated income tax rate structure, despite the fact that this is one of the defining characteristics of the U.S. individual income tax. The argument seldom goes beyond the bald assertion that as income rises, tax rates must increase accordingly. However, fair-minded individuals of good faith can and do disagree on this. One can just as easily posit that "equity" and "fairness" dictate that all citizens ought to bear the burdens associated with citizenship equally – suggesting that a "head" tax is appropriate or that political equality dictates that taxes ought to be imposed in direct proportion to one's "ability to pay," pointing toward a flat tax.[24] Likewise, one could support the position that equity demands nothing more than that the tax laws be applied equally and uniformly to

---

21. This policy underlies the deduction for medical expenses provided at IRC section 213.

22. Deductions for dependents provide some tax relief for larger families and hence provide limited compensation for the "unequal" situations. IRC secs. 151 and 152.

23. See, e.g., Conlan, Wrightson, and Beam, *Taxing Choices,* 26 n. 21: "[A]ccording to [the principle of vertical equity], fairness is a matter of progressivity: treating unequals differently; that is, taxing the wealthiest more."

24. For a discussion and critique of early-twentieth-century theories holding that tax rates must be related to "ability to pay" (i.e., must be progressive), see John F. Witte, *The Politics and Development of the Federal Income Tax* (Madison: University of Wisconsin Press, 1985), 50.

all taxpayers alike, with no special privileges (e.g., exclusions or exemptions) recognized for wealth, social standing, office, and the like.[25] Such a notion of fairness, or equity (referred to as "interstitial" equity), will be strictly confined to "process"—holding that the outcomes of a system of taxation are fair so long as the process by which they are made is unbiased and impartial.[26]

The point here is not to argue in favor of either uniform or progressive tax rates but only to suggest that when tax academics posit propositions such as vertical and horizontal equity as the fundamental principles of taxation, couching them in the seemingly neutral, scientific language of economics, they mask the extent to which these propositions are inherently political and normative.[27] Indeed, the most perceptive students of the income tax recognize and acknowledge the "perennial and unrelenting controversy" surrounding the concepts of horizontal and vertical equity.[28]

While economic analysis may decide which tax system is most "efficient," economic principles do not dictate that an income tax must redistribute income from wealthy taxpayers to those with less. In the end, one can do little better than Henry Simons, who recognized that the

25. This echoes Michael Walzer's conception of equality and distributive justice in *Spheres of Justice: A Defense of Pluralism and Equality* (New York: Basic Books, 1983).

26. See, e.g., Leslie Green, "Concepts of Equity in Taxation," in *Fairness in Taxation*, ed. Maslove, 91–93. Green builds upon this notion, which she takes from Brian Barry's assertion that interstitial equity requires that "whatever should be done should be done equally to all who are alike in what the rule itself declares to be the relevant respects." Brian Barry, *Political Argument* (London: Routledge & Kegan Paul, 1965), 153–61.

27. Economist Arthur Okun justified progressive tax rates in traditional "liberal" political rhetoric. Arthur M. Okun, *Equality and Efficiency: The Big Tradeoff* (Washington, D.C.: Brookings Institution, 1975). Perhaps the classic critique of progressive taxation is found in Friedrich A. Hayek, *The Constitution of Liberty* (Chicago: University of Chicago Press, 1960), 306–23.

28. See, e.g., Break and Pechman, *Federal Tax Reform*, 3. A defense of the principles of vertical and horizontal equity from the perspective of the economist is found in Musgrave, *The Theory of Public Finance*. Others recognize the "ambiguity" and "subjectivity" of measuring the fairness of a tax system by reference to vertical and horizontal equity, but fail to comprehend that the problem is not measurement but rather the confusion of economic concepts with normative political choices. See, e.g., Minarik, *Making Tax Choices*, 47: "Absolute conclusions about tax fairness are hard to come by. . . . Although there is an apparent consensus for a progressive income tax, the degree of progressivity that we want cannot be determined scientifically; it is a matter of public choice."

argument simply does not rest upon economic proof, but rather upon normative propositions: "The case for drastic progression in income taxation must be rested on the case against inequality—on the ethical or aesthetic judgment that the prevailing distribution of wealth and income reveals a degree (and/or kind) of inequality which is distinctly unlovely."[29] Simons himself went on to assume that progressive tax rates are in fact justified on "ethical" and "aesthetic" grounds. To the uninitiated, such a justification is hardly more convincing than those same arguments Simons so thoroughly refuted.

If the principles of vertical and horizontal equity are assumed to be objective principles dictated by the science of economics, it follows logically that tax policy itself must be judged by the extent to which it conforms with these principles of fairness: "Fairness in the tax system is defined by economists in terms of horizontal and vertical equity."[30] In this way, the question of the fairness of a tax system becomes conceptually bound up with notions of progressivity.[31] Conversely, if the structure of a tax is deemed to be "fair" only if progressive, then any statutory provision or judicial doctrine that defeats the progressivity of the income tax or affords special tax treatment for different sources of income is deemed contrary to the ideal income tax and, hence, an item for "reform." Lowering tax rates destroys the progressivity of the rate structure and, hence, is contrary to vertical equity. Any legislation that creates distinctions between different sources of income must be a tax preference and, hence, offensive to the concept of horizontal equity.

It must be said that beyond the community of tax academics, there is little dedication to the principles of vertical and horizontal equity. Regressive taxes, such as virtually all sales and employment taxes, flourish in clear violation of the principle of vertical equity and yet

29. Simons, *Personal Income Taxation,* 17–18. Simons himself scolded those who believe that such questions can be answered with slogans—such as "Taxes must be determined by reference to the taxpayer's 'ability to pay'"—arguing that such is little more than a statement that "the writer prefers the kind of taxation that he prefers," and that such a principle amounts to no more than a "conjurer's hat" from which "anything may be drawn at will."

30. Thomas J. Reese, *The Politics of Taxation* (Westport, Conn.: Quorum Books, 1980), xii.

31. See, e.g., Steuerle, *Tax Decade,* 10: "In summary, a *fair and progressive* tax system—defined as one that imposes low or zero rates of tax on low-income individuals, that increases tax rates as income rises, and that taxes equally those with equal income . . ." (emphasis added).

apparently are not abhorrent to the citizenry—at least not on grounds of equity. Likewise, the significant political success achieved by proponents of a flat (or flatter) tax rate, as evidenced in the 1986 tax act as well as more recent political events, suggests that the commitment to vertical equity and progressive tax rates is not so much a part of the public philosophy as the subjective preferences of academic tax reformers.

The Worldview of Tax Experts

To the extent that tax reform has become equated with the realization of horizontal and vertical equity in the tax code, as well as attainment of a comprehensive tax base, tax professionals share a common political agenda. There is a strong consensus among tax professionals regarding which policy goals are on the tax reform agenda: "Experts generally agree which changes in income tax laws are properly labeled as 'tax reforms.' Those changes reduce or eliminate tax expenditures which are provisions conferring deductions, credits, exemptions, or special timing or treatment of taxable income. Reductions in tax expenditures, all else being equal, produce a broader and more uniform income tax base and a less complex tax system."[32] These policy goals define the ideological worldview of tax academics, as well as most tax professionals in the executive bureaucracy and congressional staffs where the tax policy agenda is first articulated and thereafter given substance.

The two most influential tax academics in the postwar period, following in the tradition of Henry Simons, were Stanley S. Surrey of Harvard Law School (as well as assistant secretary of the treasury for tax policy) and Joseph A. Pechman of the Brookings Institution. The enduring legacy of Surrey and Pechman is found in their substantial and important contributions to the academic tax literature. It is there that they helped to refine and propagate the orthodoxy of tax reform: broadening the tax base to include previously excluded or exempt sources of income, eliminating unjustifiable preferences and tax expenditures, reducing erosion of the revenue-raising capacity of the tax laws and other sources of leakages of tax revenue, while simultaneously closing the vast array of special tax loopholes bestowed upon

32. John F. Witte, "The Tax Reform Act of 1986: A New Era in Tax Politics?" 19 *Am. Pol. Q.* 438, 438 (1991).

favored special interests. Generations of economists and tax attorneys have been schooled on the vast and important literature produced by Pechman and Surrey.[33]

As recounted in Chapter 3, Surrey's own venture into government service, holding the top tax-policymaking position in the Treasury Department in the Kennedy and Johnson administrations, inspired several political speech's for tax reform but considerably less in the way of substantive reform legislation. Ironically, the movement for tax reform provided concrete political results during the Reagan administration. The intellectual principles of the movement for tax reform that succeeded in 1986 can be traced directly to the untiring efforts of the postwar generation of academic tax reformers.

Other influential academics and tax professionals who adhere to much the same the vision of tax reform, many of whom also served in top policymaking positions in the federal government, include Henry Aaron, director of the Economic Studies Program at the Brookings Institution; Charles E. McLure Jr., senior fellow at the Hoover Institution and former deputy assistant secretary for tax analysis in Treasury from 1984 to 1985; Ronald Pearlman, a tax attorney who served in the Treasury Department during the Reagan years and thereafter as chief of the staff of the Joint Committee on Taxation (JCT); Eugene Steuerle, an economist at the Urban Institute and former deputy assistant secretary for tax analysis in Treasury from 1987 to 1989 (having previously assisted Pearlman and McLure in drafting Treasury I, the original proposal for tax reform); and Michael Graetz of Yale University Law School, who served as deputy assistant secretary for tax policy in Treasury during the Bush administration. The vision of tax reform that these academics and tax professionals advanced from their positions in American law schools, graduate programs, and high-level policymaking posi-

---

33. The most important academic works of Stanley Surrey include *Pathways to Tax Reform: The Concept of Tax Expenditures* (Cambridge: Harvard University Press, 1973); "Our Troubled Tax Policy," 12 *Tax Notes* 179 (February 2, 1981); "The Congress and the Tax Lobbyist – How Special Tax Provisions Get Enacted," 70 *Harv. L. Rev.* 1145 (1957); "Complexity and the Internal Revenue Code: The Problem of the Management of Tax Detail," 34 *Law & Contemp. Probs.* 673 (1969); and, with coauthor Paul McDaniel, *Tax Expenditures* (Cambridge: Harvard University Press, 1985). The many important works by Pechman include *Federal Tax Policy,* 5th ed. (Washington, D.C.: Brookings Institution Press, 1987); *Tax Reform, the Rich and the Poor* (Washington, D.C.: Brookings Institution, 1989); *Who Pays the Taxes?* (Washington, D.C.: Brookings Institution, 1985); and, with coauthor Benjamin A. Okner, *Who Bears the Tax Burden?* (Washington, D.C.: Brookings Institution, 1974).

tions in the federal government helped shape federal tax policy in the 1980s.

Steuerle has described the deep roots of the ideology of tax reform among tax professionals within the bureaucracy: "Within the government, the Office of Tax Policy at the Department of Treasury had become an institutional base for promoting the view that different forms of income and consumption should be treated equally for both efficiency and equity reasons. The office, comprised of mainly economists and lawyers trained in public finance and tax law, gave testimony year after year about the difficulties created when income from different sources was taxed differently."[34] Tax professionals within the Treasury Department, as well as those on the staffs of the tax committees on the Hill, adhere to the vision of tax reform derived from Henry Simons and given substance by Surrey and Pechman. As such, the commitment to tax reform plays an important role within the government. Tax lawyers and economists on the professional staffs frame policy options and choices for policymakers, and hence, the academic's understanding of tax reform indirectly shapes the way these policymakers view the federal income tax.

Tax lawyers have dominated strategic tax-policymaking positions, such as assistant secretary for tax policy in the Treasury Department and chief of staff of the Joint Committee on Taxation. In addition, most of the staff of the Office of Tax Legislative Counsel (TLC) in Treasury is made up of tax lawyers. The overwhelming majority of those who have held these positions have been tax attorneys schooled in the tradition of tax reform, although obviously the extent to which these key advisers support tax reform depends upon the background and training of the particular individual. Those attorneys with a background in academics tend to be more committed tax reformers than those coming from private practice.[35]

Economists hold most of the staff positions on the Office of Tax Analysis (OTA) in Treasury. Even more so than the tax lawyers, these economists adhere to the basic principles of tax reform: "The highest concentration of tax reformers in the government is in the Office of Tax Analysis. . . . Economists who have been hired by OTA are still influenced by the economic principles they learned as students and propagated as scholars. Their policy preferences, which they have formed

34. Steuerle, *Tax Decade,* 91.
35. For a discussion of how the background of such officials correlates with their stance toward tax reform, see Reese, *Politics of Taxation,* xviii.

through their study of public finance, are oriented toward tax reform, and their presence in the Treasury provides an important institutionalized voice for tax reform."[36] Economists have also played an important role as tax-reform proponents in the Office of Tax Policy and the Congressional Budget Office, as well as the Office of Economic Policy. On account of the critical expertise of economists in such areas as economic modeling and forecasting, skills that cannot be replicated by noneconomists, the role of economists in the tax-policymaking arena has been greatly magnified. For instance, the role of economic-revenue estimators in the critical negotiations of 1985 and 1986, during committee markup of the tax bill, was exaggerated beyond the usual on account of the strict requirements for revenue neutrality.[37]

While tax experts (both lawyers and economists, but especially the lawyers) would likely describe their own commitment in terms of "professional" standards and objective principles derived from economics or the science of public policy, their shared values really constitute an ideology, or "worldview," that can influence the political decisionmaking process. In the 1980s, this translated into support for very specific changes to the federal income tax. As the authors of the leading academic study of the Tax Reform Act of 1986 put it:

> The movement for tax reform rested above all else on the shared conviction of knowledgeable experts that the federal income-tax system had grown indefensible from the standpoint of professionally salient values. Furthermore, the ideas and activities of tax policy professionals—notably economists, but also reform-minded tax attorneys—strongly influenced the content of tax reform throughout the policymaking process. Professionals had come to agree on both the need for and, to a lesser but still important extent, the proper design of tax-reform legislation. They worked both outside and inside the government for its

36. Ibid., 3.

37. The revenue estimates produced by David Brockway's staff on the Joint Committee on Taxation were crucial in supporting the policy positions advanced by Congress. See Conlan, Wrightson, and Beam, *Taxing Choices*, 204–5: "Indeed, JTC's findings demonstrated yet again the remarkable power of professional revenue estimators to give and take away from politicians in a revenue-neutral environment and, in so doing, to direct the policy debate. . . . Moreover, JTC estimates brought heavy pressure on [Senate Finance Committee chairman] Packwood and his conferees." For a general description of the role of revenue estimates in tax policymaking, see Michael J. Graetz, "Reflections on the Tax Legislative Process: Prelude to Reform," 58 *Va. L. Rev.* 1389, 1415–22 (1972).

inclusion on the policy agenda. They devised proposals conforming to professional standards, thus establishing the parameters of debate. Finally, through the uniquely professional status of the Joint Tax Committee, they exerted influence over many details of the legislation.[38]

As the first initiatives for tax reform gained political support in 1984 and 1985, the tax professionals within the federal bureaucracy played an instrumental role in pushing along the various reform proposals and in formulating specific legislative proposals, such as Treasury I. In this way, proponents of tax reform had a significant impact upon policy outcomes.

As recounted in Chapters 4 and 6, tax reformers found themselves in the mid-1980s in an unusual position and supported by a peculiar political coalition. Tax reform became a convenient political issue for *both* the traditional political leadership in Congress (e.g., Dan Rostenkowski and Bob Packwood) and supply-siders in the White House—the former searching for a practical political issue and the latter ideologically committed to achieving lower marginal income tax rates. This convergence of political interests produced a political victory for tax reformers in 1986. An equally peculiar coalition of academic policy entrepreneurs (Hall and Rabushka) and partisan interests (the Republican leadership of the 104th Congress) is behind the more recent campaign to replace the income tax with a flat consumption tax. Both the success of tax-reform efforts in 1986 and the unlikely crusade for the flat consumption tax are political events that contradict what would be predicted by the dominant social science models most commonly employed to describe the politics of the federal income tax—pluralism and incrementalism. The strengths and weaknesses of the incrementalist/pluralist model as applied to the federal tax-policymaking process are considered in Chapter 9.

---

38. Conlan, Wrightson, and Beam, *Taxing Choices,* 242.

9

The Development of the Federal Income Tax

The tax code offers a variety of easily grasped levers. In this sense, it is an incrementalist paradise, susceptible and seductive to political tinkerers.
— John Witte (1985)

I have never viewed taxation as a means of rewarding one class of taxpayers or punishing another. If such a point of view ever controls our public policy, the traditions of freedom, justice and equality of opportunity, which are the distinguishing characteristics of our American civilization, will have disappeared and in their place we shall have class legislation with all its attendant evils.
— Andrew Mellon (1924)

The federal income tax has developed over the past century through a complex process involving many different factors and taking many different forms. From a broad historical perspective, no single model seems adequate to describe the changing politics of the federal income tax. During the relative prosperity and political stability of the past half century, the tax laws have mostly evolved through a process of incremental changes to existing policy. This process of incremental development has been linked to the pluralist structure of American politics and the related interest-group politics with which it is associated. Notwithstanding this general trend, for the past decade tax policymaking has displayed relative instability and at times extreme departures from existing policy. Furthermore, tax policy periodically has taken on an unusually strong partisan character—most particularly, during the late 1940s and the early 1990s. In 1995, the chairman of the House Ways and Means Committee repeatedly expressed his desire to "throw the income tax overboard" and dismantle the IRS altogether. None of this is what would be predicted from the dominant model of federal tax policymaking—the incrementalist/pluralist model described further below. This model fails adequately to explain many of the most significant innovations in the federal income tax as well as some of the most important and radical developments in contemporary tax policy. On the other hand, the incrementalist/pluralist model does explain a good deal about the development of the income tax and, hence, cannot be discounted.

The strengths and limitations of the incrementalist/pluralist model as applied to U.S. tax policymaking are considered in this chapter, as is an alternative typology to account for those aspects of U.S. income tax policymaking that the incrementalist/pluralist model fails adequately to address or explain.

Pluralism

For the past three or four decades, pluralism has been the dominant model applied by political scientists to describe the structure of the American political system.[1] The pluralist model is highly descriptive of the decentralized policymaking and structures of power that character- ize American political institutions. In a pluralist political structure, power is widely dispersed, and the apparatus of policymaking is readily accessible to numerous groups and interests, with no single group or interest capable of dominating the institutions of decisionmaking or the outcomes arising thereunder. Policy outcomes are generally dictated by bargaining among those groups that are organized and represented in the political decisionmaking process. As such, pluralist power struc- tures tend to produce a distinctive politics to the extent that numerous interest groups possess, or potentially possess, the power to influence specific and narrow aspects of policymaking, with no single group capa- ble of imposing upon the rest wholesale or radical departures from existing policy.

Critics of the pluralist theory have long argued that because a pluralist politics is most responsive to well-organized groups represent- ing the most important economic interests (most particularly, "big busi-

1. Robert A. Dahl is the preeminent proponent of the application of pluralist theory to the analysis of American politics, incorporating pluralism into his broader theory of "polyarchy." Dahl's most important writings include *A Preface to Democratic Theory* (Chicago: University of Chicago Press, 1956); *Who Governs?* (New Haven: Yale University Press, 1961); *Polyarchy* (New Haven: Yale University Press, 1972); *Dilemmas of Pluralist Democracy* (New Haven: Yale University Press, 1982); *Democracy and Its Critics* (New Haven: Yale University Press, 1989).

ness" and the "wealthy"), legislative outcomes are skewed in favor of these special interests at the expense of the "public interest."[2] This critique of pluralist theory rests upon the premise that special economic interests are overrepresented through the political process. But that is an empirical proposition that must be verified. The account here of federal income tax policy over the past century suggests that the story is much more complicated than that. Business and the wealthy have played a major role in shaping tax policy at various times, but they have hardly controlled the tax-policymaking process, and just as often they have been the big losers in the struggle over tax policy—for instance, in 1986. The real problem is not that the pluralist structure of political power favors the wealthy and business interests in tax policy, but rather that the policymaking process is so porous that virtually every interest has had its way with tax policy at one time or another.

The formal institutions of policymaking (i.e., Congress and the tax committees) are readily accessible at multiple points to the pressures of a wide range of organized interests. Policymakers respond with narrow policy decisions in order to accommodate dominant, organized interests with favorable new policies or modifications of existing policies. Congressmen are especially exposed to these pressures, since they must compete in the electoral arena for the right to hold office. As a result, the long-term tendency is for congressional policymakers to preserve special benefits that already have been granted to those organized interests with access to the institutions of decisionmaking and at every opportune moment enact new ones in response to the almost constant political pressures exerted upon them. The tax policymaking characteristic of congressmen acting within the parameters of such a pluralist politics constitutes the traditional "politics-as-usual" that takes place within the tax committees.[3] This pluralist interest-group politics of the federal

2. See, e.g., E. E. Schattschneider, *The Semi-Sovereign People: A Realist's View of Democracy in America* (New York: Holt, Rinehart & Winston, 1960); Grant McConnell, *Private Power and American Democracy* (New York: Vintage, 1966); Theodore J. Lowi, *The End of Liberalism* (New York: W. W. Norton, 1969); Jack L. Walker, "The Origins and Maintenance of Interest Groups in America," 77 *Am. Pol. Sci. Rev.* 390 (1983). Robert Dahl has responded to these critics in *Dilemmas of Pluralist Democracy* and *Democracy and Its Critics;* see also the introduction to the 1992 edition of Robert A. Dahl and Charles E. Lindblom, *Politics, Economics, and Welfare* (New Brunswick, N.J.: Transaction Publishers, 1992).

3. For example, Truman took as given that in tax policy, well-financed special-interest groups with a great stake in outcomes will tend to prevail in the legislative

income tax was succinctly described by T. S. Adams in his presidential address to the 1927 Annual Meeting of the American Economic Association: "[M]odern taxation or tax making in its most characteristic aspect is a group contest in which powerful interests vigorously endeavor to rid themselves of present or proposed tax burdens."[4] What was already recognized as the "normal" politics of the federal income tax in 1927 is now described by reference to the pluralist model of interest-group politics.

However, not all of the politics of the income tax is so easily explained by the pluralist model. During various historical periods, tax policy has reflected a more partisan, ideologically coherent politics, as opposed to the instrumental, nonpartisan politics of logrolling and vote trading. The success of tax reform in 1986, as well as the emergence of a dominant and highly partisan Republican tax policy following the 1980 and 1994 elections, is a reminder that political patterns that have persisted for decades can change suddenly. In the case of the 1994 elections, the partisan character of the entire Congress changed dramatically and unexpectedly as decades of uninterrupted control of the tax legislative process by Democrats came to an abrupt end. This could not but have had a profound impact upon the direction and character of tax policy given the strength of commitment of the new House Republicans to a well-defined partisan tax policy agenda.

In part, the problem is that the pluralist model is time-bound, since it presupposes the stability and persistence of those structures of politics within which tax policy has been made for the past half century or so. In other words, the pluralist model explains fairly well the normal tax politics that has generally prevailed since the defeat of the congressional Republican Party and its tax policies in the 1930s, but fails adequately to describe the sudden and dramatic changes periodically experienced in the tax-policymaking arena at crucial historical junctures. The limits of the pluralist model were most evident during the 1980s, when a pattern of unstable and highly partisan tax politics overwhelmed the normal tax politics of prior decades. Most especially, the pluralist model failed to predict, and fails to explain retrospectively, the dramatic success of the politics of tax reform in 1986.

The pluralist model focuses upon Congress and its committees and assumes a dynamic interest-group politics that drives tax policymaking.

---

arena. David Truman, *The Governmental Process,* 2d ed. (New York: Knopf, 1971), 361, 422.

4. T. S. Adams, "Ideal and Idealism in Taxation," 18 *Am. Econ. Rev.* 1 (1928).

To this extent, the influence of partisanship and ideology are slighted. The pluralist and incrementalist models are blind to the possibility of radical departures from existing policy resulting from ideological commitments or shifts in partisan allegiance that lead to (or reflect) "critical realignments" of the prevailing party system. Thus, notwithstanding the great descriptive power of the pluralist model during periods of normal tax politics, limitations in the model are evident as applied to the long-term history of U.S. fiscal policy—which is a history of long periods of stable pluralist politics punctuated by dramatic and sudden changes and radical policy innovations, of which the income tax was undoubtedly one of the most important. This suggests that some modifications and accommodations in the pluralist model are warranted.

Incrementalism

Political scientists have observed that within the prevailing pluralist structure the federal income tax has developed over time through a process of "incremental" decisionmaking.[5] The term "incrementalism" apparently was first introduced to public-policy analysis in 1953 by Charles E. Lindblom and Robert A. Dahl.[6] Incrementalism purports to describe the way in which decisionmakers actually reach solutions to problems of public policy, but it also suggests a design for problem solving. As John Witte has put it: "The model was presented as an empirical description of how the vast majority of real life world decisions are made, particularly in government, and it was justified normatively as the most rational, if still imperfect, method of reaching decisions."[7] One intellectual history of the discipline of political science describes Dahl and Lindblom's conceptual formulation of incrementalism as a *strategy* for decisionmaking: "By incrementalism, Dahl and Lindblom meant a series of policy adjustments starting from the basis of existing policy, recognizing its advantages and disadvantages, and continuing in small steps via calculated risks, where immediate additions to old policy

    5. The most important recent study of the federal income tax relies upon a incrementalist/pluralist model to explain major patterns of tax policymaking. John F. Witte, *The Politics and Development of the Federal Income Tax* (Madison: University of Wisconsin Press, 1985), 3–23, 244–70.

    6. Robert A. Dahl and Charles E. Lindblom, *Politics, Economics, and Welfare* (Chicago: University of Chicago Press, 1953); see also Charles E. Lindblom, "The Science of 'Muddling Through,'" 19 *Pub. Admin. Rev.* 79 (1959).

    7. Witte, *Politics*, 6.

will not at once achieve all goals but at the same time will not unduly invite unforeseen consequences."[8] In this respect, incrementalism is a useful model both to describe and evaluate a wide range of federal policymaking, including that of the federal income tax.[9]

As a descriptive model of decisionmaking, incrementalism holds that policymaking generally evolves through evolutionary or incremental departures from existing policies, rather than through radical breaks in, or the adoption of, wholly new policies.[10] This mode of decisionmaking has been associated with pluralist structures of political power, wherein interest-group pressures most often lead to incremental modifications of existing policies. As such, the theory describes a good deal of American policymaking. Perhaps the most notable example of the application of the incrementalist model to public policymaking is Aaron Wildavsky's seminal account of the budgeting process. According to Wildavsky: "Budgeting is incremental. The largest determining factor of the size of this year's budget is last year's budget."[11] The process of budgeting is one of marginal adjustments and departures from existing budgetary appropriations.

Another area of policymaking that readily fits the incrementalist mode is that of the U.S. Social Security program, which has developed gradually over the last fifty years through periodic additions to, and expansions upon, existing programs. Martha Derthick has described the usual pattern of policymaking for Social Security as follows: "Policy planning in the Social Security Administration has always consisted of planning for changes within the framework of established programs. . . . To the extent that executive leaders of the program have articulated a

8. David M. Ricci, *The Tragedy of Political Science* (New Haven: Yale University Press, 1984), 167.

9. Lindblom himself applied the theory of incrementalism to budgeting in Charles E. Lindblom, "Decision-Making in Taxation and Expenditure," in *Public Finance: Needs, Sources and Utilization* (Princeton: National Bureau of Economic Research, 1961), 295–336.

10. Dahl and Lindblom expressly disavowed the notion that incrementalism always means growth through gradual change. Rather, they argued that incrementalism is a theory of *growth* through "relatively small adjustments in existing reality." In many cases, incremental changes are minor; however, in other cases, the increments can be more significant. See Dahl and Lindblom, *Politics, Economics, and Welfare* (1992), 82–85.

11. See Aaron B. Wildavsky, *The Politics of the Budgetary Process* (Boston: Little, Brown, 1964), 13; see also idem, *The New Politics of the Budgetary Process* (Glenview, Ill.: Scott, Foresman & Company, 1988), and idem, "A Theory of the Budget Process," 60 *Am. Pol. Sci. Rev.* 529 (1960). A similar application of incrementalism to budgeting is found in John Wanat, "Bases of Budgetary Incrementalism," 67 *Am. Pol. Sci. Rev.* 1221 (1974).

philosophy of policy formation, this philosophy stresses gradualism."[12] The general pattern of policymaking over the course of the first three decades of the program is best described by reference to an incrementalist model; that is, policymaking consisted in making marginal additions and modifications to existing Social Security programs.

Although incrementalism is highly descriptive of Social Security policymaking during the first three decades of the program, certain limitations show up in the incrementalist model as applied to specific aspects and phases in Social Security policymaking. For example, incrementalism fails to explain why the Roosevelt administration in 1935 adopted the Social Security program in the first place. Even this relatively modest and limited initial legislation was a radical departure from traditional federal policy, and incrementalism's failure to explain it represents a serious shortcoming in the model.

Derthick has described one radical (and largely unsuccessful) Social Security policy that also represents a departure from the normal pattern of incremental policymaking—the enactment of the supplemental security income program (SSI), which was thrust upon the Social Security Administration by Congress in 1972.[13] Derthick's explanation of this nonincremental development in the Social Security program looks to factors external to the traditional Social Security decisionmaking process itself—for example, to an atypical intrusion into the Social Security policymaking process by Congress, as well as broad political initiatives from the executive. In addition, overzealous courts seized from the agency much of the policymaking initiative with respect to this particular policy program. Thus, even while incrementalism is highly descriptive of the decisionmaking process for Social Security during most of its history, the model does not adequately describe the policymaking prevailing during all periods or with respect to this particular program.

Furthermore, if the legitimacy of the Social Security program continues to be undermined and the revenue from the payroll tax no longer supports expansion or even maintenance of existing programs, incremental policymaking could cease altogether.[14] Use of general revenue

12. Martha Derthick, *Policymaking for Social Security* (Washington, D.C.: Brookings Institution, 1979), 25.

13. Martha Derthick, *Agency Under Stress: The Social Security Administration in American Government* (Washington, D.C.: Brookings Institution, 1990).

14. Steuerle and Bakija describe the fiscal imbalance inherent in the Social Security system. C. Eugene Steuerle and Jon M. Bakija, *Retooling Social Security for the Twenty-*

from the Treasury to fund Social Security deficits is an unattractive option for policymakers confronting significant annual federal budget deficits. In addition, unforeseen and unintended consequences of the program, such as the massive redistribution of resources from current younger workers to retired (and in many cases wealthier) beneficiaries, could further undermine public confidence in the program. These kinds of changes in the broader political system and external environment could impose a new framework on the politics of Social Security and, hence, modify the present dominant pattern of incremental policymaking for the program. Derthick was already aware in the mid-1970s that the prior pattern of incremental *growth* for Social Security might be nearing an end; she correctly perceived that the political climate had changed by that time – before the imposition of severe budgetary constraints on policymaking: "Growth of the system through the 1950's and 1960's depended crucially on the politician's calculations that incremental additions were advantageous, but the context was highly favorable to expansion. . . . The pattern of ad hoc incremental expansion may still continue, even with an automatic formula in place and even in the presence of heightened resistance to expansion, but if so it is likely to be attended by much higher levels of conflict than were characteristic of the past."[15] Should conditions change and the political landscape shift further away from the post–New Deal liberalism characteristic of the 1960s, unchallenged support even for such "sacred-cow" policy programs as Social Security could end. If the federal deficit ever forces policymakers to implement significant cuts in federal expenditures earmarked for so-called entitlement programs such as Social Security,[16] then all bets will be off, and prior patterns of incremental expansion may very well cease. Quite simply, incrementalism is a model that may be descriptive of a particular policy program during specific periods and under certain circumstances (namely, economic prosperity and expansion) but inade-

---

first Century: Right and Wrong Approaches to Reform (Washington, D.C.: Urban Institute Press, 1994), chap. 3 ("The Inevitable Reform of an Imbalanced System"), 39–71.

15. Derthick, *Policymaking for Social Security,* 428.

16. While the term "entitlement" is bandied about so often as to feel familiar, its etymological origins can be traced back only to the early 1980s. Although the term was used in the text of the Budget and Impoundment Control Act of 1974, it was Ronald Reagan who popularized the term during his first term as president. See Norman Ornstein, "Roots of 'Entitlements,' and Budget Woes," *Wall St. J.,* December 14, 1993, A16.

quate to describe political change or development under less favorable economic conditions.[17]

Policymaking for the federal income tax, like policymaking for Social Security, has been particularly amenable to incremental decisionmaking during the period of economic expansion following World War II; during this period, changes to existing tax laws have generally been made at the "margins" of the tax code. The most prominent account of the politics of the postwar federal income tax has emphasized the incremental nature of the tax-policymaking process: "Legislative changes in tax policy usually begin as marginal adjustments to the existing tax structure. . . . The tax code offers a variety of easily grasped levers. In this sense, it is an incrementalist paradise, susceptible and seductive to political tinkerers. As a result, most changes in tax bills consist of simple adjustments in existing policy provisions."[18] The policymaking for the federal income tax is well described by the incrementalist model, since most of the major tax bills enacted during the postwar period have been little more than collections of minor modifications to existing provisions of the tax code, modifications produced by the logrolling and vote trading of the pluralist, interest-group politics that prevails in Congress. As was suggested in Chapter 3, this type of tax bill became the norm during the 1950s.

Thus, the tax laws have generally developed through incremental adjustments as politicians accommodate salient interest groups, individuals, or economic classes. In the long run, this incremental policymaking works to the benefit of special interests as congressional policymakers amend the tax code over time to provide more and more exemptions to constituents feeling the adverse effects of particular tax provisions. This results in the legislative outcomes typical of incremental policymaking set within the context of a pluralist power structure—that is, tax preferences. The main restraint upon the tendencies of this incrementalist/pluralist policymaking is the federal government's constant need to raise revenue. Of course, the structure of the tax code also readily lends itself to legislating tax increases through relatively simple marginal adjustments to the most revenue-sensitive provisions of the

17. As Allan Schick has put it: "Incremental budgeting requires incremental resources supplied either by a growing economy, as was the case in the 1950s and 1960s, or deficit financing, as occurred in the 1980s." Allen Schick, *The Federal Budget: Politics, Policy, Process* (Washington, D.C.: Brookings Institution, 1995), 54.

18. Witte, *Politics,* 244–45.

tax code (tax rates and exemptions). This too is one manifestation of incremental policymaking—one considerably less popular among constituents (as George Bush learned in 1992 and Bill Clinton learned again in 1994).

This dominant incremental policymaking process contributed to the postwar rise in "special-interest" provisions grafted onto the tax code. The overall tendency of incremental tax policymaking in a pluralist political structure is the adoption of more and more exemptions and special-interest provisions by congressional policymakers. Likewise, incremental policymaking has contributed to expanding the tax base—gradually bringing more and more of the population and nearly all economic income under the income tax as policymakers search for revenue.

So if tax policymaking is an "incrementalist paradise," it should be the ideal case against which to test the premises, possibilities, and limits of the incrementalist/pluralist model. On the other hand, if the model cannot explain or account for tax policymaking during such periods as the 1980s and 1990s, then its usefulness as a description of policymaking must be called into question. Nevertheless, even if incrementalism fails to describe all aspects of tax policymaking, it may retain particular relevance as a normative strategy for tax decisionmaking, as considered below.

Strategic Incrementalism

Although incrementalism is mostly applied as a model descriptive of how policymakers actually legislate, especially in such policy areas as income taxation, budgeting, and Social Security, it was also originallyput forth as a *strategy* for decisionmaking. As such, incrementalism provides a vantage point from which to evaluate contemporary tax policymaking. Indeed, the greatest strength of incrementalism may well lie in providing a strategy for a more rational approach to tax policymaking.

The underlying premise of incrementalism as a normative theory is that "rational, comprehensive policy-making is an impossible and even dangerous ideal."[19] As a normative strategy, incrementalism stresses the *preferability* of marginal and gradual changes in policy. This prefer-

---

19. Ronald F. King, *Money, Time, and Politics: Investment Tax Subsidies and American Democracy* (New Haven: Yale University Press, 1993), 31.

ence is attributable to a recognition of the inherent limitations of human knowledge and experience, as well as the impossibility of policymakers ever comprehending all of the many contingencies that inevitably follow from radical policy experiments. Incrementalism is a model for a limited form of "rational" decisionmaking – or, more properly, a series of strategies for decisionmaking in the face of the limits of human reason – and by implication, policymaking. "The problems of rational-comprehensive decision-making lie in its demands on the human intellect and the unresolvability of political disputes. Rational decision-making fails to take into account the limitations of time, intelligence, and policy-discretion that are available to public officials. Limitations of time and intelligence prevent the identification of the full range of alternatives and resources that are available at the point of decision."[20]

The essence of the incrementalist strategy should be familiar and comfortable to those schooled in the legal tradition, especially that derived from the English common law. Incrementalism bears a strong resemblance to, and is consistent with, theories of the law advanced by leading defenders of the common law, such as Burke and Coke.[21] Advocates of the common-law tradition praise the inherent rationality of "the Law" because it evolves through a kind of incremental decisionmaking (i.e., the long succession of court decisions made by common-law judges providing rules to govern the nearly infinite number of conflicts and situations that arise from human interaction in society and economy). As the law develops through incremental decisionmaking over time, it purportedly rises to a level of rationality beyond that which any single human being is capable of attaining. In the words of Justice Holmes: "The life of the law has not been logic: it has been experience. . . . The law embodies the story of a nation's development through many centuries."[22] This common-law legal tradition, much as incrementalist theory itself, is hostile to any suggestion that "Reason" is capable of attaining a final or complete stage of understanding, a belief characteristic of Continental thought. Of course, this was very much the basis for Burke's

20. Ira Sharkansky, *The Politics of Taxing and Spending* (Indianapolis, Ind.: Bobbs-Merrill, 1969), 200.

21. See J.G.A. Pocock, *Politics, Language, and Time: Essays on Political Thought and History* (New York: Atheneum, 1973), especially chap. 6 ("Burke and the Ancient Constitution: A Problem in the History of Ideas"), and idem, *The Ancient Constitution and the Feudal Law: English Historical Thought in the Seventeenth Century* (New York: W. W. Norton, 1967), chaps. 2 and 3.

22. Oliver Wendell Holmes, *The Common Law* (Boston: Little, Brown, 1881), 1.

hostility to the French Revolution, expressed in his great essay *Reflections on the Revolution in France* (1790).

Incrementalism is thus a strategy for a process of limited, gradual tax policymaking.[23] After several decades of instability and radical changes in tax policy, the propriety of marginal and gradual changes to the tax code should be all the more obvious. Those who urge radical tax policy proposals, such as the complete abandonment of the federal income tax and the adoption of some entirely new mode of taxation (e.g., a national sales tax or a consumption tax) should heed the warning of Chairman Rostenkowski: "Fundamental reform almost always runs the risk of making things worse."[24] Nothing could better express the essence of strategic incrementalism, and no advice is more often ignored by proponents of wholesale "tax reform" as well as partisans who would rewrite the entire tax code to implement the Republican Party platform. Much the same can be said of those who would reform the entire U.S. health-care system at one sitting.

The Limits of the Incrementalist/Pluralist Model

Before the 1980s, it was commonly argued that interest-group politics so thoroughly dominated tax policymaking that any serious effort to enact "reform" legislation would inevitably be doomed to failure. Likewise, many observers of the federal income tax concluded that tax-reform efforts were simply incapable of transcending the pattern of incremental policymaking attributable to the pluralist power structure of American politics.[25] Because tax policymaking was thought to be part and parcel of

---

23. "Incremental decision-making is most clearly operative in spending decisions. But incrementalism is also apparent in federal tax-policy. When changes are made in taxes, Congress and the Administration have changed certain rates or added provisions to the existing regulations instead of introducing new taxes or overhauling the present code. The major revenue source of the federal government [the income tax] lends itself to incremental change." Sharkansky, *Politics of Taxing and Spending*, 82.

24. Quoted in *Daily Tax Rep.* (Bureau of National Affairs), no. 193, October 7, 1993, G-3.

25. This view was best expressed by Surrey in his classic statement of the domination of interest-group politics over tax policymaking. Stanley S. Surrey, "The Congress and the Tax Lobbyist—How Special Tax Provisions Get Enacted," 70 *Harv. L. Rev.* 1145 (1957). Surrey's account fully describes how some tax policies reflect special interests represented through lobbyists, but it totally ignores all other legislation that reflects ideological

a pluralist, interest-group politics, it was easy to conclude that efforts to reform the tax code to conform more closely to the tax reformers' vision of a comprehensive income tax were "simply outside the realm of political possibilities."[26] Indeed, most scholars and informed observers of the federal income tax took just that position, declaring that tax policymaking had reached a serious impasse on account of the adverse impact of pluralist politics on the decisionmaking process. As a consequence of adopting this view, most scholars ended up widely missing the mark when various tax-reform proposals began circulating about Washington in the fall of 1984. Most adhered to the view that pluralism, interest-group politics, and the concomitant incremental policymaking associated with it thoroughly dominated the politics of the federal income tax laws. Some of the most perceptive students of tax policy denied the possibility of reformist impulses ever succeeding.[27]

This failure to predict or account for the passage of the 1986 tax act exposes the limits of the incrementalist/pluralist model as well as the difficulty in predicting the future course of federal tax policymaking.

---

commitment to specific policies (such as the Republican tax policies of the 1940s and 1990s, as well as the supply-side economics pursued in ERTA), tax-reform legislation that is entirely at the expense of such interests (such as the 1986 act), and the impact of public-interest groups on tax policy.

26. Witte, *Politics,* 246.

27. For instance, John Witte wrote in 1985: "There is nothing, absolutely nothing in the history or politics of the income tax that indicates that any of these [tax-reform] schemes have the slightest hope of being enacted in the forms proposed." Witte, *Politics,* 380. Witte addressed the shortcomings of his prediction in "The Tax Reform Act of 1986: A New Era in Tax Politics?" 19 *Am. Pol. Q.* 438 (1991) and "A Long View of Tax Reform," 39 *Nat'l Tax J.* 255 (1986). Michael J. Graetz of Yale University Law School, assistant deputy secretary of the treasury for tax policy in the Bush administration, wrote in 1984 the following assessment of the possibilities of reform: "[P]rospects for structural tax reform have been dimmed by recent 'reforms' in congressional practices; public pressure to enact income tax reforms seems nonexistent; political leadership on tax matters has become increasingly diffuse. . . . In short, for those who would urge massive tax reforms, there is more than ample cause for despair." Michael J. Graetz, "Can the Income Tax Continue to Be the Major Revenue Source?" in *Options for Tax Reform,* ed. Joseph A. Pechman (Washington, D.C.: Brookings Institution, 1984), 39, 42. Likewise, Duke University economist David Davies wrote in 1986: "Meaningful [tax] reform, something beyond a multitude of political trades, under present political institutions essentially is doomed to failure." David G. Davies, *United States Taxes and Tax Policy* (New York: Cambridge University Press, 1986), 287.

According to the incrementalist model, a successful tax-reform movement propelled by players and interests outside the "normal" political
arena of congressional tax policymaking was not possible. The incrementalist model simply could not accommodate radical, ideologically
driven departures in tax policy. Based upon prior experience with the
federal income tax laws across three decades, this was entirely under-
standable. However, any model of political behavior based solely upon
extrapolation from past events will likely be inadequate to predict what
are, by definition, radical departures from politics-as-usual. And of
course, if past behavior allowed for easy predictions of future events, the
world of politics would be infinitely dull and mechanical. In fact, the
politics of tax policymaking in the 1980s and 1990s turned out to be
much more interesting and unpredictable than incrementalism would
ever have suggested.

Thus, the methodological problem with the incrementalist/pluralist
model is that even while it may be descriptive of tax policymaking much
of the time, it is inherently blind to those rare bursts of ideological
enthusiasm and "crisis politics" that, although outside the course of
politics-as-usual, nevertheless have periodically characterized the tax-
policymaking process and have had the most significant impact upon the
development of the federal income tax. If the dynamics of the legislative
process most often conforms with the prevailing pluralist politics, pluralist theory still does not represent the whole story, nor are Congress
and "special interests" the only sources of tax policy initiatives. The
congressionally based politics has been overwhelmed at critical historical moments. Likewise, changes in the party system such as those
experienced in November 1981 and November 1994 have had a significant impact upon the course of tax policy, overriding the general tendency for tax policymaking to proceed through incremental departures
from existing policy.

In other words, tax policy reflects more than just the dynamic interplay of interest groups and the tax committees, and not all the provisions
in the tax code are the product of incremental development. Whether
this is desirable is an entirely different question—one that should be
approached with considerable caution given recent experience with tax
legislation imposing dramatic departures from existing policy. Incrementalism as a normative theory or strategy for achieving rational
policymaking may very well be even more important in an age of
nonincremental tax policy.

The conclusion here is that contemporary tax policymaking has
departed too often from the strategy suggested by incrementalism (i.e.,

strategic advances through relatively minor, incremental departures from existing policies). Contemporary tax policy has been running wild. Incremental policymaking qua "marginal adjustments to the existing tax structure" has been submerged by a more extreme politics of the federal income tax during the past decade. The irony is that the erratic course of contemporary tax policymaking has also been ascribed to the very same pluralist structure of American politics that is supposedly responsible for incrementalism. It is said that the inability of pluralist politics and incremental policymaking to resist change deprives tax policy of coherence, stability, and direction. "Incrementalism thus causes not too little policy change, but too much change. It bestows favors not solely on the wealthy, but instead quite widely, with nearly every group receiving something especially tailored to appeal to its interest."[28] The result is that public policy can quickly shift direction, since the institutions of decisionmaking cannot resist the pressures and demands of particular interests, lacking a vision of the public interest and coherent principles of tax policy. "[T]he democratic impulse to represent broad and diverse sets of interests, which is facilitated by an incremental/pluralist process, in the long run jeopardizes the basic purpose and legitimacy of tax policy."[29]

In the end, this may be the most damning critique of a pluralist politics—that it is responsible for *both* the stability and gradualism in tax policymaking *and*, alternatively, "too much change." In other words, both the relative stability of incremental tax policy *and* the great instability and flux that periodically invade the tax legislative process are attributable to the pluralist structure of political power. What the pluralist model lacks, then, is the ability to account for the more radical expressions of tax policymaking, as well as political change itself—that is, tax policymaking during periods other than those of "normal" politics.

Normal and Crisis Tax Politics: An Alternative Typology

Normal U.S. tax politics may be that of pluralism and incrementalism, but the most significant developments in the tax laws and fiscal policy have occurred during periods of institutional instability—specifically, political crises, both those internal to the political system and those

28. King, *Money, Time, and Politics*, 33.
29. Witte, *Politics*, xxii.

attributable to external pressures. The former are typified by the challenges to the extant political regime expressed by the more radical parties of the late nineteenth century and during the Great Depression. The latter include the military crises of the War of 1812, the Civil War, and the two world wars of the twentieth century. The contrast between normal tax politics and that during such periods of systemic crisis is useful in explaining the long-term development of the U.S. income tax and suggests a basis for modifying the incrementalist/pluralist model.

As recounted in Chapter 2, American political leaders made fundamental political decisions concerning the fiscal organization of the central state at various critical junctures in American history. For instance, one of the central issues of the constitutional period, from 1783 to 1789, was financing the central government. This was reflected in the political negotiations between the state governments and national political elites over the power to be granted to the national institutions—most particularly, federal fiscal powers. Later, the highly charged political struggles over the tariff and excise taxes, as well as the subsequent battles over adoption of income taxation in 1860 and 1913, were of similar importance to the regime. These kinds of fundamental issues raise questions about the "constitution" of the regime and are typically thrust upon political elites during periods of crisis. Such constitutional decisions must be contrasted with the normal political decisionmaking ("politics-as-usual") that otherwise prevails during periods of institutional, political, and economic stability.

For the past four decades, such a normal politics has characterized most of congressional tax policymaking, as reflected in the logrolling and vote trading typically associated with the politics of the income tax. The broad consensus that has marked the postwar politics of the past half century reflects the general stability of the post–New Deal party system in which the Democratic Party maintained hegemony over the legislative process. Within the context of this political system, normal tax politics has been the congressionally based politics of logrolling and tax expenditures. This tax politics-as-usual fits into the mold of a "distributive" public policy as set forth nearly thirty years ago by political scientist Theodore J. Lowi.[30]

Lowi described three distinct types of politics—distributive, redistributive, and regulatory—each of which generates its own distinct

---

30. Theodore J. Lowi, "American Business, Public Policy, Case Studies, and Political Theory," 16 *World Pol.* 677 (1964). Lowi further developed his analysis in "Four Systems of Policy, Politics, and Choice," 33 *Pub. Admin. Rev.* 298 (1972).

"arena of power" and mode of public policymaking. In other words, Lowi's insight was that the particular type of policy generates a related pattern of policymaking, and not vice versa. The politics associated with distributive policies is characterized by logrolling and vote trading in which special benefits are provided to constituents and interest groups.[31] Congressmen support subsidies earmarked for the constituents of fellow representatives as reciprocity for votes in favor of legislation that serves their own political needs and interests. This is the normal politics that has been ascribed to the federal income tax, at least within the context of the prevailing party system and institutional structure that normally govern the conduct of congressional tax policymakers. But at other times, very different politics has characterized tax policy. The problem is to account for the "abnormal" tax politics and explain how and why tax policymaking moves from one mode to the other. Contrary to Lowi's theory, according to which the type of policy dictates the attendant mode of policymaking, policymaking for the income tax at any given moment has largely been determined by the prevailing institutional structures and external environmental pressures imposed upon the political system from without.

During specific periods of crisis, tax politics has not followed the pattern of a distributive politics. Instead, crisis tax politics has more closely resembled the redistributive politics described by Lowi. Redistributive politics involves transfers in favor of the interests of significant social or economic interests or classes at the expense of others. The policies that are associated with redistributive politics reflect and often exacerbate underlying social or economic cleavages—for instance, pitting labor against capital, agrarian interests against industry, or the poor against the wealthy. The politics of redistribution can achieve long-term stability only as these dominant interests reach some measure of societal equilibrium. Characteristic of the policies associated with redistributive politics is a higher degree of ideological rhetoric and greater levels of intensity, since those policies that favor a particular economic group or interest do so at the expense of other clearly defined (and often well-organized) economic or social groups.[32] This is the "zero-

31. See Allen Schick, "The Distributive Congress," in *Making Economic Policy in Congress,* ed. Allen Schick (Washington, D.C.: American Enterprise Institute, 1983), 257–74.
32. For a more detailed description of redistributive politics, see John Ferejohn, "Congress and Redistribution," in *Making Economic Policy,* ed. Schick, 131–57.

sum" politics expressed in the battle over the initial adoption of an income tax, as well as in the partisan politics of progressive tax rates to be used for redistributive purposes. It also applies to the persistent partisan divisions over tax rate reduction and the preferential rate for capital gains.[33]

Lowi's typology also provides for a regulatory politics generating policies that are relatively unstable because the interests of one interest group or industry are pitted against the interests of all others. The direction of regulatory politics tends to shift over time as various ideological positions come to dominate the preferences of regulators. The political institutions associated with regulatory policy are often highly insulated from the pressures and input of special-interest groups, since the key actors in the regulatory process tend to be professionals who are not exposed to the pressures of the electoral connection and who likewise are less susceptible to the pressures and entreaties of lobbyists. This is the politics of tax reform pursued by tax professionals on the congressional staffs, but especially those in the bureaucracy of the Treasury Department. At various moments political conditions have permitted this regulatory politics to overwhelm and supplant the normal pluralist tax politics; such was the case from 1985 to 1986. At that time, in the wake of the budget deficits resulting from the 1981 tax cuts, the political interests of congressional policymakers converged with the goals of the tax professionals in Treasury. According to John Kingdon, with the convergence of three "streams"—politics, problems, and policy—the precondition was established for tax reform to rise off the "governmental" policy agenda and become a bona fide political issue.[34] On the other hand, during periods of normal tax politics, the policy stream works against the political impulses of politicians.

Political historian Dall Forsythe applied Lowi's typology to American fiscal and tariff policy from 1781 to 1833.[35] Forsythe found that Lowi's

33. In many respects, the Social Security program is a redistributive policy (especially across generations), but its impact is not readily grasped by the citizenry at large. As the intergenerational effect of the program becomes better understood, the intensity of the politics surrounding it will likely heighten.

34. In the second edition of his well-known study, Kingdon has added a chapter applying his model to the enactment of the Tax Reform Act of 1986. John W. Kingdon, *Agendas, Alternatives, and Public Policies,* 2d ed. (New York: Harper Collins, 1995), chap. 10, 213–17.

35. Dall W. Forsythe, *Taxation and Political Change in the Young Nation, 1781–1833* (New York: Columbia University Press, 1977), especially chap. 5 ("Patterns of Politics") and chap. 6 ("Political Change in the United States").

categories did not fully comport with the various forms of tariff policy in evidence throughout this period, leading him to propose an alternative typology emphasizing the role of "crisis" and the behavior and responses of political elites at key historical moments. Forsythe's alternative typology, along with Lowi's original categories, is useful as well in classifying and explaining the various phases in the politics of the U.S. income tax during the past 150 years. The refinement of Lowi's typology incorporates attention to external environmental threats and internal regime crises as mechanisms and stimuli for change in tax politics.

Forsythe's typology fits American tariff and revenue policy into four categories modeled on Lowi's original scheme: regime politics, authority crisis, environmental crisis, and normal politics. According to Forsythe, "normal politics is characterized by a limited number of established participants, by a well-defined institutional arena for decision-making, patterns of logrolling, negotiation, and compromise, and by implementation of decisions through routine administration."[36] This distributive politics of logrolling and interest-group pressures dictated tariff policy during the first decades of the twentieth century.[37] Likewise, this has been the dominant politics of the federal income tax during most of the post–World War II period.

Regime politics "involves the most fundamental kinds of political questions. . . . If conflict in normal politics is muted and contained, conflict in regime politics is highly visible, dramatic, and difficult to circumscribe."[38] This mode has surfaced in the past two centuries of American politics only during intermittent outbursts of political enthusiasm—for instance, during the pitched political battles over the adoption of an income tax (heard in the intense political debate on the floor of Congress in 1860, 1894, and 1913) and during the radical agrarian parties' late-nineteenth-century campaign for a steeply graduated income tax, whose objective was no less than an egalitarian politics and a radical restructuring of the American regime. "In regime conflicts (and especially in tax disputes) . . . the patterns useful for the resolution of normal disputes are no longer applicable. Logrolling cannot settle an argument if participants see the conflict in zero-sum terms."[39]

36. Ibid., 119.
37. This politics of the tariff was the subject of the classic study by E. E. Schattschneider, *Politics, Pressures, and the Tariff* (New York: Prentice-Hall, 1935).
38. Forsythe, *Taxation and Political Change,* 120.
39. Ibid., 121.

Although Forsythe focused his attention on regime conflicts such as the Whiskey Rebellion and the struggle between Southern agricultural interests and Northern industrial interests over the tariff, much the same analysis can be applied to the political disputes from 1783 to 1789 over the fiscal organization of the new regime. Likewise, regime conflicts surfaced during the pitched political battle over income taxation waged from 1880 to 1913. This conflict raised fundamental issues concerning the nature of the regime and was eventually resolved only through the ratification of the Sixteenth Amendment, the adoption of the compromise income tax bill in 1913, and the gradual rollback of the tariff—in other words, a minor reconstitution of the American fiscal state.

The politics of authority crisis is pertinent in describing the systemic crisis of the Civil War, in which the very foundation of the regime was at stake. The military crisis that began in 1860 was over the authority of the American regime, and the threat to the regime forced even the most ardent opponents of income taxation to acquiesce in its adoption—at least until the military crisis was resolved on the battlefield. Likewise, the external environmental crisis experienced during the two world wars of the twentieth century also resulted in a crisis politics that compelled political elites to accept radical innovations in American fiscal policy. The sharp increases in the income tax from 1918 were only justified by, and accepted on account of, the environmental crisis of World War I. As Treasury secretary Andrew Mellon subsequently put it from the vantage point of the peace and tranquillity of the 1920s: "During [World War I] the highest taxes ever levied by any country were borne uncomplainingly by the American people for the purpose of defraying the unusual and ever-increasing expenses incident to the successful conduct of a great war. . . . In time of war or great public necessity, unusual tax measures can always be justified."[40] In other words, the intensified revenue imperative exerted upon policymakers during periods of crisis (authority and environmental) suppresses the politics of interests and thus becomes the agent of change in fiscal policy, thereby establishing the preconditions for radical departures and expansions in existing tax policies. One of the most peculiar and interesting aspects of tax policy is that its importance and scope actually expands during periods of military conflict, precisely while other domestic policies suffer retrenchment as spending cuts for such programs are necessitated by the fiscal crises and diversion of revenue to the military. This

40. Andrew W. Mellon, *Taxation: The People's Business* (New York: Macmillan, 1924), 12, 72.

expansion is necessitated by, and justified by policymakers on account of, the military conflict itself. Accordingly, the pattern of development of the income tax is quite different from that of most other public policies.

For instance, the radical expansion and transformation of the income tax during both world wars was justified by policymakers and condoned by the populace in light of the grave national emergency. The attendant crisis politics led to extraordinary increases in tax rates (reaching the historic high of 92 percent by 1944), reduced personal exemptions (subjecting more citizens to the income tax), and broad expansions of administrative powers (including the introduction of "withholding at the source"–an innovation that, although initially preferred, was beyond the reach of congressional policymakers during peacetime in 1913 but readily adopted in 1943).

The impact of wartime crisis on the income tax has generally persisted beyond the events that originally justified the expansion. In his comparative study of the factors that lead incrementalist policymakers to depart from base levels of government spending, Sharkansky concluded, "Generally speaking, the major trauma of depression, war, and postwar reconversion upset established patterns of spending and set new bases from which incrementalists began subsequent calculations."[41] Following both world wars, as well as the Great Depression, the politics of the federal income tax generally returned to the normal politics to which we have become accustomed in recent decades. However, the structure of the federal income tax was permanently changed by the politics that prevailed during these crises. Many crisis innovations are retained during peacetime, even if subsequently weakened and modified. This was the case following World War II, when wartime rates were retained beyond the cessation of overt military conflict. The revenue pressures occasioned by the Cold War and the expansion of the social welfare state in the Great Society programs of the 1960s continued to distort the politics of the income tax, and tax rates persisted at wartime levels until finally withdrawn in the face of the "Reagan Revolution."

Why, however, did this normal distributive politics of the federal income tax seem to come unglued during the 1980s? Both the strong partisan tax policies advanced by the Republican Party in 1981 and 1995 and the politics of tax reform that prevailed in 1986 were outside the realm of the "normal" nonpartisan distributive policymaking typically

---

41. Sharkansky, *Politics of Taxing and Spending,* 174.

associated with a pluralist political structure. There clearly was no regime crisis during the period, nor was there any external environmental crisis in any way comparable to the Great Depression, the Civil War, or the two world wars. Nevertheless, there were significant departures from what would be expected during a period of a normal politics for the income tax. The decline in the economic growth rate experienced after 1973 changed the environment within which tax policy was made and revenue raised. Beginning in 1981, a newly emergent budget crisis began to impinge upon the normal distributive politics of the income tax. Consequently, the politics of the income tax in the 1980s departed from a pure distributive politics that would otherwise have been predicted by a incrementalist/pluralist model.

Other peculiar factors that influenced and intruded into the congressional tax-policymaking process during the 1980s (described in Chapter 6) include the rise of the media as an influence over the tax-policymaking process, the effect of public-interest groups in swaying public opinion as well as that of legislators, and the weakening of the party and committee hierarchy in Congress, which unleashed the tax policy entrepreneurs and opened the door to other new players in the tax game. The odd coalition of tax reformers and supply-siders that came together in 1986 also evidenced aspects of a nondistributive politics of the income tax that surfaced during the decade. This all suggests that highly partisan, ideologically motivated tax policies are possible even within the context of the prevailing pluralist structures of power.

One must also consider the possibility that the success of the Republican Party in the 1994 elections was a harbinger of some "critical realignment" of the party system that will generate a new tax politics in the years to come.[42] In retrospect, the unstable tax politics of the 1980s might have been attributable in part to an impending shift or critical realignment of the post–New Deal party system in place for the past half century. Whether the Republican victory in 1994 marked a critical election leading to a long-term realignment of the party system and permanent changes in tax policy remains to be seen. While there has

---

42. The theory of critical elections was developed by Walter Dean Burnham in *Critical Elections and the Mainsprings of American Politics* (New York: W. W. Norton, 1970); see also William Nisbet Chambers and Walter Dean Burnham, eds., *The American Party Systems: Stages of Political Development* (New York: Oxford University Press, 1967), especially the essays by Burnham and Theodore J. Lowi. A considerable literature since the late 1970s follows Burnham's suggestion that the weakening of the party system itself makes another critical realignment impossible.

been the inevitable talk of such an impending realignment, some commentators have wisely cautioned that the 1994 elections more likely evidenced the deterioration (i.e., "dealignment") of the party system per se than a new era of Republican hegemony.[43]

If the politics of the 1994 elections persists through a realignment of the party system, the 1980s will appear as a period of regime politics during which the parameters of tax policymaking were radically altered. This will be the case if the Republican tax agenda is embraced, implemented, and retained as the new orthodoxy. Conversely, if it turns out that such a critical realignment is no longer possible given the overall weakening and deterioration of the party system itself, as was suggested by the original theorists of critical elections, then the instability and volatility of tax policy in the 1980s will likely continue. The weaknesses of the political institutions will persist, and the integrity of the tax-policymaking process will be undermined by radical (albeit temporary) swings in the electorate *and* by the pluralist interest-group politics that flourishes in the absence of strong countervailing political power. If so, tax policy will continue to reflect the failure of American politics to achieve a stable consensus over the nature and organization of the regime and, hence, tax policy. Most tragically, this failure of American politics arises out of the structural weaknesses of the regime itself and is likely to endure.

43. See, e.g., Arthur Schlesinger Jr., "Election '94: Not Realignment but Dealignment," *Wall St. J.,* November 16, 1994, A28.

Conclusion

[W]e must bid adieu to the golden era in our history in which we were scarcely conscious that we had a Government, so lightly did its burdens rest upon us, and enter upon that in which the almost sole problem of a statesman will be to make the credit balance the debt side of the national ledger.

—New York Times (1862)

Internal Revenue regulations will turn us into a nation of bookkeepers. The life of every citizen is becoming a business. This, it seems to me, is one of the worst interpretations of the meaning of human life history has ever seen. Man's life is not a business.

—Saul Bellow, *Herzog* (1964)

Several themes run throughout this study of federal tax policy. The first is that the U.S. income tax has been used by federal policymakers for a variety of conflicting purposes, much to the detriment of the stability and coherence of tax policy. These uses of the income tax are broadly dictated by the structures of a democratic electoral political system in which politicians are largely responsible for making tax policy. Congressional tax policymakers serve as constituency ombudsmen, legislators of national economic policy, and leaders of their major national political parties within Congress. On top of this, the same policymakers are charged with raising the enormous revenue required to finance the activities of the U.S. government. The revenue function of the income tax is largely at odds with the instrumental, political uses of the tax.

The structures of the political system impose conflicting demands upon tax policymakers—impelling them *both* to raise revenue and to implement policies that are functionally equivalent to direct budgetary expenditures (i.e., tax expenditures). As a result of the diverse and conflicting roles of policymakers and the related uses of the federal income tax to serve the conflicting functions thrust upon them, the tax laws have in recent decades become increasingly unstable, incoherent, and excessively complex. When the income tax is used by policymakers to implement public policies and to cull favor with local constituents, the Treasury is inevitably deprived of revenue.

Moreover, the politics of the federal income tax has expressed the prevailing partisan politics that otherwise characterizes the American party system. The divisions and ideologies of the major political parties, and periodically those of the minor parties as well, are reflected in the debate over the income tax and translated into a distinct rhetoric expressed through tax policy. In the decades following the New Deal, tax policymaking was played out within the context of a two-party political system dominated by a Democratic majority. Throughout this period, a strong antitax ideology pervaded American politics – most typically given voice by the minority Republican Party. At various moments, such as in the late 1940s and early 1980s, that antitax rhetoric prevailed in the political contest between the two major parties. It is too early to tell, however, whether the electoral victory of the Republican Party in the 1994 elections was the herald of the long-term ascendancy of this antitax ideology. If so, such a dramatic shift and realignment of the party system could fundamentally alter the dynamics of the tax-policymaking process in favor of tax reductions – or even the abandonment of the income tax altogether in favor of a flat consumption tax. But even if that unlikely event were to transpire, strong institutional forces would still exert pressure on policymakers for revenue; the revenue imperative of the state is largely oblivious to partisan politics. And the same political structures would continue to impose much the same incentives for politicians to use a consumption tax for political purposes – just as they have used the current income tax. Strong partisan ideology may be sufficient to contain and suppress those political incentives in the short run, but they would be reasserted over time, and the same familiar dynamics of tax policy would eventually reappear.

In recent decades, income tax policy has often reflected structural changes imposed from without the formal political system. For instance, since the late 1970s and early 1980s, the national economy has no longer provided federal policymakers with the "easy financing" of automatic tax increases attributable to inflation and bracket creep, as was the case in the 1950s and 1960s. The new economic reality that tax policymakers must confront is that of budget deficits and revenue-neutral tax policymaking. This has resulted in modifications to the tax-policymaking process. Likewise, the progressive weakening of the congressional committee system, exacerbated by the post-Watergate reforms adopted by Congress in the mid-1970s, had a great impact upon the tax-policymaking process. The consequent weakening of congressional policymaking institutions such as the House Ways and Means Committee opened the door of the tax policy arena to a cast of new political actors and interest groups who entered the tax game and began to compete with the traditional congressional tax policymakers for influence over the tax policy agenda. This has resulted in a tax-policymaking process that is both more susceptible to outside pressures and influences and more volatile and unstable as those pressures are translated into tax policy.

The second theme of this study is that the federal income tax has developed over time through a pattern of sudden departures from existing policy followed by periods of relative calm and stability. During the periods of calm and fiscal stability, a mostly distributive politics has informed income tax policymaking. At such times, the income tax has generally developed through incremental departures from existing policies. Conversely, the most radical innovations and departures from existing fiscal policy have occurred during periods of regime crisis – most particularly, during wartime. During periods of military crisis, policymakers have been forced to cope with increased expenditures and the related pressures for new revenues. The income tax itself was adopted by policymakers and became the primary source of federal revenue during and on account of such crises. During the Civil War, the extraordinary demand for revenue forced otherwise reluctant Republicans to accept the nation's first income tax. During the concluding decades of the nineteenth century, strong ideological pressures coupled with regional hostility to the tariff stimulated a political movement that challenged the nineteenth-century order, eventually culminating in the adoption of a new federal income tax in 1894. Notwithstanding the Supreme Court's defense of the old order, both major national political parties eventually acquiesced in the basic premises of income taxation and supported the formal ratification of a new constitution for the American regime – one financed by the federal income tax.

Following the adoption of the income tax in 1913, the most significant developments in tax policy occurred during periods of military crisis. Even the steeply graduated rate structure for the income tax, often assumed to reflect egalitarian principles, was really a product of the increased demand for revenue during the First and Second World Wars. Wartime crisis, rather than egalitarian politics, was the midwife of the progressive income tax. The revenue crisis of the First World War occasioned a fundamental restructuring of the fiscal organization of the American state, leading to the decline of the tariff and the concomitant rise of the income tax. This had profound implications for the development of the American state itself. The federal government was able to extract significant revenue through the income tax without provoking the same intense regional conflict engendered by high tariffs. Since the 1930s, the income tax has been the primary source of federal revenue and has been the most important fiscal tool of the American state, financing both the American military during the long Cold War and the great experiments in social engineering commencing with the New Deal and continuing in the Great Society programs of the 1960s.

The effects of military crises on the income tax (i.e., sharp increases in rates and the expansion of the tax base) must be contrasted with the effects of policymaking that dominate during periods of "normal" politics. During periods of normal politics, the pluralist politics of the American political system has generally held sway over the income tax. In this pluralist politics of the income tax, outside interest groups (both public and private) have ready access to the tax-policymaking process. As a result of the "openness" of the congressional policymaking process, the ideological coherence and consistency of tax policy is undermined as so many competing interests and claims are successfully translated into tax policy. Many of the problems of contemporary tax policy can be traced to these weaknesses and failures of American politics and institutions.

The dominant social science model applied to this politics of the income tax assumes a pluralist power structure and an incrementalist mode of policymaking. Incremental tax policymaking is closely associated with, and said to be a product of, the pluralist structure of American political institutions. As such, a incrementalist/pluralist model has been applied (mostly successfully) to the politics and policymaking of the federal income tax. Yet, incrementalism and pluralism fail to explain the peculiar dynamics of federal income tax policymaking witnessed in recent decades. Ideology and partisanship have resurfaced as strong, even dominant forces shaping contemporary tax policy—most recently when supply-side economics dominated tax policy in 1981, when the ideological movement for tax reform virtually rewrote the tax code in 1986, and then again when the conservative Republican majority took control of the tax policy agenda in 1995. In all these cases, radical political ideologies dominated the tax-policymaking process in ways very much at odds with what would be predicted by an incrementalist/pluralist model.

The previous chapter presented the outline of an alternative model to account for these more radical departures from incrementalist decisionmaking and pluralist politics. This model stresses military crisis as the stimulus for the most important political developments in the income tax, differentiating these developments from the incremental changes to tax policy made during periods of normal politics. However, if this alternative model provides a more comprehensive description of past tax policymaking, it is of little value in predicting future tax policy developments. The policymaking of the federal income tax remains at once a perplexing and revealing enterprise that defies easy explanations or predictions. Though incrementalism and distributive politics dominate tax policymaking during periods of normal politics, it is the radical departures that are of most importance and interest – and most difficult to predict. In this respect, tax policy is but a reflection of the structure of American political institutions.

POSTSCRIPT: Some Further Reflections on Flat Tax Fever

As the 1996 Republican presidential campaign kicked into high gear with the Iowa caucuses and the New Hampshire primary, the flat tax improbably emerged as the "hot" issue of the new political season. Equally improbable, political newcomer Malcolm S. ("Steve") Forbes Jr. emerged as a serious contender for the Republican nomination. Armed with the flat tax and a pledge to dismantle the Internal Revenue Service, Forbes sought to knock Senate majority leader Robert Dole from his tenuous position as front-runner in the race. While the chances of that evaporated as soon as the Republican faithful went to the polls in Iowa and New Hampshire, the flat tax and the broader theme of major tax reform were thrust into the political debate and onto the policy agenda.

The Origins of the Flat Tax

Interest in the flat tax had been brewing for nearly two years before candidate Forbes even came on the political scene. During the summer of 1994, Representative Richard Armey of Texas introduced a bill (the "Freedom and Fairness Restoration Act of 1994") providing for a uniform 17 percent tax stripped of all the deductions allowed under the current income tax. Armey campaigned tirelessly for his flat tax proposal throughout the 104th Congress and virtually singlehandedly brought the flat tax onto the policy agenda. Armey rests his case for the flat tax on two claims: "fairness" and "simplicity." The claim for fairness derives from the proposition that all citizens ought to be taxed at the same (uniform) rate. At the same time, the flat tax is held out as a simpler system under which "individuals would fill out a tax form the size of a postcard."

The Armey flat tax proposal was modeled on that first advanced in the early 1980s by economist Robert E. Hall and political scientist Alvin Rabushka, both of the Hoover Institution at Stanford University. Notwithstanding the disincentives created under the current income tax, Hall and Rabushka were industrious enough to produce a new edition of their 1985 book, *The Flat Tax*, as interest in their plan resurfaced a decade later. The Hall-Rabushka flat tax plan is a thoughtful attempt to present a comprehensive explanation and defense of a flat consumption-based tax to a popular (nonacademic) audience. But it is one thing to write a book on the flat tax and another to muster the political will to abandon the U.S. income tax (the primary source of revenue for the federal government) in favor of an entirely untried system of taxation. Nevertheless, armed with the Hall-Rabushka flat tax bible, Armey sought precisely that.

The Armey (Hall-Rabushka) flat tax is really a two-tier tax. The first element is a business tax that closely resembles a subtraction-method valued-added tax (VAT). The tax is imposed on a business's "gross active income"—essentially the gross receipts of the business derived from its sales less its purchases from other businesses. But unlike a traditional VAT, the flat tax allows for a deduction for the wages (but not fringe benefits) paid to the business's workers. Most significant, the business would be allowed to expense immediately the cost of its capital investments, as opposed to recovering the outlay over time through amortization as under an income tax system. The effect of an immediate deduction is effectively to exempt from taxation the return on capital. Of course, that is precisely the intention of flat tax proponents who would exempt from taxation the return on capital in order to avoid creating disincentives to savings that the current regime imposes by taxing the return on capital.

One other defining characteristic of the business component of the flat tax is that it is an "origin-based" tax. This means that the tax applies to any business located in the United States—whether conducted through a corporation, partnership, or sole proprietorship. Under an origin-based tax, a domestic business pays tax on all of its goods produced (whether for domestic use or export), while imported goods are exempt from tax. This is in contrast with most VATs based on the European model, which is "destination-based." Under a destination-based VAT, imported goods are subject to tax while exported goods are exempt ("zero-rated"). To implement these principles, tax is imposed at the border on imported goods, and in the case of exports either a border adjustment (tax rebate) is provided or in the case of a "credit-invoice"

VAT, the exporter is allowed a refundable credit (to offset the VAT paid on the goods purchased by the exporter). These border adjustments are consistent with the General Agreement on Tariffs and Trade (GATT), to which the United States recently became a signatory party. On the other hand, rebating the flat tax on exports (as well as allowing a deduction for wages) would not be allowed under GATT rules. That the flat tax is an origin-based consumption tax has been widely criticized as an apparent impediment to U.S. businesses exporting their goods. Because of the border adjustments, a destination-based VAT appears to subsidize exports and create a protective barrier from imports, while an origin-based tax appears to put domestic producers at a relative disadvantage compared to foreign producers. But economists argue that it really makes no difference. In the case of an origin-based tax such as the flat tax, there will be a corresponding adjustment in currency rates and/or wages that in the long run will correct for the absence of border adjustments.

In addition to the VAT-like tax imposed at the business level, the flat tax also includes a uniform 17 percent tax imposed on the wages and pension income distributions of an individual in excess of the relatively high standard deductions and generous dependent allowances. In the original Armey bill, the standard deductions were set at $13,100 for a single taxpayer and $26,200 for a married couple filing jointly, and the dependent allowance was $5,300—with the result that no tax at all would be owed for a family of four until income reached approximately $36,000. Under the two-tier system, the wages paid to a worker would be deductible by the business and subject to the same rate of tax in the hands of the worker. However, the economic impact of the individual tax would be somewhat different than that under the business tax on account of the high personal exemptions. Because of these, the flat payroll tax would be a "progressive" tax in the sense that a worker with total annual wages (and pension distributions) below the threshold levels would not be subject to tax at all. In effect, the tax on individuals would have the structure of a two-bracket payroll tax with a "zero-rate tax" imposed on wages up to the exemption levels and a 17 percent tax on wages above the exemption levels. Interest, dividends, and capital gains would not be taxed at the individual level, having been previously taxed when earned at the business level.

Armey's flat tax proposal didn't get much attention when it was first introduced. But that was before the Republican landslide in the November 1994 elections and before Armey became House majority leader. After that, interest in the flat tax increased dramatically. Likewise, attacks from within the ranks of the GOP against the current income tax and the Internal Revenue Service have reached an all-time high. Fringe "tax protesters" have long questioned the legitimacy of the federal income tax—notwithstanding the fact that the Sixteenth Amendment and the Supreme Court settled questions over its constitutionality more than eighty years ago. But Armey and his fellow Texan Bill Archer brought the antitax movement into the mainstream. From his pulpit as chairman of the powerful House Ways and Means Committee, where all revenue bills originate, Archer repeatedly declared his preference to "rip the income tax out by the roots and throw it overboard."

Although Armey's became the main flat tax proposal before Congress, there has been no lack of competitors. It seems that any congressional leader or would-be presidential contender needs only a few hours and some energetic staff members to draft an entirely "new" tax system. In January 1995, House minority leader Richard A. Gephardt came out in support of a flat (or flatter) income tax imposed at a 10 percent to 11 percent rate on all but the wealthiest 20 percent of American taxpayers. Only six months later, under pressure from Democrats on his left, Gephardt did an about-face and proposed five tax brackets with a progressive rate structure ranging from 10 percent to 34 percent. In a July 6 speech to the Center for National Policy, Gephardt suggested the revenue lost under his plan through the lowering of the top rate to 34 percent from the current 39.6 percent would be funded by drastically reducing "corporate welfare." This is familiar rhetoric from Democrats. When pressed for details by reporters at his press conference for the proposed tax, Gephardt could only make vague references to going after corporations that "avoid" paying U.S. income tax by shifting income to foreign jurisdictions with lower income taxes. Unfortunately, that is not as easy as it sounds. Candidate Bill Clinton made similar charges in the 1992 presidential campaign, but he never did anything about it once in office. Indeed, Treasury has been investigating this complex issue for decades and still cannot come up with a scheme that both works well and doesn't impose oppressive compliance costs on businesses.

During spring 1994, presidential hopeful Arlen Specter, the moderate Republican senator from Pennsylvania, also jumped on the flat-tax bandwagon in what seemed an overnight conversion. The long-shot presidential candidate introduced a flat tax proposal that lamely copied Armey's bill. The only distinguishing feature of Specter's proposal was that it retained limited deductions for charitable contributions and interest on a home mortgage. Lacking support among the rank and file of the Republican Party, Specter himself soon dropped out of the presidential race and his flat tax proposal was heard of no more.

In July 1995, Armey (along with Richard Shelby of Alabama in the Senate) introduced a slightly modified rendition of the Freedom and Fairness Restoration Act in the 104th Congress. This revised version would phase in (over three years) a flat 17 percent tax on the wages and pensions of individuals earning more than $10,700 and couples earning more than $21,400. By so reducing the exemption levels, the flat tax would raise considerably greater revenue. As under the original model, the revised Armey flat tax would allow none of the traditional deductions or credits of the current income tax system except that for dependents. Under the new plan the tax would be withheld from the wages and pensions of each individual taxpayer. Of course, the revised flat tax remained much "fairer" and "simpler" than the current income tax.

The Flat Tax in 1996

While Representative Armey was most responsible for stirring up the flat tax fever in 1995, it was Steve Forbes who seized the helm of the flat tax campaign in 1996. Forbes entered the race in September 1995 with a simple and persistent message, urging voters to "[scrap] the income tax. Don't fiddle with it. Junk it. Throw it out. Bury it. Replace it with a pro-growth, pro-family tax cut that lowers tax rates to 17 percent across the board." The flat tax provided a focal point for Forbes's "outsider," anti-Washington rhetoric—in many ways a replay of the same themes that Bill Clinton had used to capture the White House four years before. Portraying the income tax as the tool of decadent Washington "politicians" who sell off tax loopholes to the highest bidders (the ubiquitous "special interests"), Forbes would present the flat tax as the ultimate cure—a uniform rate and no deductions at all allowed.

Once the primary season commenced, Forbes waged a blitzkrieg campaign of television advertising in Iowa and New Hampshire, financed largely by his own considerable personal wealth. Without ever actually presenting a concrete written plan for his flat tax, Forbes succeeded in staking out the issue of "major tax reform" as his own. His campaign also included a radical proposal for the partial privatization of the Social Security system (a position that would have spelled certain death for any political candidate only years before, but which ironically was given serious consideration by the Clinton administration's own Advisory Council on Social Security). But it was the flat tax that brought Forbes his fifteen minutes of fame as a presidential contender.

The sudden rise in Steve Forbes's standing in the polls in New Hampshire and Iowa focused all eyes on the flat tax. In mid-January, with new polls showing Forbes on the way up, *Time* and *Newsweek* simultaneously put out cover stories on the candidate and the flat tax. As if on cue, virtually every major newspaper in the country (and many abroad) ran stories on the flat tax. At that point, replacing the current income tax regime with the flat tax became the dominant issue in the GOP primaries. Forbes effectively preempted the field with his well-financed media blitz, forcing the other candidates (along with the media and countless political journalists) to genuflect before the flat tax.

Bob Dole, the ever cautious front-runner, from the first was appropriately critical of Forbes's portrait of the flat tax as a cure for all that ails America. But with Forbes pushing him in the polls, Dole too eventually came out for a flatter, gentler income tax. Trailing in the polls, Phil Gramm introduced his own flat tax plan–besting Forbes's 17 percent rate by one percentage point. That did nothing to save Gramm's floundering candidacy, but it did make clear that for the moment the flat tax was the foremost campaign issue.

Forbes and Armey were not alone in promoting major tax reform in 1996. In January, the National Commission on Economic Growth and Tax Reform (chaired by Jack Kemp, former secretary of Housing and Urban Development) made public its recommendations on how to reform the federal income tax. The summer before, Senate majority leader Robert Dole and House Speaker Newt Gingrich had appointed the so-called Kemp Commission (organized as a private group rather than a formal congressional body) to investigate the various tax-reform proposals floating around Washington. Reports were that Kemp was pressured by Dole to stay clear of a full-blown endorsement of any specific tax-reform plan–in particular, that hawked by Forbes, Dole's new rival for the Republican presidential nomination. As anticipated, the commission took a moderate, noncommittal stance on what form major tax reform should take.

In its report, the Kemp Commission paid homage to all the requisite political clichés of the tax-reform debate–"flatness," "fairness," "simplicity," and "growth"–but would only commit itself to an improved *income* tax. In doing so, Kemp and company implicitly rejected the more radical proposals for a consumption tax, such as the flat tax plan championed by Armey, the "USA tax" proposed by Senators Sam Nunn and Pete Domenici during the 103rd Congress, the value-added tax (VAT) favored by so many economists (as well as Sam Gibbons, ranking Democrat on the House Ways and Means Committee), and the national sales tax (one form of consumption tax) touted by Senator Richard Lugar (himself a long-shot and highly ineffective candidate for the Republican presidential nomination). While not expressly endorsing the flat tax, the Kemp Commission further stimulated voter and media interest in the overall issue of major tax reform. In this way, the Forbes campaign benefited from all the attention generated by the commission.

Why Not a Flat Tax?

Because each flat tax plan differs somewhat from the rest, it is difficult to generalize. Nevertheless, all the flat tax plans share certain common features and their proponents make similar claims for their plans. These claims warrant more reflection (and critical response) than the candidates seem willing to provide.

Simplicity. All of the proponents of the flat tax begin their case by stressing the extreme complexity and overall impenetrability of the present income tax. They point out that the Internal Revenue Code and income tax regulations go on for thousands of pages. This is true enough. And reducing the complexity of the tax code is an admirable goal. But it must be recognized that the great complexity of the income tax is in no way a product of its progressive (graduated) rate structure. The tax code is complicated because politicians in Washington have used the income tax to implement so many social and economic policies rather than just to raise revenue—which it is actually quite effective in doing. Admittedly, simplifying the current income tax is quite difficult, but surely no more so than finding the political will to junk the income tax altogether.

The problem is that the same political impulses that led congressmen to use the tax code to curry favor with constituents, implement their favorite social policies, and fine-tune the economy would also soon result in an increasingly complicated flat tax. Lobbyists would soon lobby for special provisions under the flat tax, just as they now do under the income tax regime. Tax attorneys also would undoubtedly push Congress to adopt complicated new provisions as they would learn to exploit the bare-bones (i.e., simplistic) provisions in the flat tax for the benefit of their clients. For the last eighty years, Congress and the IRS have responded to this kind of "tax avoidance" by enacting new statutes and regulations designed to shut down abusive tax-motivated transactions with no economic substance. These anti-abuse rules would be "thrown overboard" and junked along with the income tax. Hardly a great result for the U.S. Treasury, which would be forced to start all over in designing rules to police the revenue laws.

Finally, one of the main selling points that Armey makes for his flat tax is that because it is a "simple" tax, individuals would fill out a tax form the "size of a postcard." But right now more than 70 percent of taxpayers claim the standard deduction rather than itemize their deductions. These taxpayers already file tax returns no more than a page or two long. While shrinking the tax return down to postcard size would be nice, it's not really such a big deal for most taxpayers. In fact, businesses would still need to fill out fairly complicated tax returns using new "cash-flow" accounting methods. The determination of "business income" would likely be less complicated than the determination of taxable income under the current income tax, but the overall enterprise would require much more than a postcard-size tax return.

Fairness. Flat tax proponents argue that a uniform tax rate will be "fairer" than the current progressive rate structure. For example, Representative Armey has justified his proposal for a flat tax on the grounds that "the great virtue of a flat tax is its fundamental fairness." Senator Specter asserted that a flat tax would "provide for fairness among all taxpayers." The clear implication is that some taxpayers are treated unfairly by the current progressive rate structure.

It may strike many as only "fair" that all taxpayers should pay taxes at the same rate. On the other hand, most recognize that the poorer among us should pay no taxes at all (a zero tax rate)–indicating an acceptance of the general principle that some differences among taxpayers justify different rates. The whole issue of whether the "Wealthy" ought to pay at a higher rate or the same rate as everyone else is a normative question that is not at all self-evident. Flat tax proponents are obliged to present a normative argument in support of their demand to change the status quo (a progressive rate structure)–just as those in the Democrat Party who believe in progressive tax rates are obliged to defend their vision of justice as income redistribution. There wasn't much of that when President Clinton in 1993 used the income tax as a weapon of class warfare by imposing a "millionaire's" surtax on those with incomes above $250,000. But by themselves failing to present clear and convincing reasons why a uniform tax rate is "fairer," flat tax proponents diminish the political debate discourse rather than enhance it. In the end, the choice of a tax rate structure is a normative choice reflecting deep-rooted political values about the role of government and how the cost of government should be shared by the citizenry. It's just not enough to just repeat over and over that a flat tax is "fairer."

Savings and Investment. Proponents of the flat tax blame the present income tax for the dangerously low savings rate in this country. They claim that the flat tax will lead to increased savings and investment in the United States. Steve Forbes predicts that thousands of new jobs and an "explosion" in productivity will materialize the moment we adopt a flat tax. Phil Gramm, Arlen Specter, and Dick Armey all make similar claims for their flat tax proposals. In the long-run, such exaggerated assertions will only work against the campaign for a genuine pro-growth fiscal policy.

Most economists predict only a modest increase in savings from adopting the flat tax. For example, Federal Reserve Board economist Eric Engen has calculated that switching to a consumption tax could increase national savings by as much as 10 percent. Based on the current level of 5 percent of GDP, that would translate into an increase to 5.5 percent of GDP–desirable to be sure, but simply not that significant an improvement. Economist William Gale of the Brookings Institution predicts the increase would be even lower than that. Why such a lackluster improvement if the income tax is really so thoroughly anti-investment? Mostly because the present income tax (really a hybrid system) already excludes from taxation a good deal of the savings of most taxpayers. This is done through tax-favored pension plans, individual retirement accounts (IRAs), and Keogh plans (for self-employed persons). Adopting an unlimited exemption from taxation for all investments (as the flat tax plan effectively would) will not increase savings by that much since most taxpayers already save all they want to–failing even to utilize their present savings exemptions. Most taxpayers do not contribute the maximum $2,000 to their IRAs or the more than $9,000 that they are permitted to contribute tax-free to their 401(k) plans and Keoghs. If the claims for an improved national savings rate cannot be counted on, maybe it's not necessary to go down the path of radical tax reform after all.

The Flat Tax Is "Pro-Family." One of the strangest arguments advanced for the flat tax is that it is somehow more "pro-family" than the present income tax. Much the same sentiment is behind the $500-per-child tax credit included in the Contract with America tax bill. Conservatives themselves should be more critical of the logic underlying this claim. If using the tax system to implement social policy is undesirable and is doomed to fail, as is charged against the present income tax, then using the flat tax to strengthen the American family may not be such a great idea either.

Anyway, since when do conservatives believe that the morality and cohesion of American families depends upon whether or not the federal government supplies the appropriate level of tax credits, deductions, and exemptions? While there are good technical reasons why the personal and dependent exemptions should be increased under the present income tax (mainly because they haven't kept pace with the overall rate of inflation) and why a tax credit is preferable to a deduction for supporting one's dependent, there simply is no reason to think that any of these attempts at social engineering through the tax system would have much impact upon the morality of the citizenry or the strength of the American family.

Side-Effects of the Flat Tax

If flat tax proponents make these and other exaggerated claims on its behalf, they also tend to underestimate the serious problems and economic upheaval that could result from junking the income tax in favor of a whole new untried tax system. These are just some of the problems that could result.

Flat Tax/Consumption Tax. The most radical and least understood aspect of the flat tax is that it really is a consumption tax. In contrast to an income tax that taxes annual income plus the return on savings and investment (e.g., dividends and interest), the return on savings is entirely exempt from taxation under the flat tax. This is what makes it a consumption tax. When you cut through all the technical language, the end result is to tax an individual's net consumption for the year.

Of course, this is what makes the flat tax so attractive to pro-growth Republicans as well as professional economists who bemoan the disincentives and inefficiencies that result from taxing the return on capital. But the effects of such a radical shift in tax policy would be dramatic and are not very well understood. Since savings would no longer be taxed, certain taxpayers would benefit—at least it looks that way on first glance. For example, wealthy individuals with high annual incomes but low consumption patterns (a rich miser such as the late Sam Walton of Wal-Mart or the relatively moderate Bill Gates of Microsoft) would likely pay less tax under a consumption tax than under the current income tax. On the other hand, their businesses would likely pay more tax, and the value of their stock portfolios (and other accumulated wealth) would likely decline on account of the adoption of a consumption tax. Princeton University economist David Bradford, a leading and long-time proponent of consumption taxes and architect of Treasury's 1977 landmark *Blueprints for Basic Tax Reform*, describes the enactment of a consumption tax such as the flat tax as equivalent to a one-time tax on all existing wealth (e.g., savings). It is highly unlikely that the typical Forbes supporter is aware that the flat tax is really a *wealth tax*.

Despite the economic reality of a consumption tax as a wealth tax (which if properly understood, would not exactly help in winning the votes of well-heeled voters), the image of some rich fat-cat sitting on his yacht and living off his investment return free of all tax will make for a powerful political image just waiting to be exploited by President Clinton and Democrats in the fall 1996 elections. For this reason, most proponents of the flat tax who actually want to win an election make exceptions to pure consumption tax principles—so it doesn't look like they are taking from the middle class and giving to the wealthy (which is precisely what they are doing if rates are kept at a flat 17 percent). In addition, some flat tax proposals retain at least some of the most politically appealing features of the income tax—the deductions for home-mortgage interest and charitable contributions, and the Earned Income Tax Credit. Among the assortment of Republican presidential candidates in 1996, only Forbes would have us go "cold turkey" and adopt a pure flat consumption tax stripped of all these deductions and credits. While this is the theoretically consistent position, the political consequences of adopting such a plan in the presidential campaign could be fatal to the GOP. While economists disdain such accommodations to popular opinion, Republican candidates are forced to cope with real-life voters in electoral campaigns. It's fine to educate the public on why the home-mortgage-interest deduction is an unwanted "inefficiency" in the capital market, but such subtle points are sure to be lost on an electorate that wants more, rather than less, in the way of deductions.

Economic Impact. Aside from the political popularity of the deductions for home mortgage interest and charitable donations, whole sectors of the national economy have grown up around and depend upon these tax preferences. Universities, museums, and city orchestras all rely upon the incentives to charitable giving created by high marginal tax rates and deductions for contributions. Predictions are that the housing industry could take a big hit if the home-mortgage-interest deduction were eliminated. For this reason, the housing industry immediately geared up for a political battle. Hall and Rabushka reassure that the loss of the deduction would be offset by the lower costs of borrowing that would result from exempting interest payments from taxation. Of course, if interest rates really do plunge, after-tax rates of return on investment will too, thus defeating one of the main justifications for adopting the flat consumption tax in the first place—creating added incentives for savings and investment. The intellectually sound argument for doing away with the home-mortgage-interest deduction is that it causes an inefficient overallocation of our national resources to home-ownership and away from other capital investment. The deduction should be repealed even under the current income tax. But try selling that one in an election year.

State and municipal governments also won't be thrilled to lose the special tax treatment now afforded to interest paid on their bonds. Since all interest would be exempt from tax under the flat tax, tax-exempt state and municipal bonds would lose their preference. This could result in as much as a 30 percent drop in the value of portfolios of tax-exempt bonds. It also would make it more difficult for state and local governments to finance their activities–the little things such as building roads, repairing bridges, or maintaining public transportation services. The economic upheaval that could ensue from switching tax systems should be good enough reason for all to pause and reconsider. Whatever its shortcomings, the income tax is so closely intertwined with the national economy that its repeal would take us into uncharted waters.

Revenue. Another serious reason conservatives should be very cautious in approaching the flat tax is revenue–or the lack of it under the flat tax. From the first it was clear that at the low rates proposed by supporters the flat tax could not raise as much revenue as the present income tax. The Treasury Department originally estimated that Armey's 17 percent flat tax would cost $244 billion in lost revenue a year and calculated that a 25.8 percent flat tax would be needed to achieve "revenue neutrality." A more recent Treasury estimate concluded that the newest version of the Armey plan (which does away with the gift and estate taxes as well as the Earned Income Tax Credit) still comes up about $138 billion a year short. Under Armey's flat tax, a rate of 20.8 percent (or significant cuts in the personal exemptions) would be necessary to raise the same revenue as the present tax system. The Forbes flat tax does no better, although it has never officially been "scored" since it has only been presented as an informal plan. Of course, at rates higher than 17 percent, the flat tax is considerably less attractive politically. And if the revenue estimators are correct, the kind of significant additions to the deficit that the flat tax would inflict on the Treasury could spell fiscal disaster.

The current income tax–the most significant source of federal revenue–will raise somewhere near $730 billion in 1995. There simply is no revenue crisis. The income tax is not broken but merely overextended by a political process that caters to the electorate's boundless appetite for public goods and tax expenditures. The source of the impending fiscal crisis lies in the government's unfunded commitment to pay future "entitlement" benefits, not the inability of the income tax to raise revenue. Among the candidates, only Forbes was willing to address this issue. But even for Forbes, the income tax and the IRS make for easier political targets than senior citizens living on social security and Medicare.

Redistribution. If the flat tax would fail to raise sufficient revenue, it also would shift the burden of taxation as presently shared. Despite the fact that the wealthy make greater use of the tax deductions that would be stripped out of the tax code, they also now pay taxes at effective (average) rates higher than 17 percent. Thus, at any of the proposed rates for the flat tax, the effect would be a slight redistribution of the tax burden to the middle class away from wealthier taxpayers. Lower-income taxpayers would also benefit as the exemption levels would be set so high. The flat tax is a popular issue with the middle class, which obviously has some difficulty following such technical points.

State Tax Systems. One of the least understood results of adopting a flat consumption tax at the national level is the impact on the tax systems of the state governments. Since many states "piggyback" on the federal income tax base (subject to certain modifications) for their own state income taxes, repeal would wreak havoc on state revenue systems. Unless these states also switch to a consumption-based tax, taxpayers would still have to determine their state tax obligations under some form of an income tax system. Furthermore, states rely on federal "information reporting" (on IRS Form 1099) to verify what interest and dividend income taxpayers have for the year. Under the flat tax, these sources of income would be exempt, and so there would be no information reporting. This would render the states at a serious disadvantage in trying to administer their own taxes. And finally, calls to abolish the IRS are not likely to sit well with state officials who presumably would be charged with the unwanted task of collecting the federal government's revenue.

Transition Problems. Beyond these many substantive objections, how would we actually switch to a consumption tax? Even if adopting the flat tax was truly desirable, the transition from an income tax to a consumption tax may be the fatal stumbling block. Most polls show widespread backing for a flat tax, but beneath this veneer of support lie powerful political constituencies who will fight it tooth and nail. Whole sectors of the national economy have grown up around, and depend upon, the kind of tax preferences that the flat tax would eliminate.

Since all current savings have already been taxed under the present income tax regime, it would be necessary to exempt these amounts from taxation under the new tax. Otherwise, the savings of all taxpayers (for instance, that of retirees who have accumulated their lifetime savings to get them through their twilight years) would be taxed a second time as they spend their savings in retirement. But any set of rules that would allow taxpayers to identify their pre-"reform" savings would be a nightmare of complexity. And exempting so much of the national wealth from the consumption tax would obviate the very benefits the new tax regime is supposed to achieve. Economists such as Gale and Bradford emphasize the relative advantages of a consumption tax over the income tax, but they also recognize the considerable barriers to switching. This is more than can be said for Forbes and company. Proponents such as Armey acknowledge such problems but generally dismiss them as "solvable." Such glib responses are not very reassuring.

If there is some extended period wherein the new tax is phased in while the income tax is phased out, there will be two tax regimes that taxpayers must confront and plan around. A truly radical break with the past is impossible, and the transition period promises to be even more complex as two tax systems are in place. Boston University economist Laurence Kotlikoff, an ardent and well-respected proponent of a flat consumption tax, offers one good reason why there should be no transition rules to avoid double taxation. Kotlikoff suggests that the older generation of taxpayers has already reaped an economic windfall from the Social Security system. He has a valid point. The Social Security program has provided seniors (as a whole the generation with the most after-tax savings) with overly generous benefits far in excess of their contributions. It takes current (and prior) retirees only a few years to recover their lifetime contributions to the system—after that, it's all gravy. Still, particular taxpayers could be devastated by a double tax on their savings—and the impact of such tax could be all out of proportion to the "excess" benefits they received from the Social Security program. In any event, the mere specter of riled-up seniors mobilizing their powerful political associations should be enough to dissuade members of Congress from embracing Kotlikoff's notion of rough economic justice. So politicians would most likely vote for transition rules—which means more complexity.

Whither the Flat Tax?

What are the chances that flat tax mania will succeed in dislodging the income tax? To date, there have been few within the Republican Party willing to express any dissent in the face of the groundswell of enthusiasm for the flat tax. One key figure who might have been able to co-opt and redirect support for radical tax reform was Oregon Senator Bob Packwood. Packwood chaired the Finance Committee during the great tax reform effort of 1986. (He also contributed mightily to the distortion of the tax laws through countless special-interest provisions, particularly those designed to benefit Oregon's timber industry.) In 1986 Packwood was one of those (along with his counterpart on Ways and Means, Dan Rostenkowski) who took control of the radical tax reform movement generated by tax professionals in Treasury and sculpted it into a more moderate and politically viable package. In April and May 1995, Packwood held hearings on the flat tax, with both Armey and Specter testifying in support of their own proposals. Packwood needed to appear supportive of the flat tax, since the scandal-plagued senator could hardly be seen as blocking his party's hottest idea. But Packwood, who understood the tax system as well as anyone in the Senate, could see the danger that a flat tax presents, and he may have been willing to work quietly to gut it. However, with Packwood's forced resignation from the Senate in September 1995, the point became moot. His successor at the helm of the Finance Committee, Delaware Senator William Roth, is much more receptive to the flat tax.

Once the flat tax was actually tested as a campaign issue in New Hampshire and Iowa, it turned out not to be such a "hot" idea after all. Of course, it was unclear whether the Republican voters in those states were rejecting the flat tax or merely Steve Forbes. In Iowa, Forbes came in a distant fourth in the caucus voting. In New Hampshire, a state notorious for its antitax ideology, Forbes ran a weak fourth, garnering just 12 percent of the vote. Indeed, polls had already indicated that the flat tax reached its peak as a campaign issue by mid-February. After that, Forbes's popularity rose a bit more even as the popularity of the flat tax began to ebb. Then came Iowa and New Hampshire; victories for Forbes in Arizona and Delaware merely delayed the inevitable. Soon after, it became obvious that the flat tax banner would have to be carried by someone other than Steve Forbes. And Bob Dole is not a likely candidate for that chore.

What did the Forbes campaign accomplish beyond putting some much appreciated cash in the pockets of some advertising consultants and television station owners in New Hampshire and Iowa? For one thing, Republicans were forced to rethink their commitment to the flat tax before actually having to front a flat-tax candidate such as Steve Forbes in a general election where the response to his tax reform proposal and Social Security privatization plan would be much more critical and could spell political suicide. As Robert Reischauer, former director of the Congressional Budget Office, has warned: "It [tax reform] may look great from a mile away, but up close, it's a political minefield." Fortunately for them, Republicans learned this lesson *before* the general election.

But the flat tax itself is not going to go away so quickly. So long as Messrs. Armey and Archer remain in the House, the issue is sure to get an extensive and prolonged hearing in the 105th Congress. And who knows, perhaps candidate Clinton will turn the tables on candidate Dole and embrace the flat tax as *his* campaign issue in the fall of 1996. Stranger things have happened where the flat tax is concerned.

Appendix

Table 1: Projected Fiscal Year 1996 Federal Receipts by Source ($ in Billions)

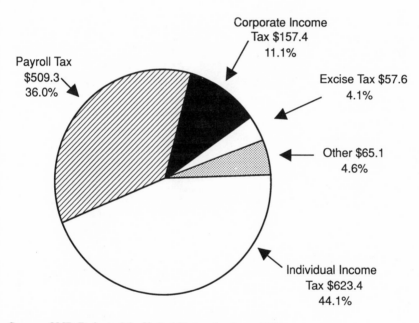

Source: OMB, Budget of the United States, fiscal year 1996

Table 2:   Aggregate Federal Receipts by Source, 1890–1994 (nominal dollars) [in billions of dollars]

Year	Individual income tax	Payroll tax	Corporate income tax	Excise taxes	Other receipts
1994	543.1	461.5	140.4	55.2	57.6
1993	509.7	428.3	117.5	48.1	50.0
1992	476.0	413.7	100.3	45.6	55.0
1991	467.8	396.0	98.1	42.4	49.9
1990	466.9	380.0	93.5	35.3	55.5
1989	445.7	359.4	103.3	34.4	47.9
1988	401.2	334.3	94.5	35.2	43.7
1987	392.6	303.3	83.9	32.5	41.9
1986	349.0	283.9	63.1	32.9	40.2
1985	334.5	265.2	61.1	36.0	37.2
1984	298.4	239.4	56.9	37.4	34.4
1983	288.9	209.0	37.0	35.3	30.3
1982	297.7	201.5	49.2	36.3	33.0
1981	285.9	182.7	61.1	40.8	28.7
1980	244.1	157.8	64.6	24.3	26.3
1979	217.8	138.9	65.7	18.7	22.1
1978	181.0	121.0	60.0	18.4	19.3
1977	157.6	106.5	54.9	17.5	19.0
1976	131.6	90.8	41.4	17.0	17.3
1975	122.4	84.5	40.6	16.6	15.0
1974	119.0	75.1	38.6	16.8	13.7
1973	103.2	63.1	36.2	16.3	12.0
1972	94.7	52.6	32.2	15.5	12.4
1971	86.2	47.3	26.8	16.6	10.2
1970	90.4	44.4	32.8	15.7	9.5
1969	87.2	39.0	36.7	15.2	8.7
1968	68.7	33.9	28.7	14.1	7.6
1967	61.5	32.6	34.0	13.7	7.0
1966	55.4	25.5	30.1	13.1	6.7
1965	48.8	22.2	25.5	14.6	5.8
1964	48.7	22.0	23.5	13.7	4.7
1963	47.6	19.8	21.6	13.2	4.4
1962	45.6	17.0	20.5	12.5	4.0
1961	41.3	16.4	21.0	11.9	3.8
1960	40.7	14.7	21.5	11.7	3.9
1959	36.7	11.7	17.3	10.6	2.9
1958	34.7	11.2	20.1	10.6	3.0
1957	35.6	10.0	21.2	10.5	2.7

Continued

Table 2: *Continued*

Year	Individual income tax	Payroll tax	Corporate income tax	Excise taxes	Other receipts
1956	32.2	9.3	20.9	9.9	2.3
1955	28.7	7.9	17.9	9.1	1.9
1954	29.5	7.2	21.1	9.9	1.9
1953	29.8	6.8	21.2	9.9	1.9
1952	27.9	6.4	21.2	8.9	1.7
1951	21.6	5.7	14.1	8.6	1.6
1950	15.8	4.3	10.4	7.6	1.4
1949	15.6	3.6	11.2	7.5	1.4
1948	19.3	3.8	9.7	7.4	1.5
1947	17.9	3.4	8.6	7.2	1.3
1946	16.1	3.1	11.9	7.0	1.2
1945	18.4	3.5	16.0	6.3	1.1
1944	19.7	3.5	14.8	4.8	1.0
1943	6.5	3.0	9.6	4.1	0.8
1942	3.3	2.5	4.7	3.4	0.8
1941	1.3	1.9	2.1	2.6	0.8
1940	0.9	1.8	1.2	2.0	0.7
1939	1.0	1.6	1.1	1.9	0.7
1938	1.3	1.5	1.3	1.9	0.8
1937	1.1	0.6	1.0	1.9	0.8
1936	0.7	0.1	0.7	1.6	0.8
1935	0.5	0.0	0.5	1.4	1.1
1934	0.4	0.0	0.4	1.4	0.8
1933	0.4	0.0	0.4	0.8	0.0
1932	0.4	0.0	0.6	0.5	0.0
1931	0.8	0.0	1.0	0.5	0.0
1930	1.1	0.0	1.3	0.6	0.1
1929	1.1	0.0	1.2	0.5	0.1
1928	0.9	0.0	1.3	0.5	0.1
1927	0.9	0.0	1.3	0.5	0.2
1926	0.9	0.0	1.1	0.6	0.3
1925	0.8	0.0	0.9	0.5	0.3
1924	0.8	0.0	0.9	0.7	0.4
1923	0.9	0.0	0.0	0.6	0.0
1922	0.7	0.0	0.0	0.6	0.0
1921	1.1	0.0	0.0	0.7	0.0
1920	1.3	0.0	0.0	0.8	0.0
1919	1.1	0.0	0.0	0.8	0.0

Continued

Table 2: *Continued*

Year	Individual income tax	Payroll tax	Corporate income tax	Excise taxes	Other receipts
1918	0.8	0.0	0.0	0.6	0.0
1917	0.2	0.0	0.2	0.4	0.0
1916	0.1	0.0	0.1	0.3	0.0
1915	0.0	0.0	0.0	0.3	0.0
1914	0.0	0.0	0.0	0.3	0.0
1913	0.0	0.0	0.0	0.3	0.0
1912	0.0	0.0	0.0	0.3	0.0
1911	0.0	0.0	0.0	0.3	0.0
1910	0.0	0.0	0.0	0.3	0.0
1909	0.0	0.0	0.0	0.2	0.0
1908	0.0	0.0	0.0	0.3	0.0
1907	0.0	0.0	0.0	0.3	0.0
1906	0.0	0.0	0.0	0.2	0.0
1905	0.0	0.0	0.0	0.2	0.0
1904	0.0	0.0	0.0	0.2	0.0
1903	0.0	0.0	0.0	0.2	0.0
1902	0.0	0.0	0.0	0.3	0.0
1901	0.0	0.0	0.0	0.3	0.0
1900	0.0	0.0	0.0	0.3	0.0
1899	0.0	0.0	0.0	0.3	0.0
1898	0.0	0.0	0.0	0.2	0.0
1897	0.0	0.0	0.0	0.1	0.0
1896	0.0	0.0	0.0	0.1	0.0
1895	0.0	0.0	0.0	0.1	0.0
1894	0.0	0.0	0.0	0.1	0.0
1893	0.0	0.0	0.0	0.2	0.0
1892	0.0	0.0	0.0	0.2	0.0
1891	0.0	0.0	0.0	0.1	0.0
1890	0.0	0.0	0.0	0.1	0.0

SOURCE: Joint Committee on Taxation; Office of Management and Budget, *Historical Tables, Budget of the United States Government, Fiscal Year 1996*; and Census Bureau, Department of Commerce, *Historical Statistics of the United States, Colonial Times to Present.*

Table 3: Federal Receipts by Source, as a Percentage of Total Revenues, 1890–1994

Year	Individual income tax	Payroll taxes	Corporate income tax	Excise taxes	Other receipts
1994	43.18	36.69	11.16	4.39	4.58
1993	44.18	37.13	10.19	4.17	4.33
1992	43.65	37.94	9.20	4.18	5.04
1991	44.37	37.56	9.30	4.02	4.74
1990	45.27	36.85	9.07	3.43	5.39
1989	44.99	36.28	10.43	3.47	4.84
1988	44.14	36.78	10.40	3.88	4.81
1987	45.96	35.51	9.83	3.80	4.90
1986	45.37	36.91	8.21	4.28	5.22
1985	45.57	36.12	8.33	4.90	5.07
1984	44.78	35.92	8.54	5.61	5.16
1983	48.11	34.80	6.16	5.88	5.05
1982	48.20	32.62	7.96	5.88	5.34
1981	47.71	30.49	10.20	6.81	4.78
1980	47.20	30.52	12.49	4.70	5.09
1979	47.02	29.99	14.18	4.05	4.77
1978	45.30	30.27	15.00	4.60	4.82
1977	44.33	29.95	15.44	4.94	5.35
1976	44.15	30.45	13.89	5.69	5.81
1975	43.85	30.29	14.55	5.93	5.37
1974	45.19	28.52	14.67	6.40	5.22
1973	44.73	27.35	15.66	7.05	5.21
1972	45.70	25.36	15.52	7.47	5.96
1971	46.08	25.29	14.31	8.88	5.44
1970	46.89	23.01	17.03	8.15	4.93
1969	46.69	20.88	19.63	8.15	4.66
1968	44.93	22.18	18.74	9.20	4.96
1967	41.34	21.92	22.83	9.22	4.69
1966	42.38	19.53	22.99	9.98	5.13
1965	41.77	19.04	21.80	12.47	4.92
1964	43.24	19.50	20.86	12.19	4.20
1963	44.66	18.58	20.25	12.38	4.12
1962	45.72	17.10	20.59	12.57	4.02
1961	43.80	17.42	22.20	12.57	4.02
1960	44.02	15.87	23.24	12.62	4.24
1959	46.33	14.79	21.84	13.35	3.69
1958	43.60	14.11	25.21	13.36	3.72
1957	44.53	12.50	26.46	13.17	3.34

Continued

Table 3: *Continued*

Year	Individual income tax	Payroll taxes	Corporate income tax	Excise taxes	Other receipts
1956	43.15	12.50	27.99	13.31	3.04
1955	43.92	12.01	27.29	13.95	2.83
1954	42.38	10.34	30.27	14.27	2.73
1953	42.83	9.80	30.51	14.19	2.67
1952	42.22	9.74	32.08	13.38	2.58
1951	41.88	10.99	27.32	16.75	3.06
1950	39.94	11.00	26.49	19.14	3.43
1949	39.46	9.59	28.40	19.03	3.52
1948	46.47	9.03	23.29	17.70	3.51
1947	46.57	8.89	22.37	18.72	3.46
1946	40.97	7.93	30.24	17.81	3.06
1945	40.68	7.64	35.40	13.87	2.40
1944	45.04	7.94	33.92	10.88	2.22
1943	27.10	12.68	39.82	17.07	3.33
1942	22.30	16.76	32.25	23.23	5.47
1941	15.08	22.27	24.38	29.29	8.98
1940	13.62	27.26	18.28	30.19	10.64
1939	16.35	25.31	17.90	29.72	10.72
1938	19.05	22.83	19.06	27.60	11.46
1937	20.27	10.77	19.27	34.82	14.87
1936	17.18	1.33	18.33	41.58	21.59
1935	14.60	0.86	14.66	39.87	30.01
1934	14.21	1.02	12.32	45.82	26.63
1933	21.79	0.00	24.32	51.79	2.10
1932	27.41	0.00	40.44	29.14	3.02
1931	34.35	0.00	42.26	21.42	1.98
1930	37.73	0.00	41.55	18.59	2.14
1929	37.29	0.00	42.06	18.37	2.28
1928	31.64	0.00	46.29	17.23	4.84
1927	31.82	0.00	45.64	16.82	5.72
1926	30.99	0.00	38.61	20.13	10.26
1925	32.70	0.00	35.45	21.01	10.84
1924	30.22	0.00	32.76	23.86	13.16
1923	32.84	0.00	0.00	23.84	0.00
1922	22.49	0.00	0.00	18.55	0.00
1921	23.39	0.00	0.00	14.91	0.00
1920	23.48	0.00	0.00	14.94	0.00
1919	29.30	0.00	0.00	21.74	0.00
1918	21.49	0.00	0.00	17.22	0.00

Continued

Table 3: *Continued*

Year	Individual income tax	Payroll taxes	Corporate income tax	Excise taxes	Other receipts
1917	22.25	0.00	25.59	47.96	4.20
1916	13.26	0.00	11.11	66.28	9.36
1915	9.86	0.00	0.00	78.85	0.00
1914	7.37	0.00	0.00	80.79	0.00
1913	0.00	0.00	0.00	89.53	10.47
1912	0.00	0.00	0.00	90.37	9.63
1911	0.00	0.00	0.00	88.85	11.15
1910	0.00	0.00	0.00	92.07	7.93
1909	0.00	0.00	0.00	99.59	0.41
1908	0.00	0.00	0.00	99.21	0.79
1907	0.00	0.00	0.00	99.26	0.74
1906	0.00	0.00	0.00	99.60	0.40
1905	0.00	0.00	0.00	99.15	0.85
1904	0.00	0.00	0.00	98.71	1.29
1903	0.00	0.00	0.00	96.54	3.46
1902	0.00	0.00	0.00	95.22	4.78
1901	0.00	0.00	0.00	95.77	4.23
1900	0.00	0.00	0.00	96.27	3.73
1899	0.00	0.00	0.00	97.07	2.93
1898	0.00	0.00	0.00	98.83	1.17
1897	0.00	0.00	0.00	99.32	0.68
1896	0.00	0.00	0.00	98.64	1.36
1895	0.00	0.00	0.00	99.30	0.70
1894	0.00	0.00	0.00	98.64	1.36
1893	0.00	0.00	0.00	98.76	1.24
1892	0.00	0.00	0.00	98.70	1.30
1891	0.00	0.00	0.00	99.32	0.68
1890	0.00	0.00	0.00	99.30	0.70

SOURCE: Joint Committee on Taxation; Office of Management and Budget, *Historical Tables, Budget of the United States Government, Fiscal Year 1996*; and Census Bureau, Department of Commerce, *Historical Statistics of the United States, Colonial Times to Present.*

Table 4:   Federal Receipts by Source, as a Percentage of GDP, 1934–1994

Year	Total receipts	Individual income tax	Payroll taxes	Corporate income tax	Excise taxes	Other receipts
1994	18.96	8.19	6.96	2.12	0.83	0.87
1993	18.43	8.14	6.84	1.88	0.77	0.80
1992	18.42	8.04	6.99	1.69	0.77	0.93
1991	18.57	8.24	6.98	1.73	0.75	0.88
1990	18.81	8.52	6.93	1.71	0.64	1.01
1989	19.15	8.62	6.95	2.00	0.66	0.93
1988	18.90	8.34	6.95	1.97	0.73	0.91
1987	19.18	8.82	6.81	1.88	0.73	0.94
1986	18.23	8.27	6.73	1.50	0.78	0.95
1985	18.50	8.43	6.68	1.54	0.91	0.94
1984	18.04	8.08	6.48	1.54	1.01	0.93
1983	18.11	8.71	6.30	1.12	1.06	0.91
1982	19.79	9.54	6.45	1.58	1.16	1.06
1981	20.22	9.65	6.16	2.06	1.38	0.97
1980	19.56	9.23	5.97	2.44	0.92	1.00
1979	19.07	8.97	5.72	2.70	0.77	0.91
1978	18.54	8.40	5.61	2.78	0.85	0.89
1977	18.55	8.22	5.55	2.86	0.92	0.99
1976	17.70	7.81	5.39	2.46	1.01	1.03
1975	18.49	8.11	5.60	2.69	1.10	0.99
1974	18.75	8.47	5.35	2.75	1.20	0.98
1973	18.12	8.10	4.95	2.84	1.28	0.94
1972	18.06	8.25	4.58	2.80	1.35	1.08
1971	17.81	8.21	4.50	2.55	1.58	0.97
1970	19.57	9.18	4.50	3.33	1.59	0.96
1969	20.19	9.43	4.21	3.96	1.64	0.94
1968	18.06	8.11	4.00	3.38	1.66	0.89
1967	18.76	7.76	4.11	4.28	1.73	0.88
1966	17.79	7.54	3.47	4.09	1.78	0.91
1965	17.41	7.27	3.31	3.79	2.17	0.86
1964	18.01	7.79	3.51	3.76	2.20	0.76
1963	18.23	8.14	3.39	3.69	2.26	0.75
1962	17.95	8.21	3.07	3.70	2.26	0.72
1961	18.26	8.00	3.18	4.05	2.29	0.73
1960	18.33	8.07	2.91	4.26	2.31	0.78
1959	16.50	7.65	2.44	3.60	2.20	0.61
1958	17.77	7.75	2.51	4.48	2.37	0.66
1957	18.25	8.13	2.28	4.83	2.40	0.61
1956	17.92	7.73	2.24	5.02	2.39	0.55

Continued

Table 4: *Continued*

Year	Total receipts	Individual income tax	Payroll taxes	Corporate income tax	Excise taxes	Other receipts
1955	17.01	7.47	2.04	4.64	2.37	0.48
1954	18.94	8.03	1.96	5.73	2.70	0.52
1953	19.13	8.20	1.87	5.84	2.71	0.51
1952	19.43	8.20	1.89	6.23	2.60	0.50
1951	16.46	6.90	1.81	4.50	2.76	0.50
1950	14.84	5.93	1.63	3.93	2.84	0.51
1949	15.00	5.92	1.44	4.26	2.86	0.53
1948	16.85	7.83	1.52	3.92	2.98	0.59
1947	17.28	8.05	1.54	3.86	3.24	0.60
1946	18.49	7.58	1.47	5.59	3.29	0.57
1945	21.30	8.67	1.63	7.54	2.96	0.51
1944	21.69	9.77	1.72	7.36	2.36	0.48
1943	13.68	3.71	1.74	5.45	2.34	0.46
1942	10.32	2.30	1.73	3.33	2.40	0.56
1941	7.74	1.17	1.72	1.89	2.27	0.70
1940	6.86	0.94	1.87	1.25	2.07	0.73
1939	7.17	1.17	1.81	1.28	2.13	0.77
1938	7.69	1.46	1.76	1.47	2.12	0.88
1937	6.21	1.26	0.67	1.20	2.16	0.92
1936	5.06	0.87	0.07	0.93	2.10	1.09
1935	5.25	0.77	0.05	0.77	2.09	1.58
1934	4.89	0.70	0.05	0.60	2.24	1.30

SOURCE: Joint Committee on Taxation; Office of Management and Budget, *Historical Tables, Budget of the United States Government, Fiscal Year 1996*; and Census Bureau, Department of Commerce, *Historical Statistics of the United States, Colonial Times to Present.*

Table 5: Distribution of Federal Tax Liability [1995 Projection]

Income Category[1]	Individual Income Tax		Total Federal Taxes[2]	
	Billions	Percent	Billions	Percent
Less than $10,000	−$5	−1.0	$8	0.7
$10,000 to $20,000	−2	−0.3	36	3.3
$20,000 to $30,000	19	3.3	73	6.6
$30,000 to $40,000	36	6.3	100	9.1
$40,000 to $50,000	43	7.5	106	9.6
$50,000 to $75,000	100	17.6	228	20.7
$75,000 to $100,000	78	13.8	156	14.2
$100,000 to $200,000	115	20.2	184	16.7
$200,000 and over	184	32.5	210	19.1
Total, all taxpayers	$567	100	$1,100	100

[1]The income concept used to place tax returns into income categories is adjusted gross income (AGI) plus: [1] tax-exempt interest, [2] employer contributions for health plans and life insurance, [3] employer share of FICA tax, [4] workers compensation, [5] nontaxable social security benefits, [6] insurance value of Medicare benefits, [7] alternative minimum tax preference items, and [8] excluded income of U.S. citizens living abroad.

[2]Federal taxes are equal to individual income tax (including the outlay portion of the EITC), employment tax attributed to employees, and excise taxes (attributed to consumers). Corporate income taxes not included due to uncertainty concerning the incidence of the tax.

NOTE: Details may not add to totals due to rounding.

SOURCE: Joint Committee on Taxation.

Selected Bibliography

Andrews, William D. "Personal Deductions in an Ideal Income Tax." 86 *Harv. L. Rev.* 313 (1971).

Becker, Robert A. *Revolution, Reform, and the Politics of American Taxation, 1763–1783*. Baton Rouge: Louisiana State University Press, 1980.

Birnbaum, Jeffrey H., and Alan S. Murray. *Showdown at Gucci Gulch: Lawmakers, Lobbyists, and the Unlikely Triumph of Tax Reform.* New York: Vintage, 1987.

Bittker, Boris I. "A 'Comprehensive Tax Base' as a Goal of Income Tax Reform." 80 *Harv. L. Rev.* 925 (1967).

Bittker, Boris I., Charles O. Galvin, R. A. Musgrave, and Joseph A. Pechman. *A Comprehensive Income Tax Base? A Debate.* Branford, Conn.: Federal Tax Press, 1968.

Blakely, Roy G., and Gladys C. Blakely. *The Federal Income Tax.* New York: Longmans, Green & Co., 1940.

Blough, Roy. *The Federal Taxing Process.* New York: Prentice-Hall, 1952.

Boskin, Michael J., ed. *Federal Tax Reform: Myths and Realities.* San Francisco: Institute of Contemporary Studies, 1978.

Bosworth, Barry P. *Tax Incentives and Economic Growth.* Washington, D.C.: Brookings Institution, 1984.

Bradford, David F. *Untangling the Income Tax.* Cambridge: Harvard University Press, 1986.

Break, George F., and Joseph A. Pechman. *Federal Tax Reform: The Impossible Dream?* Washington, D.C.: Brookings Institution, 1975.

Brennan, Geoffrey, and James M. Buchanan. *The Power to Tax: Analytical Foundations of a Fiscal Constitution.* Cambridge: Cambridge University Press, 1980.

Buenker, John D. *The Income Tax and the Progressive Era.* New York: Garland Publishing Co., 1985.

Burnham, David. *A Law Unto Itself: The IRS and the Abuse of Power.* New York: Vintage Books, 1989.

Chirelstein, Marvin A. *Federal Income Taxation.* 4th ed. Mineola, N.Y.: Foundation Press, 1985.

Conlan, Timothy J., Margaret T. Wrightson, and David R. Beam. *Taxing Choices: The Politics of Tax Reform.* Washington, D.C.: Congressional Quarterly Press, 1990.

Dahl, Robert A., and Charles E. Lindblom. *Politics, Economics, and Welfare.* Chicago: University of Chicago Press, 1953.

Davies, David G. *United States Taxes and Tax Policy.* New York: Cambridge University Press, 1986.

Derthick, Martha. *Agency Under Stress: The Social Security Administration in American Government.* Washington, D.C.: Brookings Institution, 1990.

——. *Policymaking for Social Security.* Washington, D.C.: Brookings Institution, 1979.

Derthick, Martha, and Paul J. Quirk. *The Politics of Deregulation.* Washington, D.C.: Brookings Institution, 1985.

Eustice, James S. "Tax Complexity and the Tax Practitioner." 45 *Tax L. Rev.* 7 (1989).

Fenno, Richard, Jr. *The Power of the Purse: Appropriations Politics in Congress.* Boston: Little, Brown, 1966.

Fiorina, Morris P. *Congress: Keystone of the Washington Establishment.* New Haven: Yale University Press, 1977.

Forsythe, Dall W. *Taxation and Political Change in the Young Nation, 1781–1833.* New York: Columbia University Press, 1977.

Goode, Richard. *The Individual Income Tax.* Washington, D.C.: Brookings Institution, 1976.

Graetz, Michael J. *Federal Income Taxation: Principles and Policies.* 2d ed. Westbury, N.Y.: Foundation Press, 1988.

Groves, Harold M. *Tax Philosophers: Two Hundred Years of Thought in Great Britain and the United States,* edited by Donald J. Curran. Madison: University of Wisconsin Press, 1974.

Haig, Robert M. *The Federal Income Tax.* New York: Columbia University Press, 1921.

Hall, Arthur P. "The Cost of Unstable Tax Laws." 65 *Tax Notes* 759 (November 7, 1994).

Hansen, Susan B. *The Politics of Taxation: Revenue Without Representation.* New York: Praeger, 1983.

Higgs, Robert. *Crisis and Leviathan: Critical Episodes in the Growth of American Government.* New York: Oxford University Press, 1987.

Isenbergh, Joseph. "The End of Income Taxation." 45 *Tax L. Rev.* 283 (1990).

Kettl, Donald F. *Deficit Politics: Public Budgeting in Its Institutional and Historical Context.* New York: Macmillan, 1992.

King, Ronald F. *Money, Time, and Politics: Investment Tax Subsidies and American Democracy.* New Haven: Yale University Press, 1993.

Kingdon, John W. *Agendas, Alternatives, and Public Policies.* New York: Harper Collins, 1984.

Klein, William A., Joseph Bankman, Boris I. Bittker, and Lawrence M. Stone. *Federal Income Taxation.* 8th ed. Boston: Little, Brown, 1990.

Leff, Mark H. *The Limits of Symbolic Reform: The New Deal and Taxation, 1933–1939*. New York: Cambridge University Press, 1984.

Levi, Margaret. *Of Rule and Revenue*. Berkeley and Los Angeles: University of California Press, 1988.

——. "A Theory of Predatory Rule." 10 *Pol. & Soc'y* 431 (1981).

Lindblom, Charles E. "The Science of 'Muddling Through.'" 19 *Pub. Admin. Rev.* 79 (1959).

Lindsey, Lawrence B. *The Growth Experiment: How the New Tax Policy Is Transforming the U.S. Economy*. New York: Basic Books, 1990.

Lowi, Theodore J. "American Business, Public Policy, Case Studies, and Political Theory." 16 *World Pol.* 677 (1964).

——. *The End of Liberalism*. New York: W. W. Norton, 1969.

Makin, John H., and Norman J. Ornstein. *Debt and Taxes*. New York: Random House, 1994.

Manley, John F. *The Politics of Finance: The House Committee on Ways and Means*. Boston: Little, Brown, 1970.

——. "Wilbur D. Mills: A Study in Congressional Influence." 63 *Am. Pol. Sci. Rev.* 442 (1969).

Martin, Cathie J. *Shifting the Burden: The Struggle over Growth and Corporate Taxation*. Chicago: University of Chicago Press, 1991.

Maslove, Allan M., ed. *Fairness in Taxation: Exploring the Principles*. Toronto: University of Toronto Press, 1993.

Mayhew, David R. *Congress: The Electoral Connection*. New Haven: Yale University Press, 1974.

McDaniel, Paul. "Federal Income Tax Simplification: The Political Process." 34 *Tax L. Rev.* 27 (1978).

McLure, Charles A., Jr. "The Budget Process and Tax Simplification/Complication." 45 *Tax L. Rev.* 25 (1989).

McLure, Charles A., Jr., and George R. Zodrow. "Implementing Direct Consumption Taxes in Developing Countries." 46 *Tax L. Rev.* 405 (1991).

Mellon, Andrew W. *Taxation: The People's Business*. New York: Macmillan, 1924.

Minarik, Joseph J. *Making Tax Choices*. Washington, D.C.: Urban Institute Press, 1985.

——. "How Tax Reform Came About." 37 *Tax Notes* 1359 (December 28, 1987).

Okun, Arthur M. *Equality and Efficiency: The Big Tradeoff*. Washington, D.C.: Brookings Institution, 1975.

Paul, Randolph E. *Taxation in the United States*. Boston: Little, Brown, 1954.

Pechman, Joseph A. *Federal Tax Policy*. 5th ed. Washington, D.C.: Brookings Institution, 1987.

——. *Tax Reform, the Rich, and the Poor*. Washington, D.C.: Brookings Institution, 1989.

——. *Who Pays the Taxes?* Washington, D.C.: Brookings Institution, 1985.

——, ed. *Comprehensive Income Taxation*. Washington, D.C.: Brookings Institution, 1977.

———, ed. *Options for Tax Reform*. Washington, D.C.: Brookings Institution, 1984.

———, ed. *What Should Be Taxed: Income or Expenditure?* Washington, D.C.: Brookings Institution, 1980.

Pechman, Joseph A., and Benjamin A. Okner. *Who Bears the Tax Burden?* Washington, D.C.: Brookings Institution, 1974.

Peters, B. Guy. *The Politics of Taxation: A Comparative Perspective*. Cambridge: Blackwell, 1991.

Pollack, Sheldon D. "Tax Complexity, Reform, and the Illusions of Tax Simplification." 2 *Geo. Mason Indep. L. Rev.* 319 (1994).

———. "Tax Reform: The 1980's in Perspective." 46 *Tax L. Rev.* 489 (1991).

Quirk, Paul J. *Industry Influence in Federal Regulatory Agencies*. Princeton: Princeton University Press, 1981.

Rabushka, Alvin. "The Tax Reform Act of 1986: Concentrated Costs, Diffuse Benefits–An Inversion of Public Choice." 9 *Contemp. Pol'y Issues* 50 (1988).

Rabushka, Alvin, and Robert E. Hall. *Low Tax, Simple Tax, Flat Tax*. New York: McGraw-Hill, 1983.

———. *The Flat Tax*. Stanford, Calif.: Hoover Institution Press, 1985.

Ratner, Sidney. *American Taxation: Its History as a Social Force in Democracy*. New York: W. W. Norton, 1942.

Reese, Thomas J. *The Politics of Taxation*. Westport, Conn.: Quorum Books, 1980.

Reinhard, David W. *The Republican Right Since 1945*. Lexington: University Press of Kentucky, 1983.

Roberts, Paul Craig. *The Supply-Side Revolution*. Cambridge: Harvard University Press, 1984.

Rudder, Catherine E. "Tax Policy: Structure and Choice." In *Making Economic Policy in Congress*, edited by Allen Schick. Washington, D.C.: American Enterprise Institute, 1983.

Savage, James D. *Balanced Budgets and American Politics*. Ithaca, N.Y.: Cornell University Press, 1988.

Schick, Allen. *The Federal Budget: Politics, Policy, Process*. Washington, D.C.: Brookings Institution, 1995.

Schumpeter, Joseph A. "The Crisis of the Tax State." 1918. Reprinted in *International Economic Papers, No. 4*. New York: Macmillan, 1954.

Seligman, Edwin R. A. *The Income Tax: A Study of the History, Theory, and Practice of Income Taxation at Home and Abroad*. New York: Macmillan, 1911.

Sharkansky, Ira. *The Politics of Taxing and Spending*. Indianapolis, Ind.: Bobbs-Merrill, 1969.

Shaviro, Daniel. "Beyond Public Choice and Public Interest: A Study of the Legislative Process As Illustrated by Tax Legislation in the 1980s." 139 *U. Pa. L. Rev.* 1 (1990).

Simons, Henry C. *Federal Tax Reform*. Chicago: University of Chicago Press, 1950.

——. *Personal Income Taxation: The Definition of Income as a Problem of Fiscal Policy.* Chicago: University of Chicago, 1938.

Skowronek, Stephen. *Building a New American State: The Expansion of National Administrative Capacities, 1877–1920.* New York: Cambridge University Press, 1982.

Slemrod, Joel. *Tax Progressivity and Income Inequality.* New York: Cambridge University Press, 1994.

Steinmo, Sven. *Taxation and Democracy: Swedish, British, and American Approaches to Financing the Modern State.* New Haven: Yale University Press, 1993.

Steuerle, C. Eugene. *The Tax Decade: How Taxes Came to Dominate the Public Agenda.* Washington, D.C.: Urban Institute Press, 1992.

Steuerle, C. Eugene, and Jon M. Bakija. *Retooling Social Security for the Twenty-first Century: Right and Wrong Approaches to Reform.* Washington, D.C.: Urban Institute Press, 1994.

Strahan, Randall. *New Ways and Means: Reform and Change in a Congressional Committee.* Chapel Hill: University of North Carolina Press, 1990.

Surrey, Stanley S. "Complexity and the Internal Revenue Code: The Problem of the Management of Tax Detail." 34 *Law & Contemp. Probs.* 673 (1969).

——. "The Congress and the Tax Lobbyist–How Special Tax Provisions Get Enacted." 70 *Harv. L. Rev.* 1145 (1957).

——. "Our Troubled Tax Policy." 12 *Tax Notes* 179 (February 2, 1981).

——. *Pathways to Tax Reform: The Concept of Tax Expenditures.* Cambridge: Harvard University Press, 1973.

Surrey, Stanley S., and Paul McDaniel. *Tax Expenditures.* Cambridge: Harvard University Press, 1985.

Thuronyi, Victor. "The Concept of Income." 46 *Tax L. Rev.* 45 (1990).

Waltman, Jerold L. *Political Origins of the U.S. Income Tax.* Jackson: University Press of Mississippi, 1985.

Wildavsky, Aaron B. *The New Politics of the Budgetary Process.* Glenview, Ill.: Scott, Foresman & Co., 1988.

——. *The Politics of the Budgetary Process.* Boston: Little, Brown, 1964.

——. "A Theory of the Budget Process." 60 *Am. Pol. Sci. Rev.* 529 (1960).

Wildavsky, Aaron B., and Carolyn Webber. *A History of Taxation and Expenditure in the Western World.* New York: Simon & Schuster, 1986.

Wildavsky, Aaron B., and Joseph White. *The Deficit and the Public Interest: The Search for Responsible Budgeting in the 1980s.* Berkeley and Los Angeles: University of California Press, 1989.

Wilson, James Q., ed. *The Politics of Regulation.* New York: Basic Books, 1980.

Witte, John F. "A Long View of Tax Reform." 39 *Nat'l Tax J.* 255 (1986).

——. *The Politics and Development of the Federal Income Tax.* Madison: University of Wisconsin Press, 1985.

——. "The Tax Reform Act of 1986: A New Era in Tax Politics?" 19 *Am. Pol. Q.* 438 (1991).

Index